Advance Praise for *A Troubled Sleep: Risk and Resilience in Contemporary Northern Ireland*

"Cutting-edge social psychologist, brilliant analyst of the Holocaust and other genocides, James Waller combines his expertise on atrocity prevention and his commitment to reconciliation in post-conflict societies to produce a penetrating and challenging account of Northern Ireland's fraught but still promising prospects. Grounded in extensive field research, including abundant interviews with people of diverse persuasions and loyalties, *A Troubled Sleep* vividly depicts the uneasy peace reached after decades of sectarian violence and insightfully discerns the risks that threaten to undo it. Beyond that immense accomplishment, this lucid and elegantly written book persuasively shows how Northern Ireland's ongoing odyssey of risk and resilience provides warning and wisdom wherever the waste of conflict and the wreckage of violence require the struggle, uncertain though its outcomes may be, to rebuild trust and sustain community. Waller and *A Troubled Sleep* are welcome companions on that hard but vital way."

John K. Roth
Edward J. Sexton Professor Emeritus of Philosophy
Claremont McKenna College
Author, *The Failures of Ethics: Confronting the Holocaust, Genocide, and Other Mass Atrocities*

"*A Troubled Sleep* is at once poetic and practical. Beautifully written and personal in tone, it is an essential guide for how practitioners in the fields of conflict prevention and transitional justice can better approach the challenges and prospects for post-conflict societies with greater hope of long-term peace. Waller provides a singularly humane analysis of contemporary social and political life in 'post-conflict' Northern Ireland, illustrating the profound and lasting legacy of the country's 30 years of conflict on its immediate victims and society at large. Drawing on extensive comparative research, Waller methodically examines risk factors that precede future violence and artfully presents an evidence-based assessment of how these risk factors may be mitigated, and resiliencies strengthened and adapted, to support prevention efforts and genuine recovery."

Elinor Stevenson, Consultant on atrocity prevention,
transitional justice, and human rights

"In this remarkable book, James Waller weaves a narrative that leads the reader to understand the complexity of the conflict in Northern Ireland, and the consequent complexity of our peace process. With affection, and a clear understanding of the nuanced paradoxes of my home country, Waller evokes the sensations of Northern Ireland and throughout its pages it is possible to hear the voices of people who have certainly been wounded, but who have found ways to create hope. With insight, compassion, and humor, Waller honors these voices, nimbly making sense of their lived experience, and giving energy and amplification to their hope."

Peter McBride, Director of the Cohen Center for
Holocaust and Genocide Studies, Keene State College

A Troubled Sleep

Risk and Resilience in Contemporary Northern Ireland

JAMES WALLER

OXFORD

UNIVERSITY PRESS

OXFORD
UNIVERSITY PRESS

Oxford University Press is a department of the University of Oxford. It furthers
the University's objective of excellence in research, scholarship, and education
by publishing worldwide. Oxford is a registered trade mark of Oxford University
Press in the UK and certain other countries.

Published in the United States of America by Oxford University Press
198 Madison Avenue, New York, NY 10016, United States of America.

Library of Congress Cataloging-in-Publication Data
Names: Waller, James, 1961– author.
Title: A troubled sleep : risk and resilience in contemporary Northern Ireland /
James Waller.
Description: New York, NY : Oxford University Press, [2021] |
Includes bibliographical references and index.
Identifiers: LCCN 2020048154 (print) | LCCN 2020048155 (ebook) |
ISBN 9780190095574 (hardback) | ISBN 9780190095598 (epub) |
ISBN 9780197558751 (oso)
Subjects: LCSH: Northern Ireland—Social conditions—21st century. |
Group identity—Northern Ireland. | Nationalism—Northern Ireland. |
Social conflict—Northern Ireland.
Classification: LCC HN398.N6 W35 2021 (print) | LCC HN398.N6 (ebook) |
DDC 306.09416—dc23
LC record available at https://lccn.loc.gov/2020048154
LC ebook record available at https://lccn.loc.gov/2020048155

DOI: 10.1093/oso/9780190095574.001.0001

1 3 5 7 9 8 6 4 2

Printed by Sheridan Books, Inc., United States of America

With deep appreciation for the people, cultures, history, land, and place of Northern Ireland.
And even deeper hope for its future.

Contents

Foreword

Senator George J. Mitchell, Independent Chairman of the Northern Ireland Peace Talks

The Good Friday Agreement, which ended the long conflict that has come to be known as "the Troubles," was signed 22 years ago. Dozens of books and documentary films and hundreds of news articles have been published and broadcast about the Agreement and the process that led to it. I have read or seen many—perhaps most of them—and have generally been impressed by their quality. Each is unique, adding detail and nuance to the long and painful history of the conflict. Most of them are largely factual and chronological, describing the actions of the men and women who conducted the conflict and ended it. No doubt there will be many more in the run up to and the aftermath of the twenty-fifth anniversary of the Agreement in 2023.

James Waller has taken a different approach. Rather than "who and when," he asks—and answers—"why and how." Importantly, his emphasis is on the future. The substance of his book is a response to the many apprehensions that exist and the questions being asked in and about Northern Ireland.

> Can the two identities at the heart of a deeply divided society ever be expected to live together without oppression, resistance or violence?
>
> Has the conflict, while perhaps managed and resolved, at least through a peace agreement, been transformed—structurally and relationally—into a win-win situation for both sides?
>
> Does Northern Ireland have the resiliency to withstand the internal and external stressors that may threaten a destabilization of its fragile peace?
>
> Has it rebuilt differently enough so as to ensure nonrecurrence of violent conflict?

These are very difficult but relevant questions to which, by their actions, the people of Northern Ireland must respond.

For his part, based on his interest, experience, and writing skill, James Waller is well-equipped to suggest answers to these questions. His interest in Northern Ireland was engaged by an educational exchange program in 2004. He has since returned often, as a visitor, researcher, and educator, including a stint as an honorary visiting research professor at the Senator George J. Mitchell Institute for Global Peace, Security, and Justice at Queen's University Belfast.

Waller obviously admires the people of Northern Ireland. In researching this book he met and talked with many of them. Most of his time was spent listening. This is both a sign of respect and a method of proceeding that ultimately gives substance and credibility to his conclusions.

The heart of the book offers a real-time analysis of Northern Ireland's latent, and manifest, vulnerabilities more than two decades after the Good Friday Agreement. Drawing on comparative research from an extensive array of post-conflict societies, Waller delves into the challenges of memory, governance, and social fragmentation. He complements this analysis of risk with a review of the points of resiliency—both within and outside the country—that help inoculate Northern Ireland against the recurrence of conflict. He offers concrete suggestions for how memory can become more inclusive, governance systems can be effectively structured, and social cohesion can be better promoted to inoculate a post-conflict society against those risk factors.

In the closing section of the book, Waller lays out in detail several alternative paths for Northern Ireland's future. On balance, he is cautiously pessimistic, deeply concerned about a return to widespread violence. I am somewhat more optimistic, but of course no one can predict the future with certainty. Whatever one's view, Waller's analysis is cogent and thought-provoking. It surely should be read by all of the political and civic leaders of Northern Ireland.

I spent a good part of 15 years in Northern Ireland, five of them (1995–1999) as a participant in the peace process and then a decade as the Chancellor of Queen's University Belfast. I came to know, respect, and love the people. While they can at times be contentious, they are warm, generous, and very energetic. I am an American and proud of it, but a large part of my heart and my emotions will forever be with the people of Northern Ireland. I hope they will heed the concerns set forth in this book.

Acknowledgments

On January 26, 2017, as I landed at Dublin airport and began my two-hour bus trip north to start my spring term appointment as an honorary visiting research professor at Queen's University Belfast, I received a voice mail from my sister telling me that our Mother, as many Native people expressively say, had walked on. It was not a surprise. I had postponed my trip to Belfast because my Mom's health, in a steady decline since a car accident several months earlier, had taken a decided turn for the worse by mid-January. With my sister and our extended family, I spent several days in a South Carolina hospital at my Mom's bedside. She was seldom conscious during that time. When she was, the conversations were brief, sometimes poignant and other times pedestrian ("Jimmy, can you get me a Frosty from Wendy's?"). In the last conversation I had with her, she asked why I wasn't already in Ireland (the political demarcation between the Republic of Ireland and Northern Ireland was a distinction without a difference for her, as it is for most Americans). Feeling it was a searching question on her part to discover how dire her circumstances really were, I responded evasively: "I just decided I didn't need to be there quite so early." Noting the quiver in my voice and downward glance of my eyes, and understanding, at some level, that this latest trip to the hospital was different from the previous ones, she replied: "Jimmy, go where you are supposed to be."

I returned home to New Hampshire that next day and repacked for the trip to Northern Ireland. I thought Mom's final gift to me, in those last words, was the maternal encouragement to keep at the work to which I devoted my professional life. She knew the rhythm of my heart longer than I have. I would soon find out, though, that her death had given me an even more profound gift: a heart open to listening, a renewed sense of empathy and compassion, and a deeper sense of humility birthed from heart-rending loss and rooted in the recognition of our shared frailties. I arrived in Northern Ireland with different eyes than when I had first planned out my research strategy for the term, more attuned to the human consequences of lives lived in such a society. I felt a need, even a hunger, to listen rather than speak; to understand more than to be understood; to genuinely feel as deeply as could be felt; to privilege, in the most humane way possible, the voice and agency of those who shared their stories and lives with me. The weight of silence, whether in times of solitude or in the companionable midst of conversations, was a welcome one; a space of reflection and of hearing things unspoken. In the midst of loss, and far away from home and loved ones, I was able to reacquaint myself with my own company. While I still feel the presence of my Mom's absence daily, this book is different—and I think more human—because of the power of the place where I was in my personal life when the research, and writing were being done.

Over the years, I have developed a deep appreciation for the wonderful pluralities of Northern Ireland—its histories, its cultures, its geographies, and, most significantly, its people. During my most recent visit there, one friend commented "you seem very much at home in Northern Ireland." Indeed, it does feel like a home of sorts. I am a child of the American South, born and raised in Georgia before moving for brief stints to Virginia, West Virginia, North Carolina, and Texas before leaving to go to college in Kentucky. It is the Deep South, though, and its myriad complexities, that defines me in many ways. And part of that definition comes from growing up in a society that still struggles on its better days, and ignores it on its worst, with the thorny legacies of conflict, exclusion, racism, and identity. So the questions, divisions, and contradictions that make up contemporary Northern Ireland do feel, in an odd sort of way, as familiar to me as sweet tea and red clay.

My first introduction to Northern Ireland was as a participant in a 2004 faculty development seminar sponsored by the Council on International Educational Exchange. Since then, I have guided two month-long student study programs to Northern Ireland (January 2006 and 2008), completed certification work in safety and security after violent conflict at Queen's University Belfast (2016), was an honorary visiting research professor in the Senator George J. Mitchell Institute for Global Peace, Security and Justice at Queen's University Belfast (2017), and have returned to Northern Ireland numerous times over the years to do additional fieldwork, research, interviews; to deliver public lectures and participate on community panels; and to just explore the wonders of a beautiful country.

While I cannot thank each of them by name, a profound "thank you" is due to those anonymous friends who generously opened their homes, hearts, histories, heartaches, and humanity to me ... and, most importantly, gave me the gift of their trust (or at least the opportunity to earn that gift). While those interviews shaped much of my thinking for this book, the views expressed in the following pages are my own. There may be some in Northern Ireland who read this book and say: "I wish he would have talked to me, I could have straightened him out!" To those, I, too, wish I would have had that chance and look forward to having it in the future.

In Belfast, I am particularly indebted to my hosts at Queen's University Belfast, Hastings Donnan and Neil Jarman, for their support of me during my stint as honorary visiting research professor in their Institute. During my time at Queen's, I also benefitted from rich conversations with Richard English, Cheryl Lawther, John Brewer, and Dominic Bryan. Paul Donnelly of DC Tours in Belfast was always quick with a reply to my endless questions and even quicker to join me for a pint and the craic. Among the many relationships I began during my time in Northern Ireland, most notable was a friendship with Peter McBride, who not only provided remarkable depth of insight at a time when I needed it most but has now, I am proud to say, also joined me as a colleague in his role of Director of the Cohen Center for Holocaust and Genocide Studies at Keene State College. I also am deeply appreciative to Katy Radford, both for opening her home to me during my time in Belfast as well as for the friendship we have developed since—she is a beacon of hope in the frontline work she does in bringing divided communities together in Northern Ireland. Finally, a note of appreciation for the Northern Ireland Statistics and Research Agency for their clear and accessible database as well as for the Northern Ireland Life and Times Survey for its diligent recording of the rhythm of everyday life in Northern Ireland since 1998.

As always, my colleagues in the Department of Holocaust and Genocide Studies at Keene State College, the only such department in the United States, have been wonderful sources of support and, where necessary, challenge. Among these are Lisa DiGiovanni, Ashley Greene, Dana Smith, and John Sturtz. Other colleagues at the College have continued to make this a wonderful professional home with their friendship and support. Among these are Darrell Hucks, Taneem Hussein, Tanya Sturtz, and Tom White. My dean, Kirsti Sandy, stepped up at a crucial time in the final stretch of writing to find the funds to purchase a new office computer . . . and helped prevent a meltdown that certainly would have ended with the destruction of college property. Finally, I also have benefitted from the opportunity to think out loud about this project over several semesters of teaching our wonderful students at Keene State and, outside the campus, at invited presentations at the Walpole International Affairs Discussion Group, Monadnock Lyceum, the Keene State College Seminar Series, Queen's University Belfast, and at the Museum of Free Derry.

My international colleagues at the Auschwitz Institute for the Prevention of Genocide and Mass Atrocities continue to be incredible partners in our shared work, and traveling the globe to do that work has given me the opportunity to develop the comparative perspectives that inform this book. So, a huge thanks is due to Tibi Galis, Jack Mayerhofer, Samantha Capicotto, Rob Scharf, Susan Braden, Eliza Fairbrother, Gary Penzell, Violet Roberts, Kerry Whigham, Ashley Greene (again), Mariana Salazar Albornoz, Stephanie Wright, Duaa Randhawa, Hannah Waller, Maria Eugenia Carbone, Sharleen Lazartes, Laura Karaskiewicz, Clara Ramirez-Barat, Amanda Petaglia, Ashad Sentongo, Kevin Lillian Nakayenga, Abbas Sekyanzi Muluubya, Laila Igitego, Gabriela Ghindea, Matei Demetrescu, and Gosia Waligora.

I also am indebted to the several anonymous reviewers who responded so promptly and with such warm encouragement to Oxford when approached with the proposal for this book. Not only did they affirm the intent of what I set out to do but also offered constructive insight into how I might do it better. My friend, Michael Mac McCaffry, read a draft of the early chapters and, likewise, helped focus my writing on the essential argument. My sister, Jan Rogers, continues to be a source of inspiration and pride. And, as always, it was a pleasure and honor to work with Oxford University Press for the fourth time. The editorial team, Abby Gross and Katie Pratt, were patient and kind throughout. Despite being the world's largest academic press, Oxford has an uncanny ability to make its authors feel like their book is the only one that matters. Finally, a special note of appreciation to a remarkable peacemaker, Senator George Mitchell, for taking time out of his very busy schedule to contribute the Foreword for this book.

My family knows that my mind dwells and, if it is not dwelling on writing, it is going to dwell on something else. For the past three years, my mind's dwelling place has been on writing but my heart, as always, has dwelt with my wife, Patti, and our three children, Brennan, Hannah, and Noah. No matter how far apart we are, you are my home. The greatest honor in my life is to be part of our family, and I still watch in awe and with deep admiration as you each continue to define yourself and your place in this world.

Finally, in his memoir of Paris in the 1920s, *A Moveable Feast*, Ernest Hemingway wrote that "the writer's job is to tell the truth" and that job begins with writing "one true sentence" and then going on from there. The multiplicities of truths in Northern Ireland makes writing even "one true sentence" about its history and current state a daunting task. Regardless, I hope there are enough sentences of truth within this book to do justice to the complicated story of the north of Ireland, its people, and its future.

—J. W.
December 21, 2020
Keene, New Hampshire

About the Author

James Waller is Cohen Professor of Holocaust and Genocide Studies and chair of that same department at Keene State College (NH-US). He is the author of five books, most notably his widely acclaimed *Becoming Evil: How Ordinary People Commit Genocide and Mass Killing* (Oxford University Press, 2nd ed., 2007) and *Confronting Evil: Engaging Our Responsibility to Prevent Genocide* (Oxford University Press, 2016). Waller has held numerous visiting professorships, most recently as an honorary visiting research professor in the George J. Mitchell Institute for Global Peace, Justice and Security at Queen's University in Belfast, Northern Ireland (2017). In the policymaking arena, Waller is also regularly involved, in his role as Director of Academic Programs with the Auschwitz Institute for the Prevention of Genocide and Mass Atrocities, as the curriculum developer and lead instructor for the Raphael Lemkin Seminars for Genocide Prevention. These seminars, held on-site and in conjunction with the Auschwitz-Birkenau State Museum, introduce diplomats and government officials from around the world to issues of genocide warning and prevention. Waller also has delivered invited briefings on genocide prevention and perpetrator behavior for the US Department of State's Bureau of Intelligence and Research, the CIA Directorate of Intelligence, the International Human Rights Unit of the FBI, and the Federal Law Enforcement Training Center. In 2017, he was the inaugural recipient of the Engaged Scholarship Prize from the International Association of Genocide Scholars in recognition of his exemplary engagement in advancing genocide awareness and prevention. Waller is frequently interviewed by broadcast and print media, including PBS, CNN, CBC, the *Los Angeles Times*, the *Washington Post*, *Salon*, *National Geographic*, and the *New York Times*.

Introduction

A Brutal Duality

Here now is a brutal duality called Northern Ireland. A brutal duality of naming as one person's "Northern Ireland" is another person's "North of Ireland." A brutal duality of geography as the six counties of the north are set apart from the 26 counties of the south. A brutal duality of social division as Protestant and Catholic live in near-complete segregation and are, for the most part, content to do so. A brutal duality of historical interpretation between Britain as "protector" and Britain as "occupier." A brutal duality of symbols and narratives coded as "orange" or "green." A brutal duality of media perspectives across the expository gulf between the British Broadcasting Corporation (BBC) and Raidió Teilifís Éireann (RTE). A brutal duality of loyalty between those who speak of "their Queen" and those who speak of "the English Queen." A brutal duality of sectarian violence between those perceived as "terrorists" by one community yet hailed as "freedom fighters" by the other. A brutal duality of death resulting from that violence as one side drapes its martyrs in the Union Jack and the other in the Irish tricolor. And, most divisively, a brutal duality of national identity between those who consider themselves proudly British, aligned with their communal partners of England, Scotland, and Wales in the United Kingdom (UK), and those who consider themselves resolutely Irish, eagerly anticipating the inevitable end of British rule and the reunification of the island of Ireland as one cohesive, independent, and sovereign nation-state.

These brutal dualities—birthed by history, geography, religion, culture, and politics, and then reified with the compromise creation of the statelet designated as Northern Ireland in 1921—have given shape to a country both wonderful and wounded. A wonderful country of 1.8 million people—less than 5,500 square miles in area, roughly the size of Connecticut but with about half its population—with alluring land and seascapes, vibrant culture, rich music and poetry traditions, and a warm and welcoming folk with a blunt and wickedly sly sense of humor. Yet also a wounded country carrying

A Troubled Sleep. James Waller, Oxford University Press (2021). © Oxford University Press.
DOI: 10.1093/oso/9780190095574.003.0001

the scars—seen and unseen, tangible and intangible, acknowledged and unacknowledged—of the aftermath of 30 years of disfiguring violence in the latter half of the twentieth century.

And there is no place where the binary oppositions of this brutal duality are more clearly evident than in Belfast, the capital city and home to more than 300,000 people (the most populous locality in Northern Ireland). Crowned, for the first time, as the best UK City by the Guardian and Observer Travel Awards in 2016, Belfast is self-described as "bursting at the seams with culture, shopping, award-winning dining and an eclectic nightlife."[1] *National Geographic Traveller*'s reader awards lauded Belfast as the "Rising Star of 2017" and *Lonely Planet* followed up in 2018 by listing Belfast, along with the Causeway Coast, as their "No. 1 region in the world to visit."[2] The city is home to two Michelin star restaurants (Northern Ireland recently was recognized as the "World's Best Food Destination" by the World Travel and Tourism Awards in London) and hosts an impressive variety of international sporting events, concerts, and other live entertainment.[3] The broader regional economic boon from the influx of tourists and their money will continue to soar with HBO's recent announcement to transform several iconic sets of their award-winning *Game of Thrones* series, filmed on location in Northern Ireland, into tourist attractions.[4] Already, Belfast hosts more than 10 million tourists annually.[5] Indeed, many locals now have an avocation, if not an outright vocation, as tour guides.

Despite the waves of tourists, Belfast remains, at heart, a small town where authentic and conspicuous civility abounds. People say "thank you" to the driver as they go on and off public buses, you can go months without hearing a honking horn in the city center, locals routinely stop to ask the few homeless people if they need anything, and, on nearly every occasion where I visited with someone for an interview or chat, I was met with generosity of heart and offers of more tea and biscuits than anyone could fairly consume, nearly always followed with a good-natured "safe home then" as I left—said with the distinctive Belfast upspeak that ends each statement with the rising inflection of a question. On a recent national well-being index for the UK, the people of Northern Ireland ranked their overall life satisfaction higher than any other region.[6] While there is no parallel index for the bovine population of Northern Ireland, one would not be wrong to think even the cows in the surrounding countryside seem unusually content. As local columnist Alex Kane writes of contemporary Belfast: "Taxi drivers are happy to drive you from [one] side of the city to the other. Buses aren't hijacked. She [his daughter] has never been evacuated during a bomb scare. Clubs stay open until the early hours. There are no locked gates; no armed patrols and no no-go zones. There's barely a week or weekend goes by without a major festival, concert, event or sporting occasion. Belfast is buzzing today. A lively, mostly lovely city. A city where people smile and someone stopping you in the street isn't scary any more—it's usually a tourist."[7]

There is also in the city, however, the low, soft, steady hum of sectarian tension. A tension that gave birth to and remains a percussive consequence of a 30-year "low-intensity" conflict whose continuing legacy belies that misleading description. Belfast was the epicenter of the violence that ruled the country from 1968 to 1998, euphemistically known as "the Troubles," with nearly half of the more than 3,500 deaths in the conflict occurring within the city's boundaries. Kane describes those years in Belfast: "I remember it as a dark and dangerous place which closed down after 7 PM. I remember the security gates and the police and army patrols. I remember ducking, as did everybody else, when a car backfired. I remember that slight air of panic when a car drove slowly past you. I remember never straying far from the university during hours of darkness. I remember the ritual of being ready to phone home after the 11 PM radio news if there had been any mention of a bomb or shooting in the general area where I lived."[8] Novelist and travel writer Paul Theroux, visiting Belfast in the summer of 1982, described the city as "the old horror . . . a city of drunks, of lurkers, of late risers. It smelled of wet bricks and burning coal. It stank. . . . When the rain came down in Belfast, it splashed through the roof and spattered through the window glass and poured into your soul. It was the blackest city in Britain and the most damaged . . . grim . . . [with an] ugly face."[9] In a 1991 report, a British government official who had lived in Belfast for several years finally visited the mainly Catholic area of West Belfast. He entitled his subsequent report "Into the Alternative Universe" and described the visit "as strange to me as the Forbidden City would have been to a Chinese before 1911."[10]

More than 20 years after the peace was made, the legacy of living in such a conflict-ridden society is clear in present-day Belfast. While overall life satisfaction may have improved in a relative sense after the end of the Troubles, the protracted conflict clearly set a low bar as suicide remains a major public health issue (in the years since the conflict ended, more people have died by suicide in Northern Ireland than were killed in the conflict), exacerbated by the negative stigma tied to seeking preventive mental health care. Prescription rates, alcohol abuse, and pathology incidences (including the prevalence of posttraumatic stress disorder) are among the highest in the Western world, and an estimated 39% of the population have experienced a conflict-related traumatic event.[11] People look raddled, older than they are, weathered by the grind of lives lived in less than ordinary times. Police, as a matter of routine, still search under their cars before they leave their homes for duty or even to take their children to school. In June and July, the height of marching season shutters restaurants and shops for weeks as Protestant bands and orders hold triumphalist displays of cultural heritage and light menacing bonfires several stories high. Graffiti tags in sectarian neighborhoods viscerally reflect the animosity; Protestant neighborhoods are peppered with FTP ("Fuck the Pope") tags while Catholic neighborhoods counter with FTQ ("Fuck the Queen"). Hatred's long-range planning is revealed in the occasional FTNP and FTNQ graffiti tag, where "N" stands for "Next." Unresolved wounds in these communities stay fresh with frequent and continuing calls for further investigation and inquest into sectarian or state-sponsored killings that occurred, in some cases, nearly 50 years ago.

If there is a middle ground in the myriad brutal dualities of contemporary Northern Ireland, few can identify it. Here, in a bifurcated society where roughly 48% grew up as Protestant and 45% as Catholic, the political is always personal. Profoundly personal. In-between spaces lie abandoned and voices of moderation have been silenced in the polarization of a society deeply fragmented by identity politics and generationally accustomed to parallel lives lived in proximity but seldom in shared space. In many areas of the country, the sale of a home or land still does not dare cross sectarian hands. Northern Ireland remains, as first described by Dervla Murphy in her travels throughout the country in the 1970s, "a place apart," filled with "an ineradicable mistrust of the other side, permeating every crevice of the victim's heart and soul." As she asks: "What could be more damaging than that?"[12]

* * *

The goal of this book is to offer an empirically and experientially informed, nonpartisan analysis of risk and resilience in contemporary Northern Ireland. Today, more than 50 years since the Troubles began and more than 20 years after they "ended," does Northern Ireland remain, in Murphy's words, "a place apart?" Are the sociopolitical vulnerabilities exposed by the Troubles still present? Or has Northern Ireland rebuilt differently enough so as to ensure nonrecurrence of violent conflict? Has the conflict, while perhaps managed and contained, at least through a peace agreement, been transformed—structurally and relationally—into a win-win situation for both sides embroiled in the conflict? Does Northern Ireland have the resiliency to withstand the internal and external stressors that may threaten a destabilization of its fragile peace?

To write a book about Northern Ireland is to be aware of how much we still do not know about the myriad obstacles facing a post-conflict society. In that spirit, this book is written out of a commitment to understand the present as well as a concern for the future. Ultimately, understanding where you are is a crucial starting point for understanding where you want to go.

During the winter and spring of 2017, as an honorary visiting research professor in the Senator George J. Mitchell Institute for Global Peace, Security and Justice at Queen's University Belfast, I had the opportunity to "ground truth" these questions by being on location for an extended period of time. Since then, I have returned numerous times to Northern Ireland for additional ethnographic fieldwork, research, and interviews and to deliver public lectures and participate on community panels. All told, I have collected more than 110 hours of face-to-face interviews drawn from more than 60 politicians, activists, community workers, former political prisoners, former (and sometimes current) paramilitary members, members of dissident groups, academics, journalists, mental health practitioners, tour guides, school teachers, museum curators, students, police and military personnel (active and retired), legal experts, and religious leaders across Northern Ireland.

In connecting with interviewees, I relied primarily on *purposive sampling* to strategically identify those people most relevant to the research questions I was asking. Many times, interviewees would then suggest, and often introduce me to, other interviewees they believed to be suitable for the project. This *snowball sampling* brought access to interviewees who may have been impossible to access otherwise. Finally, the small, welcoming community of Northern Ireland also opened up pathways for *convenience sampling*—the frequent, usually daily, accidental opportunities for "interviews" with people on the street; in buses, trains, and taxis; and in the restaurants and pubs and coffee stands with whom I would strike up an informal conversation that would, at some point quickly, turn to the questions surrounding contemporary Northern Ireland.[13]

Throughout these mixed sampling approaches, I remained intentional in the diversity of voices I sought in terms of political and national leanings, geographic and professional distribution, and age and gender representation.

Some self-defined as victims, others as survivors, and yet others as victim-survivors. Still others resisted any language that defined them based on what was done to them by others and focused, rather, on an empowered identity born from self-definition. Among the interviewees were those who killed and those who lost loved ones to the violence, some even falling into both categories as "guilty victims." For others, the old shadows of a country long at odds with itself stretched out and found them in more indirect ways.

Each person I spoke with in these various contexts had, over the course of their lives in Northern Ireland, been touched by the Troubles and its legacy in some significant manner. The death toll of that 30-year period was 3,532 persons, with another 42,216 injured as a direct result of that conflict. Each person killed in the Troubles loved someone else and was loved by someone else. Each had hopes, dreams, and aspirations that would never be fulfilled simply because of what they believed or did not believe, who they were or were not, or, simply, where they happened to be or not be at a given moment. While to the outside eye it may be tempting to assume that the suffering of living under prolonged conflict is confined only to those directly victimized, such an assumption is recklessly misleading. The suffering is multidirectional. Thousands upon thousands of others are scarred—physically, psychologically, and emotionally—by the violence. Everyone in a conflict society is a victim of a collective traumatization; there is a population-level impact. In Argentina, for instance, where upward of 30,000 people were killed or disappeared during the military dictatorship of 1976–1983, the reality was that everyone lived in fear that they *could* be killed or disappeared. So the death toll itself is dwarfed by the collective societal traumatization in which all Argentines lived under the terror of violence.[14] It was the destruction of a society from within. Even if they did not choose conflict, the conflict could choose them.

Similarly, in Northern Ireland, there were no sidelines during the Troubles, only sides; no winners, only victims. The violence was routinized, normalized, and, far too often, indiscriminate. Because of this reality, the impact of violence also was inescapable for anyone living in Northern Ireland during the Troubles. As one shopkeeper in West Belfast told me, "every Catholic family was impacted by loss or imprisonment during the Troubles." A mental health practitioner I interviewed pointed out that "the psychic impact of the Troubles is disproportionate to the number of lives lost, in part because the violence was up close and personal for so many people." Even for those who have come since, the legacy of the conflict seeps into daily consciousness and life for everyone in Northern Ireland. The transgenerational wounds caused by the transmission of traumatic events and loss bear witness to the continuing secondary legacy of conflict in an allegedly post-conflict society.[15]

Recognizing this, I abided by the guideline that there is no better research methodology than actively and deeply listening to the people living the reality of a post-conflict society. They certainly had more to teach me than I had to offer them, and recognizing that truth went a long way toward opening doors of understanding. These interviews were not intended to be systematic data collection. There are scores of works, many referenced as notes in this book, where such data can be found. Rather, these interviews were in-depth chats in an environment of the interviewees' own choosing (home, café, pub, public park, office, etc.). We began with a broad framing question ("To what degree do you see Northern Ireland as a post-conflict society?") to open spaces for conversation to flow uninterrupted by a predetermined script. It was the natural rhythm of conversation, directed primarily by the interviewees' reflections and tangents, that allowed them—and me—to open doorways of access to thoughts and opinions that would have been inaccessible in a standard prescribed interview format. More than dates, times, and events, I wanted traces of their thoughts, feelings, and reflections about contemporary Northern Ireland. Listening to people think out loud about their lives and how they make sense of the world in which they live can offer a profound depth of understanding, both in what is said as well as unsaid. It can move the interesting to the important, breathing life into the research.

My search for understanding was not the pursuit of "a Truth" but the unpacking of many kinds of "truths." Indeed, to restrict oneself to the notion that there are only two kinds of truth in Northern Ireland—Protestant or Catholic—is to vastly underestimate the multiplicity of how "truth" is interpreted and internalized across segments of that society. In pursuit of these many kinds of truth, even biased misinformation—often framed as a "true story" but smacking more of a "strong opinion"—was helpful in understanding how people receive and transmit (intentionally and unintentionally) the truths that are central to their personal and collective narratives of identity. Here, my positionality as a "cultural outsider" meant that I had a clearer lens—or at least a lens less clouded by personal investment, family history, or cultural upbringing—through which I could critically approach, with clarity and focus afforded by distance and a broader perspective, the competing narratives of mutual exclusivity that underlie the deep cisterns of fear, suspicion, and resentment.

When welcomed to these conversations, trust was not always quick in coming. Northern Ireland has long been seen as the paradigmatic case study of intergroup (mis)relations (often included in the disciplinary canon with South Africa and Israel/Palestine), so it has drawn its fair share of researchers collecting interviews over the years. At times, some of those researchers have made questionable ethical decisions that have compromised the safety and security of those they interviewed. Most notable was the recent controversy in which 46 former paramilitary members provided testimonies to a Boston College oral history project on the grounds that the testimonies would only be made public after they died. In 2011, the Police Service of Northern Ireland (PSNI), using an obscure legal assistance treaty, applied to US authorities for subpoenas to gain access to some of those testimonies. Eventually, Boston College, bowing to the legal pressure, reneged on the comprehensive guarantees under which the testimonies had been collected and released transcripts and tapes of some interviews to the PSNI (which ultimately led to the arrest and brief detention of then Sinn Fein leader Gerry Adams in relation to the 1972 murder of Jean McConville). Some of those whose interviews had been released faced threats of physical violence and ostracism from their communities. All of those who had been interviewed for the project—even if their interviews had not been released to the PSNI—recognized that their confidentiality and control over their testimonies, promised by Boston College, were now null and void.

Caught in the flotsam of these recent events, not everyone, particularly in the Catholic community, readily agreed to be interviewed by yet another American researcher (and most cited the Boston College controversy as the reason for their hesitation or refusal). For people who did agree to be interviewed, and that was the vast majority of those I approached, all were assured that their individual identities would be protected in this book. Too many of them have suffered too much for me or any researcher to expose them to any additional pain, shame, threat, condemnation, or, even, civil or criminal liability. While some remained hesitant to take my word on those ground rules of anonymity and confidentiality, most came to recognize my interest was less on their activities in the past (criminal or otherwise) and more on their subjective insights on the present and future in Northern Ireland. The secrets they shared with me, and then tucked back into their hiding place, are owned by them, not by me. A very few, at the end of an interview, even backtracked and asked that I not use any of the specific information they shared with me, and I have honored those requests in full. So, in this book, quoted material attributed directly to a named source comes either from previously published writings, publicly accessible statements (e.g., a speech, pamphlet, or poster), or with the direct and explicit permission of the person named.

The interviews collected for this book have profoundly shaped my thinking and reflections on contemporary Northern Ireland. Even where these voices are not directly quoted, their presence can be felt between the lines of these pages as rich, original, primary source material that brings the lived experience to my evidence-based analysis of risk and resilience. As historian and political scientist Richard English of Queen's University Belfast notes: "Interviews can unveil otherwise unavailable and invisible views and experiences, through evidence acquired from people who are less salient and powerful than those who are usually quoted; such evidence can also lead one to re-evaluate other kinds of data in fresh and stringent fashion."[16]

In addition, this dialogue with the voices of the interviewees is complemented by a dialogue with a range of primary source archival material, representing both sides of the sectarian divide, from depositories at libraries and museums throughout Northern Ireland. Particularly valuable were the voices of on-the-ground local and regional columnists and commentators from the *Belfast Telegraph*, *Belfast News Letter*, the *Irish Times*, the *Irish News*, BBC, RTE, *The Detail* (an investigative news and analysis website based in Belfast), and open-source analysis from the blogosphere. All of this intensive fieldwork is buttressed by a deep dive into the wealth of secondary research material surrounding Northern Ireland from a wide range of academic disciplines.

Having the opportunity to "ground truth" also means you live with more nontraditional "voices" of ethnographic witness—landscapes and soundscapes, murals and memorials, commemorations and parades, neighborhoods and rituals, food and humor, sport and folklore, and the everyday rhythm of life in a post-conflict society. There is no substitute for being "there" in person. By being fully present, embedded, and attentively observing—being in a country but not of it—you see and hear things that you could not see and hear from a distance. As an itinerant child of divorce who moved from town to town every two years or so, I developed the survival skills of an outsider's eyes and ears that served me well during my time in Northern Ireland.

To this wealth of fieldwork and primary and secondary source research material, I bring to bear a career of teaching and scholarship in intergroup relations, conflict, large-scale violence, and political psychology. My work on perpetrator behavior, published as *Becoming Evil: How Ordinary People Commit Genocide and Mass Killing* (Oxford University Press, 2nd ed., 2007), is part of an ongoing research project that now includes more than 225 face-to-face interviews with alleged and convicted perpetrators of war crimes, crimes against humanity, and genocide from around the globe—including fieldwork in post-conflict societies in Germany, Israel, and several countries in the former Yugoslavia (Bosnia-Herzegovina, Republika Srpska, Serbia, and Croatia), the African Great Lakes Region (Rwanda, Uganda, and Tanzania), Latin America (Argentina, Guatemala, Uruguay, Colombia, and Chile), and southeast Asia (Thailand, Cambodia, and Burma). These international experiences in a diverse range of post-conflict societies give me a valuable and unique comparative lens to bring as another entry point to understanding contemporary Northern Ireland.

More recently, I have directly addressed issues of conflict prevention in my *Confronting Evil: Engaging Our Responsibility to Prevent Genocide* (Oxford University Press, 2016). Of particular relevance in that work is my focus on understanding the underlying risk factors that place a society at peril for violent conflict. Among these, I include risk factors related to memory, governance, and social fragmentation. These are cross-cutting and intersecting issues that, when contextually understood, give us an informed probability of violent conflict emerging in a society. In addition, these risk factors give us insight into the types of strategies to be developed to foster resilience in a society. That is, if we have a good understanding of the issues that put a society at risk, it also opens us to a more constructive understanding of how conflict history can be remembered, governance systems can be structured, and social cohesion can be promoted to inoculate a society against those risk factors. This work allows me to contextualize contemporary Northern Ireland's risk and resilience in a broader global context of evidence-based knowledge about deeply divided societies and how they recover from prolonged conflict.

Finally, my lived experience as someone born and raised in the United States also opens up windows of connection and resonance with the Irish experience. The number of US residents who claim Irish ancestry is more than 33 million, about 10% of our total population and more than seven times the population of Ireland itself. That Irish diaspora has retained a strong interest in the island of Ireland. The Ireland Funds, for example, is a global philanthropic organization, with its largest chapter in the United States, that has raised more than $600 million since 1976 to promote and support peace, culture, education, and community development throughout the island of Ireland. Much of Irish-American interest is directed toward a united Ireland, and this is reflected in contributions of nearly $13 million to Sinn Fein since they began fundraising operations in America in 1994. In a June 4, 2020 online conversation hosted by USA-based Friends of Sinn Fein, Gerry Adams called on Irish-American supporters to begin lobbying for a referendum on a united Ireland.[17] As Ted Smyth, a former Irish diplomat, has said: "There has been the tradition since at least 1916 of the Irish in America being more militant than the Irish in Ireland."[18] That militancy aside, it was, though, the US civil rights movement that was the original catalyst for the nonviolent protests for civil rights and equality of citizenship in Northern Ireland. Successive presidential administrations, from Carter through Obama, were actively involved in supporting and sustaining the peace process and, as co-guarantors of the Good Friday Agreement, the United States joins the British and Irish governments in having a continuing vested interest in a peaceful Northern Ireland.

In recent years, unfortunately, the Trump administration reversed course and no longer maintained a policy of active engagement in the peace process and, in so doing, weakened the intergovernmental relations that have been so crucial to maintaining the peace. Moreover, the administration's renewed focus on domestic issues ("America First") pulled it away from the international engagement necessary to provide the support and leverage to ensure the stability of Northern Ireland's post-conflict present and future.

In February 2019, taking a more engaged approach, a bipartisan group of more than 40 American politicians and business leaders and foreign policy experts came together to form the Ad Hoc Committee to Protect the Good Friday Agreement. The following August, the most powerful US Democrat, Nancy Pelosi, declared: "If Brexit undermines the Good Friday accord, there will be no chance of a US–UK trade agreement passing the Congress."[19] A House resolution reaffirming support of the Good Friday Agreement was passed in December 2019.[20] Most recently, the incoming Biden administration has reemphasized the United States' commitment to the peace process in Northern Ireland and pledged itself to rebuilding the international relationships necessary to ensure that the peace holds.[21]

The deepest resonance for me, as an American, is that I see myself and my divided country reflected in Northern Ireland. As *The Irish Times* columnist Fintan O'Toole writes: "Over more than two centuries, the United States has stirred a very wide range of feelings in the rest of the world: love and hatred, fear and hope, envy and contempt, awe and anger."[22] And, as an American, I know we stir the worst of those feelings when we claim the high ground and lecture others on how memory, governance, and social cohesion ought best be promoted. This book is not meant to be judgmental or pejorative. Rather, it comes from a place of recognizing a common, shared predicament of living in a deeply divided society caught in the long-running grip of a culture war and fraught with contested memory, dysfunctional governance, and social fragmentation.

* * *

At the simplest level, contemporary Northern Ireland can be viewed through a peace lens or a conflict lens. A peace lens recognizes that "by whatever un-certain and circuitous route, the peace process is advancing" and tends to privilege those advances over the retreats.[23] I absolutely appreciate the no-tion that peace is a winding, dynamic journey and not a destination. I have an even deeper appreciation for the important work of peace done over the years in Northern Ireland, particularly at the grassroots level. But I also ap-preciate the fact that, as one interviewee described to me, "there is nothing 'post' about Northern Ireland's post-conflict society." The Good Friday Agreement was not the culmination of a peace process: it was simply one part of a prolonged and ongoing peace process. The road to conflict transforma-tion is a long one, and, in my opinion, it is too soon to look with unqualified optimism at contemporary Northern Ireland through a peace lens.

So, this book, while recognizing that the peace process continues, is written through a conflict lens. This is not born from a sense of pessimism or negativity or a verdict about the darkness of human nature. I do believe there are more things to admire in people than to abhor. I also believe, however, that peace cannot be reduced simply to an absence of violence. While armed conflict has dissipated to a large degree, the transformation in contemporary Northern Ireland has not been from armed conflict to peace but from armed conflict to political, social, and cultural conflict.

Using that conflict lens, this book—while recognizing that the long slow processes of rebuilding a post-conflict society include work at the grass-roots level—operates from the perspective that those processes draw their oxygen from a much broader macro-context that enables, or hinders, their development. This approach, more akin to critical ethnography, interrogates higher level social structures and systems of power relationships from the perspectives of the participants involved, with the belief that the transition from conflict to peace is, in the final analysis, driven mostly at that higher level. While that top-down approach is not sufficient for such change to occur, it is necessary and, too often, neglected in micro-level analyses that privilege the bottom-up approaches to rebuilding a post-conflict society. Today, in contemporary Northern Ireland, many of the civil society actors and organizations that proved so pivotal in building peace from below are now, in large part, absent.

Part I of the book, "Wounded Identities," reviews the deep divisions within the north of Ireland and contextualizes them within the theoretical frameworks of deeply divided societies and social identity (Chapter 1). This book is not a rehashing of the complex history of the Troubles nor is it an attempt to place blame for their origin or continuation. It is necessary, however, to understand how the history of the north of Ireland, in all its complexity and contestation, gave shape to the social identities that still deeply divide contemporary Northern Ireland (Chapter 2). Over that time, two conflicting cultures, built on group-based social identities, emerged with little community of feeling, common citizenship, or unity of being.

Part II of the book, "Risk and Resilience in Contemporary Northern Ireland," analyzes Northern Ireland's current vulnerabilities and points of resilience as an allegedly "post-conflict" society. The vulnerabilities are analyzed through a model of risk assessment I developed that examines the longer term and slower moving structures, measures, society-wide conditions, and processes that leave societies vulnerable to violent conflict.[24] Such risk factors include the interpretation of conflict history (Chapter 3), how authority in a country is exercised (Chapter 4), and the susceptibility to social disharmony, isolation, and fragmentation (Chapter 5). Resilience is examined from a survey of the countering influences, both within and outside Northern Ireland, that are working diligently to confirm humanity by reducing or reversing these vulnerabilities. So, while I will argue that contemporary Northern Ireland is clearly a fragile state, the reality must be acknowledged that it has not crossed the line to becoming the world's newest failing or failed state. Understanding the reasons why the teetering, however precipitous, has not become a calamitous fall, including a return to violence, is a vital part of understanding the complexity of factors at play in contemporary Northern Ireland.

Part III of the book, "A Troubled Sleep," concludes by examining the accelerating factors in contemporary Northern Ireland that may lead to an escalation of crisis as well as the triggering factors that could spark the onset of violent conflict itself (Chapter 6). Accelerants and triggers help us understand the transformation of possibilities for violent conflict into probabilities. In the face of escalating risk and fading resilience, how possible is it that the children's future does not mirror their parent's and grandparent's and great-grandparent's past? Must the past always be in front of Northern Ireland?

On display in the permanent visitor exhibition in Belfast City Hall is an "Inter-Schools Peace Capsule" with a placard reading: "Schools representing the two main traditions created a Peace Capsule for posterity. It contains items representing their peace and reconciliation projects and their aspirations and hopes for a peaceful future in Northern Ireland at the start of the new Millennium. To be opened during 2025." This book opens that capsule a bit early and measures the obstacles to, and opportunities for, that peaceful future.

* * *

Sitting on a bench one brisk gray afternoon in Dunville Park on Falls Road in West Belfast, a predominately Catholic area, I strike up a conversation with an older woman who had taken her dog for a walk. Inevitably, our chat turns to my reason for being in Belfast (many locals, particularly those who lived through the Troubles, are still surprised that people voluntarily choose to visit Belfast). I explain to her my interest in how a society recovers from conflict and some of the places in which I had worked on that question around the world. With a wry smile, she replies: "You picked an easy one here, didn't you? Hasn't anyone told you that the more you learn about Northern Ireland, the less you understand?" As we talk more (and I understand less), we discuss the strides the country has made but also the ways in which Northern Ireland might still be at risk for the recurrence of violent conflict. It is clear, both from what she says as well as what is unsaid, that her heart is taken back to the 30 years of her life that she lived in such conflict; even, to her mind, as a lifelong resident of West Belfast, a life lived under military siege. There is a long period of quiet only interrupted by the occasional bark of her dog. And then, gazing in the distance far past the city center and toward the River Lagan, she asks: "Do you think we have any hope?"

On the other side of the sectarian divide, just a few hundred yards away in the Protestant enclave of Shankill Road, there is a monument with a large stone slab reading "In Memory of Five Innocent Protestants Slaughtered

Here by a Republican Murder Gang on 13th August 1975." This memorial commemorates a bomb and gun attack on the local Bayardo Bar. Behind the memorial is a small fenced area, nestled next to a former drug addiction treatment center, titled "The Garden of Hope and Reflection." On the fence surrounding the garden is posted a user notice reading: "Users of The Garden of Hope and Reflection do so at their own risk. FASA [Forum for Action on Substance Abuse] cannot and will not accept responsibility for any injury obtained in The Garden of Hope and Reflection. FASA will also not accept any liability for any personal belongings brought onto the premises. No pets permitted in The Garden of Hope and Reflection. Thank you."

Hope. *Nada* in Bosnian. *Nadzieja* in Polish. *Esperanza* in Spanish. *Ikizere* in Kinyarwandan. *May hayaar laint hkyet* in Burmese. *Ta Suil* in Irish. Whatever language we use, hope is fervently sought in all post-conflict societies. Rather than dwelling on the nightmares of the past, hope summons the buoyant dreams of an optimistic future. Hope is less about what has been and more about what is to come. In contemporary Northern Ireland, though, hope comes qualified. Hope is a fragile entity in this place, and you engage it at your own risk. But choosing not to engage it brings even greater risk. While there certainly are times when there seems little reason to be optimistic about the future of Northern Ireland, there is still yet every reason to be hopeful. To find those reasons to be hopeful, however, requires an honest analysis of the current vulnerabilities in Northern Ireland related to memory, governance, and social fragmentation, as well as an assessment of the actors, organizations, and strategies that can reduce or reverse those vulnerabilities. Engaging these coupled realities of risk and resilience, situated in a contextual understanding of contemporary accelerators and triggers of potential conflict, is where reasons for hope, however fragile, will be found.

Notes

1. For news of the Guardian and Observer Travel Award, see https://www.independent.ie/life/travel/travel-news/belfast-is-named-best-uk-city-at-guardian-and-observer-travel-awards-34521629.html, accessed on September 29, 2018. Quoted material comes from the *Northern Ireland Visitors Journal* (Spring 2017), p. 10.
2. For *National Geographic Traveller's* award, see http://www.natgeotraveller.co.uk/readerawards/reader-awards-2017/, accessed on September 29, 2018. For the Lonely Planet designation, see https://www.lonelyplanet.com/best-in-travel/regions, also accessed on September 29, 2018.

3. See http://www.irishnews.com/business/2018/12/05/news/belfast-restaurants-named-among-world-s-best-in-prestigious-list-1500878, accessed on December 5, 2018.

4. David Barden, "'Game of Thrones' Filming Locations to Become Tourist Attractions," accessed on September 25, 2018, at https://www.huffingtonpost.com/entry/game-of-thrones-tourist-attractions-northern-ireland_us_5ba9d5e9e4b0375f8f9ff8ef

5. See Claire McNeilly, "Reborn Belfast Now a Magnet for Close to 10M Visitors a Year," *Belfast Telegraph*, accessed on September 21, 2018, at https://www.belfasttelegraph.co.uk/news/northern-ireland/reborn-belfast-now-a-magnet-for-close-to-10m-visitors-a-year-35623706.html

6. Accessed on September 21, 2018, at https://www.theguardian.com/world/2016/sep/27/northern-ireland-happiest-place-uk-ons-wellbeing-survey

7. Alex Kane, "A Tale of Two Belfasts," *The Irish News* (May 25, 2018), accessed on October 27, 2018, at http://www.irishnews.com/opinion/columnists/2018/05/25/news/alex-kane-a-tale-of-two-belfasts-1336917/

8. Ibid.

9. Paul Theroux, *The Kingdom by the Sea: A Journey Around Great Britain* (Boston, MA: Houghton Mifflin, 1983), 248–249, 254.

10. Eamon Phoenix, "West Belfast an 'Alternative Universe' Says Government Official," *The Irish News* (August 25, 2017), accessed on September 21, 2018, at http://www.irishnews.com/news/northernirelandnews/2017/08/25/news/west-belfast-an-alternative-universe-says-government-official-1120314

11. Brendan Bunting, Finola Ferry, Sam Murphy, Siobhan O'Neill, Gerard Leavey, and David Bolton, "Troubled Consequences: A Report on the Mental Health Impact of the Civil Conflict in Northern Ireland" (October 2011), prepared for the Commission for Victims and Survivors by the Bamford Centre for Mental Health and Wellbeing at the University of Ulster in partnership with the Northern Ireland Centre for Trauma and Transformation and Compass, accessed on June 1, 2020, at https://www.cvsni.org/media/1435/troubled-consequences-october-2011.pdf

12. Dervla Murphy, *A Place Apart: Northern Ireland in the 1970s* (London: Erland Books, 2014; first published 1978), 121.

13. For additional information on these forms of sampling, see Alan Bryman, *Social Research Methods*, 5th ed. (New York: Oxford University Press, 2016).

14. See Daniel Feierstein, *Genocide as Social Practice: Reorganizing Society Under the Nazis and Argentina's Military Juntas* (Brunswick, NJ: Rutgers University Press, 2014).

15. Siobhan O' Neill, Cherie Armour, David Bolton, Brendan Bunting, Colette Corry, Barney Devine, Edel Ennis, Finola Ferry, Aine McKenna, Margaret McLafferty, and Sam Murphy, "Towards a Better Future: The Trans-Generational Impact of the Troubles on Mental Health" (March 2015), prepared for the Commission for Victims and Survivors by Ulster University, accessed on June 1, 2020, at https://www.cvsni.org/media/1171/towards-a-better-future-march-2015.pdf

16. Richard English, *Does Terrorism Work?: A History* (London: Oxford University Press, 2016), 22.

17. The entire conversation can be found at https://www.youtube.com/watch?v=8QZD5qcv3aE&t=656s, accessed on June 6, 2020.

18. Liam Stack, "New Sinn Fein Leader Has a Familiar Task: Wooing Irish-Americans," *The New York Times* (March 17, 2018), accessed on June 1, 2020, at https://www.nytimes.com/2018/03/17/world/europe/sinn-fein-ireland-mcdonald.html

19. Susan Heavey, "US-British Trade Pact Won't Pass Congress if Good Friday Deal Harmed," *Reuters* (August 14, 2019), accessed on June 1, 2020, at https://www.reuters.com/article/uk-britain-eu-pelosi/u-s-british-trade-pact-wont-pass-congress-if-good-friday-deal-harmed-pelosi-idUSKCN1V419I

20. Text of the resolution can be found at https://www.congress.gov/bill/116th-congress/house-resolution/585/text, accessed on June 1, 2020.

21. See Jennifer Duggan, "Biden Says Irish Border Must Remain Open as Brexit Talks Continue," *Time* (November 25, 2020), accessed on December 14, 2020 at https://time.com/5915513/biden-brexit-ireland-coveney/

22. Fintan O'Toole, "Donald Trump Has Destroyed the Country He Promised to Make Great Again," *The Irish Times* (April 25, 2020), accessed on May 31, 2020, at https://www.irishtimes.com/opinion/fintan-o-toole-donald-trump-has-destroyed-the-country-he-promised-to-make-great-again-1.4235928

23. Vicky Cosstick, *Belfast: Toward a City Without Walls* (Belfast: Colourpoint, 2015), 23.

24. See James Waller, *Confronting Evil: Engaging Our Responsibility to Prevent Genocide* (New York: Oxford University Press, 2016), particularly chapter 4.

PART I
WOUNDED IDENTITIES

In a lecture delivered at the University of Oxford in 1978, Irish historian F.S.L. Lyons, outlining the conflicting cultures which exist in Ireland, spoke of "an anarchy in the mind and in the heart, an anarchy which forbade not just unity of territories, but also 'unity of being,' an anarchy that sprang from the collision within a small and intimate island of seemingly irreconcilable cultures, unable to live together or to live apart, caught inextricably in the web of their tragic history."[1]

Part I of this book opens by contextualizing the absence of a "unity of being" within the theoretical frameworks of deeply divided societies and social identity. A central defining feature of deeply divided societies is binary division based on class, caste, religion, language, race, ethnicity, clan, political beliefs, or a variety of other social identities. Deeply divided societies, delineated by difference from the "other," breed communities of fear and isolation that often are the cause of, or justification for, intractable social identity conflicts. To reduce the complexity of social identities in Northern Ireland to religion—Protestant or Catholic—is dangerously simplistic and misleading. In reality, the dividing, and defining, social identity cleavage is one of national identity—those supporting Northern Ireland's constitutional status with the United Kingdom aligned against those believing that Northern Ireland should more rightly be part of a united Ireland.

Part I then unpacks how the wounded history of the north of Ireland, in all its complexity and contestation, gave shape to the social identities that still deeply divide contemporary Northern Ireland. This historical survey is not a rehashing of the complex history of the north of Ireland nor is it an attempt to place blame for the origin or continuation of the sectarian divide that defines it. A legion of scholars far more adroit than I have addressed the former and the latter—"the conflict about the conflict"—is a daily exercise for most everyone in Northern Ireland. Rather, a broad survey of that scarified history is offered in recognition that understanding the origins of those competing social identities, and the ways in which they became cemented over generations, is essential context, and a necessary reference point, for Part II's analysis of risk and resilience in contemporary Northern Ireland.

Note

1. F.S. L. Lyons, *Culture and Anarchy in Ireland, 1890–1939* (Oxford: Clarendon Press, 1979), 177.

1

"You're One or the Other"

Social Identities in Deeply Divided Societies

In the decades following the devastation of World War II, the stability and durability of liberal democracies had become a significant concern among political scientists. Increasing attention was being paid to the factors that built an
enduring and resilient democracy, as well as to the forces that worked against
them. Of particular concern were identity threats related to "fragmented systems" or "plural societies." Arend Lijphart, for instance, wrote of "segmental
cleavages . . . of a religious, ideological, linguistic, regional, cultural, racial
or ethnic nature" that had to be overcome in order to establish political stability.[1] Similarly, Eric Nordlinger addressed the challenges of conflict regulation in what he defined as "deeply divided societies" where "a large number
of conflict group members attach overwhelming importance to the issues at
stake, or manifest strongly held antagonistic beliefs and emotions toward the
opposing segment, or both."[2] Nordlinger's concept of "deeply divided societies" rapidly became embedded in academic discourse, even as its defining
characteristics were debated and, as academics are wont to do, wordsmithed
to the point of being arcane. Ian Lustick, for instance, considered a society to
be deeply divided "if ascriptive ties generate an antagonistic segmentation of
society, based on terminal identities with high political salience, sustained
over a substantial period and a wide variety of issues. As a minimum condition, boundaries between rival groups must be sharp enough so that membership is clear and, with few exceptions, unchangeable."[3]

Lijphart, Nordlinger, and Lustick each make some reference to "segmental," "segment," or "segmentation." Embedded in these references is the
recognition that a central defining feature of deeply divided societies is binary
division: two contrasting segments of a population that represent a cleavage
significant enough to impact a wide range of issues. These binary fault lines
can arise from class, caste, religion, language, race, ethnicity, clan, or political identity. They also can come from "settler versus native; immigrant
versus indigenous population; pastoralist versus cultivator; peasant versus

A Troubled Sleep. James Waller, Oxford University Press (2021). © Oxford University Press.
DOI: 10.1093/oso/9780190095574.003.0002

landowner; urban versus rural; and centre versus periphery."[4] The destabilizing polarization that is so typical of deeply divided societies is embedded in a black-and-white binary division—"us" and "them." While there are some cases of deeply divided societies where the divisions involve more than two competing groups (e.g., Bosnia-Herzegovina and Iraq), generally, more diverse societies are less prone to the types of polarizing dynamics that characterize deeply divided societies.

The binary divisions inherent in deeply divided societies breed communities of fear and isolation. In a deeply divided society, incentives for trust, cooperation, dialogue, and long-term social exposure are reduced. As Belfast-based columnist Malachi O'Doherty writes: "This is the big problem with a divided society; every issue is presumed to be sectarian at heart. And every issue ends up being appropriated by one side and opposed by the other."[5] The binary identities are manipulated by powerholders to exacerbate social dismemberment and advance their own partisan interests. These divisions become particularly destructive when paired with differential access to "power and wealth, services and resources, employment, development opportunities, citizenship and the enjoyment of fundamental rights and freedoms."[6] It is discrimination based on the binary differences, and a persistent pattern of it, that dictates differences in quality of life and entrench the segmentation in a deeply divided society. The discrimination becomes both a cause of, and a justification for, the walls that divide the two groups.

Between 1959 and 1962, a revolution in Rwanda led to a dramatic reordering of social relations between the country's two dominant identity communities—Hutu, making up roughly 85% of the population, and Tutsi, about 14% of the population. The Tutsi minority, previously empowered by colonial favoritism, now found itself politically and socially marginalized with the rise to power of the Hutu majority. After declaring its formal independence in 1962, the Hutu president of Rwanda's First Republic, Gregoire Kayibanda, paid lip service to tolerance and respect for minority rights even as Tutsi civilians became frequent targets of discrimination and significant violence at the hands of the Hutu majority. Kayibanda's authoritarian regime consolidated, by policy and practice, a narrative that cemented the binary divisions of Rwanda's deeply divided society. Kayibanda described the Hutu and Tutsi as "two nations in a single state. . . . Two nations between whom there is no intercourse and no sympathy, who are as ignorant of each other's habits, thoughts and feelings as if they were dwellers of different zones, or inhabitants of different planets."[7] These rigidified differences would continue to be embraced by Hutu elites after the birth of Rwanda's Second Republic in 1973, eventually culminating in the genocide of 1994 in which more than 800,000 Tutsi and moderate Hutus were killed by Hutu extremists over a three-month period.[8]

In Northern Ireland, there is a similar tyranny of social identity that leaves little room for shades of gray. There are two tribes, a binary division definitory of a divided society. As one local, born and raised in Belfast, told me "you're one or the other." The use of the word "other" is telling because it exposes the depersonalization that is at the heart of group-based social identities. The nature of human relations shifts "from *inter-personal* (interaction between people is determined by their personal relationship and their respective individual characteristics) to *inter-group* (the behavior of individuals towards each other is determined by their membership of different groups)."[9] When that relational shift happens—from interacting with you based on who you are as an individual to interacting with you based on the group to which you belong—it can move us along a continuum of tension with the "other" from group comparison to group competition to group hostility to, possibly, inter-group conflict.

Derry Girls, the critically acclaimed television sitcom set in early-1990s Northern Ireland, paints sharp and often hilariously irreverent depictions of lives lived in a society defined by difference from the "other." In the opening episode of its second season, titled "Across the Barricade," a Catholic Priest, Father Peter, is leading a peace initiative retreat ("No hate, no hate, let's integrate!") for Catholic and Protestant teenage students. As part of an opening group exercise, Father Peter asks the students to give him examples of things that Catholics and Protestants have in common and things they do not have in common. He begins by asking for similarities. The question is met with silence until one student gives it a go but, after a few stumbling attempts, ends with "I'm actually drawing a blank here to be honest." The second response follows from another student: "Protestants are British and Catholics are Irish." Father Peter patiently points out: "That's actually a difference . . . quite a . . . quite a big difference." He allows it, though, to be written on the chalkboard labeled "Differences." After asking the students to get "back to similarities," Father Peter is again met with rapid-fire answer after answer illustrating "differences." "Protestants are richer." "Catholics really buzz off statues and we don't so much." "Protestants like to march and Catholics like to walk." By the end of the scene, despite a defeated Father Peter's best effort, the chalkboard labeled "Differences" is crammed full ("Catholics have more freckles,"

"Protestants hate ABBA") while the board labeled "Similarities" is tellingly barren.

Deeply divided societies, delineated by difference from the "other," can be seen as intractable identity conflicts. Rather than being thought of as a discrete category, intractable identity conflicts are better viewed as lying along on a continuum of conflict. On that continuum, intractable identity conflicts are defined by the following attributes: they are long-standing, pervasive or chronically salient to those involved, have conflict-intensifying features that go far beyond the original dispute, simplify stereotypes, and are mired in zero-sum conceptualizations (whatever is gained by one side is lost by the other) and mutual disidentification (defining who we are based on who we are not).[10]

Intractable identity conflicts, while not literally unresolvable, are stubbornly resistant to resolution. Often enduring and existing over generations, such conflicts are fanned by the flames of "hot, direct, unambiguous prejudices" that "advocate segregation, containment, and even elimination of outgroups."[11] There is an "ascendancy of military terms," or "war-talk" (for instance, "no-go areas"), which dehumanizes the "other," mitigates against resolution, and even justifies (and often glorifies) harm-doing.[12] Indeed, it is the escalating potential for violence, born not simply from incompatibility but from a deep sense that each group is an intractable existential threat to the other, that is the flesh-and-blood consequence of living in a deeply divided society. As Adrian Guelke, a professor of comparative politics at Queen's University Belfast, writes: "in a deeply divided society conflict exists along a well-entrenched fault line that is recurrent and endemic and that contains the potential for violence between the segments."[13] A World Bank policy research report found compelling evidence of the realization of this potential: "A completely polarized society, divided into two equal groups, has a risk of civil war around six times higher than a homogenous society."[14]

The canon of case studies considered as "deeply divided societies" is voluminous and ever-growing. Most cases include situations where the deep divisions "have given rise to violent conflict, or at the very least to the threat of violent conflict."[15] These cases include South Africa, Cyprus, Kosovo, Sri Lanka, Nepal, Belgium, Iraq, Lebanon, Rwanda, Bosnia-Herzegovina, Israel/Palestine, and, as I have argued elsewhere, the contemporary United States.[16] The archetype of all case studies of deeply divided societies, though, is most commonly taken to be Northern Ireland. Even predating its birth in 1921, as we will see in Chapter 2, the new statelet, by whatever name it was called—Northern Ireland, the Six Counties, the North of Ireland, or Ulster—had deep divisions needled into the fabric of its lived experience. Those deep divisions give us insight into the ongoing sectarian divide in contemporary Northern Ireland. They also, however, beg an even deeper psychological question: How, and why, do group-based social identities become so divisive?

* * *

There are a multitude of sources of intergroup conflict—scarcity of and competition for vital natural resources (agricultural land, forests, water, food, energy, minerals, metals, oil, etc.), inequities in the allocation of such resources, rampant poverty and economic depression, state-sponsored abuse of human rights, political and social inequalities, state crises, fragile political systems transitioning from dictatorships to democracies, territorial disputes, and a history of grievances and provocations between groups.[17] Perhaps, however, the most increasingly potent source of the divisions and conflict that rattle our contemporary world are issues of identity. As journalist Fareed Zakaria has observed: "The questions that fill people with emotion are 'Who are we?' and, more ominously, 'Who are we not?' "[18] At the turn of the twenty-first century, international relations scholar Mary Kaldor argued that identity, along with globalization, would be the key concepts for understanding the new conflicts of the post-Cold War era.[19] Indeed, a review of armed conflicts from around the world in 2013 cited identity as a main cause of conflict in 21 of the 35 reported cases.[20] As I write this chapter, populist and nationalist parties—many with xenophobic tendencies—are enjoying a resurgence of political power across the globe. Ethnic and racial tensions continue to deface the landscape of community after community. A January 2014 Pew Research Center report found that the share of countries with a high level of social hostilities involving religious identities had reached a six-year peak—increasing in every major region of the world except the Americas.[21] Today, there is widespread agreement that it is identity groups and the organizations claiming to represent such groups that are the core of contemporary violent conflicts.[22]

So, what do we mean by identity and why does it play such a significant role in intergroup conflict? On one level, we can think of identity as a personal construct; the self-conceptualizations that define us in relation to or in comparison with other individuals. When asked who we are, this level of personal identity—"I-identity"—focuses on characteristics that are relatively unique to how we define ourselves as an individual. On another level, however, identity is tied to our social worlds; a conceptualization of the self that derives from membership in emotionally significant social categories or groups to which we perceive ourselves as belonging. On this level, when asked who we are, we focus on social identities—"we-identity"—tied to memberships in groups that are important to us at that particular moment in our lives.[23] Our social identities allow the groups with which we identify to enter into our sense of who we are. These personal and social identities subsumed under our self-concept are inherently and reciprocally related, the former built on our perceived individual uniqueness and the latter on our shared group sameness.[24] Different contexts prime different constructs of our identities: personal I-identity may be salient in one context and we may readily shift to we-identity in another context.

For we-identities, the ambiguous nature of how groups are defined means that the issue is less one of objective group membership and more one of a subjective psychological sense of symbolic attachment, togetherness, or be-longingness to a specific social identity. In defining the attachment charac-teristics of ethnic or national group identity, for instance, social psychologist Herbert Kelman speaks of "its enduring characteristics and basic values, its strengths and weaknesses, its hopes and fears, its reputation and conditions of existence, its institutions and traditions, its past history, current purposes, and future prospects."[25] Social identities include groups or categories based on race, socioeconomic status or social class, religion, gender, sex, age, sexual orientation, ethnicity, nationality, ability/disability, language, etc. These so-cial identity markers are a preexisting part of the structured societies into which we are born. Over the course of our lives, our social identities become central to the integrity of who we are and also, when applied to others, help us make sense of a very complex social world. In this sense, groups are more than simply a collection of individuals: groups also are rich avenues of un-derstanding who we, and others, are.

The sources of our social identities are multiple. Some are ascribed, written on us at birth. Such we-identities—race, biological sex, ethnicity, etc.—are seen as relatively impermeable and fixed. Other social identities are achieved, earned, or chosen throughout the course of our lives. Such we-identities—socioeconomic status, religion, nationality, etc.—are seen as more plastic and transient. A far greater number of modern social identities are subject to choice than in the past. Moreover, many social identities have a fluid, perme-able nature to their boundaries and straddle both the ascribed and achieved categories. In some caste-like societies, for instance, you can be born into a profession or craft, an ascribed identity that modern societies would more commonly see as achieved. A family's socioeconomic status could be achieved but would be an ascribed identity for its children. In Northern Ireland, religious identity, which some across the world may see as achieved, is really better understood as ascribed—you are the religious identity into which you are born. Denominational switching is seldom between Protestant and Catholic; rather it is a transfer within Protestant denominations or, like-lier, an out-migration to "none." Some we-identities—whether ascribed or achieved—give us power and privilege in some environments, and others leave us feeling vulnerable and unsafe in other environments.

At certain times and in certain places, some social identities are subor-dinated to a broader common superordinate social identity. During spells of patriotic fervor, for instance, the larger unitary national identity of "American" may be more operative for how individuals answer who they are than the subordinate identity of African American, Asian American, Latino American, Native American, etc. In contemporary Rwanda, the common su-perordinate social identity of "Rwandan" is now legally compulsory in place of the proscribed "Hutu" and "Tutsi" designations of social identity. Similarly, when Ukraine achieved independence in 1991, it scrapped ethnicity from all official documents, believing that ethnic social identities were not conducive to the creation of an inclusive state.

At other times and in other places, superordinate social identities may be dissembled into competing subordinate identities that give rise to inter-group conflict. For instance, the disintegration of the former Yugoslavia following the death of Marshal Tito in 1980 saw a devolution from a superordinate social identity of "Yugoslavian" to the triggering of a host of divisive subordinate ethnic identities (with strong nationalist overtones) of Serbian, Croatian, Slovenian, etc. When all was said and done, iden-tity conflicts in the former Yugoslavia would claim the lives of more than 100,000 people and leave a region still plagued by division, mistrust, and hostility.

Finally, some social identities simply indicate an affiliate relationship, not necessarily one in which we actively contribute to the performance of the group. For instance, fans of a national football team during the World Cup find that affiliate social identity very emotionally significant and tie a large part of their self-esteem to the successes and failures of the team with which they have aligned themselves—their triumphs become our triumphs and their failures our failures.

The activation of our various social identities—whether ascribed, achieved, superordinate, subordinate, or affiliate—is context-dependent. That is, our we-identity is influenced by where we are, who we are with, and what we are doing in our daily lives. In addition to being contextual, social identity is dynamic and changeable. It is "multitiered and quite malleable under certain circumstances."[26] At any given moment, the social identity relevant to us at that point in time is about what we have in common with a group—"us" and "we"—rather than what is unique about us as a person. From a social identity perspective, our uniqueness is drawn from the fact that our various social identities are multiple and overlapping—interwoven threads that answer the complex question of who we are. We can be Chilean, a woman, a politician, an activist, wealthy, and gay all at the same time. Our social identity is not a zero-sum game in which holding one negates holding any others. That is, we can hold one social identity without detracting from or giving up on other social identities which—in different circumstances and settings—may be more important to us. The salience of our identification with a particular social identity even varies over time—while religion may have been the defining social identity marker at one point in my life, it may not have been at another point.

In itself, group-based social identity is not problematic. It can be a healthy source of self-understanding as well as social understanding; it gives us a sense of who we, and others, are based on group memberships. Social identity can become dangerous, however, when it begins to essentialize and draw evaluative and emotional boundaries between those in my group and those not (the "other"), when there is a "crystallization of difference" that cements and fixes the social identities.[27] Social psychologists refer to these groups as "in-groups" (us) and "out-groups" (them). The in-group is any group to which we belong or with which we identify. In-groups can range from small, face-to-face groupings of family and friends to larger we-identities such as race, ethnicity, gender, or religion. Out-groups are any groups to which we do not belong or with which we do not identify. We should recognize that who we are is very strongly tied to who we are not; it is easier to be Hutu if there is someone else to be Tutsi. Defining who we are based on who we are not is called "disidentification" and becomes a primary mechanism for building the walls between "us" and "them."[28] Assigning people to in-groups and out-groups—that is, social categorization—has important consequences for how we-identity can become a source of intergroup conflict.

On one level, the power of social identity leads us to perceive other in-group members as more similar to us than out-group members. We solidify this perception, known as the *assumed similarity effect*, by exaggerating the similarities within our own group. Even in laboratory experiments, when we have been arbitrarily assigned to a nominal group, we assume other in-group members are similar to us on a surprisingly wide range of thoughts, feelings, and behaviors. We complement this in-group similarity with a cor-responding belief that all members of the out-group are alike as well. This *out-group homogeneity effect* leads us to believe that if we know something about one out-group member, we know something about all of them; they are all interchangeable. This overgeneralization, ignoring the potential plu-rality of out-group members' identities, can even extend to perceptual rec-ognition. Research has found, for instance, that people of other races are perceived to look more alike than members of one's own race.[29] We then am-plify our assumed similarity of in-group members and homogeneity of out-group members by drawing ever starker lines between "us" and "them." We draw these lines by exaggerating the differences between our group and the out-group. This exaggeration of differentness, termed the *accentuation effect*, leaves us biased toward information that enhances the differences between groups and less attentive to information about similarities between members of different groups.

To this point, all our discussion of social identity has done is reveal our tendencies as cognitive misers—we think in-group members are similar to us and out-group members are all alike, and we overestimate the differences between "us" and "them." These seem like fairly innocuous cognitive biases that are, at worst, depersonalizing—both for the ways in which we forfeit our uniqueness in favor of the assumed similarity of our in-group as well as for the ways in which we exaggerate the perceived sameness of out-group members. Unfortunately, however, as social psychologist Gordon Allport argued in his 1954 classic *The Nature of Prejudice*, there is a psychological primacy to the survival value of in-groups—"We live in them, by them, and, sometimes, for them"—that leaves such biases seldom affectively neutral.[30] Indeed, experi-ence and research have demonstrated that we generally like people we think are similar to us and dislike those we perceive as different. That is, the mere act of dividing people into groups inevitably sets up a bias in favor of the in-group and against the out-group. The bias has been defined broadly as "an unfair evaluative, emotional, cognitive, or behavioral response toward another group in ways that devaluate or disadvantage the other group and its members either directly or indirectly by valuing or privileging members of one's own group."[31] Such in-group favoritism, labeled the *in-group bias*, has been demonstrated across a wide range of groups, ages, contexts, and tasks.[32]

Why is in-group bias so prevalent in intergroup relations? The search for a theoretical understanding to this question began in the mind of Henri Tajfel, a Polish Jew studying at the Sorbonne, in Paris, at the outset of World War II. After volunteering to serve in the French Army, he was captured by the Germans and became a prisoner of war. During that time, Tajfel was struck by the ways in which simple social categorization—for example, being a French Jew as opposed to a Polish Jew—had direct life and death consequences. Tajfel saw firsthand how social identities fundamentally changed the ways people saw and related to others. After his release, and his discovery that his entire family had been killed during the Holocaust, Tajfel focused his professional career as a social psychologist "on a life-long quest to understand what happens psychologically when people categorize themselves and others into groups."[33]

Tajfel, joined by his colleague, John Turner, believed that the major underlying psychological motive for in-group bias was the need to improve self-esteem. In their social identity theory, we enhance our self-esteem by allowing the in-group to become an extension of ourselves.[34] To maximize this avenue to develop (or borrow) positive self-esteem, however, we must see our group as not only distinct but superior to other groups. We can do this by boosting the status of the group to which we belong, as well as by denigrating and discriminating against the groups to which we do not belong. That is, since we derive part of our self-esteem from the groups with which we identify, we are motivated to perceive "the in-group and the out-group on dimensions that lead the in-group to be judged positively and the out-group to be judged negatively."[35] This evolved competitive dynamic, while not inherently conflictual, may certainly lead to discriminatory intergroup behavior.

To test this theory, Tajfel devised a unique methodology known as the "minimal group paradigm." While there have been decades of research involving this methodology, and a wide range of variations, the heart of it is based on one simple, yet brilliant, insight: the minimal condition needed for in-group favoritism is simply categorization into a group. Where others had assumed that in-group bias had to be born from preexisting groups with emotional investments, histories of dislike or hostility, or in competition for the same resources, Tajfel argued that the mere fact of being assigned to a group would be enough to prompt in-group bias at the expense of others.

The most common variant of his "minimal group paradigm" methodology would assign participants to groups on an arbitrary, trivial, or even explicitly random basis—for instance, the flip of a coin. Each participant recognized the meaningless nature of their group assignment as well as that of every other group member's assignment. Then, before any type of face-to-face group interaction began, Tajfel asked the participants to complete a survey rating their own group, as well as the other group, on a series of positive and negative traits. In other variants, participants were asked to assign points on matrices, distribute rewards or penalties, or allocate resources to members of their group and the other group. Results show that groups, assigned on an arbitrary or trivial or random basis, start to act in ways that favor the in-group and discriminate against the out-group.[36] So, in groups with as little social meaning as possible, having no past histories or shared futures, the power of social identity led to in-group bias. In summarizing a robust research program of experiments using this methodology, Tajfel and Turner state: "The basic and highly reliable finding is that the trivial, ad hoc intergroup categorization leads to in-group favoritism and discrimination against the out-group."[37]

Why is in-group bias and out-group discrimination so extraordinarily easy to trigger? Recent interdisciplinary research suggests there is an underlying biology to "us" and "them." Robert Sapolsky, a neuroscientist at Stanford University, writes: "Our brains distinguish between in-group members and outsiders in a fraction of a second, and they encourage us to be kind to the former but hostile to the latter. These biases are automatic and unconscious and emerge at astonishingly young ages."[38] While specific biases are acquired through social experience and can be modified by other social experiences, the cognitive structures on which they are built already are preset. This is an evolutionary adaptation that allows us "to detect any potential cues about social coalitions and alliances—to increase one's chance of survival by telling friend from foe."[39] Certainly, these cognitive presets can lead to a range of behaviors that affirm our capacity for cooperative, caring, nonviolent relations, particularly with those to whom we feel an identity connection—including love, friendship, preferential and reciprocal altruism, nurturance, compassion, communication, a sense of fairness, and, even, self-sacrifice. In short, the things that hold society together. In this light, in-group loyalty can even be cast as a moral virtue.

Self-congratulation about our human nature, though, is premature. There are some darker sides to these cognitive presets—such as intergroup competition for dominance, boundary definition, prejudice, social exclusion, and, even, dehumanization—that often tear society apart by leading to intergroup conflict with those whom we identify as the "other." It is this innate tribalism, manifest as in-group bias—particularly when based on group membership perceived as impermeable and fixed—that helps us understand why social identity matters as a source of intergroup conflict.

To be sure, discrimination *for* in-groups and *against* out-groups is not necessarily and inevitably two sides of the same coin. However rarely, it is possible to have an in-group preference for those that we acknowledge to be "us" without the reciprocal presence of hostile thoughts, feelings, or behaviors toward out-groups of "them." Even in these exceptional instances, however, in-group favoritism is anything but benign over the long term. As social psychologist Marilynn Brewer summarizes: "The very factors that make in-group attachment and allegiance important to individuals also provide a fertile ground for antagonism and distrust of those outside the in-group boundaries. The need to justify in-group values in the form of moral superiority to others, sensitivity to threat, the anticipation of interdependence under conditions of distrust, social comparison processes, and power politics all conspire to connect in-group identification and loyalty to disdain and overt hostility toward out-groups."[40] These factors are likely to be especially powerful when in-group members fear, realistically or not, that what makes them distinct and superior is under threat from out-group members. As peace scholar Jay Rothman argues, identity becomes "conflictual when two identities are negatively interdependent, in a zero-sum or threatening relationship. When my being me depends on you not being you, or when your being you threatens my being me."[41]

Moreover, as social psychologists Sonia Roccas and Andrey Elster point out, there is a "conflict-enhancing feedback loop" between social identity and intergroup conflict. In a tragically symbiotic relationship, the effects of social identity on conflict are reciprocated by the effects of conflict on social identity. Conflict can increase the salience of social identity in such a way as to intensify the sense of commitment and loyalty to the in-group as well as antagonism toward the out-group. As they write: "intergroup conflict is likely to lead to a simplified social identity, which in turn might lead to less tolerance and to intensification of conflict. . . . Simple identities increase conflict, and conflict simplifies identities."[42] So the calcification of social identities can be more than simply a cause of intergroup conflict: it can also be a consequence of such conflict.

In sum, group-based social identity is *a* source—but far from *the* only source—of intergroup conflict. It does remind us, however, that not all conflict is reducible simply to competition for vital natural resources, political power, economic gains, territorial expansion, or historical memory. Rather intergroup conflict—particularly in a world in which no country is perfectly homogenous—can also be about competition between social identities seeking to maintain, restore, or claim a favored identity status. We-identities—and how they are manipulated by "identitarians"—matter greatly in understanding the etiology of intergroup conflict, particularly in a deeply divided society like contemporary Northern Ireland.

* * *

What are the we-identities at play in Northern Ireland? Historically, discussions of "us" and "them" in Northern Ireland have been abbreviated to one of two simplified group-based religious social identities: *Protestant* or *Catholic*. These identities carry such meaning, are so part and parcel of everyday life, that a religion question has been included in every Northern Ireland census, most often for the purposes of monitoring the delivery of public services as well as compliance with discrimination legislation. And the baggage attached to those identities is so significant that "mixed marriages" between a Protestant and Catholic often lead to the generational breakdown of family relationships and the loss of social networks and even jobs. One person I interviewed said that, after her marriage to someone from "the other side of the divide," both sets of parents disowned the newlyweds and that building a different social network of friends and having to find new employment left them feeling like they "had moved to another country." Even the children of mixed marriages suffer from the social shame of being born from what another interviewee described as "an unnatural union."[43]

Today, from a demographic perspective, Christianity remains the largest religion in Northern Ireland. In the 2011 census, 82.3% of respondents in Northern Ireland identified themselves as "Christian."[44] This is a bit lower than the response rate in Ireland (90.5% identified as Christian), but substantially higher than response rates in England and Wales (59.3%) and Scotland (53.8%). In that same census, 45.14% of the Northern Ireland population identified as either Catholic or brought up as Catholic, with the highest prevalence rate in Newry, Mourne, and Down, southern areas fast by the Irish border. Those identifying as Protestant (mainly Presbyterian Church in Ireland, Church of Ireland, or Methodist Church in Ireland) and other Christian (e.g., Pentecostal, Free Presbyterian, or Jehovah's Witness), or either brought up as Protestant or in other Christian-related denominations, accounted for 48.36% of respondents, with the highest prevalence rate in Mid and East Antrim, northeast sections of the country. Significantly, the 2011 census, following decades-long demographic trajectories, was the first time that "belonging to or brought up in Protestant or other Christian-related denominations" represented less than half of Northern Ireland's population.

While most census respondents will self-identify as "Catholic" or "Protestant" in terms of their community background, that does not necessarily mean the practice of those religions is flourishing in contemporary Northern Ireland. Lately mirroring a pattern of secularization in Western Europe, Christian churches in Northern Ireland are seeing substantial declines in membership and attendance, particularly in the urban areas. In various churches I attended during my time in country, deserted pews and an aging faithful few (particularly noticeable in Protestant churches) were the rule. The 2019 Northern Ireland Life and Times (NILT) survey, interviewing more than 1,200 adults across Northern Ireland, found the highest percentage of respondents indicating they attended church "once a week" or "several times a week" to be in the 65 and older age range. Conversely, the highest percentage of respondents reporting "never" attending church were disproportionately clustered in age ranges younger than 45.[45] While some, especially within the Catholic community, are likely to retain a formal religious identification, the meaning of the church, for both communities, has receded. In the more than 110 hours of interviews I collected, the only people even mentioning the role of the church in daily life or in healing the fractures with Northern Ireland were church officials—and even then it smacked as a half-hearted obligatory requirement of their job rather than a deeply committed affirmation of reality. Today, despite their ubiquitous presence as group identifiers, "Protestant" and "Catholic" have become nebulous descriptors that lie somewhere in a gray area between nominal and notional. "Protestant" and "Catholic" exist in name only; their social meaning having become a confession less of religious identity and more of national identity.

This reality is perhaps best captured in a well-worn joke that has left most folk in Northern Ireland worn out at the telling—and hearing—of it. Two men are sitting in their local pub enjoying a pint and the craic. A stranger comes in and has a seat by the two of them. Conversation ensues and the two men, uncertain which side of the sectarian divide the stranger falls on but deciding he will bring variety to their day, practice the "art of telling" by querying him in ways meant to sidestep the social inelegance of the direct question. What town are you from? What street did you grow up on? Where did you go to school? What football team do you support? Finally, still unsure, one of the men blurts out: "What foot do you kick with, lad?" Realizing the stranger is completely befuddled, the other man asks: "Are you a Protestant or a Catholic?" "Neither," the stranger replies, "I am a Jew." There is a pause: after all, the number of Jews in Northern Ireland is so small that it is a struggle to find a minyan to take part in synagogue services. The silence is broken when one of the men then asks: "Yes, but are you a Protestant Jew or a Catholic Jew?"

The joke is rooted in the pervasiveness of simplified social identities in Northern Ireland. It also, though, reveals a deeper truth about what lies at the heart of those competing dualities. To reduce our understanding of social identities in Northern Ireland to religion—Protestant or Catholic— is dangerously misleading. In reality, the issue is one of national identity, where Protestant becomes shorthand for *unionist* (those supporting Northern Ireland's constitutional status within the United Kingdom and opposing the involvement of the Irish Republic in Northern Ireland) and Catholic for *nationalist* (those believing that Northern Ireland is part of the Irish nation and opposing the imposition of British rule that prevents a united Ireland).[46] So, the Jewish man in the joke—like the recent immigrants to Northern Ireland from Poland, India, Pakistan, Portugal, and China—still find themselves at play in this game of binary identity. They are "Protestant" or "Catholic," not based on religious identity, but based on notions of national identity.

A former republican political prisoner I interviewed described it this way: "What, for instance, if Spain had colonized Ireland? We wouldn't be talking about a Catholic versus Catholic split; rather, we'd be correctly talking about a colonial issue of national identity—Spanish versus Irish. So, why don't we just admit that's what it's about in Northern Ireland? A colonial issue of national identity—English versus Irish." The predominant role of national identity in understanding contemporary Northern Ireland is graphically displayed on the lower Newtownards Road, a Protestant neighborhood of East Belfast. There, four murals (Figure 1.1), standing in relief against the Samson and Goliath gantry cranes in the neighboring shipyard of Harland & Wolff, form the self-proclaimed "Ulster's Freedom Corner." On one of the murals, superimposed over iconic badges of Ulster, Scotland, the UK, England, and Wales, stands the bolded phrase: "The Ulster conflict is about nationality. This we shall maintain."

The duality, even plurality, of national identities in contemporary Northern Ireland and how closely they align with religious identities are plainly reflected in a range of survey data. In the 2011 census, for instance, respondents were asked to self-identify their national identity and could choose between British, Irish, Northern Irish, or any four combinations of those three national identities (along with "other"). In this measure of segmented citizenship, 81% of those who choose "British only" as their national identity were or had been brought up as Protestants, compared with only 12% of those who were or had been brought up as Catholics. In contrast, 94% of those who choose "Irish only" as their national identity were or had been

Figure 1.1 Loyalist mural along Newtownards Road in East Belfast reading "The Ulster Conflict is About Nationality. This We Shall Maintain." In the background are the Samson and Goliath gantry cranes in the neighboring shipyard of Harland & Wolff, famous for having built the *Titanic*.
Photo by author, February 3, 2017.

brought up as Catholics, compared with only 4.4% of those who belonged to or had been brought up in Protestant denominations. More recently, the 2019 NILT survey found Protestants (61%) were much more willing than Catholics (2%) to identify as "British not Irish," with Catholics (55%) being much more willing than Protestants (1%) to identity as "Irish not British." In a related question, 20% of Protestants saw themselves as "More British than Irish," compared to only 1% of Catholics. Conversely, 25% of Catholics saw themselves as "More Irish than British," compared to only 2% of Protestants. Only 11% of Catholics and 12% of Protestants identified as "Equally Irish and British."[47]

Following the Good Friday Agreement of 1998, the plurality of national identity was formally institutionalized as it recognized "the birthright of all the people of Northern Ireland to identify themselves and be accepted as Irish or British, or both, as they may so choose, and accordingly [the two governments] confirm that their right to hold both British and Irish citizenship is accepted by both Governments and would not be affected by any future change in the status of Northern Ireland."[48] Since the UK is a party to United Nations conventions to prevent statelessness at birth by allowing children to acquire the nationality of the country in which they are born, British citizenship is presumed to be the default for people born in Northern Ireland. So, those who opt for Irish citizenship typically do so in addition to British citizenship and not instead of it (unless they choose to go through the process of formally renouncing British citizenship).[49] At least 700,000 people born in Northern Ireland now hold an Irish passport, with more than 200,000 of those making application after the 2016 Brexit referendum.

With a multiplicity of national identities from which to choose in contemporary Northern Ireland, the country offers a compelling test of the hypothesis that nations must possess a cohesive, exclusive sense of national identity in order to survive and thrive. Must there be a profound desire for a common life in order for there to be a "nation?" Does a nation have to have, in the words of historian Benedict Anderson, "a deep horizontal comradeship" in order to have an "imagined community?" Clearly, there is no one "imagined community" when it comes to national identity in Northern Ireland; rather there are multiple imagined communities, contingent on social constructions imbued with historical legacies and composed of members for whom "in the minds of each lives the image of their communion."[50] Indeed, in contemporary Northern Ireland, these communities are steeped in such deeply embedded worldviews that to call them "imagined" or "constructed" is to underestimate their potent influence on we-identity and the ways in which they are mobilized as a resource to achieve a wide variety of political and social goals.[51]

With this plurality of national identities at play, the blurring of them—intentionally or otherwise—by outsiders is inevitable. In July 2019, for instance, Britain's most successful female golfer, Laura Davies, in reference to Irish golfer Shane Lowry's lead at the Open Championship, said: "It would be lovely for the home fans . . . to see a British winner of The Open." She felt Twitter's wrath as outraged Irish people from both sides of the border questioned her conception of "home fans," as the Open was being played in Portrush, Northern Ireland, as well as her appropriation of a born-and-bred Irishman as "British." As Twitter user @KaneClarke sarcastically pointed out: "Shane Lowry is winning The Open so he's now British."[52]

Assessing political attitudes, the 2019 NILT survey also asked respondents if they thought of themselves as unionists, nationalists, or neither. Fifty-nine percent of Catholics were willing to identify as "Nationalists" (the highest figure in any NILT survey since 2003), compared to only 1% of Protestants. Conversely, 67% of Protestants identified as "Unionists" (compared to 55% the previous year), while no Catholic respondents identified as such. Likely reflecting a frustration with the contentious political climate and perhaps a desire to separate religious and national identities, a significant number of both Catholic and Protestant respondents simply responded "Neither" (39% and 29%, respectively).[53]

So, as shorthand, data reveal that these pairings of religious and national identity have their limitations: while few and far between, one can find Protestant nationalists as well as Catholic unionists within Northern Ireland. Generally, however, the fusion of the two identities—Protestant-unionist and Catholic-nationalist—is universal enough in practice to ensure that knowing one side of the hyphen allows you to safely assume the other. This fusion of identities is not uncommon in deeply divided societies. In the former Yugoslavia, for instance, ethnic identifiers came to elide so commonly with religious identifiers (Croat with Roman Catholic, Serb with Orthodox Christian, and Bosnian with Muslim) that new ethnoreligious identities emerged. The complexity of multiple identities (ethnic and religious) was reduced by merging into simplified ethnoreligious identifiers (Croat, Serb, or Bosniak); not always 100 percent accurate, but close enough to determine who to align with and against.

In Northern Ireland, the fusion of identities is most commonly described in ethnonational terms, a form of merged identity in which the nation is defined in terms of ethnicity (in this case, ethnicity based on a shared cultural heritage of religious identification). Self-determination lies at the core of ethnonational identity, an exclusivist belief that "the ethnic community should form the basis for the governance of independent states."[54] This ethnic definition of nationhood—Protestant-unionists self-identifying with the United Kingdom and Catholic-nationalists with a united Ireland—lies at the heart of the constitutional status division in Northern Ireland. In reality, Northern Ireland is a land of two nationalisms battling for the right of self-determination—British nationalism and Irish nationalism.[55] Both sides are about "union"—one focused on its union with the United Kingdom and the other on its (re)union with the Republic of Ireland. Each are competing to define the membership boundaries of the "nation" and the territory that nation has a right to control.[56]

Centuries of intergroup conflict have concretized these simplified social identities of Protestant-unionist and Catholic-nationalist, turning them "into something hard, unchangeable, and absolute."[57] Slavenka Drakulic, a Croatian journalist, spoke of this transformation as the war neared her town of Zagreb in January 1992. Comparing her contextually imposed new national social identity to an ill-fitting shirt, she wrote: "You may feel the sleeves are too short, the collar too tight. You might not like the colour, and the cloth might itch. But there is no escape; there is nothing else to wear. . . . So right now, in the new state of Croatia, no one is allowed not to be a Croat."[58] Similarly, in contemporary Northern Ireland, particularly in public spaces, very few are allowed not to be Protestant-unionist or Catholic-nationalist. There is little to no space between.

To the Protestant-unionist and Catholic-nationalist identities are often added a third identity category: *loyalist* or *republican*. Loyalists are uncompromising unionists (mostly Protestant) who see themselves, as one former political prisoner showed me on his arm tattoo, as "British and proud." As their name suggests, they are fiercely loyal to unionist cultural traditions and the ties that bind them to the British crown and state. Generally, the term "loyalist" is used in particular reference to paramilitary groups who endorse physical violence as the surest route to defend the union with the United Kingdom. Moreover, loyalism also carries with it a perceived class differentiation from unionism; the former is seen as working class and the latter as more affluent middle class. Over the years, loyalists trace their lineage back centuries to the Peep O'Day Boys and the Orange Order. More recently, loyalist paramilitary groups have included the Ulster Volunteer Force, Red Hand Commando, Ulster Defence Association, South East Antrim Ulster Defence Association, Ulster Freedom Fighters, and the Loyalist Volunteer Force.

Republicans (mostly Catholic) have deep and profoundly romanticized roots in constitutional Irish nationalism. Those shared roots include an appreciation for Irish cultural traditions, particularly the Irish language, and a desire to remove the imposition of British rule in the north of Ireland. Republicanism diverges from nationalism, though, in advocating the use of physical, not simply political, force to break the union with Britain and reunify with Ireland (some use "physical force nationalism" as synonymous with "republicanism"). Republican paramilitary groups are steeped in the narrative traditions of violent struggle and sacrifice against British rule in Ireland. Prefigured centuries earlier by the Defenders and the United Irishmen, these groups have included the Official Irish Republican Army (IRA), Provisional IRA, the Irish National Liberation Army, and a host of so-called *dissident republican* paramilitary groups who reject the 1998 Good Friday Agreement— among them, Oglaigh na hEirann ("Soldiers of Ireland"), the Continuity IRA, and the "New" IRA.[59]

The loyalist and republican paramilitaries represent the violent extreme of a long-standing extraconstitutional continuum of achieving political change in Northern Ireland. This extraconstitutional tradition "seeks to achieve political goals through the use of force, either through protest activity (and an implicit threat of physical force) or through the use of armed force itself (the explicit threat of physical force)."[60] Given the success of this extraconstitutional tradition over the years, particularly the major political changes attributed to republican violence, it is little surprise that paramilitaries enjoyed significant levels of support in their respective communities. This is especially true in nationalist circles where ex-combatants are generally regarded as hero deities who were defenders of their community.

While all loyalist and republican paramilitary organizations are illegal in contemporary Northern Ireland, most are still in existence, with varying semblances of a militaristic command structure even if centralized control has become fragmented. Since most of those groups have been on ceasefire since 1994, the scale of the violence has reduced over the course of the peace process. Some groups even have transitioned their energies into positive political and community engagement. As we will see, however, some hard-line subgroups of paramilitaries on both sides of the divide actively continue to recruit in order to carry on with their violent campaigns of intimidation, criminality, and sectarian attacks.

Some scholars capture the various facets of these identities with the aggregate acronyms of *PUL* (Protestant-unionist-loyalist) and *CNR* (Catholic-nationalist-republican). I believe this muddies more than it clarifies. It is a crude pruning of the multiplicity of identity, a broad brush-stroke sweeping away any nuance. Many of the people I interviewed, for instance, were particularly adamant about drawing the line between what they perceived as a legitimate political label (unionist or nationalist) and a disparaging criminal or violent designation (loyalist or republican). Claims of "I'm unionist but not a loyalist" or "I'm nationalist but not a republican" were common.

In this book, I want to bring clarity by using the terms as accurately as possible. Outside of quoted material, where I will remain faithful to the source's use of identifiers, my default terminology for the two sides of the divide will be "unionist" and "nationalist," capturing the reality that the current divisiveness is over the constitutional question of national identity and state sovereignty. When I use "loyalist" and "republican," it will be in specific reference to paramilitary units that advocate violence as a means to solve the question of national identity. Finally, when I refer to "Protestant" and "Catholic," it will be to specific religious dimensions of the conflict, usually historical, or in reference to community demographics where one identity or the other predominates.

Notes

1. Arend Lijphart, *Democracy in Plural Societies: A Comparative Exploration* (New Haven, CT: Yale University Press, 1977), 3.
2. Eric Nordlinger, *Conflict Regulation in Divided Societies* (Cambridge, MA: Harvard University Center for International Affairs, 1972), 9.
3. Ian S. Lustick, "Stability in Deeply Divided Societies: Consociationalism Versus Control," *World Politics* (1979), 31 (3), 325.
4. Adrian Guelke, *Politics in Deeply Divided Societies* (Cambridge, UK: Polity Press, 2012), 14.
5. Malachi O'Doherty, *Fifty Years On: The Troubles and the Struggle for Change in Northern Ireland* (London: Atlantic Books, 2019), 352.

6. Accessed on September 8, 2014, at http://www.un.org/en/preventgenocide/adviser/genocide_prevention.shtml and "Prevention of Genocide," (August 17, 2014), accessed on August 18, 2014, at http://venitism.blogspot.com/2014/08/prevention-of-genocide.html

7. Cited in Rene Lemarchand, *Rwanda and Burundi* (New York: Praeger, 1970), 169.

8. See chapter 9, "Fighting for the Hutu Revolution in Rwanda," in Scott Straus, *Making and Unmaking Nations: War, Leadership, and Genocide in Modern Africa* (Ithaca, NY: Cornell University Press, 2015).

9. Jolle Demmers, *Theories of Violent Conflict: An Introduction* (New York: Routledge, 2012), 43.

10. Characteristics drawn from C. Marlene Fiol, Michael G. Pratt, and Edward J. O'Connor, "Managing Intractable Identity Conflicts," *Academy of Management Review* (2009) 34 (1), 32–55.

11. Susan Fiske, "What We Know Now About Bias and Intergroup Conflict, the Problem of the Century," *Current Directions in Psychological Science* (2002) 11 (4), 127.

12. Quoted material taken from John Agnew, "Beyond Reason: Spatial and Temporal Sources of Ethnic Conflicts," in Louis Kriesberg, Terrell Northrup, and Stuart Thorson (eds.), *Intractable Conflicts and Their Transformations* (New York: Syracuse University Press, 1989), 51.

13. Guelke, *Politics in Deeply Divided Societies*, 30.

14. Paul Collier, V. L. Elliott, Haard Hegre, Anke Hoeffler, Marta Reynal-Querol, and Nicholas Sambanis, *Breaking the Conflict Trap: Civil War and Development Policy* (Washington, DC: The World Bank, 2003), 58.

15. Guelke, *Politics in Deeply Divided Societies*, 9.

16. James Waller, "It Can Happen Here: Assessing the Risk of Genocide in the US" (March 20, 2017), accessible at http://www.wfm-igp.org/content/it-can-happen-here-assessing-risk-genocide-us-dr-james-waller-keene-state-college and James Waller, "'I Didn't Know If I Was Going to Be Seen Again:' The Escalating Risk of Mass Violence in the United States" (November 2020), accessible at https://stanleycenter.org/wp-content/uploads/2020/10/AIMVA-Waller-US-Risks1020.pdf

17. For a broad review, see Frances Stewart, "The Causes of Civil War and Genocide: A Comparison," in Adam Lupel and Ernesto Verdeja (eds.), *Responding to Genocide: The Politics of International Action* (Boulder, CO: Lynne Rienner, 2013), 47–83.

18. Accessed on September 19, 2014, at http://fareedzakaria.com/2014/07/06/identity-not-ideology-is-moving-the-world/

19. Mary Kaldor, *New and Old Wars: Organized Violence in a Global Era* (Stanford, CA: Stanford University Press, 1998). The book was released in a third edition in 2012.

20. Institute for Economics and Peace, "Five Key Questions Answered on the Link Between Peace & Religion," (October 2014), 6. Available for download at http://www.economicsandpeace.org

21. Pew Research Center, "Religious Hostilities Reach Six-Year High," (January 2014).

22. See Demmers, *Theories of Violent Conflict*, 9.

23. "I-identity" and "we-identity" are taken from the work of German sociologist Norbert Elias (1897–1990). See his *What Is Sociology?* (New York: Columbia University Press,

1978) and *The Civilizing Process: State Formation and Civilization* (Oxford: Basil Blackwell, 1982).

24. Demmers, *Theories of Violent Conflict*, 20. See also Jeffrey R. Seul, " 'Ours Is the Way of God': Religion, Identity, and Intergroup Conflict," *Journal of Peace Research* 36 (1999), 554.

25. Herbert C. Kelman, "The Place of Ethnic Identity in the Development of Personal Identity: A Challenge for the Jewish Family," in Peter Y. Medding (ed.), *Studies in Contemporary Jewry: Coping with Life and Death: Jewish Families in the Twentieth Century* (New York: Oxford University Press, 1999), 16.

26. I. William Zartman and Mark Anstey, "The Problem," in I. William Zartman, Mark Anstey, and Paul Meerts (eds.), *The Slippery Slope to Genocide: Reducing Identity Conflicts and Preventing Mass Murder* (New York: Oxford University Press, 2012), 6.

27. "Crystallization of difference" taken from Alexander Hinton's *Why Did They Kill?: Cambodia in the Shadow of Genocide* (Berkeley: University of California Press, 2005).

28. Fiol et al., "Managing Intractable Identity Conflicts," 34.

29. The research literature on what is known as "cross-race recognition deficit" is robust. See, for instance, Siri Carpenter, "Why Do 'They All Look Alike'?" *American Psychological Association Monitor on Psychology* 31 (December 2000), 44; and Daniel B. Wright, Catherine E. Boyd, and Colin G. Tredoux, "Inter-racial Contact and the Own-Race Bias for Face Recognition in South Africa and England," *Applied Cognitive Psychology* 17 (2003), 365–373.

30. Gordon W. Allport, *The Nature of Prejudice* (Boston, MA: Beacon Press, 1954), 42.

31. John F. Dovidio and Samuel L. Gaertner, "Intergroup Bias," in Susan T. Fiske, Daniel T. Gilbert, and Gardner Lindzey (eds.), *Handbook of Social Psychology*, 5th ed., vol. 2 (Hoboken: John Wiley & Sons, 2010), 1084.

32. See James Waller, *Becoming Evil: How Ordinary People Commit Genocide and Mass Killing*, 2nd ed. (New York: Oxford University Press, 2007), 173–179.

33. Alexa Ispas, *Psychology and Politics: A Social Identity Perspective* (New York: Psychology Press, 2013), vii.

34. Henri Tajfel and John C. Turner, "The Social Identity Theory of Intergroup Behavior," in Stephen Worchel and William G. Austin (eds.), *Psychology of Intergroup Relations*, 2nd ed. (Chicago: Nelson-Hall, 1986), 7–24.

35. Jan E. Stets and Peter J. Burke, "Identity Theory and Social Identity Theory," *Social Psychology Quarterly* 63 (2000), 225.

36. See, for instance, Henry Tajfel, "Experiments in Intergroup Discrimination," *Scientific American* 223 (1970), 96–102.

37. Tajfel and Turner, "The Social Identity Theory of Intergroup Behavior," 14.

38. Robert Sapolsky, "This Is Your Brain on Nationalism: The Biology of Us and Them," *Foreign Affairs* (March/April 2019), 42.

39. Ibid, 46.

40. Marilynn B. Brewer, "The Psychology of Prejudice: Ingroup Love or Outgroup Hate?" *Journal of Social Issues* 55 (1999), 442.

41. Jay Rothman, "The Insides of Identity and Intragroup Conflict," in Zartman et al., *The Slippery Slope to Genocide*, 156.

42. Sonia Roccas and Andrew Elster, "Group Identities," in Linda R. Tropp (ed.), *The Oxford Handbook of Intergroup Conflict* (New York: Oxford University Press, 2012), 115, 116.

43. The Northern Ireland Mixed Marriage Association exists to support those contemplating, or in, a mixed marriage. See http://www.nimma.org.uk, accessed on June 5, 2020.

44. Information on the 2011 Census in Northern Ireland, including how to access the data and supporting documents, can be found at https://www.nisra.gov.uk/statistics/census/2011-census (accessed on March 17, 2019). In the 2011 census, 17% of usual residents either had no religion or no stated religion and 0.8% were "other religions." The next census is scheduled for 2021.

45. Northern Ireland Life and Times (NILT) data taken from https://www.ark.ac.uk/nilt/2019/Background/CHATTND2.html, accessed on June 18, 2020. The precursor of the NILT was the Northern Ireland Social Attitudes (NISA) survey.

46. Parenthetical descriptions taken from Accord, *Striking a Balance: The Northern Ireland Peace Process* (London: Conciliation Resources, 1999), 6–7.

47. NILT data taken from https://www.ark.ac.uk/nilt/2019/Political_Attitudes/IRBRIT.html, accessed on June 18, 2020.

48. The complete text of the Good Friday Agreement was accessed on June 5, 2020, at https://peacemaker.un.org/sites/peacemaker.un.org/files/IE%20GB_980410_Northern%20Ireland%20Agreement.pdf. The quoted material is taken from p. 3.

49. As of this writing, a legal case to challenge the presumption of British identity as the default in Northern Ireland remains pending.

50. Quoted material related to imagined communities is taken from Benedict Anderson, *Imagined Communities* (London: Verso, 1991, revised and extended edition), 7, 6.

51. Duncan Morrow, "The Rocky Road from Enmity," in Cillian McGrattan and Elizabeth Meehan (eds.), *Everyday Life After the Irish Conflict: The Impact of Devolution and Cross-Border Cooperation* (Manchester: Manchester University Press, 2012), 23.

52. Liam Bryce, "Shane Lowry Blooper as Laura Davies Backs 'British When He Wins' Star for Glory at The Open," *Daily Record* (July 20, 2019), accessed on July 22, 2019, at https://www.dailyrecord.co.uk/sport/golf/shane-lowry-blooper-laura-davies-18458950

53. NILT data taken from https://www.ark.ac.uk/nilt/2019/Political_Attitudes/UNINATID.html, accessed on June 18, 2020.

54. Guelke, *Politics in Deeply Divided Societies*, 32.

55. The notion of "two nationalisms" is taken from John F. Clark, "Rwanda: Tragic Land of Dual Nationalisms," in Lowell W. Barrington (ed.), *After Independence: Making and Protecting the Nation in Postcolonial and Postcommunist States* (Ann Arbor: University of Michigan Press, 2006), 71.

56. See Lowell W. Barrington, "Nationalism & Independence," in Barrington (ed.), *After Independence*, 10–11.

57. Demmers, *Theories of Violent Conflict*, 27.

58. Cited in Demmers, *Theories of Violent Conflict*, 27; original quote may be found in Slavenka Drakulic, *The Balkan Express: Fragments from the Other Side of the War* (New York: W. W. Norton, 1993), 52.

59. Much of the information on the names of the loyalist and republican paramilitary groups is taken from an assessment commissioned by the Secretary of State for Northern Ireland, titled "Paramilitary Groups in Northern Ireland," (October 19, 2015), accessed on June 4, 2020, at https://cain.ulster.ac.uk/issues/police/docs/psni_2015-10-19_paramilitary-groups.pdf

60. Berndette C. Hayes and Ian McAllister, "Sowing Dragon's Teeth: Public Support for Political Violence and Paramilitarism in Northern Ireland," *Political Studies* 49 (2001), 912.

2

"Two Eyes on the Past"

Northern Ireland's Wounded History

For more than four centuries, public houses, or "pubs," have occupied a central role in the social life of Ireland. Similarly, they often occupied a central role in my research for this book while in Northern Ireland. On most occasions, when arranging to interview someone outside of regular working hours, the meeting place was a pub (actually, on more than a few occasions, a pub was a meeting place during regular working hours as well). Sometimes, the pub was a local one in which the person I was interviewing felt comfortable, at ease, and in a safe space for what could be a difficult conversation. At other times, they requested a more neutral space where friends and family would be less likely to see them chatting with a stranger and subsequently less likely to ask the inevitable "What were you on about?"

In Belfast, the accepted neutral space is the city center, and one of the most well-known and well-liked pubs in the city center is the Garrick, established in 1870. "They pour a nice pint," as a friend told me, "and leave you alone to enjoy it." Often the recipient of Belfast's "Best Kept Small Building Award," the Garrick is noted for refined tiling and woodwork. It also is noted, by passersby, for a quote painted on the exterior of its gable end: "A nation that keeps one eye on the past is wise. A nation that keeps two eyes on the past is blind."

The past in Northern Ireland is always present and always contested. It intrudes into radio and television shows, songs, murals, education, flags, symbols, architecture, sports, religion, daily conversation, and, most notably, communities in which who you are and who you are not defines inclusion or exclusion. The present is, in many ways, a prisoner of the past. As Duncan Morrow, the Director of Community Engagement at Ulster University, has said: "To live in Northern Ireland is to live in a place haunted by its own memories of violence and discrimination."[1] So, in Northern Ireland, to keep one eye on the past is more than wise; it is absolutely necessary to understand what made "now." How did the wounded history of the north of Ireland, in

A Troubled Sleep. James Waller, Oxford University Press (2021). © Oxford University Press.
DOI: 10.1093/oso/9780190095574.003.0003

all its complexity and contestation, give shape to the social identities that still deeply divide contemporary Northern Ireland?

* * *

To depict the deep divisions within the north of Ireland as an early twentieth-century phenomenon is to, as one academic told me, "begin in the middle of things." In truth, those deep divisions have an origin story spanning eight centuries—from the coming of the English in the twelfth century through the arrival of Protestantism in the sixteenth century and through the birth of the contemporary statelet of Northern Ireland in the early twentieth century. A host of historians have done outstanding work tracing the serrated intricacies of those centuries—the conquests, rebellions, wars, uprisings, insurrections, revolts, massacres, counter-massacres, and, even, blending and integration, that defined the island of Ireland and, particularly, the region of what would come to be called Ulster.[2] (Or, for those desiring a more concise understanding, you can, as a Belfast taxi driver said to me, distill the entire history of the north of Ireland into two simple sentences capturing the centuries of contentious interaction between Protestants and Catholics: "Feck off! No, you feck off!".)

To begin at the beginning of things requires going back to the arrival of the neighboring English in the twelfth century (indeed, I lost track of how many nationalists recited to me some variant of "the Troubles really began over 800 years ago with the English invasions"). Plans for the Anglo-Norman invasion—and the first serious attempt at Ireland's colonization—began in 1169. Colonization was only partly successful over the next few centuries, with many of the descendants of the first Norman invaders adopting the native language and social system and, through intermarriage and assimilation, becoming "more Irish than the Irish themselves."[3] By the fifteenth century, this half-conquest of Ireland left a country "divided up into a patchwork of individual supremacies with varying degrees of loyalty to the English crown."[4]

By the end of the sixteenth century, however, political concerns (the threat that Catholic France and Spain could pose through a Catholic Ireland) and economic opportunities (increasingly close trading ties between southwestern Scotland and northeastern Ireland) convinced Protestant England that the complete (re)conquest of Ireland was a strategically advantageous, even necessary, foreign policy objective. Unfortunately, because the Protestant Reformation had bypassed Catholic Ireland, the takeover of the country would have to be done differently. If Ireland would not become Protestant, then Protestants would have to be brought into Ireland.[5] So, London began a series of attempts to establish, through aggressive colonization, a Protestant population in Ireland. Known as "plantations," the aim of this social engineering exercise was to "plant" strategic areas of Ireland with English and Scottish Protestants, civil and obedient subjects loyal to the British crown, to defend English influence from the threats posed by indigenous Catholics. In practice, however, as historian Ian Gregory and colleagues argue: "The plantation system was anything but neat, it was more often reactive than proactive, it was disorganized and incoherent in its approach, and the geographies that it left were often disjointed and contested."[6]

A large part of the contestation came from native Irish resistance, both armed and cultural, to English colonization. Seemingly every generation had its own uprising or Gaelic resurgence that, however fruitless the result, provided a glorious failure that kept burning the flame of Irish defiance and the will to independently control their own national destiny and identity.[7] Of particular concern to London, however, was the intransigence in the northernmost province of Ulster, one of four provinces on the island of Ireland (along with Connacht, Munster, and Leinster). Ulster had a chieftain tradition of powerful native clans and a landscape, with myriad natural barriers and blockades, shaped for isolation. It was the most Gaelicized and least Anglicized of the provinces, effectively an independent and often rebellious realm relatively unimpacted by English power and a bit too cozy with other continental powers. English officials in Dublin even referred to Ulster as "the Great Irishry."[8]

By the beginning of the seventeenth century, the British crown was in need of a radical solution to address its "Ulster problem" and permanently remove the threat of rebellion. In 1608, believing they could improve on the shortcomings of previous plantation settlements, London began making detailed plans for the plantation of several colonies in Ulster. Meant to increase rule over its most unruly province, the "Plantation of Ulster" would be called by one historian "the most ambitious colonizing project to be carried out in western Europe in modern times" and, by another, "the greatest single act of confiscation that had ever been inflicted by the English on the Irish."[9] "Underpopulated and underdeveloped," Jonathan Bardon, the preeminent historian of Ulster, writes, "Ulster offered prospective colonists a secure title to cheap land, bountiful fisheries and great tracts of valuable woodland."[10] Starting in 1610, droves of settlers drawn from every class of society in England and Scotland, "Protestant in faith and English in attitude," began arriving in Ulster.[11] By 1622, there were about 13,000 of them, half English and half Scots (some there from informal settlements of previous years).[12] For the plantation system, "separation was the essence of the scheme . . . [colonists] had to clear their estates completely of native Irish inhabitants" to make room for a network of new, entirely Protestant communities.[13]

Australian historian Patrick Wolfe has described the purpose of such "settler colonialism" as premised on a logic of elimination: "settler colonizers come to stay; invasion is a structure, not an event. . . . Settler colonialism destroys to replace."[14] While not completely successful in destroying, and replacing the native Catholic Irish population, the plantation of Ulster was successful in establishing two inimical nations within one geographical space, each with its own unmistakable cultures, political allegiances, and economic histories. As John Darby, who helped develop the Centre for the Study of Conflict at the University of Ulster, outlined: "The sum of the Plantation was the introduction to Ulster of a community of strangers who spoke a different language, worshipped apart and followed an alien culture and way of life . . . [with] close commercial, cultural and political ties with Britain."[15]

Divisions into "us" and "them" are an inevitable consequence of settler colonial societies. The authority to govern is often built on the demonization and destruction of "them." In the words of Bardon, the Plantation, coupled with a time of intense religious conflict between supporters of the Reformation and those of the Counter-Reformation in Europe, left Ulster with: "Hostility, suspicion and uncertainty [creating] an unstable atmosphere of fear and division which was to persist to our own times."[16] Over the next two centuries, the unstable atmosphere descended into outright sectarian violence in the region—massacres, counter-massacres, and wars that, as we will see in Chapter 3, remain politicized, even weaponized, in how they are taught and remembered in contemporary Northern Ireland. A series of Penal Laws, enacted across the island between 1695 and 1720, imposed devastating discriminatory measures against Catholic clergy and laity. These acts, akin to making it a crime to be Irish in Ireland, included prohibiting Catholics from buying land or inheriting land from Protestants, from practicing law or holding public office, from teaching or running schools within Ireland, from going overseas for purposes of education, from intermarriage with Protestants, and from voting or being Members of Parliament (MPs). The last of the Penal Laws would not be repealed until 1829.

By the time of the 1851 census, famine and emigration had combined to reduce Ulster's population by 374,000 over the course of the previous decade, a drop of 15.7%.[17] For those who remained, the echoes of a deeply divided society reverberated to the point of normalization. The identity divisions, though, were no longer purely religious: they had transcended religion and become issues of national identity—particularly centered on the constitutional status of Ireland. In this regard, there were "two nations" within Ulster: "nationalists" wanting self-government for Ireland and "unionists" desiring for Ireland to remain part of the United Kingdom (as it had been since being absorbed into the United Kingdom of Great Britain and Ireland in 1801). Nationalists "argued that the political Irish nation was coextensive with the geographical island of Ireland."[18] In response, Ulster unionists denied that nationalists even had a right to call Ireland a nation because it was already "part of a nation, the British nation."[19] Unionists doubted the Irish could run their own country and were wary of "the perfidious influence of the Catholic Church and its insidious doctrines."[20]

With the highest concentration of Protestants in Ireland, the dualities of identity in Ulster were strikingly apparent both to foreign visitors as well as lifelong residents. Writing in 1887, Paschal Groussett, an exiled French journalist, told of a "Scottish Ireland" in "loyal Ulster" that "belongs to the same geological, ethnological, commercial, and religious [Protestant] system" of neighboring Scotland.[21] Similarly, in 1896, Thomas MacKnight, a unionist Anglo-Irish newspaper editor, opined: "The plain, the undeniable truth, is that there are two antagonistic populations, two different nations on Irish soil. To speak of one of them only, as is so often done, as the Irish people, is a mischievous fallacy, a political and social untruth. To put the one under the feet of the other, and this is what is meant by governing Ireland by an Irish Legislature and according to Irish ideas, would be a shameful and cruel injustice. Whatever may be pretended, it never would, it never could, come to good. There is no community of feeling, and therefore no common citizenship between the two sections of the Irish people."[22]

These competing dualities of identity suggested a soil fertile for sectarian violence. In 1914, Irish novelist F. Frankfort Moore, describing Ulster as "like a piece hacked out of Britain somewhere between the Tweed and the Tyne," warned: "Ulster today resembles one of those volcanic basins which only need a single stone to be flung into them to produce such an eruption as may change the whole face of the landscape . . . anyone passing through these localities will perceive, on being made aware of the respective creeds of the inhabitants and of the spirit of animosity which is inhaled by all from their earliest years, how easy it is for a riot to be started."[23] That same year, unionist politician Sir Edward Carson observed: "I see no hopes of peace. I see nothing at present but darkness and shadows."[24]

Despite this palpable "spirit of animosity" in the "darkness and shadows" of an increasingly contentious Ulster, large-scale violence was, for a time, averted by the Great War of 1914–1918. After the end of the war, however, the UK General Election of 1918 made clear that Irish nationalism was on the rise, particularly in the south of Ireland. The move to establish a national assembly in Ireland, asserting Ireland's right to independence, became a reality on January 21, 1919, with the extralegal seating of the Assembly of Ireland, or "Dail Eireann" in Irish, in Dublin. A Declaration of Independence was passed asserting: "English rule in this country is, and always has been, based upon force and fraud and maintained by military occupation against the declared will of the people."[25] The securing of that unilaterally declared independence would, however, not come easily. British authorities did everything in their power to bring down the new government of the Irish Republic. The resulting two-year armed struggle would become known as the Anglo-Irish War or, in the south, the Irish War of Independence.

In the midst of that conflict, Britain decided it would be easier to deal with the revolt and manage its own interests if it could at least partially reconcile some of the conflicting desires of Irish nationalists and Ulster unionists. In pursuit of that objective, the British government proposed a bill to partition Ireland into two separate parliaments in Dublin and Belfast. Irish nationalist powerholders in the south rejected the plan and carried on with their war for independence until a ceasefire was called on July 11, 1921. In Ulster, however, unionist powerholders reluctantly accepted the plan for limited self-government as the best alternative to remaining part of the United Kingdom. The bill, passed as the Government of Ireland Act of 1920 and sometimes known as the Partition Act, would give a home, however contested, to the deeply divided society of the north of Ireland in the new statelet of Northern Ireland.

In the runup leading to partition of the north from the south of Ireland, there was heated debate about who would—and would not—be included in the new statelet. Sometimes, all nine counties of Ulster were to be included; other times, just the four counties around Belfast. Eventually, to preserve a unionist majority, the borders of Northern Ireland included only six of Ulster's nine counties—Fermanagh, Armagh, Tyrone, Londonderry,

Antrim, and Down (bequeathing to generations of schoolchildren the catchy mnemonic acronym of FATLAD). The three excluded counties (Cavan, Monaghan, and Donegal), while containing some unionists, enclosed such a large block of nationalist voters that a unionist majority in the new parliament would be in immediate jeopardy. "A couple of members sick," said one unionist defending the exclusions, "or two or three members absent for some accidental reason, might in one evening hand over the entire Ulster parliament and the entire Ulster position."[26] So, those three counties, still looking north to their historical connection with the region of Ulster, would become part of "Southern Ireland" (renamed the Irish Free State in 1922). In the six-county gerrymandered statelet of Northern Ireland, nationalists would become members of a country in which they made up less than a third of the population. To be precise, as political scientist Brendan O'Leary points out, Northern Ireland, unlike its southern neighbor, never has been or is a state; rather it is a devolved entity of the United Kingdom of Great Britain and Northern Ireland. Moreover, "Northern Ireland is in Union with Great Britain but it is not part of Great Britain, which refers to England (incorporating Wales) and Scotland."[27]

In May 1921, elections were held within the six counties of Northern Ireland and the country seated its first parliament, with, as expected from "little more than a sectarian headcount," 40 out of the 52 seats taken by unionists.[28] The opening of the Parliament of Northern Ireland was held in Belfast City Hall on June 22, 1921, with its unionist members enthusiastically swearing an oath of allegiance to King George V even as its nationalist members refused to take their seats. The devolved parliament of Northern Ireland would now be self-governing in terms of controlling most domestic affairs and internal law and order. All other areas, however, would be specifically reserved to the British crown (e.g., foreign trade, defense, major taxation, customs and excise, and the High Court).[29] The "two antagonistic populations" with a lack of a "community of feeling" and "common citizenship," referred to by MacKnight just two decades before, now constituted the world's newest country.

* * *

In the new six-county artificial entity of Northern Ireland, the majority (unionists) were faced with a disappointed and alienated minority (nationalists) who refused to recognize the British state and its devolved institutions. As historian Sean Duffy writes: "It [Northern Ireland] catered for the needs of a minority in Ireland [Protestants], but had within its own boundaries a very substantial minority of its own [Catholics] who wanted nothing to do with it."[30] For the first four years of its existence, believing, as one nationalist leader said, "it [Northern Ireland] was a very temporary thing and that the house of cards would crumble," nationalists refused to take their seats in the Northern Ireland parliament—effectively making the country a one-party state.[31] Signaling a mainstream rather than extremist opposition, Catholic church leaders were vocal in their public support of the nationalist rejection of the new state, while "Catholic school managers refused to accept grants from the state and some Catholic school teachers actually refused to take their state salaries."[32] In turn, this fueled unionist anti-Catholic rhetoric and effectively freed unionist politicians of any perceived responsibility to protect the rights of the minority and "govern all the people."

In effect, the young Northern Ireland parliament had become, as boasted by Sir James Craig, the first Prime Minister of Northern Ireland, "a Protestant Parliament" leading "a Protestant state."[33] Although Northern Ireland would maintain some form of formal democratic institutions from its birth until 1972, the deck was stacked against any semblance of equality between the two dominant identity groups. As a result, it was a democracy in name only, "a fiefdom run by an interlocking cadre of mutually supportive elites."[34] As sociologists Bernadette Hayes and Ian McAllister write: "The province was not a competitive democracy in the conventional sense, since there was no possibility that the Protestant and unionist majority would ever lose an election, nor that the Catholic and nationalist opposition could ever win."[35] Moreover, the civil and police services of the new statelet also were over-whelmingly Protestant and unionist. This Protestant and unionist unre-lenting hold on power reflected well the lines from Rudyard Kipling's 1912 poem titled *Ulster*: "We know, when all is said, We perish if we yield."[36]

Perhaps unsurprisingly, these rival communities descended into wide-spread sectarian violence as the newly partitioned state was emerging. Between July 1920 and July 1922, 557 people were killed: 303 Catholics, 172 Protestants, and 82 members of the police and British army.[37] The govern-ment responded with the Special Powers Act of 1922, emergency legislation giving wide powers of arrest and detention to the Royal Ulster Constabulary (RUC), a largely Protestant armed police force. The act (allegedly admired by both Adolf Hitler and Johannes Vorster, one of the architects of apart-heid in South Africa), used almost exclusively against Catholics, allowed for the imposition of curfews, arrest and detention without trial, flogging, and even death for the possession of firearms.[38] Fearful of their fate in a unionist-dominated country, many nationalists gave their support to the Irish Republican Army's (IRA) campaign of terror against the government of Northern Ireland. This "disloyalty," an assault on the very existence of Northern Ireland, stoked the fears of unionists and further deepened the birth pangs within the still-coalescing statelet.

The political and sectarian strife would decline for a period of time as republican activism was pulled south during the Irish Civil War of 1922–1923. It would rise again, however, and be compounded by economic distress as the staple industries of linen, shipbuilding, and agriculture faced severe hardship after the collapse of the postwar boom. In August 1920, the Dail Eireann in the south of Ireland, responding to recent attacks on Catholics in Belfast, ordered a boycott of Belfast-based banks and insurance companies. This quickly expanded into a wider campaign to exclude Northern Irish goods from the nationalist-dominated south. Meant to show the unfeasibility of partition, the boycott actually cemented its reality. By the time the boycott ended in 1922, it had significantly weakened banking and commercial links between the north and south. That same year, nearly 23% of Northern Irish were unemployed "and for the rest of the decade on average around one fifth of all insured workers had no jobs."[39] Beginning in 1929, the global economic depression devastated an already vulnerable Northern Ireland. By February of 1938, 29.5% of insured industrial workers were unemployed in Northern Ireland, the highest figure for any region in Britain.[40] Poverty and sickness were unrelenting. Maternal mortality rates rose by one-fifth between 1922 and 1938.[41]

When war between Britain and Germany broke out in September 1939, however, the economic fortunes of Northern Ireland would reverse. Ireland, exercising its right as an independent state, would choose to remain neutral throughout the war. In his 1945 response to Churchill's criticism about Ireland's neutrality, Irish Taoiseach (head of government) Eamon de Valera came back with a defense born and bred in Irish nationalism. Citing the "already bloodstained record of the relations between England and this country" as well as the "mutilation" and partition of his country by the British government, de Valera defended Ireland's neutrality: "With our history and our experience after the last war and with a part of our country [Northern Ireland] still unjustly severed from us, no other policy was possible."[42]

Conversely, for the unionist-dominated government of Northern Ireland (now commonly referred to as "Stormont" because its purpose-built parliament building was opened in 1932 in the Stormont estate area on the outskirts of Belfast), no other policy was possible apart from siding with Britain and the allied forces. Northern Ireland became invaluable to the Allied war effort, not only as an important source of workforce but also in providing ports and strategic staging areas for air sorties and convey escorts, as well as industrial and agricultural production supporting the war effort. Tens of thousands of British, American, and Canadian troops passed through Northern Ireland during the course of the war, with many going on to theaters of combat in North Africa and, later, the D-Day landings in Normandy. The workforce of Harland and Wolff tripled to about 35,000 as the shipyard built three aircraft carriers but also specialized in the construction of convoy escort vessels and merchant ships. Short's aircraft factory helped produce 1,200 Stirling bombers and 125 Sunderland Flying Boats. Mackie's Foundry manufactured some 75 million artillery shells, while the linen and textile factories of Northern Ireland produced more than 200 million yards of cloth for the mass production of uniforms. Agricultural and food production roughly doubled relative to prewar levels and unemployment across the country was significantly reduced.[43]

While these wartime production levels were lower than any other part of the United Kingdom, Northern Ireland's willingness to step up for Britain and her allies, as well as the suffering loosed on Belfast in April–May 1941 by four German air raids, did not go unnoticed. Winston Churchill, British Prime Minister: "But for the loyalty of Northern Ireland we should have been confronted with slavery and death and the light which now shines so strongly throughout the world would have been quenched. The bonds of affection between Great Britain and the people of Northern Ireland have been tempered by fire and are now, I believe, unbreakable."[44]

This fraternal, unbreakable connection with Britain became a rallying cry for the Protestant unionist majority in Northern Ireland intent on further cementing the relationship in the postwar years. To do so, however, required a united front, particularly inclusive of working-class Protestants. By catering to the needs of working-class Protestants, unionism was able to stave off any internal division based on class. By favoring one side, however, it also disfavored the other side. Accusations of anti-Catholic discrimination and even civil rights abuses were common in nationalist communities. These accusations, regularly repeated, included discrimination against Catholics in housing and employment (particularly in the public sector), gerrymandering of electoral boundaries to favor unionist voters, and abuses of civil power against Catholics (particularly the Special Powers Act of 1922). This was an intersection of oppressions that left Catholics, relative to Protestants, disenfranchised across the country.

Unionists, of course, denied the existence of any anti-Catholic discrimination at all. While there remains debate over how widespread such discrimination was and too little acknowledgment of how discrimination also impacted some working-class or poor Protestants, there is little debate that discrimination against Catholics existed.[45] Even in a society as generally disadvantaged as Northern Ireland, Protestants held relative positions of privilege over their Catholic counterparts, particularly in certain regions of the country (e.g., west of the River Bann, epicenter of the seventeenth-century plantation scheme). As Bardon argues: "The lower socioeconomic status and educational attainment of Catholics in Ulster were evident long before the creation of Northern Ireland. Protestants had always dominated the skilled trades . . . [making] it difficult for Catholics to find work."[46] Similarly, Edmund A. Aunger wrote in his analysis of occupational status in Northern Ireland in the 1960s and 1970s: "While a clerk may be Catholic, it is more likely that the office Manager will be a Protestant; while a skilled craftsmen may be a Catholic, it is more likely that the supervisor will be a Protestant; and while the nurse may be a Catholic, it is more likely that the Doctor will be a Protestant."[47] Actor and singer Bronagh Gallagher, in recalling the experience of what it meant to be poor and Catholic for her father's generation in Northern Ireland, said: "There's no point in covering it up. You were a second- or third-class citizen. All the jobs were going to people who had connections to the middle-class, the upper-class, the Orange Order. That's just the way it was."[48] Also helpful in unpacking the relative group differences in socioeconomic status and employment opportunities was larger Catholic family size, often negatively impacting wealth and its generational transmission, as well as "relatively poor standards of education in Catholic-run schools [with] lower levels of state subsidy."[49]

Central to maintaining Protestant privilege, however, was political control, particularly at the level of local government. Political control was self-perpetuating as it made certain those in power could make the allocations—in housing and public sector employment—to ensure they would remain in control. In the words of author and activist Adrian Kerr: "The Unionist Government ran the North on the basis that to give something to Catholics was to take it away from Protestants, and nothing was ever willingly given to Catholics."[50]

For unionists, maintaining political control required particular creativity in cities and counties with a nationalist majority. In those cases, the
challenge was to take the numerical superiority of nationalists and turn it
into a political minority. One means to accomplish this was the allocation
of voting rights. In Northern Ireland, while all residents older than 21 years
of age could vote in national elections, voting in local government elections
was restricted to the owners or tenants of a house and their spouses.
Children older than 21 living in the house, or subtenants in a house, had no
voting rights in local elections. This was particularly disenfranchising for
Catholics who, generally, tended to have a markedly higher percentage of
people living at densities of more than two per room than did Protestants.[51]
Moreover, some large property owners, most often Protestant businesses,
might have up to six votes. Overall, these practices of deciding who did
and did not have voting rights disproportionately favored unionists and
disfavored nationalists. In effect, one unionist vote was roughly equivalent
to two and a half nationalist votes.

With voting rights so directly tied to house ownership or occupancy, the
means by which public housing was allocated—who received it and where—
became an important tool in wielding political power. Controlling those
allocations effectively meant controlling voting. So, allocation decisions regarding public housing were political decisions; to give someone a house was
to give them, and their spouse, a local government vote. In this way, unionist
politicians could continue to cement political control in nationalist-majority
cities and counties by ensuring that public housing allocations did not
threaten the continuation of unionist political control. This could be done by
withholding public housing in nationalist communities or, more commonly,
simply ensuring that the location of the housing allocated to Catholics did
not disrupt the electoral balance by endangering unionist majorities. As
Austin Currie, a nationalist politician from County Tyrone, said: "The purpose of the exercise was to ensure that Unionists had continued supremacy
in the areas where in fact they were in the minority."[52]

* * *

The starkest case study of these inequalities and discriminatory practices
was in Londonderry, the second largest city in Northern Ireland and the
largest city in the country with a nationalist majority. Originally known
as Derry (from the Irish "Doire Cholm Chille," meaning the oak grove of
Colmkille), the town's name was changed to Londonderry in 1613, when the

city was granted a royal charter by King James I. Adding the prefix "London" was a colonizing nod to the funding of the city's construction by London guilds.

(Still today, the duality of the name is a source of contention, with unionists preferring the official name, "Londonderry," and nationalists opting for the historic Irish name of "Derry." Road signs within Northern Ireland use "Londonderry," but the majority of the time "London" has been painted over by vandals. In 1984, the British government attempted to mollify the situation by changing the name of the city council and the municipally owned airport from "Londonderry" to "Derry," while keeping the official name of the city and county as "Londonderry." Despite repeated attempts by local nationalist politicians to change the official city and county name back to "Derry," it remains, as it has been since 1613, officially "Londonderry." And, as has been true since 1613, the name you use for the city is often a not-so-subtle political statement. Folk outside the town or county try to avoid the controversy by referring to it as Derry/Londonderry or "Stroke City," a reflection of the dividing slash between the two names. Not abiding by that implicit social compromise can lead to awkward encounters, as I found out when I stepped into a Belfast taxi to the bus station for what I described to the driver as "a trip to Derry" and he testily responded: "In this cab, it's Londonderry." Ironically, though, local residents of Derry/Londonderry, both unionist and nationalist, commonly use the name "Derry" as a shorthand term in everyday speech. As one unionist activist told me, "If the name was good enough for the Apprentice Boys of Derry [a Protestant/loyalist organization set up in memory of the group of apprentice boys who shut the gates of Derry on the approaching army of Catholic King James II in December of 1688], it's good enough for me." So, in respect for how most of the town's residents commonly refer to their city, I will use the name "Derry," without inferring any political or ideological statement, while recognizing that the city's official name remains "Londonderry.")

At the time of the 1961 national census, Derry's total population was 53,744, with 36,049 of those identifying as Catholic and 17,695 as Protestant. Voting restrictions meant only 14,325 Catholics were entitled to vote in local elections, with the remaining 21,724 disenfranchised. This number, however, was still significantly higher than the 9,235 Protestants who were eligible to vote in local elections in Derry.[53] Fortunately for unionists, the city had been divided into three electoral wards, one of which was predominately Catholic (the South Ward, including the Bogside, Brandywell, and

Creggan neighborhoods) and the other two of which were predominately Protestant (the North and Waterside Wards). These wards, born of a set of gerrymandering policies and practices first established shortly after the birth of the state in 1922 and then refined through 1936, were sufficient to allow unionists to retain political control even while living amid a majority nationalist voting electorate.

Central to the success of Derry's gerrymandering was the allocation of public housing, delegated to the mayor of the city. As Eamonn McCann, a local resident, describes in his memoir: "The mayor, on his own, allocated the houses. . . . The operation was completely secret. There were no set criteria to guide him. The only way to get a Corporation house, therefore, was to convince the mayor that you *ought* [emphasis in original] to get one, and members of his local Orange lodge were obviously better placed than Bogsiders to do this."[54] With this unilateral power, the unionist mayor could confine nearly all Catholics to the nationalist South Ward. When building land began to run out in the grossly overcrowded South Ward, the city decided to build upward in multistory apartment buildings. Very seldom was a Catholic allocated housing in the unionist North and Waterside Wards.

This discriminatory pattern of housing allocation led to an effective gerrymandering of electoral boundaries, with the majority of the larger Catholic population corralled into one ward (South) which returned eight seats, while the majority of the smaller Protestant population were in two wards (North and Waterside) which returned twelve seats. In effect, it took many more individual votes to elect a Catholic than it did to elect a Protestant. So, even with Catholic voters in Derry outnumbering Protestants by 5,000, this gerrymandering ensured that, election after election, there was a Protestant and unionist majority on the Londonderry Corporation even as that majority was receiving only a minority of the general vote. In fact, only 18% of the employees of the Londonderry Corporation were Catholic, and none of those was employed in senior positions.[55]

* * *

As historian Sean Duffy argues: "It was inevitable that the worldwide radicalization of the sixties would have profound consequences in the six counties."[56] Indeed, the zeitgeist of the times—resonating in the voices of freedom rising in Paris to Prague to Chicago to Mexico City—found fertile soil among Catholic and nationalist communities in Northern Ireland who believed the state was neither legitimate nor fair. "In Northern Nationalist eyes," as historian and political scientist Richard English argues, "the state's illegitimacy and its unfairness were interwoven: since this British state had been wrongly carved out of Ireland to serve Unionist interests, what else could be expected there but pro-Unionist political and economic bias?"[57]

In response to this perceived bias as well as rising sectarian tensions following the impassioned 1966 commemorations of the fiftieth anniversaries of the Easter Rising and the Battle of the Somme, the Northern Ireland Civil Rights Association (NICRA) was formed in early 1967. Animated by the civil rights movement in the United States (even borrowing the gospel anthem "We Shall Overcome"), NICRA was formed by a diverse coalition of trade unionists, communists, radical socialists, republicans, nationalists, unionists, leftwing student activists, and members of the Northern Irish Labour and Liberal political parties. Bernadette McAliskey (née Devlin), a well-known civil rights activist and politician from Country Tyrone, recalls: "NICRA was formed by people who were members of political parties and groups who united, despite other differences, to collectively campaign for basic reforms which they believed would provide basic equality of citizenship within the political structures of the north."[58] NICRA was a nonsectarian and nonpolitical organization committed to nonviolent methods of civil disobedience (including protests, marches, and sit-ins). They did not seek to end the existence of the British government in Northern Ireland; rather, they sought to change that government's behavior. Rather than bringing about social change through conflict meant to overthrow the existing political system, they pursued social change within the institutions provided by that political system. NICRA had six demands: a call for "one man [sic], one vote" for all people over the age of 18, an end to discrimination and gerrymandering, a formal procedure to deal with complaints against public authorities, the disbandment of the B-Specials, fair play in public housing allocation, and an end to the Special Powers Act.[59]

As the burgeoning US civil rights movement found its catalyst event in the 1955 arrest of Rosa Parks for refusing to surrender her seat on a bus to a white passenger, so, too, would the summer of 1968 see NICRA finding its catalyst event in Caledon, a nationalist village in County Tyrone with a severe housing shortage. Fifteen new houses had been built by the unionist-dominated housing council in Caldeon, with an informal understanding that they would be allocated as evenly as possible between Protestant and Catholic families. Upon allocation, however, 14 of the 15 high-demand houses were granted to Protestant families, including a three-bedroom house to a young, single, Protestant woman, Emily Beattie, who worked for a unionist parliamentary candidate—even as more than 250 Catholic families remained on a waiting list. In protest, a local Catholic family squatted in one of the houses and, allowed by a judge to remain for six months, waited futilely for a new house to be allocated to them. On June 19, they were forcibly evicted from the house. The following day, nationalist MP Austin Currie, along with two other local men, decided to protest by squatting in the vacated house until evicted a few hours later by RUC officers (one of whom happened to be Emily Beattie's brother). On August 24, 1968, in a public demonstration to support Currie's protest (now known as the "Caledon Squat"), NICRA organized its first march. Going between the towns of Coalisland and Dungannon in Country Tyrone, the march of more than 4,000 people passed without incident (though it was prohibited from entering the town center).

On October 5, 1968, building on the publicity drawn from the previous march, NICRA organized a second civil rights march to protest the Londonderry Corporation's record of inequality in the allocation of public housing. The march would begin at 3:30 PM at the Waterside Railway Station in Derry. The march would conclude at the Diamond, Derry's main square, where hastily made posters said "a PUBLIC METTING [sic] will take place." Two days before it was to be held, the march was officially banned by William Craig, Minister for Home Affairs in the Stormont Parliament and a staunch unionist who saw the civil rights movement as a political front for violent republicanism. In defiance, a small group of 400 marchers decided to proceed with the march. Just as they began their march on Duke Street, they were met with water cannons and unrestrained baton-wielding members of the RUC, resulting in injuries to 96 of the marchers. In Austin Currie's recollection, there were "policemen to the front of us, policemen to the back of us . . . no way out."[60] The excessive and violent state response to this peaceful march was captured in 60 seconds of unforgettable Raidió Teilifís Éireann (RTE, the Irish national broadcaster) footage. The events in Derry galvanized the world's attention and brought international pressure to bear on Northern Ireland's government. In addition, it spurred greater commitment to the cause from the nationalist community. Magnetic leaders such as John Hume and Bernadette Devlin emerged to further highlight the cause of constitutional nationalism. In Derry, a subsequent march the next month, over the same route, would draw 15,000 marchers.

Reflecting on the events of 1968 in Derry, a prominent unionist politician, Edmund Warnock, acknowledged: "If ever a community had a right to demonstrate against a denial of civil rights, Derry is the finest example. A Roman Catholic and Nationalist city has for three or four decades been administered (and none too fairly administered) by a Protestant and Unionist majority secured by a manipulation of the Ward boundaries for the sole purpose of retaining Unionist control."[61]

* * *

Asking anyone in Northern Ireland when the Troubles began will provide a variety of responses ranging across centuries. As most will agree, however, the events of 1968 were a pivotal turning point. As Bardon describes: "At a stroke the television coverage of the events of 5 October 1968 destabilised Northern Ireland, and as the sectarian dragon was fully reawakened, the region was plunged into a near-revolutionary crisis, characterized by bitter intercommunal conflict and protracted violence and destruction."[62]

The exact role of the civil rights movement in the complicated historical narrative of Northern Ireland is, like so many other events in that narrative, contested. I think it too simple to depict the movement, as some do, as the origin of the Troubles. The intent of the civil rights movement was to change the behavior of the British government in Northern Ireland by peaceful means, not to remove that government. What the unrest prompted by the movement did do, however, was open a space, a window of opportunity, through which other actors with other motives could enter. And it was those actors, both state and non-state, and their actions that better explain the origin of the Troubles.

More than one person I interviewed described the civil rights movement, always remorsefully, as a "lost moment" when reform could well have gone down a peaceful, constitutional path rather than the violent, extraconstitutional path it was to take. "We had it [a peaceful means to transformation] in our hands," one nationalist interviewee said, "and we let it slip away. So many lives were destroyed because we lost control of what we wanted to achieve." The transformation from a peaceful strategy of nonviolent civil resistance to a social and political strategy of violence did not occur in a vacuum. It was shaped by the state's response to calls for change—sometimes violent, at other times dismissive, and at yet other times compliant, but at a glacial pace—as well as the rise of intense unionist counter-demonstrations and loyalist paramilitary violence. Richard English: "Protestant loyalists saw the civil rights project as merely another anti-Unionist ploy and so responded in hostile—at times, violent—fashion. The Belfast government did produce reforms, but these managed to be simultaneously too little and too tardy for nationalist appetites, and yet too much for many unionists to stomach."[63] So began a cyclical pattern of rising nationalist impatience with resistance to reform leading to increasing unionist resistance to that impatience. Reservoirs of fear, resentment, threat, and even hatred were being released on all sides.

The path between the most commonly identified beginning and end points of the Troubles—the civil rights movement in 1968 and the signing of the Good Friday Agreement in 1998—was anything but linear and certainly anything but inevitable. It was a precipitous path with numerous twists and turns that could easily have twisted and turned in different directions. In differential calculus, such turning points are known as "inflection points," or points at which a curve changes from upward to downward (or vice versa). Following that concept, we can trace the path of the Troubles through its inflection points, those times of significant change in the country's social and political situation that altered the path of the Troubles. Doing so allows us focus on those crucial moments when state and non-state actors made policy and practice decisions that altered the course of Northern Ireland's history. After 1968, we can identify five inflection points that, from the perspective of a broad overview, can help us understand the 30 years of violence that would be bookended by the civil rights movement and the peace agreement: deployment of British troops (1969), introduction of internment (1971), Bloody Sunday (1972), implementation of direct rule (1972), and the Hunger Strikes (1981).

(1) *Deployment of British Troops.* On August 14, 1969, a third combatant was added to the already volatile mix when British troops were deployed to the streets of Northern Ireland to restore security after a series of riots triggered by Protestant parades. "Operation Banner" was a supposed "limited operation" to restore law and order. Planned to be in place only until law and order had been restored, but certainly for no longer than six months, British troops would remain for 38 years. At its peak in 1972, there were 25,700 British troops deployed in Northern Ireland, making the British military presence larger than the population in all but a handful of Northern Ireland's towns.[64] At the beginning, nationalist communities cautiously welcomed the presence of British troops as protectors in the face of rising loyalist violence. British soldiers were often greeted with cups of tea and appreciative smiles. For republicans, however, the presence of British troops on Irish soil was a visible, and visceral, reminder of a British occupation that went back eight

centuries. It would not be long before nationalist communities also withdrew their welcome as they recognized the British Army's presence was primarily in a support role for an exhausted and depleted RUC; rather than being protective, their presence was, in fact, repressive. As one former republican political prisoner told me, "British soldiers assumed that people in nationalist areas were one of three things—either in the IRA, supportive sympathizers of the IRA, or going to be in the IRA one day."

In 1969, the republican movement consisted of about 120 men in the IRA.[65] Despite its ties to a proud historical lineage of republicanism, the IRA had become largely dormant. In Belfast, its total arsenal was a machine gun, a pistol, and some ammunition.[66] At that time, the IRA was mocked by nationalist communities as "I Ran Away" due to its ineffectiveness in defending Catholics and nationalists over recent years (and particularly their conspicuous absence during the rioting over the past two years). As one republican argued, this was "the logical outcome of an obsession in recent years with parliamentary politics, and the subsequent undermining of the Irish Republican Army."[67] As sectarian violence escalated, however, an influx of young men and women, intent on action rather than staid discourse about Marxist ideology and politics, began to push the movement to regain its legitimacy as the physical defender of the Catholic community in Northern Ireland.

Brendan Behan once quipped that at IRA meetings the first item on any agenda was usually "the split."[68] Indeed, in mid-December 1969, an acrimonious IRA "General Army Convention," convened in the Republic of Ireland, effectively sealed a split within the organization between, on one side, those who favored more radical leftist politics and steered away from violence and, on the other, the more conservative traditionalists who favored paramilitary action and anti-state violence. The latter formed a breakaway group, naming themselves the "Provisional IRA" (a term connecting with the 1916 Easter Rising leaders who had declared a "Provisional" government of Ireland). Also known as the "Provos," or the PIRA, this new dissident wing within the IRA sought to reclaim the "fundamental republican position." In their first public statement, released on December 28, the PIRA affirmed their "allegiance to the thirty-two-country Irish Republic . . . suppressed to this day by the existing British-imposed six-county and twenty-six-county partition states."[69] The PIRA, grown weary and suspicious of relying on political activity to change the status quo, was explicitly committed to the use of violence to both defend Catholic communities as well as remove the British presence from the island of Ireland. The following month, on January 10–11, 1970, in Dublin, the IRA split would be mirrored politically at the Sinn Fein Ard Fheis (party conference), with the political wing of the IRA formally splitting into two groups—the Dublin-based "Official Sinn Fein" and the Belfast-based "Provisional Sinn Fein." As Brian Hanley describes: "Friendships were sundered, old comrades fell out and in Belfast, from an early stage, both organisations were fighting each other."[70]

For a period of time, the "Officials" retained both a military and political presence. On May 29, 1972, however, the paramilitary wing of their organization, the Official IRA (OIRA), would declare a conditional ceasefire. Hoping to avoid a sectarian civil war, the Officials would come to focus their energies predominantly on political activity and mass movements of nonviolent civil agitation. As the OIRA moved away from a systematic campaign of violence, dissidents from its ranks who wanted to continue with the use of force left the organization to form the Irish National Liberation Army (INLA), the military wing of the Irish Republican Socialist Party (IRSP). With the OIRA ceasefire in 1972, and the defection of some of its members into the INLA, the Provisionals, who already had inherited most of the IRA structural organization in the north, continued to grow in influence and soon became the dominant faction of IRA life. Reflecting this, the word "Provisionals" eventually would drop and the "IRA" became the accepted shorthand designation for the organization previously known as the PIRA (and this book follows that convention). Similarly, Provisional Sinn Fein soon became simply known as Sinn Fein.

The reorganized and reenergized IRA—with sophisticated intelligence, quartermaster, finance, and engineering branches—would remain the dominant force in violent Irish republicanism for the next 30 years. The IRA's guerrilla strategy, as described in their training and induction manual, focused on "hit and run tactics against the Brits while at the same time striking at the soft economic underbelly of the enemy, not with the hope of physically driving them into the sea but nevertheless expecting to effect their withdrawal by an effective campaign of continuing harassment." Depicting themselves as legal representatives of the Irish people, the IRA claimed a moral justification for "carrying out a campaign of resistance against foreign occupation forces and domestic collaborators."[71] Over the years of the Troubles, Martin McGuinness believed that close to 10,000 people were involved in the ranks of the IRA, while others put the figure at closer to 8,000.[72] Many in the communities in which the IRA was embedded turned a blind eye while others offered safe houses, hid weapons, or, as one former republican political prisoner told me, "keep front and back doors always unlocked so we could run through as we evaded the Brits and security forces."

Likewise, loyalist paramilitaries were mobilized by attacks on their Protestant state and their Protestant privileges. These loyalist paramilitaries used violence to strengthen unionist domination and protect their communities from the menace of Catholic agitation. The most active group was the Ulster Volunteer Force (UVF), first emerging in 1966 under the leadership of Gusty Spence. Also active and, despite frequent cooperation, often at odds with the UVF, was the larger Ulster Defence Association (UDA), founded in September 1971. At the height of its power, it is estimated that the UDA could, given an hour or two of notice, put 20,000 men on the streets of Belfast.[73] As a cover for its violent acts and to protect itself from proscription, the UDA formed a surrogate force, the Ulster Freedom Fighters (UFF), in May 1972. The secretive Red Hand Commando (RHC), formed the same year, was closely associated with the UVF.

Political, religious, and social rhetoric inflamed the tensions. Reverend Ian Paisley, an evangelical Protestant clergyman speaking to Protestant, unionist, and loyalist audiences, emerged as the most vocal voice raising concerns about the sinister influence of Catholicism. With a Bible seemingly always in hand, he told spellbound audiences how Catholics consumed "the bones, body, blood and sinews of Jesus Christ" at Mass and had to be instructed not to chew "the wafer" but "simply let him melt away on the roof of your mouth."[74] In his mind, anything that promoted Catholicism directly threatened Protestantism supremacy and what he saw as the Protestant basis of Northern Ireland. Paisley twinned the Vatican with the IRA in a "plot marked by darkness, secrecy, violence, and sexual perversity."[75] As journalist Patrick Radden Keefe describes him: "Paisley was a Pied Piper agitator who liked to lead his followers through Catholic neighborhoods, sparking riots wherever he went. . . . He was a flamboyantly divisive figure, a maestro of incitement. In fact, he was so unsympathetic, so naked in his bigotry, that some republicans came to feel that on balance, he might be *good* [emphasis in original] for their movement."[76]

One former UVF member I interviewed spoke directly of Paisley's appeal to working-class Protestants who felt the escalating threat of Catholicism, nationalism, and republicanism. Born and bred in East Belfast, his family were avid followers of Paisley, particularly an uncle who was a self-described "Paisleyite" who regularly took him to Sunday evening meetings featuring Paisley's fiery oratory. He admits to "being led by the nose by Ian Paisley" into believing that, since the appeasing British government did not want to take on the IRA, loyalist paramilitaries needed to. So, as a teenager, he quit school and entered the youth wing of the UVF. He later would be arrested and convicted for acts of paramilitary violence and sentenced to multiple life terms totaling several hundred years, eventually being granted early release under the Good Friday Agreement.

Catholic, nationalist, and republican audiences were not left without their own firebrands warning of continued British colonial occupation, local police collusion with the British Army, the illegitimacy of the Northern Ireland state, and the need for violence as the only response strategy the British would ever understand. Leaders and strategists such as Martin McGuinness, Gerry Adams, and Danny Morrison, drawing on centuries of Irish nationalism and republicanism, advocated for one last heave to get the British out of Ireland. During the 1970s, each January saw republican leaders declaring this was the year for victory. One republican leader I interviewed wryly remembered: "We had a victory in '74 slogan, a victory in '75 slogan, a victory in '76 slogan . . . finally, someone suggested we hold off on the slogans for a while."

The sectarian divide further needled its way into the political structures of Northern Ireland as 1970 saw the birth of the Alliance party, a cross-community group of moderate and largely middle-class Protestants and Catholics. That same year saw the formation of the Social Democratic and Labour Party (SDLP), made up of moderate nationalists. More extreme voices also moved into the political fray. To protect the Protestant basis of the state, and believing that the long-standing Ulster Unionist Party (UUP) had become far too elitist and moderate, Paisley formed the Democratic Unionist Party (DUP) in the latter part of 1971. It would be another decade before Sinn Fein (Gaelic for "Ourselves Alone"), commonly understood by members of both nationalist and unionist communities as the political arm of the IRA, began to actively pursue Irish self-determination through the political route.[77] Sinn Fein would quickly emerge as the more extreme nationalist counterpoint to the DUP. The intransigence of the DUP and Sinn Fein, still felt in the politics of contemporary Northern Ireland, would only widen the sectarian divide.

(2) *Introduction of Internment.* Often, the state's response to violence is worse than the violence itself. In response to the alarming rise in sectarian violence, and as an attempt to impose control, August 1971 saw the introduction of internment without trial. Used in every decade since Northern Ireland was established in 1921, internment meant that suspected terrorists

could be held indefinitely without charge, proof, or evidence. In the early morning hours of August 9, 1971, under the name "Operation Demetrius," Catholic homes across the country were raided and 342 men suspected of republican sympathies or paramilitary ties were forcibly detained. (It would be February 1973 before the first loyalist paramilitaries were interned. By the time the policy of internment was discontinued in December 1975, 1,874 republicans and 107 loyalists had been detained).

Fathers Denis Faul and Raymond Murray immediately began a campaign to highlight the torture and ill treatment of the internees. They were particularly concerned with the experience of 14 high-value targets, "The Hooded Men," who were transported to a secret detention facility for "deep interrogation." There, later revealed to be a British Army camp outside of Derry, they were subjected to sensory deprivation techniques over four to seven days— including standing for hours against the wall in a stress position, continuous high-pitched white noise, sleep deprivation, food and drink deprivation, and hooding.[78] A subsequent Amnesty International report stated: "Many prisoners felt they were on the brink of insanity—one alleges he prayed for death, another that he tried to kill himself by banging his head against some metal piping in the room."[79]

Internment did the opposite of what it was supposed to do as violence escalated across Northern Ireland. Twenty-five people were killed in the four days after internment was introduced. On August 9–11, in the Ballymurphy area of West Belfast, anti-internment riots turned deadly as 10 civilians, including a Catholic priest and a mother of eight, were killed by the First Battalion of the Parachute Regiment of the British Army. Another man died of heart failure after allegedly being subjected to a mock execution. Across the country, 7,000 people, the majority of them Catholics, fled their homes. Many moved to the Republic of Ireland and have never returned to the north. Membership in the PIRA skyrocketed, far surpassing that of the OIRA and signaling a decided shift in nationalist support toward violent republicanism. As a British Ministry of Defence reported admitted in 2006: "Put simply, on balance and with the benefit of hindsight, it [Operation Demetrius] was a major mistake."[80]

(3) *Bloody Sunday*. In the face of the chaos surrounding the introduction of internment, the civil rights movement still remained committed to nonviolent methods of civil disobedience. To protest internment, a series of marches were organized around the country. On January 30, 1972, an anti-internment march in Derry, banned by the new northern Prime Minister

Brian Faulkner, drew about 10,000–15,000 people to the Creggan estate with a plan to march to the city's Guildhall Square. As the march entered the Bogside, they encountered 26 army barricades erected to stop the march from going into the city center. In addition, the First Battalion of the Parachute Regiment, an "elite" regiment of the British Army that also was present at the Ballymurphy massacre the previous year, was in place to bolster security—even though it was generally understood that the IRA stood down during civil rights marches. As sporadic rioting broke out, members of the Parachute Regiment opened fire with live rounds around 4:10 PM. In the resulting chaos, taking less than half an hour, 14 civilians were killed or mortally wounded and a further 18 injured. None of the victims was armed and, indeed, no arms were found among the marchers. Many of the victims were shot in the back, leading Derry's coroner, Hubert O'Neill, to state: "I say it without reservation—it was sheer, unadulterated murder."[81]

The Parachute Regiment's massacre, known as Bloody Sunday, marked an irreversible turn in the nationalist relationship to the state. It effectively marked the end of the civil rights movement as it "unleashed a conflict with battle lines different from those they had anticipated, and a struggle that they could not direct."[82] Bloody Sunday radicalized those no longer satisfied with simply a change in the behavior of the state but now wanting the outright removal of what they perceived as a terrorist state. It, for once and all, moved the conflict outside of Derry to the whole of Northern Ireland. As one member of the nationalist community told me: "Bloody Sunday was the biggest turning point in the Troubles because it showed they were prepared to exterminate us. So, in turn, we had to be prepared to defend ourselves." The Bloody Sunday Inquiry would conclude in 2010: "What happened on Bloody Sunday strengthened the Provisional IRA, increased nationalist resentment and hostility towards the Army and exacerbated the violent conflict of the years that followed. Bloody Sunday was a tragedy for the bereaved and the wounded, and a catastrophe for the people of Northern Ireland."[83]

(4) *Implementation of Direct Rule.* Following Bloody Sunday, the situation in Northern Ireland was now so grave—indeed, so catastrophic—that London doubted Stormont was capable of maintaining law and order. The Northern Ireland parliament met for the last time on Tuesday, March 28, 1972. The next day, London temporarily suspended the Northern Ireland parliament and introduced what would become known as "direct rule." Direct rule meant that Northern Ireland was ruled directly from the parliament at Westminster in London. While Northern Ireland would continue

to be represented by its elected members in British parliament (only 12 members in a House of Commons that numbered some 600), the country would no longer have its own assembly or executive government. A team of ministers, led by the new post of Secretary of State for Northern Ireland, took over the functions of the Stormont Cabinet and the day-to-day administration of Northern Ireland. After 50 years of limited self-government, albeit effectively one-party rule, Northern Ireland could no longer be trusted to rule itself.

Direct rule exacerbated the sectarian tension rather than soothing it. Unionists saw direct rule as a clear indication that violent republicanism had achieved its aim of making Northern Ireland ungovernable. The unionist-dominated parliament that had served as a barrier against a united Ireland was no more. Unionists, recognizing Britain had been moving out of the business of colonialism for decades, felt betrayed by London and were suspicious that attempts to restore local government would involve yet more concessions to nationalists, particularly in the form of forced power-sharing, or cross-community arrangements, with both Protestant and Catholic elected representatives. Spurred by this fear of the loss of their single-party domination and the privileges that went with it, enlistment in loyalist paramilitaries soared by the thousands. There was a palpable sense that their national identity was under threat and needed to be defended.

On the other side, Catholic responses to direct rule were mixed. Many nationalists welcomed the fall of Stormont as a "new beginning," believing direct rule from London certainly could not be worse than what they currently had and might well be even better in terms of addressing some of the burdens of discrimination and violence faced by Catholic communities. Republicans, however, saw direct rule as a(nother) colonial takeover of Ireland by London, a deeper entrenchment of the British presence on Irish soil. In response to direct rule, as well as the rise in loyalist attacks against Catholics, the IRA escalated its campaign of violence, detonating 30 bombs across the country on April 14, 1972. On July 21 of that same year, in what would come to be known as "Bloody Friday," the IRA set off 22 bombs in bus stations, railway depots, and shopping areas across Belfast in the space of 75 minutes, killing nine people and seriously injuring 130 others. Journalist Alf McCreary recalls scenes of fire and rescue workers "scraping up the remains of human beings into plastic bags, like lumps of red, jellied meat from pavement."[84]

All told, 1972 would stand as the bloodiest year of the Troubles, with 480 people killed, more than 10,000 bombs planted, and an average of around 30 shootings a day.[85] Local press photographer Stanley Matchett recalls: "That year, after each atrocity, we all thought, this is the one that will finish it. We had no idea of what was to come."[86]

While direct rule originally was intended to be a temporary measure, the violence of 1972 moved London to formally abolish the Northern Ireland parliament the following year. A 1973 initiative, known as the Sunningdale Agreement, attempted to establish a power-sharing Northern Ireland Assembly to take over the political governance of the country. Described as "the first creative attempt to take a political initiative in Northern Ireland since 1922," the agreement was derided by Paisley as "nothing less than the first instalment and down payment on an eventual united Ireland scheme."[87] Eventually, the agreement was brought down by unionists through a series of regular public protests, culminating in the two-week Ulster Workers' Council Strike in May of 1974. Led by an umbrella grouping of Protestant trade unionists and supported by loyalist paramilitaries, this strike "demonstrated the depth and strength of unionist opposition to the Sunningdale Agreement" and served as its death knell.[88]

On the third day of the Ulster Workers' Council Strike, on May 17, 1974, violence crossed the border into the Republic of Ireland via a loyalist bombing spree, allegedly carried out by the UVF with assistance from British security forces, in which three car bombs in Dublin and one in Monaghan killed 33 people and an unborn child. Another 258 people were injured. The bombings resulted in the greatest loss of life in a single day in the conflict.[89]

For noted Northern Irish poet Seamus Heaney, hope disappeared after 1974. "The violence from below," he writes, "was then productive of nothing but a retaliatory violence from above, the dream of justice became subsumed into the callousness of reality, and people settled in to a quarter century of life-waste and spirit-waste, of hardening attitudes and narrowing possibilities that were the natural result of political solidarity, traumatic suffering and sheer emotional self-protectiveness."[90]

(5) *Hunger Strikes.* In May 1972, following a 35-day hunger strike in Crumlin Road Jail in Belfast, the British government granted paramilitary prisoners "Special Category Status." This status gave such prisoners a relative sense of autonomy—placed in special wings of the prison, they could wear their own clothes, did not have to do prison work, could receive extra visits and parcels (food and tobacco), and, most importantly, were housed within their paramilitary factions and free to associate with other paramilitary prisoners. As a result, prisons housing Special Category prisoners

became ideological training grounds that reinforced commitment to "the cause" on both sides of the sectarian divide. Special Category prisoners maintained militaristic command structures inside the prisons, even drilling with dummy wooden guns, and often exerted centralized control outside the prisons through a complex series of surreptitious communication networks (including, for example, "messages written on sheets of toilet paper in microscopically small handwriting, folded into little pellets, wrapped in cling film and brought out in the mouth of a prisoner's relative").[91] Social identities—republican and loyalist—were further cemented through language, history, art, music, and culture classes taught by the prisoners. A former prison guard I interviewed even described how Special Category prisoners team-taught the instructional mechanics of bomb-making, guerrilla tactics, and self-defense. From where he stood, each of the prisons to which Special Category prisoners had been assigned was best described as a "University of Terrorism."

For Special Category prisoners, their status was an affirmation of involvement in a legitimate political-military struggle, de facto prisoners of war. In London, however, the incoming Labour government wanted to reframe the situation in Northern Ireland as a law-and-order crisis rather than a "war." As one former IRA member I interviewed summarized: "Political prisoners meant political problems that necessitated political solutions and the Brits wanted no part of that." So, after March 1, 1976, as part of the government's new policy of "criminalisation," those convicted of terrorist offenses were now categorized as common criminals. In protest, incoming prisoners, mainly republicans, refused to wear prison uniforms and, instead, draped themselves in blankets. Kieran Nugent, the first republican to be sentenced under the new policy, said: "If they want me to wear a criminal uniform, they will have to nail it to my back."[92] By late 1980, about 340 prisoners were "on the blanket." For every day on the blanket, one was added to their sentence. When prison authorities decided to withhold the right to use the washroom or toilet facilities unless the prisoner was wearing a prison uniform, prisoners responded with the "no wash protests" and the "dirty protests." In these protests, prisoners refused to bathe or slop out their "piss pots" and smeared the walls of their cells with their own excrement.

Eventually, the prisoners decided to escalate their protests by embarking on "a long-standing tradition of Irish resistance"—a hunger strike.[93] In so doing, they were attempting to redefine who they were perceived to be: ordinary criminals would not go on a hunger strike, but political prisoners of conscience would. In October 1980, seven republican prisoners (their number a nod to the seven signatories of the 1916 Proclamation), led by Brendan Hughes, began a hunger strike in order to reclaim "political status." They were later joined by three female republican prisoners in Armagh jail and then another 30 republican prisoners in the H-Blocks of the Maze/Long Kesh.[94] The hunger strike was called off in December when the British government appeared to concede the prisoners' right to wear their own clothes.

When it became clear, though, that the government had misled the prisoners, a second hunger strike began on March 1, 1981, the fifth anniversary of the repeal of Special Category status. Continuing the refrain of the 1980 hunger strike, republican prisoners claimed the right to be granted political status "as captured combatants in the continuing struggle for national liberation and self-determination."[95] With Margaret Thatcher, the British prime minister, refusing to concede to their demands, the first republican prisoner died on May 5, after 66 days of hunger strike. That prisoner, the 27-year-old Bobby Sands, had, just the month before, been elected as a Member of Parliament for Fermanagh/South Tyrone. Even with such popular support, however, the British government had let a Westminster MP starve himself to death. Thatcher was unapologetic: "Mr. Sands was a convicted criminal. He chose to take his own life. It was a choice his organization [the IRA] did not allow to many of its victims."[96] Sands's Belfast funeral drew 100,000 people, and he is well-remembered as one of the leading icons of republican history.[97] Over the next eight months, nine other republican prisoners, each of whom had joined the protest at staggered intervals so as to maximize its impact, would die on hunger strike.[98]

While the British government never officially regranted Special Category status (though they did eventually implement many of the demands requested by the hunger strikers), the strikes were a huge propaganda victory for the IRA. "These hunger strikes," writes security studies expert Caroline Kennedy-Pipe, "were a turning point in internal, European, and international perceptions of the British government's position on Ireland."[99] The strikes politicized a new generation of young nationalists on both sides of the border. Republicans now were standing in every election possible, North and South. The hunger strikes also drew widespread regional and international condemnation of the British government's handling of the situation. For republicans, where bombs drew negative publicity, the hunger strikes showed how nonviolence could garner enormous popular public attention and support.

This is not to say that the hunger strikes were the sole catalyst in beginning to move republicanism away from its violent campaign and in a more political direction. Republican leadership was trying to do that well before 1981. As English summarizes in his insightful analysis of the 1981 hunger strike, it is wrong to see it "as *beginning* a process of republican politicization; it would be more accurately understood as an unintended *accelerator* of a process already favoured by the leaders of the movement [emphasis in original]."[100] Those who survived the hunger strikes certainly recognized their role in this process. In 2006, one of the hunger strikers, Paddy Quinn, reflected: "If Sinn Fein had remained hard-line and military, then I think the sacrifices made on the hunger strike would have been a complete waste. It was Sinn Fein going into politics that made it worthwhile."[101]

Indeed, the hunger strikes became a rich source of political capital for Sinn Fein in that process of acceleration. Many nationalists had grown increasingly disillusioned with the middle-class focus of the SDLP and were growing increasingly appreciative of Sinn Fein's connection with the working class. Even if they were tired of IRA violence, they could at least find common ground in the same ideals of Irish nationalism. Speaking in 1987, Martin McGuinness said: "Not since the declaration in arms of the Irish republic on the steps of Dublin's GPO in 1916 has any event in modern Irish history stirred the minds and hearts of the Irish people to such an extent as the hunger strike of 1981."[102]

Recognizing the opportunity to accelerate a political complement to its campaign of violence, Sinn Fein "sought to displace the SDLP as the main voice of nationalists and win political support for its 'Brits out' approach."[103] At its 1981 party conference, senior republican leader Danny Morrison asked: "Who here really believes we can win the war through the ballot box? But will anyone here object if, with the ballot paper in one hand and the Armalite [rifle] in the other, we take power in Ireland?"[104] This diversification—not reversal—of strategy was affirmed by the *Republican News*: "Not everyone can plant a bomb, but everyone can plant a vote."[105] Similarly, as one former republican political prisoner told me: "Being in the struggle was like being on a football team. You had to find the best position for you to play. Not the one you wanted to play, necessarily, but the one the team needed you to play."

For Sinn Fein, the value of the IRA became its role in creating space for political advances. As Belfast journalist Malachi O'Doherty wrote: "Having an armed campaign behind you and the power to end it is an enormous political advantage."[106] In 1982, Sinn Fein began to draw on this advantage by contesting a Stormont election for the first time. They won 5 of the 78 seats, with Gerry Adams and Martin McGuiness representing two of those five victories. In the 1983 general election, Sinn Fein received 13.4% of the vote compared to SDLP's 17.9%. This was the beginning of a quick ascendency of political power for Sinn Fein, one that would see it become the major force within the republican movement and soon overtake the SDLP as the voice of nationalist voters. As a result, the British government "now found themselves fighting on two fronts, militarily and politically" against the IRA.[107] That fight would continue over the next decade as the IRA's long war of attrition was now conjoined with an ever-evolving nonmilitary political strategy.

* * *

As Moya Cannon writes of the Troubles: "The violence was local, intimate, not international. The killer lives, not in a distant country, but in a neighbouring village or street. Revenge is instinctive, peace-making counter-intuitive."[108] Despite that, several sporadic attempts at making peace emerged over the years of the Troubles—most notably, the short-lived Northern Ireland Assembly (July 1973–May 1974), the Sunningdale Agreement (December 1973), the Constitutional Convention (May 1975–March 1976), a little longer lived Northern Ireland Assembly (November 1982–June 1986), the Anglo-Irish Agreement (November 1985), the Brooke/Mayhew talks (April 1991–November 1992), and the Downing Street Declaration (December 1993). Each of these dealt, in some way, with a variety of initiatives meant to ensure political accommodation; the reduction of inequality in housing, employment and education; improvements in human rights and the administration of justice; the cessation of violence; or the encouragement of conciliation and cultural diversity.[109] These political initiatives were accompanied by a wide range of civil society peace initiatives as well.[110] While none of these proved equal to the task of bringing a full stop to the conflict, they did, collectively, improve cooperation between the British and Irish governments and prefigure the spirit of the agreement that would eventually spell the end of the Troubles.

Throughout the Troubles, the British government continued to believe that a military solution to the conflict was possible. Covert intelligence gathering, counter-intelligence, and double agents supplemented more traditional military maneuvers, often at the expense of civilian lives. Eventually, however, it became clear none of the three groups—the British Army, IRA, or loyalist paramilitaries—could militarily defeat the others. Further conflict would only end in a stalemate. In November 1989, British Secretary of State for Northern Ireland, Peter Brooke, publicly admitted that the IRA could not be beaten by military means. Paisley called Brooke's statement "treachery and surrender" while another unionist leader, William Ross, demanded Brooke's "dismissal in the wake of this new incitement to the IRA to go on bombing and murdering their way to the conference table."[111] Similarly, the IRA, riddled with informers, had come to realize that they could not, militarily, get the British out of the north of Ireland, let alone deliver a united Ireland.[112] As one former republican political prisoner told me, "We began to realize that the best we could hope for was a very successful draw." Richard English: "The IRA could go on fighting, but so too could the British state, and so too could Ulster loyalists."[113] In a perpetual war with no winners but only victims, there had to be a different way forward.

On August 31, 1994, believing its use of force had now positioned it for substantive political gains related to the right of self-determination, the IRA called for a complete cessation of its campaign of violence. Six weeks later, on October 13, loyalist paramilitaries followed suit. Gusty Spence, speaking for the Combined Loyalist Military Command (including the UDA, UVF, and RHC paramilitaries), announced the "Union is safe" and "that the democratically expressed wishes of the greater number of people in Northern Ireland will be respected and upheld" and further warned that "the permanence of our ceasefire will be completely dependent upon the continued cessation of all nationalist/republican violence."[114] While the violence did not cease completely—in a number of communities, republican and loyalist paramilitaries continued with a policing role that included punishment beatings and killings—it did subside enough to provide the working space for a peace process to begin to unfold.

Blaming the unionist politicians and British government's reluctance to move the peace process forward and no longer willing to negotiate on the decommissioning of its weapons, the 17-month IRA ceasefire ended in February 1996 with a series of terrorist activities in Britain and Europe. Most loyalist paramilitaries continued to maintain their ceasefire, though violence erupted in other ways. In July 1996, for instance, a Protestant parade from the Drumcree parish church outside Portadown, routed along a mainly nationalist road, led to several days of intimidation, violence, and rioting throughout Northern Ireland. More than 600 Protestant and Catholic families moved out of their homes, and damage in excess of £50 million was done to properties.[115] The following week, echoing the refrains of a deeply divided society, political commentator Barry White wrote: "We have no common nationality to rediscover, and the two mother countries we look to regard us as aliens . . . if we can't learn to tolerate our differences, and find some way of accommodating our conflicting aspirations, we'll destroy ourselves, either in an all-out conflagration or a slow death."[116]

Eventually, the IRA declared a second ceasefire on July 19, 1997, expressing an intent "to enhance the search for democratic peace settlement through real and inclusive negotiations."[117] Sinn Fein depicted the next phase of the republican struggle as a political one, leaving behind the IRA's campaign of violence against British rule in Northern Ireland and repackaging itself as a historical extension of Northern Ireland's civil rights movement.[118] Substantive all-party peace talks, or at least "talks about talks," would pick up again in September of that same year.[119] The peace talks occurred in and were influenced by an era of peace processes, most notably the end of the Cold War and the beginning of conflict resolution efforts in South Africa and Israel/Palestine. They were also influenced by a fatigue that opened room to find a different way forward. As Duncan Morrow argues: "Peace when it arrived was a peace based on military-political exhaustion rather than a peace shaped by transformed political relationships."[120]

Chairing the peace negotiations was former US Senator George Mitchell (D-ME). British Prime Minister Tony Blair and his Irish counterpart, Taoiseach Bertie Ahern, were to play significant roles in the negotiations as well. The two main political parties in the negotiations were the Ulster Unionist Party, led by David Trimble, and the SDLP, led by John Hume. The two political leaders would jointly share the 1998 Nobel Peace Prize in recognition of "their efforts to find a peaceful solution to the conflict in Northern Ireland."[121]

Despite the complexity of the negotiations, the team was eventually able to develop a peaceful and democratic framework for power-sharing in Northern Ireland. The lengthy 11,000-word agreement stated that Northern Ireland would remain part of the United Kingdom unless and until a majority of the people in both Northern Ireland and the Republic of Ireland (50% + 1) voted otherwise. For Northern Ireland's internal governmental structure, devolved government returned in the form of a new democratically elected 108-member National Assembly, "inclusive in its membership" (Strand 1). Cross-community power-sharing also was ensured at the executive level, with unionist and nationalist Ministers appointed based on the number of seats a party won in the election. The joint office of the First and deputy First Ministers, one unionist and one nationalist, were granted equal governmental powers, and one could not be in position without the other. The agreement also created opportunities for north–south cooperation be-tween Northern Ireland and the Republic of Ireland (Strand 2) as well as for east–west connections between the Republic of Ireland and the United Kingdom (Strand 3). Finally, in terms of more immediate practical issues, the agreement called for prisoner releases within two years for those associated with paramilitary groups on ceasefire, the decommissioning of all weapons held by paramilitary forces, reform of the police service, and a reduction in the number and role of British armed forces in Northern Ireland.

The agreement, bringing an end to the Government of Ireland Act of 1920, was reached at 5:00 PM on Good Friday, April 10, 1998. As then-Prime Minister Tony Blair recalled: "I didn't know we were going to get an agree-ment until literally minutes before it happened. We thought we had lost it several times."[122] The 35-page agreement, commonly known as the Good Friday Agreement, was settled between the British and Irish governments and eight political parties or groups in Northern Ireland. The DUP, protesting that republican and loyalist paramilitary weapons had not been decommissioned, was the only major political group in Northern Ireland to oppose the Good Friday Agreement. (Still signaling its opposition today, both to the spirit of the agreement as well as its perceived misappropria-tion of religious language, DUP leaders routinely refer to it as the Belfast Agreement). In announcing the agreement, an emotional Mitchell, who later remarked of the process, "we had about 700 days of failure and one day of success," said: "The agreement proves that democracy works, and in its wake we can say to the men of violence, to those who disdain democ-racy; whose tools are bombs and bullets: Your way is not the right way. You will never solve the problems of Northern Ireland by violence. You will only make them worse. It doesn't take courage to shoot a policeman in the back of the head, or to murder an unarmed taxi driver. What takes courage is to compete in the arena of democracy, where the tools are persuasion, fairness, and common decency."[123]

On May 22, voters were given the chance to claim the courage to com-pete in that arena of democracy. The agreement was put to referendum in both the north and south of Ireland. With billboards reminding the voting public, "It's Your Decision," the agreement was endorsed by 71.12% in the north and by 94.39% in the south. In Northern Ireland, polls estimated that close to 97% of nationalists supported the agreement with 52% of unionists offering support.[124] Commonly marked as the end of the Troubles, the passage of the Good Friday Agreement was the signature event that opened up a space of hope, at least a ledge to step out upon, for a deeply divided society to find a new beginning. The first elections to the Northern Ireland Assembly took place on June 25, 1998, though it would "take almost a decade for the institutions envisaged in the Good Friday Agreement to begin operating in a manner that even appeared to be sustainable."[125]

The Good Friday Agreement nominally marked the end of one struggle and the beginning of another; it made history but did not end it. "Ultimately," Morrow writes, "the Agreement did not represent the end of division over sovereignty in Ireland. But it did abolish any significant prospect of using violence to constitutional ends with support from outside Northern Ireland."[126] Similarly, John Hume, speaking at the SDLP's annual conference in November 1998, urged attendees to "Think of what we have decommissioned. We have decommissioned the reality of violence. We have decommissioned in a profound way the prospect of conflict leading to more victims . . . we live now in the prevalence of peace, not the prevalence of violence. We have decommissioned mind-sets that saw only difference and division. We have decommissioned the political paralysis of direct rule and the exclusion of local politicians from power and responsibility."[127]

To be certain, the implementation of a peace agreement is more difficult than making the agreement itself, and, as George Mitchell admitted, making this particular peace agreement was "the longest, most difficult years of my life."[128] Peace is an incremental, winding, dynamic, long-term protracted process with an ebb and flow, not a one-time static event or end-game. Peace is a trade-off in which all sides abandon their top preference (outright victory) and settle, instead, for mutually agreed-upon compromise. Some have a hard time letting go of their preference for outright victory and find ways, direct and indirect, to oppose the peace settlement.

As a result, after approving the Good Friday Agreement, that process of peace in Northern Ireland proceeded, and still proceeds, in halting fits and starts. To be sure, the violence did not, and still has not, come to a full stop. In fact, the single worst incident of violence would come on a sunny Saturday afternoon of August 15, 1998, when a car bomb planted in Omagh by the Real IRA, a dissident republican group, resulted in 29 deaths (plus two unborn children) and hundreds of injuries. Decommissioning of paramilitary arms would take years beyond the original deadline of May 2000, and the last actively deployed British troops would not be withdrawn from Northern Ireland until midnight July 31, 2007.[129] The central legacy of the Good Friday Agreement, however, is that it effectively removed the politically motivated violence that had been an everyday feature of life in Northern Ireland for decades. According to one estimate, 2018 would find around 2,400 Northern Irish people alive who would have long since been dead had the Good Friday Agreement not passed two decades earlier.[130]

* * *

Threaded throughout this brief review of the contested history behind a contested country are the lives of the men, women, and children who were killed and those who killed them. There is no single, official list of Troubles-related deaths and attributions of responsibility. Police reports, often skewed toward recording their own fatalities and misrecording attributions of responsibility, never publicly provided sectarian breakdowns of civilian or noncivilian victims. Civil society and academic tabulations vary in what is included and excluded as well as when the death count begins and ends. Nonetheless, as Brendan O'Leary argues: "Where these databases are comparable, over the same periods, the results are strongly convergent . . . the similarities are more important than the differences . . . and their cumulative impact therefore inspires confidence."[131]

Of these various databases, one of the most well-respected is maintained by independent researcher Malcolm Sutton on Ulster University's CAIN web site (*Conflict Archive on the INternet*).[132] Beginning in the mid-1980s, Sutton has scoured scores of newspaper clippings, coroner's and inquest records, books and pamphlets, and has visited cemeteries and funerals, all in an attempt to compile a comprehensive list of deaths related to the conflict in Northern Ireland. His records begin on July 14, 1969, with the death of Francis McCloskey, a 67-year-old Catholic beaten by a baton-wielding RUC officer during street disturbances in Dungiven. They end in December 2001, with the death of Derek Lenehan, a 27-year-old civilian from Dublin who was killed in County Armagh by the INLA. Over the three-plus decades encompassing those two fatalities, Sutton attributes a cumulative total of 3,532 deaths related to the Troubles.[133] Proportionally, if a similar level of violence had taken place in the United States, the death toll would have been more than 500,000—more than the number of Americans who died in World War II, nearly 10 times the American war dead in Vietnam, and about 100 times the number of Americans killed in Iraq after 2003. Extrapolating to Britain, the number of deaths would have been more than 111,000 people, just under half of all British deaths during World War II.[134]

Of those killed, and fairly reflective of late twentieth-century warfare, the majority were civilians caught in the crossfire of violence. As Jake O'Kane, a Belfast-based stand-up comedian, recounts of those dark times: "We came to live with the reality that survival was a matter of luck and nothing to do with being good or bad, involved or uninvolved. Death waited, and all you had to be was in the wrong place at the wrong time."[135]

Rather than deal in percentages, which remove us one step further from the individual victims, I think it best to remain with actual numbers. In Sutton's dataset, 1,840 of the people killed were civilians, most in the wrong place at the wrong time. The remainder of the dead included 1,114 British security (including the British Army, the Ulster Defence Regiment, and the RUC), 397 republican paramilitary, 170 loyalist paramilitary, and 11 Irish security. The single highest risk factor for an individual was gender. Of the total deaths, 3,210 were male and only 322 were female. Geography also played a role with more than 9 out of every 10 deaths taking place in Northern Ireland, and those living in Belfast or Londonderry significantly more likely to die as victims of violence. Death was no respecter of age. Journalists Joe Duffy and Freya McClements chronicle that 186 children (aged 16 and under) were killed in Troubles-related violence. Ten percent of those were fatally injured in the "safety" of their own homes; many more were killed on the streets outside their homes. Throughout Northern Ireland, childhoods were steeped in daily expectations of death amid the ubiquitous presence of funerals.[136] In terms of religious identity, Catholic deaths numbered 1,521 and Protestant 1,289. The remaining 722 deaths represented victims not from Northern Ireland who were killed in Northern Ireland (505) or those conflict-related victims who were killed in Britain (120), Ireland (83), or elsewhere in Europe (14).

Regardless of their social identity—civilian, security forces, or paramilitary—each one of the 3,532 victims was an individual. Each loved someone else and was loved by someone else. Each had hopes, dreams, and aspirations that would never be fulfilled simply because of what they believed or did not believe, who they were or were not, or, simply, where they happened to be or not be at a given moment. To lose the individual nature of each victim is to revictimize them by turning them into a statistic. Recognizing this, digital humanist John Barber has created an online listening gallery, "Remembering the Dead," where he humanizes the loss with the names, ages, locations, and days of death for each of the victims.[137] Sitting and listening, even for a few minutes, as the names are spoken, one is moved by the reminder of lives lost.

Lives lost. As if they were simply misplaced. In reality, they were lives taken. Death did not come passively to Northern Ireland; it was an active destruction. For every one of those lives taken, there was a killer. In terms of those who killed, Sutton attributes responsibility for 2,057 of the deaths to killings perpetrated by republican paramilitary groups, with 721 of those being civilian, 1,080 British security, 188 republican paramilitary, 57 loyalist paramilitary, and 11 Irish security. Killings attributed to loyalist paramilitary groups totaled 1,027, with 878 of those victims being civilian, 14 British security, 41 republic paramilitary, and 94 loyalist paramilitary. British forces were responsible for 363 deaths, including 186 civilians, 13 British security, 146 republican paramilitary, and 18 loyalist paramilitary. Five deaths were attributed to Irish security forces (all of the victims were republican paramilitary), and responsibility for the remaining 80 deaths is "not known" (though it is known that 55 of those deaths were civilian, 7 British security, 17 republican paramilitary, and 1 loyalist paramilitary).

Death was not the only measure of destruction in the Troubles. The effects of violence extended to Northern Ireland society as a whole and had a population-level impact on the everyday lives of substantial numbers of individuals. During the Troubles, there were more than 35,000 shooting incidents and another 15,000 bomb explosions. A total of 42,216 were injured as a direct result of the conflict, about 3% of the population.[138] By 1998, one in seven of the population of Northern Ireland reported being a direct victim of violence, one in five reported being intimidated at some point during the Troubles or having a family member or close relative killed or injured, more than half personally knew someone who had been killed or injured, and one in four had been caught up in an explosion or riot. This exposure to violence—whether direct, indirect, or collective—was unevenly distributed across communities, with Catholics reporting substantially higher levels of exposure.[139] There was profound and traumatic moral injury—the wounding of moral and ethical expectations pertaining to the sanctity of life—among those who perpetrated, witnessed, or failed to prevent the violence. All told, around 500,000 people in Northern Ireland were impacted by the Troubles.[140] Indeed, it is difficult to find anyone who lived in Northern Ireland during those years who is more than one degree removed from family members or friends who were impacted by the Troubles. Twenty years after the Good Friday Agreement was signed, a 2018 survey conducted for the Commission for Victims and Survivors even found that more than a quarter of Northern Ireland's population said they or a family member continued to be affected by a Troubles-related incident.[141]

* * *

To complement Sutton's work, research fellow Martin Melaugh of Ulster University continues to compile an ongoing list—approaching 100 names—of deaths related to the conflict from 2002 on.[142] While some of those deaths may yet be found to be unrelated to the Troubles, many of the victims did have paramilitary ties in their past or were involved with ongoing feuds within paramilitary organizations. Some were also involved in criminal activity.

At the time of this writing, however, the most recent death included in that list was yet another civilian caught in the wrong place and at the wrong time. On April 18, 2019, the week of the twenty-first anniversary of the Good Friday Agreement, 29-year-old investigative journalist Lyra McKee was on scene for a massive security operation in a nationalist Creggan area of Derry. In the midst of a riot with bottles and more than 50 petrol bombs being thrown by masked youths, a lone gunman emerged firing shots indiscriminately in the direction of police vehicles. Positioned behind one of those Land Rovers, Lyra McKee was shot in the head and killed. Police, treating it as a terrorist incident, attributed the killing to the New IRA, a dissident republican group formed several years ago from the merger of several splinter groups. The New IRA later admitted their role in the killing but released a statement laying the killing "squarely at the feet of the British crown forces, who sought to grab headlines and engineered confrontation with the community."[143]

When I first met Lyra McKee at an event four years ago, there was not a place so dark and hopeless in me to think that I was meeting an eventual victim of the conflict. There was a brightness about her that pulled you into a shared light of hope and optimism. Her death moved many back, at least temporarily, into the shadows of despair. For others, it steeled their resolve to find a different way forward. In a moving remembrance, journalist Leona O'Neill wrote: "The people rioting on the night Lyra was shot were young themselves. They were born after the Good Friday Agreement into peace. They know nothing of the brutality and barbarity of our Troubles and how we are still suffering from its aftermath even today. Yet they want to drag us back to that place, to bring violence back on to our streets, to make murder commonplace again. This is not us. This is not who we should be. We have fought for our hard-earned peace, too hard and for too long to gift the next generation the horrors that we are still scarred by. We are letting our peace slip through our fingers. Our politicians have let our progress on the path to normality stall and in the abyss that this void has created, malicious groups have been allowed to thrive and grow. These groups are leading a new generation on to a dangerous path that could destroy the bright future we were promised and we promised to our own children."[144]

Less than a year after the shooting, Joan McKee, Lyra's mother, passed away—a tragedy after a tragedy. A surviving daughter, Nichola McKee Corner, said her mother died "of a broken heart" over Lyra's death. "The bastards who murdered my baby sister should also be tried for the murder of my mother," tweeted Nichola. "They killed her the day they killed her precious baby girl." As journalist Ruth Dudley Edwards reflected: "The bullet, or the bomb, that kills one person does incalculable damage to so many more."[145]

* * *

We know the cessation of conflict is not the solution to all the drivers of that conflict. Moreover, prolonged conflict exacerbates the potency of many of those drivers, leaving them even more entrenched in a post-conflict society. To complicate matters, the violence often leaves gaping holes in the infrastructure necessary to rebuild that society. In the case of Northern Ireland, it is far too much to expect that slightly more than 20 years of "peace"— faltering and hesitant throughout—somehow has counteracted completely the prior 30 years of destabilizing conflict (let alone the 800 years of deep identity divisions). In this current moment, while many elements of the peace agreement have held fast, the peace seems more fragile than ever.

Part II of this book offers a nonpartisan real-time assessment of the degree to which contemporary Northern Ireland is letting its hard-earned peace slip through its fingers. What are the new generation of Northern Ireland, those born in the post-peace agreement era, inheriting? How dangerous is the path the country is on? Can these two identities at the heart of a deeply divided society ever be expected to live together without oppression, resistance, or violence? Has the conflict, while perhaps managed and resolved, at least through a peace agreement, been transformed—structurally and relationally—into a win-win situation for both sides? Does Northern Ireland have the resiliency to withstand the internal and external stressors that may threaten a destabilization of its fragile peace? Has it rebuilt differently enough to ensure nonrecurrence of violent conflict?

To approach an answer to those complex questions requires an honest analysis of the current vulnerabilities in Northern Ireland related to memory, governance, and social fragmentation, as well as an assessment of the actors, organizations, and strategies that can reduce or reverse those vulnerabilities. Engaging these coupled realities of risk and resilience in the context of contemporary accelerators and triggers of potential conflict will help us understand the challenges and opportunities a society faces in moving from conflict to a stable, enduring, and sustainable peace.

Notes

1. Cited in Tony Gallagher, "Identities in Northern Ireland: Nothing but the Same Old Stories?," in Maurna Crozier and Richard Froggatt (eds.), *What Made Now in Northern Ireland* (Belfast: Northern Ireland Community Relations Council, 2008), 114.
2. For readers interested in a fuller understanding of the history of the north of Ireland, the definitive text remains Jonathan Bardon's *A History of Ulster* (Belfast: Blackstaff Press, new updated edition, 2005). Brendan O'Leary's more recent three-volume analysis, *A Treatise on Northern Ireland* (London: Oxford University Press, 2019), embeds the historical analysis within a rich social scientific theoretical context.
3. Jonathan Bardon, "From the Earliest Times to the Union," in *What Made Now in Northern Ireland*, 4.
4. Art Cosgrove, "The Gaelic Resurgence and the Geraldine Supremacy," in T. W. Moody and F. X. Martin (eds.), *The Course of Irish History* (New York: Weybright and Talley, 1967), 160.
5. See Aiden Clarke, "The Colonisation of Ulster and the Rebellion of 1641," in Moody and Martin (eds.), *The Course of Irish History*, 189–203.
6. Ian N. Gregory, Niall A. Cunningham, C. D. Lloyd, Ian G. Shuttleworth, and Paul S. Ell, *Troubled Geographies: A Spatial History of Religion and Society in Ireland* (Bloomington: Indiana University Press, 2013), 11.
7. For a broad overview of Irish resistance, see Kevin Kenna's *All the Risings: Ireland 1014–1916* (Dublin: Currach Press, 2016).
8. Jonathan Bardon, *The Plantation of Ulster* (Dublin: Gill Books, 2012), 9.
9. Bardon, "From the Earliest Times to the Union," 6; and T. W. Moody, *The Ulster Question, 1603–1973* (Dublin: The Mercier Press, 1974), 6.
10. Bardon, *The Plantation of Ulster*, 145.
11. Quoted material from F. J. M. Madden, *The History of Ireland* (London: Hodder Education, 2005), 33.
12. Robert Kee, *Ireland: A History* (London: Abacus, 2003).
13. Bardon, *A History of Ulster*, 125.

14. Patrick Wolfe, "Settler Colonialism and the Elimination of the Native," *Journal of Genocide Research* 8 (2006), 388.

15. John Darby, *Scorpions in a Bottle: Conflicting Cultures in Northern Ireland* (London: Minority Rights Group, 1997), 21.

16. Bardon, "From the Earliest Times to the Union," 6–7.

17. Bardon, *A History of Ulster*, 307.

18. Thomas Hennessey, *A History of Northern Ireland* (New York: St. Martin's Press, 1997), 2.

19. Ibid., 4.

20. Madden, *The History of Ireland*, 85.

21. Paschal Grousset, *Ireland's Disease: The English in Ireland 1887* (London: George Routledge and Sons, 1887), 271, 273.

22. Thomas MacKnight, *Ulster As It Is or Twenty-Eight Years' Experience as an Irish Editor* (London: Macmillan and Co., 1896), Vol. II, 380–381.

23. F. Frankfort Moore, *The Truth About Ulster* (London: Eveleigh Nash, 1914), 70, 15, 48.

24. Bardon, *The Plantation of Ulster*, 344.

25. Sean Duffy, *The Concise History of Ireland* (Dublin: Gill & Macmillan, 2005), 195.

26. Quoted in Bardon, *A History of Ulster*, 478.

27. O'Leary, *A Treatise on Northern Ireland: Consociation and Confederation, Volume 3*, xli.

28. Quoted material taken from Bardon, *A History of Ulster*, 480.

29. For more detail, see "Systems of Government, 1968–1999," in Sydney Elliott and W. D. Flackes, *Conflict in Northern Ireland: An Encyclopedia* (Santa Barbara, CA: ABC-CLIO, 1999).

30. Duffy, *The Concise History of Ireland*, 198–199.

31. Quoted material taken from Kee, *Ireland: A History*, 226.

32. Ibid.

33. Cited in Madden, *The History of Ireland*, 127.

34. Donald Clarke, "Dealing with All the Bumps in the Road," *The Irish Times Magazine* (October 5, 2019), 10.

35. Berndette C. Hayes and Ian McAllister, "Sowing Dragon's Teeth: Public Support for Political Violence and Paramilitarism in Northern Ireland," *Political Studies* 49 (2001), 915.

36. Accessed on May 17, 2019, at https://www.poetryloverspage.com/poets/kipling/ulster.html

37. Bardon, *A History of Ulster*, 494.

38. See Peter Berresford Ellis, *Eyewitness to Irish History* (New York: John Wiley & Sons, 2004), 8.

39. Bardon, *A History of Ulster*, 515.

40. Ibid., 529.

41. Ibid., 531.

42. Quoted material taken from https://speakola.com/political/eamon-de-valera-churchill-criticism-1945, accessed on April 25, 2019.

43. Data in this paragraph taken from "Northern Ireland and World War II," https://www.qub.ac.uk/sites/irishhistorylive/IrishHistoryResources/Shortarticlesandencyclopaed

iaentries/Encyclopaedia/LengthyEntries/NorthernIrelandandWorldWarII/, accessed on April 23, 2019, and Duffy, *The Concise History of Ireland*, 212.

44. Quoted in William A. Carson, *Ulster and the Irish Republic* (Belfast: William W. Cleland, Ltd., 1947), 47.

45. For the minority opinion that anti-Catholic discrimination was less systematic and widespread than widely believed, see, for instance, Dennis Kennedy, "The Partition of Ireland," in *What Made Now in Northern Ireland*, 55–57.

46. Bardon, *A History of Ulster*, 641.

47. Edmund A. Aunger, "Religion and Occupational Class in Northern Ireland," *Economic and Social Review* 1 (1975), 8.

48. Clarke, "Dealing with All the Bumps in the Road," 10.

49. Marc Mulholland, *Northern Ireland: A Very Short Introduction* (New York: Oxford University Press, 2002), 40.

50. Adrian Kerr, *Free Derry: Protest and Resistance* (Derry: Guildhall Press, 2013), 27.

51. For instance, the percentage of people living at densities of more than two per room in 1961 in Derry was 21.1% in the largely Catholic South Ward, markedly higher than figures for the Protestant North (5.7%) and Waterside (7.9%) Wards. See Bardon, *A History of Ulster*, 647.

52. Tim Pat Coogan, *The Troubles: Ireland's Ordeal and the Search for Peace* (New York: Palgrave, 2002), 35.

53. Ibid., 37–38.

54. Eamonn MCann, *War and an Irish Town*, 3rd ed. (Chicago: Haymarket Books, 2018; first edition published 1974), 50.

55. Adrian Kerr, "Recording the Revolution," in Eamon Melaugh, *Derry's Troubled Years* (Derry: Guildhall Press, 2018), 13.

56. Duffy, *The Concise History of Ireland*, 226.

57. Richard English, "Explaining the Northern Ireland Troubles," in *What Made Now in Northern Ireland*, 63.

58. John Manley, "Bernadette McAliskey Rejects Claim That Civil Rights Movement Was Inspired by the Republican Movement," *The Irish News* (February 9, 2018). Accessed on June 6, 2019, at https://www.irishnews.com/news/2018/02/09/news/bernadette-mcaliskey-rejects-claim-that-civil-rights-movement-was-inspired-by-the-republican-movement-1252355/

59. Coogan, *The Troubles*, 67.

60. Accessed on May 10, 2019, at https://www.rte.ie/archives/exhibitions/1031-civil-rights-movement-1968-9/1034-derry-5-october-1968/319378-background-to-march/

61. Letter to Terence O'Neill included in Cabinet Conclusions, Public Record Office of Northern Ireland (PRONI), November 13, 1968, CAB/4/1414/5. Also quoted at https://www.irishtimes.com/news/o-neill-was-given-civil-rights-warning-1.142116, accessed on April 28, 2019.

62. Bardon, *A History of Ulster*, 655.

63. English, "Explaining the Northern Ireland Troubles," in *What Made Now in Northern Ireland*, 63.

64. Population data from the 1971 Census for Northern Ireland was accessed on May 11, 2019 at https://www.nisra.gov.uk/sites/nisra.gov.uk/files/publications/1971-census-towns-villages-booklet.PDF

65. Ministry of Defence, "Operation Banner: An Analysis of Military Operations in Northern Ireland" (July 2006), 3–1. More recently, Brian Hanley has argued that British Intelligence estimate the IRA had as many as 500 people in Northern Ireland in 1969 and even more in the Republic of Ireland. See his "'I Ran Away?' The I.R.A. and 1969: The Evolution of a Myth," *Irish Historical Studies* (November 2013), 671–687.

66. Bardon, *A History of Ulster*, 675.

67. Brian Hanley, *The IRA: A Documentary History* (Dublin: Gill & MacMillan, 2015), 159.

68. David McKittrick, "Obituary: Cathal Goulding," *Independent* (December 29, 1998). Accessed on May 17, 2019 at https://www.independent.co.uk/arts-entertainment/obituary-cathal-goulding-1194751.html

69. Quoted material cited in Richard English, *Armed Struggle: The History of the IRA* (London: Pan Books, 2012), 106.

70. Hanley, *The IRA: A Documentary History*, 159.

71. Quoted material in this paragraph taken from the IRA *Green Book*, accessed on May 16, 2019, at https://cain.ulster.ac.uk/othelem/organ/ira/ira_green_book.htm

72. McGuinness figure of 10,000 is taken from Ed Moloney, *A Secret History of the IRA* (UK: Penguin Books, 2002), xiv; the figure of 8,000 is taken from Patrick Bishop and Eamonn Mallie, *The Provisional I.R.A.* (UK: Corgi, 1996).

73. Moloney, *A Secret History of the IRA* (UK: Penguin Books, 2002), xiv.

74. Quoted material taken from Kee, *Ireland: A History*, 232.

75. Simon Prince, *Northern Ireland's '68: Civil Rights, Global Revolt and the Origins of the Troubles* (Newbridge: Irish Academic Press, 2018), 28.

76. Patrick Radden Keefe, *Say Nothing: A True Story of Murder and Memory in Northern Ireland* (New York: Doubleday, 2019), 20.

77. For an accessible history of the movement, see Brian Feeney, *Sinn Fein: A Hundred Turbulent Years* (Madison: University of Wisconsin Press, 2003).

78. Denis Faul and Raymond Murray, *The Hooded Men: British Torture in Ireland August, October 1971* (Dublin: Wordwell, 2016; work first published 1974). For a brief history of sensory deprivation research, see Mical Raz, "Alone Again: John Zubek and the Troubled History of Sensory Deprivation Research," *Journal of the History of the Behavioral Sciences* 49 (2013), 379–395.

79. Amnesty International, "A Report on Allegations of Ill-Treatment Made by Persons Arrest under the Special Powers Acts after 8th August 1971" (October 30, 1971). Accessed on May 10, 2019, at https://cain.ulster.ac.uk/events/intern/docs/amnesty71.htm. A 2019 judgment by the Court of Appeal in Belfast would affirm that the treatment to which "The Hooded Men" were subjected, if it occurred today, would properly be characterized as torture.

80. Ministry of Defence, "Operation Banner," 2–7.

81. Bardon, *A History of Ulster*, 688.

82. English, *Armed Struggle*, 92–93.

83. The complete text of the "Report of the Bloody Sunday Inquiry" can be found at https://www.gov.uk/government/publications/report-of-the-bloody-sunday-inquiry (accessed on May 10, 2019). The quoted material comes from "Principal Conclusions and Overall Assessment of the Bloody Sunday Inquiry," 5.5, p. 58.

84. Alf McCreary, *Survivors* (Belfast: Century Books, 1976), 244.

85. David McKittrick and David McVea, *Making Sense of the Troubles: A History of the Northern Ireland Conflict* (London: Viking, 2012), 96.

86. Stanley Matchett, "The Camera Was Always on My Desk with a Fresh Roll of Film in It," in *Shooting the Darkness: Iconic Images of the Troubles and the Stories of the Photographers Who Took Them* (Belfast: Blackstaff Press, 2019), 14.

87. Initial quoted material taken from Kee, *Ireland: A History*, 248; Paisley quote taken from Tom Kelly, "John Hume's Formidable Legacy Should be Honoured in Euro Vote," *The Irish News* (May 20, 2019).

88. Madden, *The History of Ireland*, 210.

89. On July 15, 1993, the UVF released a statement admitting sole responsibility for the bombings. Families of the victims continue their pursuit of justice, including calling for a full, impartial investigation into the complicity of British state forces in the bombings.

90. Seamus Heaney, "Crediting Poetry," in *Nobel Lectures: From the Literature Laureates, 1986 to 2006* (New York: The New Press, 2007), 157–158.

91. Crispin Rodwell, "There's Intuition and Instinct, But on Top of That There's Luck," in *Shooting the Darkness*, 96.

92. Quoted in Gerry Adams, *A Farther Shore: Ireland's Long Road to Peace* (New York: Random House, 2003), 14.

93. Keefe, *Say Nothing*, 149.

94. H-Blocks refers to the shape of the wings in the officially titled HM Prison Maze; often referred to colloquially as Long Kesh (particularly by republicans).

95. F. Stuart Ross, "Bobby Sands on the 1980 Hunger Strike: 'Fuair Muid Faic' – 'We Got Nothing,'" *The Irish Times* (December 18, 2015), accessed on May 19, 2019, at https://www.irishtimes.com/culture/heritage/bobby-sands-on-the-1980-hunger-strike-fuair-muid-faic-we-got-nothing-1.2468371

96. McKittrick and McVea, *Making Sense of the Troubles*, 167.

97. In 1981, the Iranian government officially changed the name of the street where the British Embassy is based in Tehran from Winston Churchill Street to Bobby Sands Street. In response, and to avoid having to put "Bobby Sands Street" on its letterhead, the British government sealed the entrance to the embassy on Bobby Sands Street and knocked through a wall into Ferdowsi Avenue to create a new entry point and street address.

98. For more information, see David Beresford, *Ten Men Dead: The Story of the 1981 Irish Hunger Strike* (London: Grafton Books, 1987) and Brian Campbell's compilation, *Nor Meekly Serve My Time: The H-Block Struggle 1976–1981* (Belfast: Beyond the Pale, 2006, first published 1994). In 2008, producer Steve McQueen released *Hunger*, a film depicting the 1981 hunger strike.

99. Caroline Kennedy-Pipe, "From War to Uneasy Peace in Northern Ireland," in Michael Cox, Adrian Guelke, and Fiona Stephen (eds.), *A Farewell to Arms?: Beyond the Good Friday Agreement* (Manchester: Manchester University Press, 2006), 48–49.

100. English, *Armed Struggle*, 206.

101. Melanie McFadyean, "The Legacy of the Hunger Strikes," *The Guardian* (March 3, 2006). Accessed June 7, 2019, at https://www.theguardian.com/politics/2006/mar/04/northernireland.northernireland

102. English, *Armed Struggle*, 204.

103. Elliott and Flackes, *Conflict in Northern Ireland*, 611.

104. Marc Mulholland, *The Longest War: Northern Ireland's Troubled History* (New York: Oxford University Press, 2002), 140.

105. Accessed on May 14, 2019, at https://www.pbs.org/wgbh/pages/frontline/shows/ira/conflict/gasf.html

106. Malachi O'Doherty, "Malachi O'Doherty on How Sinn Féin Leader Gerry Adams Has Played the Long Game," *The Irish News* (August 24, 2017), accessed on June 7, 2019, at http://www.irishnews.com/arts/2017/08/24/news/malachi-o-doherty-on-how-sf-leader-gerry-adams-has-played-the-long-game-1115268

107. Paul Dixon and Eamonn O'Kane, *Northern Ireland Since 1969* (London: Pearson, 2011), 52.

108. Moya Cannon, "On the Nobility of Compromise," *Irish Pages* 10 (2018), 78.

109. Darby, *Scorpions in a Bottle*, 75.

110. See Fergal Cochrane, "Two Cheers for the NGOs: Building Peace from Below in Northern Ireland," in Cox, Guelke, and Stephen (eds.), *A Farewell to Arms*, 253–267.

111. R. C. Longworth, "British Official Hints at Talks with IRA," *Chicago Tribune* (November 4, 1989). Accessed on May 13, 2019, at https://www.chicagotribune.com/news/ct-xpm-1989-11-04-8901280155-story.html

112. See Thomas Leahy's *The Intelligence War Against the IRA* (London: Cambridge University Press, 2020) for a nuanced analysis on the role of British intelligence and their informers during the conflict.

113. English, *Armed Struggle*, 307.

114. Cox, Guelke, and Stephen, *A Farewell to Arms*, 495.

115. Dick Grogan, "Scarcely Anything but Trouble from Beginning to End," *The Irish Times* (December 28, 1996), accessed on December 15, 2020 at https://www.irishtimes.com/news/scarcely-anything-but-trouble-from-beginning-to-end-1.119666

116. Barry White, "Drumcree's Volatile Mix Threatens Unionism with a Terminal Illness," *Belfast Telegraph* (July 19, 1996), accessed on December 15, 2020 at https://www.belfasttelegraph.co.uk/imported/drumcrees-volatile-mix-threatens-unionism-with-a-terminal-illness-28381463.html

117. Cox, Guelke, and Stephen, *A Farewell to Arms*, 509.

118. See, for instance, Kevin Bean, *The New Politics of Sinn Fein* (Liverpool: Liverpool University Press, 2007).

119. With Sinn Fein now included, the DUP withdrew from the talks.

120. Duncan Morrow, "The Meaning of History and Experience for the Future," in *What Made Now in Northern Ireland*, 178.

121. The Nobel Peace Prize 1998. Accessed on June 19, 2019, at https://www.nobelprize. org/prizes/peace/1998/summary

122. Stephen Castle, "With Good Friday Agreement Under Threat, Voters Urged to 'Stand Up,'" *The New York Times* (April 9, 2018), accessed on September 17, 2019, at https://www.nytimes.com/2018/04/09/world/europe/peace-in-ireland-blair.html

123. Initial quote taken from Castle (Ibid.); the remainder of the quoted material taken from George J. Mitchell, *Making Peace* (New York: Alfred A. Knopf, 1999), 182.

124. Madden, *The History of Ireland*, 246. See also, Dixon and O'Kane, *Northern Ireland Since 1969*, 92.

125. Colin Coulter and Peter Shirlow, "From the 'Long War' to the 'Long Peace:' An Introduction to the Special Edition," *Capital & Class* 43 (2019), 5.

126. Duncan Morrow, "The Rocky Road from Enmity," in Cillian McGrattan and Elizabeth Meehan (eds.), *Everyday Life After the Irish Conflict: The Impact of Devolution and Cross-Border Cooperation* (Manchester: Manchester University Press, 2012), 29.

127. Speech accessed at https://cain.ulster.ac.uk/events/peace/docs/jh141198.htm on June 9, 2020.

128. Mitchell, *Making Peace*, 188.

129. Esther Addley, "British Troops Leave After 38 Years," *The Guardian* (July 31, 2007), accessed on May 11, 2019, at https://www.theguardian.com/uk/2007/aug/01/ northernireland.military

130. Steven McCaffery, "Key Legacy of Good Friday Agreement: Lives Saved," *The Detail* (April 10, 2018), accessed on June 4, 2020, at https://thedetail.tv/articles/the-legacy-of-the-good-friday-agreement-how-the-peace-dividend-has-saved-lives

131. O'Leary, *A Treatise on Northern Ireland, Volume 1: Colonialism*, 105, 82, 104.

132. See https://cain.ulster.ac.uk/, accessed on January 24, 2020.

133. Malcolm Sutton, *Bear in Mind These Dead: An Index of Deaths from the Conflict in Ireland 1969–1993* (Belfast: Beyond the Pale Publications, 1994). Data are taken from revised and updated material (October 2002) accessible on the CAIN Web Service at https://cain.ulster.ac.uk/sutton/. Sutton's database excludes accidental shootings, deaths due to heart attacks brought on by conflict-related incidents, suicides, deaths from casual street violence, and deaths from road and helicopter accidents. David McKittrick and colleagues set the total number of deaths from 1966–2000 at 3,638 in their *Lost Lives: The Stories of the Men, Women and Children Who Died as a Result of the Northern Ireland Troubles* (Edinburgh: Mainstream Publishing, 2004). Richard English, bounding the time frame from 1966–2001, puts the death toll at 3,665 in his *Armed Struggle: The History of the IRA*. Sydney Elliott and W. D. Flackes put the death toll from 1969–1998 at 3,289 in their *Conflict in Northern Ireland: An Encyclopedia*. Finally, Michael McKeown also has maintained a private individual study indicating a death toll of 3,623 as end of the end of 2001 (https://cain.ulster.ac.uk/victims/mckeown/index.html).

134. See Sydney Elliott and William D. Flackes, *Northern Ireland: A Political Directory, 1968–99* (Belfast: Blackstaff Press, 1999) and O'Leary, *A Treatise on Northern Ireland*, 37.

135. Jake O'Kane, "A Familiar Feeling from the Troubles is Back—and It's Not a Good One," *The Irish News* (March 21, 2020), accessed on March 22, 2020, at http://www.irishnews.com/lifestyle/2020/03/21/news/jake-o-kane-a-familiar-feeling-from-the-troubles-is-back-and-it-s-not-a-good-one-1872319/

136. See Joe Duffy and Freya McClements, *Children of the Troubles: The Untold Story of the Children Killed in the Northern Ireland Conflict* (Dublin: Hachette Books Ireland, 2019).

137. John Barber, "Remembering the Dead," http://remembering.newbinarypress.com/, accessed on May 8, 2019.

138. Elliott and Flackes, *Conflict in Northern Ireland*, 638, 684.

139. Data regarding 1998 taken from Hayes and McAllister, "Sowing Dragon's Teeth," *Political Studies* 49 (2001).

140. Kenneth Lesley-Dixon, *Northern Ireland: The Troubles* (Barnsley, UK: Pen & Sword Books, 2018), 10.

141. John Monaghan, "Quarter of Northern Ireland's Population Continue to be Affected by a Troubles-Related Incident," *The Irish News* (April 11, 2018), accessed on June 5, 2020, at https://www.irishnews.com/news/northernirelandnews/2018/04/11/news/quarter-of-northern-ireland-s-population-continue-to-be-affected-by-a-troubles-related-incident-according-to-new-research-1301262/

142. See https://cain.ulster.ac.uk/issues/violence/deaths2019draft.htm, accessed on June 16, 2020.

143. Ed O'Loughlin and Richard Perez-Pena, "Lyra McKee, Northern Ireland Journalist, Is Killed in 'Terrorist Incident' Police Say," *The New York Times* (April 19, 2019), accessed on May 9, 2019, at https://www.nytimes.com/2019/04/19/world/europe/lyra-mckee-northern-ireland-violence.html

144. Leona O'Neill, "Lyra McKee's Death Shows We Are Letting Peace Slip Through Our Fingers," *The Irish News* (April 23, 2019), accessed on May 8, 2019, at http://www.irishnews.com/lifestyle/2019/04/23/news/leona-o-neill-lyra-s-death-shows-we-are-letting-our-peace-slip-through-our-fingers-1603224/

145. Quoted material taken from Ruth Dudley Edwards, "Why the Killers of Lyra McKee Took Her Beloved Mother Joan's Life Just as Surely as If They Had Shot Her Too," *Belfast Telegraph* (March 11, 2020), accessed on March 17, 2020, at https://www.belfasttelegraph.co.uk/opinion/columnists/ruth-dudley-edwards/why-the-killers-of-lyra-mckee-took-her-beloved-mother-joans-life-just-as-surely-as-if-theyd-shot-her-too-39037627.html

PART II

RISK AND RESILIENCE IN CONTEMPORARY NORTHERN IRELAND

Each year, from Easter Monday until the end of August, brings "marching season" to Northern Ireland. This is a time of Protestant triumphalism where Orange Order parades, under the banner (literally and figuratively) of celebrating cultural identity, take to the streets of Northern Ireland to trumpet their heritage and identity.[1] The Orange Order inaugurated its founding in 1795 with its first parade and that same year also saw the first Catholic protests of parades as well as the first parades-related death. The militaristic parades include Orangemen in full regalia (black suits and bowlers along with orange sashes and white gloves), marching fife and drum bands, a creatively wide array of British symbols, and, often, the ground-shaking rhythm of large Lambeg drums beaten with canes. As Brendan Behan wrote of the drummers: "They keep it up for hours and it is said that a man is not a good drummer unless his knuckles bleed profusely as he keeps on drumming."[2] Many of them—particularly the ones routing near or through Catholic neighborhoods—require high levels of police oversight to avoid outbreaks of violence. In 2013–2014 alone, the Police Service of Northern Ireland spent an estimated $76 million on policing controversial marches and street protests.[3]

The crescendo of marching season begins on the "Eleventh Night" of July, the eve of the commemoration of Protestant King William of Orange's defeat of Catholic King James II at the Battle of the Boyne in 1690. On that evening, in preparation for the largest marches of the season on the following day, loyalists light huge bonfires throughout Protestant neighborhoods across the country. These bonfires, built primarily of wooden pallets that begin collecting in vacant neighborhood lots as early as April, can be several stories high. Sometimes incorporating tires and other rubbish, the bonfires often include offensive images or effigies of opposing politicians as well as Irish flags,

Catholic icons, and nationalist symbols. Recognizing that there is no such thing as a safe bonfire, firefighters douse the roofs of surrounding homes to protect people and property. No firefighters dare douse the fire itself because doing so would be seen as an attack on Protestant cultural heritage and lead to an even larger and more heated social and political conflagration that would consume the following weeks and months.

The larger the stacks of wood in these bonfires, the larger the risk posed to the community where the fire is located. If the risk is not addressed by at least removing some of the pallets, and we passively wait for the wood to be soaked in petrol and then set alight, the greater potential we have for a large, perhaps even uncontrollable, fire. Similarly, we can think of the stacks of wood that bring these bonfires to life as analogous manifestations of risk factors for violent conflict in a society. Risk factors are the longer term and slower moving structures, measures, society-wide conditions, and processes that leave a society vulnerable to fragmentation and strife. The more risk factors we have in a society, and the less to which they are attended, the greater the potential for a large, perhaps even uncontrollable, violent conflict.

Understanding the underlying risk factors that place a society at peril for violent conflict is the backbone of an "early warning system." The concept of early warning systems has been in existence since the 1950s, primarily used by military strategic intelligence to predict attacks but also used by international altruistic organizations to forecast humanitarian and natural disasters such as earthquakes, drought, food shortages, and famine. Only recently have we been developing early warning systems for forecasting a range of violent conflict situations. Some of these systems are heavily quantitative, relying on systematic empirical data collection or the use of other preexisting large data banks (often from previous conflicts). Other systems are more qualitative, relying on field-based reports or special envoys that often privilege civil society and the experientially informed "eyes and ears" of local sources on the ground (such qualitative data are often, for instance, at the heart of the advocacy work of Human Rights Watch, Amnesty International, and the International Crisis Group). Still other systems blend quantitative and qualitative approaches.

This diversity of methodologies, coupled with competing and even contradictory views of what constitutes a risk factor, has led to the proliferation of several dozen models of early warning systems for violent conflict. These models are built on a wide range of risk factors and an even greater number of corresponding objective indicators to help determine the degree to which any risk factor is present in a given situation. Illustrating the complexity involved in risk assessment, a 2008 report from the Center for Strategic and International Studies, surveying only 30 such models, found more than 800 indicators of risk used by those models alone.[4] Similarly, in my consulting work with the Economic Community of West African States, I have seen how their alert and response structure for early warning has evolved to rely on 66 indicators—ranging from declining student attendance in schools or an outbreak of crop disease to the abuse of power or misuse of public resources by a chieftaincy or traditional institution.

In the work of risk assessment, regardless of how many risk factors any particular model relies on, no one risk factor or set of risk factors is taken as predominant in contributing importance. Rather, they are contextually understood, in conjunction with the presence of other risk factors, as associated with increasing the probability of violent conflict. The actors behind these risk factors can be the state, proxies of the state, or nonstate parties from which the state has failed to protect its population.

Rather than being understood in causal terms, it is best to think of the risk posed by these factors as probabilistic predictions, not infallible, that maximize our forecasting power for violent conflict. That is, a high prevalence of risk factors increases the preconditions of risk or susceptibility to violent conflict, but does not equate to its inevitable occurrence. A second analogy: a person may have several of the major risk factors for cardiovascular disease (e.g., risks related to age, sex, heredity, smoking, blood cholesterol, physical inactivity, and so on) without necessarily ever succumbing to a stroke—though, certainly, from a probability standpoint, the more risk factors you have, the greater your chance of developing some form of coronary heart disease. Careful monitoring of those background risk factors, however, places us in a better position to lower the chance of subsequent disease.

We can broaden this individual disease analogy to a collective level through the public health concept of *syndromic surveillance*. The US Centers for Disease Control and Prevention describe syndromic surveillance as the continuous and systematic collection, analysis, and interpretation of health-related data in order to "precede diagnosis and signal a sufficient probability of a case or outbreak."[5] The development of this type of early warning system to detect unusual health trends or anticipate disease outbreaks allows public health officials to monitor and target at-risk situations before a public health crisis fully develops. In so doing, they also can document the impact of any interventions that may promote resilience or counter the disease. Syndromic surveillance allows policy priorities to be set that inform public health practices and, when necessary, mobilize a rapid response.

Similarly, a periodic scan based on background risk factors, a "syndromic surveillance" of a country's stability-related data, allows us to monitor at-risk countries for future signs of instability before a crisis fully develops. Regular monitoring of risk—taking care to separate it from "background noise"— gives us an ongoing situational awareness that allows us to respond to potentially violent conflict before it becomes deadly. Understanding how, why, where, and when these factors place a society at risk for violent conflict also helps us understand the forms of resilience and countering influences that can be fostered to keep them in check.

In my previous work on violent conflict prevention, I reviewed the mostly widely utilized early warning systems for violent conflict, drawn from a broad range of multidisciplinary research. From that comprehensive review, I distilled the most well-supported (quantitatively and/or qualitatively) risk factors and grouped them into risk categories related to (1) the interpretation and remembering of conflict history, (2) how authority in a country is exercised, and (3) a country's susceptibility to social disharmony, isolation, and fragmentation.[6] The risk factors in these categories, interlaced throughout by social identity issues, are real-time cross-cutting and intersecting issues, not easily confined to one discrete category. Taken together, however, they offer a robust and reliable picture of a society's susceptibility to violent conflict.

Part II of this book is structured around these three categories of risk factors for violent conflict. In each of the three chapters, we will assess contemporary Northern Ireland's latent and manifest vulnerabilities on the various risk factors for a given category, as well as the points of resiliency—both within and outside the country—that help inoculate it against the recurrence of conflict. If we have a good understanding of the issues that put a society at risk, it also opens us to a more constructive understanding of how memory can become more inclusive, governance systems can be effectively structured, and social cohesion can be better promoted to inoculate a society against those risk factors.

Balancing volatility with stability, particularly in the face of internal and external stressors that threaten its brittle peace, is the existential reality of contemporary Northern Ireland. So, while I will argue that contemporary Northern Ireland is clearly a fragile state, the reality must be acknowledged that it has not crossed the line to becoming the world's newest failing or failed state. Understanding the reasons why the teetering, however precipitous, has not become a calamitous fall, including a return to violence, is a vital part of understanding the complexity of historical, political, and social factors at play in contemporary Northern Ireland.

Part II of this book is born out of a commitment to understand this present moment in Northern Ireland as well as a deep and abiding concern for the country's future in our global community. We each have an investment in that future because it is in that future where we, and the citizens of Northern Ireland, are going to spend the rest of our collective lives. And the lessons to be learned from Northern Ireland are lessons applicable far beyond its borders. As Belfast-based journalist Malachi O'Doherty writes: "Be warned. We used to think that Northern Ireland was a strange backward place out of step with the modern world. Now we see our division mirrored everywhere."[7]

Notes

1. While the Orange Order is the most active group, Protestant parades also are held by groups such as the Ancient Order of Hibernians, the Apprentice Boys of Derry, and the Royal Black Institution.
2. Brendan Behan, *Brendan Behan's Island: An Irish Sketchbook* (Chicago, IL: Bernard Geis Associates, 1962), 162.
3. Henry McDonald, "Orange Order March in Belfast Begins Peacefully," accessed April 22, 2019, at https://www.theguardian.com/uk-news/2014/jul/12/orange-order-march-belfast-northern-ireland
4. Frederick Barton and Karin von Hippel, "Early Warning? A Review of Conflict Prediction Models and Systems" (Washington, DC: Center for Strategic and International Studies, 2008).
5. Centers for Disease Control and Prevention, https://www.webcitation.org/5LKEYsrRT, accessed on April 22, 2019.
6. See James Waller, *Confronting Evil: Engaging Our Responsibility to Prevent Genocide* (New York: Oxford University Press, 2016). The fourth category of risk factors discussed in that book—a country's degree of economic stability—does not have as much of a robust level of empirical support and, given Northern Ireland's embedded economic interrelationship with the United Kingdom, is more difficult to tease out in this particular case. So, issues related to Northern Ireland's economic stability or lack thereof will be discussed in the context of an accelerant or trigger in Chapter 6.
7. Malachi O'Doherty, "Foreword," *Brexit and Northern Ireland: Bordering on Confusion?* (Goring on Thames, UK: Bite-Sized Books, 2019), 13.

3

"Was There Ever a Before?"

The Tyranny of Memory

Hyperthymesia, or "highly superior autobiographical memory" (HSAM), is a rare condition in which people remember an abnormally large number of their life experiences in vivid detail. Regardless of how insignificant or trivial, these memories include every conversation and emotion ever experienced as well as every person and object encountered. While it may have its advantages, being unable to forget also has its drawbacks. One person with HSAM describes the difficulties of being absorbed in the past: "It can be very hard to forget embarrassing moments. You feel [the] same emotions—it is just as raw, just as fresh. . . . You can't turn off that stream of memories, no matter how hard you try." Another agrees: "It is like having these open wounds—they are just a part of you."[1]

Irish history offers its own form of collective HSAM which makes it difficult to lay the past to rest. "It has often been observed that Irish history," Jonathan Bardon writes, "even from the earliest times, is current affairs. Whatever the truth of this statement, it cannot be denied that popular historical memory in Ulster is particularly long and that growing conditions for the cultivation of myths are particularly favourable there."[2]

Indeed, popular historical memory and the myths that it cultivates may be the most potent factor in understanding risk and resilience in contemporary Northern Ireland. Every day, from Belfast to Bangor from Newry to Coleraine from Omagh to Portrush, people walk side by side with their wounded past of sectarian conflict. There are cultures of memory littered throughout Northern Ireland—in landscapes and soundscapes, murals and memorials, commemorations and parades, songs and poetry, neighborhoods and rituals, food and humor, sport and folklore, and in the everyday rhythm of life. Here the past and present are not separate places. "Before" and "Now" are synonymous. The departed stay present. Tomorrow is less important than yesterday. There is no right, or wrong, to be forgotten. Confrontations

A Troubled Sleep. James Waller, Oxford University Press (2021). © Oxford University Press.
DOI: 10.1093/oso/9780190095574.003.0004

with the past arrive unbidden and are always present. The past is a thread that cannot be unwoven from the fabric of the present. The past is not a foreign country where things are done differently; the past is present where things are always as they have been.[3] As Belfast columnist Alex Kane writes: "The past is always in front of us in Northern Ireland. No matter how much we talk about addressing it, nor how hard we try to free ourselves from it, we always return to it. And the reason we always return to it, is because there is nowhere else to go when there is no agreement on the present or future. The past is our comfort zone."[4]

The "comfort zone" afforded by the cramped space of history, however, is illusory. As one interviewee told me: "The problem with the past in Northern Ireland is that it's never where you think you left it." While there is certainly a shared past, there is not a shared narrative or memory of that past. It is a country with a contested biography. There is a common history, but not a common memory. Rather, there are multiple contested, conflicting, and competing memories, each an electrified wire. Northern Ireland produces more memory that it can consume, and it consumes a hell of a lot of memory. In versions of historical—and sometimes hysterical—revisionism, some peddle memory myths and call it history. A war of historical narratives— individual, collective, and institutional—has replaced a war of weapons. As Paul Nolan, research director at the *Northern Ireland Peace Monitoring Report*, writes: "Each political side wishes not only to see its historical inter- pretation validated, but the other side's account invalidated."[5] In contested situations like that, memory is vulnerable. And it is that very vulnerability that endows memory, memory-makers, and memory-entrepreneurs with singular power in contemporary Northern Ireland.

* * *

To return to our cardiovascular disease analogy from the introduction to Part II, some of the risk factors—age, sex, heredity—are nonmodifiable. Whether part of your genetic heritage or simply part of the process of getting old, these risk factors are the organic burden we carry. While these particular risk factors are nonmodifiable, there are a host of other modifiable risk factors— smoking, blood cholesterol, and physical inactivity—that can help moderate the risk saddled on us by the nonmodifiable factors. So, while recognizing our nonmodifiable history, we do not have to be unremitting slaves to it; we can understand that history in the context of other modifiable factors.

Similarly, the long-running history of intergroup conflict in Northern Ireland is a nonmodifiable risk factor—what happened cannot be unhappened. What can, and often is, modified, however, are the ways in which that history is remembered, taught, processed, and understood. As novelist Jonathan Safran Foer argues, memory is not simply "a second order means of interpreting events."[6] Rather, memory is an active past that gives shape and meaning to our present. Memory changes the tense from past to present. In that regard, the past continually intrudes on the present. Many times, the human mind moves on, it does not dwell. In Northern Ireland, however, it not only dwells, but it also resides and abides. As one interviewee responded, only partly tongue in cheek, when I asked about how Northern Irish think about the past and what has come before: "Was there ever a before?"

At the level of group-based social identities, memory is commonly referred to as *collective memory*. Collective memory is the communal shared past, framed in the present, binding social identity group members together and connecting successive generations with one another. In essence, collective memory "is not simply synonymous with the way in which the past is represented in the present; it is itself constitutive of the present. Meaning and identity go hand in hand."[7] The past gets its meaning through its link to the present. There is a "past present" in each of us. It is a negotiated outcome, a cognitive map, of interaction between multiple social identities—national, racial, ethnic, political, gender, religious, professional, familial, class, and so on.

Collective memory is not organic in the sense that it is a "group mind" passed on through genetic transmission. That does not mean, however, that collective memory is just a conceptual construct without implications for real life. Rather, collective memory is born of the social construction and transmission of a distinctive shared memory drawn from stories, artifacts, food and drink, symbols, traditions, images, and music—the cultural birthright that one inherits as a member of a social identity group. Collective memory also includes the traumas, both suffered and perpetrated, of a social identity group. In this sense of "soul wounds" or "blood memories," collective memory transmits the staggering loss of an assumptive world that grounded, secured, stabilized, and oriented people; a past fragmented by "a dramatic loss of identity and meaning, a tear in the social fabric."[8] As sociologist Ron Eyerman describes: "Collective memory specifies the temporal parameters of past and future, where we came from and where we are going, and also why we are here now."[9]

In a sense, collective memory runs parallel to the late historian and geographer David Lowenthal's conception of "heritage." "Heritage," he writes, "should not be confused with history. . . . Heritage exaggerates and omits, candidly invents and frankly forgets, and thrives on ignorance and error. . . . Heritage uses history traces and tells historical tales. But these tales and traces are stitched into fables closed to critical scrutiny. Heritage is immune to criticism because it is not erudition but catechism—not checkable fact but credulous allegiance. Heritage is not a testable or even plausible version of our past; it is a *declaration of faith* [emphasis in original] in that past."[10]

Similarly, as a declaration of faith in that past, collective memory is a selective embodiment of pasts and their meanings. "Out of many possible pasts, some are lost, while others are the subjects of careful strategies of maintenance and reproduction."[11] That is, the collective memory of a constant past is not preserved with objective facticity but is instead subjectively reconstructed in the variable social context of the needs of the present. This social context not only defines what is remembered but also what is forgotten; there are some "unknown knowns" that we repress because they are too painful to know through admission. What is remembered is not simply the past as it was; rather, it is the past, at best, half-remembered and, at worst, actively misremembered. As scholar Andreas Huyssen states: "The past is not simply there in memory . . . it must be articulated to become memory."[12] Memory is human and social. As a result, the significance of collective memory lies in its socially constructed meaning, not in its historical accuracy. Lowenthal: "Hence it is futile to vilify heritage as biased. Prejudiced pride in the past is not the sorry upshot of heritage but its essential aim."[13]

For historian Pierre Nora: "Memory is life, borne by living societies founded in its name. It remains in permanent evolution, open to the dialectic of remembering and forgetting, unconscious of its successive deformations, vulnerable to manipulation and appropriation, susceptible to being long dormant and periodically revived."[14] The vulnerability of memory means that "collective memories often become embroiled in . . . disputes as they are strategically manipulated by social actors to alter the balance of power between groups."[15] Memory-makers—government, religious, education, community, and media actors—compete to construct collective memory by establishing the social frames that will accommodate only those memories that suit their agenda. This is a "meaning struggle" for power rather than truth; a mobilization to control a master narrative that fits a group's subjective interests rather than an objective account of historical processes. As George Orwell famously wrote about the dangers of totalitarian society in his novel *1984*: "Who controls the past controls the future: who controls the present controls the past."[16] In this sense, memory-makers use collective memory the way a drunk uses a lamppost, for support rather than illumination. As historian Michael Kammen asserts: "societies in fact reconstruct their pasts rather than faithfully record them, and that they do so with the needs of contemporary culture clearly in mind—manipulating the past in order to mold the present."[17] In such cases, collectives live by memory rather than truth, and such "memory is never shaped in a vacuum" and its motives "are never pure."[18]

In Rwanda, for example, government and social institutions control much of the collective memory—in the minds of some critics, a clear manipulation of the past in order to mold the present. Transitional justice scholar Katherine Conway writes of contemporary Rwanda: "Limits to memory include restrictions on the freedom of speech, a focus on minimizing ethnic identity, methods of memorialization, and control over the versions of memory that are taught in schools, celebrated during the month of April, and discussed in public spaces."[19] As she points out, such restrictions not only limit memory but also serve to limit the debate about the past. Historian Peter Novick's work on the Holocaust and collective memory warns of the dangers of limiting memory and debate about the past: "If there *are* lessons to be extracted from encountering the past, that encounter has to be with the past in all its messiness; they're not likely to come from an encounter with a past that's been shaped and shaded so that inspiring lessons will emerge."[20]

In a post-conflict society, the messiness of the past will be attended to— whether we make an active decision to agree on it or not. To attend to the past constructively can build bonds of social cohesion between competing social identities. To leave it unattended, however, is to leave space for the sparring—and scarring—narratives that feed deep social divisions. As historian Jill Lepore argues: "Nations are made up by people, but held together by history, like wattle and daub or lath and plaster or bricks and mortar. . . . Nations, to make sense of themselves, need some kind of agreed upon past. They can get it from scholars or they can get it from demagogues, but get it they will."[21]

* * *

In 2003, on the thirtieth anniversary of Pinochet's coup, Chilean president Ricardo Lagos challenged his country to continuing facing their violent past. Twelve years after the conclusion of Chile's National Commission on Truth and Reconciliation, Lagos announced the formation of a second truth commission specific to a group of victims largely left out of the first Commission's purview: former prisoners illegally detained and tortured for politically motivated reasons during the period of military rule. Lagos told his fellow Chileans that they had to, again, collectively confront this traumatic past because "without yesterday there is no tomorrow."[22]

With "tomorrow" in mind, we will review five specific risk factors related to "yesterday" and the ways in which collective and contested memories impact contemporary Northern Ireland: (1) history of identity-related tension, (2) prior genocides or politicides, (3) past cultural trauma, (4) legacy of vengeance or group grievance, and (5) record of serious violations of international human rights and law.

History of Identity-Related Tension

For social psychologist Ervin Staub, a history of identity-related tension serves as a risk factor for violent conflict because it leads to "ideologies of antagonism" that are "the outcome of a long history of hostility and mutual violence. Such ideologies are worldviews in which another group is perceived as an implacable enemy, bent on one's destruction. The welfare of one's own group is best served by the other's demise." These ideologies, steeped in a history of identity-related tensions, can be a significant risk factor even if only a segment of a population holds the ideology. In Staub's view, ideologies of antagonism in which the "other" is perceived as a threat "seemed to have roles in the start or maintenance of violence in the former Yugoslavia, between Israelis and Palestinians, and in Rwanda."[23]

As we saw in Chapter 1, in-group bias leaves us predisposed to in-group favoritism and out-group discrimination. Since not all out-groups are equivalent, however, we need some metric to determine which out-groups pose the most danger to "us." Clearly, a history of identity-related tension and conflict is one such metric, and the previous chapter reviewed how deep that history has run between the two sectarian communities in Northern Ireland. In many respects, and at various times, the two groups posed an actual threat to each other, and that threat was sufficient to ignite and sustain intergroup conflict.

In addition, however, psychologists Walter Stephan and Lausanne Renfro suggest *perceived threat* as another metric by which we can understand how a particular out-group becomes a target of hostility. That is, it is not only the actual threat posed by the "other" that matters in understanding intergroup conflict; it also is the degree to which threats posed by the "other" are perceived to exist. In their *intergroup threat theory* (ITT), perceived threats come "when members of one group perceive that another group is in a position to cause them harm."[24] Such perceived threats, leading to a fear of in-group destruction, take two forms. *Realistic threats* are tangible threats to the physical well-being and the economic and political power and resources of the in-group. *Symbolic threats* are intangible threats to the in-group's meaning system (i.e., their values, morals, beliefs, religion, ideology, philosophy, standard, attitudes, and worldview). Perceived threats, whether realistic or symbolic, do not have to be accurate, nor do they have to be fulfilled, to have a negative impact on intergroup behavior. The perception of threat becomes its own reality and helps us understand whether a specific out-group remains merely an object of indifference or becomes, instead, a target of hostility.

As we will discuss in Chapter 6, there are any number of actual threats to the stability, and even existence, of contemporary Northern Ireland. At the group–group level, however, it is the perceived threats to one's own group identity and survival, built on and reinforced by a history of identity-related tension and conflict, that best help us understand the deep divisions within Northern Ireland's society. As Walter and Cookie White Stephan summarize: "There are a number of studies that provide evidence supporting the proposition that negative prior intercultural relations are positively correlated with perceived threats."[25] The perceived threats posed by the out-group have significant emotional, cognitive, and behavioral consequences on both sides of the divide—manifest in avoidance, biases, stereotyping, prejudice, discrimination, competitiveness, fear, anxiety, stress reactions, intolerance, passive aggression, hatred, anger, mistrust, contempt, resentment, and, ultimately, open intergroup conflict.[26] Even if the other group does not have actual power to do harm to "us," the overriding influence of perceived threats can move intergroup relations from out-group disregard to out-group hostility. Hatred is held on to like a hard-won prize. And, in a debilitating interactive and recursive feedback loop, this hostility can nurture even higher levels of perceived threat as "the behavior of each group affects the responses and perceptions of the other group . . . [and] the ingroup's own responses to threat will feed back into its perceptions of the outgroup, usually augmenting them."[27]

To spend time in the sectarian divide of contemporary Northern Ireland is to be immersed in the overtones, and undertones, of the perceived threats— both realistic and symbolic—of the "other." The internalization of perceived threat is a tangible post-conflict legacy. As one local Catholic told me about Protestants: "We love outsiders [visitors from outside Northern Ireland], it's just them'uns we can't stand!" Unionist and nationalist communities each believe they have a great deal to lose from perceived threats posed by the "them'uns" on the other side. Both frame themselves as low-power groups at the perilous mercy of a more powerful group. In sectarian communities there is a constant awareness, even a hypervigilance, of the "other" as a threat. In a nationalist neighborhood of West Belfast, for instance, you can find a poster depicting armed British soldiers with the ominous warning "They Haven't Gone Away You Know." A few streets away, in a unionist neighborhood of East Belfast, you can find a poster with the exact same words of warning, but depicting armed Irish Republican Army (IRA) volunteers as the perceived threat.[28] And those perceived threats, however accurate or inaccurate, are ruinous for hopes of improving intergroup relations. Perceived threats come to be constructs, or frames, that reduce a complex world into a simpler understanding of "us" and "them." In this simplified social world, the frames afford by perceived threats become engrained one-dimensional portrayals of the "other" and heighten our sensitivity to anything that is perceived to threaten our physical well-being or symbolic meaning systems.

As just one example, ITT suggests "threats to the symbol system of the group go to the very core of group identity—the way in which the group defines itself and the symbols it chooses to mark that identity." Those identity symbols include "religion, cultural values, belief systems, ideology, philosophy, morality, and differing worldviews."[29] Also among these identity symbols is language. Language is a symbol of whom a group considers themselves to be, a memory of a people, a means of expression as well as thinking. When a symbolic threat is actualized and language is removed or prohibited, as has been done to indigenous peoples around the world, a sense of meaning and group identity and history is erased. The harsh truth is that nation-states use symbols, like language, as clear markers of who belongs and who does not. On July 19, 2018, for example, Israel's "Jewish Nation-State Law" went into effect, abolishing Arabic as an official language of the state of Israel. Affirming Israel as the national, and exclusive, home of the Jewish people, Prime Minister Benjamin Netanyahu boasted: "Today we made it a law: This is our nation, language, and flag."[30] The law also, however, can be seen as part of a process of ethnic exclusion with a clear message of threat to Israeli Arabs who make up one-fifth of Israel's 9 million citizens: you do not belong here.

Similarly, in contemporary Northern Ireland, language has come front and center as a symbolic threat and deeply divisive social and political issue. With the Irish language suppressed under much of British colonial rule, English became the primary language of most Irish people. From the birth of Northern Ireland, English remained in favor as the official language of successive unionist-dominated governments. The Good Friday Agreement, however, drawing on the recently enacted European Charter for Regional or Minority Languages, afforded some protections for the Irish language and placed a statutory duty on authorities (still largely unfulfilled) to encourage Irish education. The St. Andrews Agreement of 2006 further called for the government to introduce legislation to enhance and protect the development of the Irish language. Since that time, nationalist leaders, under the banner of an "equality agenda" (also including same-sex marriage and abortion rights), have doggedly pursued legislation attempting to give the Irish language official and equal status with English in Northern Ireland. An Irish Language Act would mean the use of Irish in the courts and state bodies, bilingual signage on public buildings and roads, the appointment of an Irish-language commissioner, and education through Irish.

The identity tug-of-war into which this initiative has devolved is often cited as one of the chief reasons for the political deadlock that shut down the government of Northern Ireland for more than three years. For nationalists, the Irish language is an important part of their meaning system, how they define themselves, and one of the ways in which they mark their group-based social identity and cultural heritage. When the 2011 census revealed that only about 10.65% of Northern Irish respondents reported having some ability in Irish, with less than 1% using it as their main home language, nationalist communities responded with a renewed focus on Irish language education as a badge of Irish identity. (Despite that renewed focus, a 2017 report on an Irish language telephone service set up by Belfast City Council found that, in the 11 years it had been in place, the service had not been used a single time.)[31] For unionists, however, an Irish Language Act is perceived as a political weapon in nationalists' ongoing pursuit for a united Ireland, as well as a symbolic threat to the "British character" of Northern Ireland. Unionist political leaders, when not outright mocking the Irish language, countered that the St. Andrews Agreement also called for Ulster-Scots language, heritage, and culture to be enhanced and developed. In their view, only a broader and more balanced act of legislation addressing the wider context of all cultural identity issues, including unionist ones, would be feasible. In reply, nationalist political leaders remained insistent that a stand-alone Irish Language Act is necessary "for an end to the rights and equality deficit that exists in the north" and that Stormont would not be restored without an agreement for such an act.[32]

The January 2020 "New Decade, New Approach" compromise deal that restored Stormont called for legislation "to create a Commissioner to recognise, support, protect and enhance the development of the Irish language in Northern Ireland and to provide official recognition of the status of the Irish Language in Northern Ireland." In the spirit of parity, the deal also called for legislation "to create a further such Commissioner to enhance and develop the language, arts and literature associated with the Ulster Scots/Ulster British tradition and to provide official recognition of the status of the Ulster Scots language in Northern Ireland."[33] As of this writing, neither post has yet to be filled.

The perception of threat and its impact on our behavior has significant evolutionary value because perceiving threats when none exists is a far less costly error than not perceiving threats when, in fact, they do exist.[34] So, it is difficult to mitigate the risk this adaptive predisposition poses. Nonetheless, while histories of identity-related tension can reify social identities in ways that perpetuate risk, we also recognize that social identities are fluid and changeable. Social identities can be reconfigured in ways to reduce, rather than exacerbate, the historical tensions and resulting ideologies of antagonism behind them. In Rwanda, for example, laws against "divisionism" now make it illegal to talk or write about the subordinate ethnic identities of "Tutsi" and "Hutu." In their place, it has been decreed: "There is no ethnicity here. We are all Rwandan."[35] This conscious choice to focus on the superordinate national identity of "Rwandan" is an attempt, however heavy-handed, to inclusively redefine social identity from above so as to diminish the considerable risk left by the history of identity-related tension in the region. (Though, as critics point out, the amputation of ethnicity may suppress the important dialogue that Rwanda requires for moving forward and, in so doing, actually increase, rather than decrease, the risk of future intergroup conflict.)[36]

Similarly, in contemporary Northern Ireland, there has been some hope placed in the belief that a superordinate shared identity of "Northern Irish" might yield a more inclusive and unifying understanding of national belonging. The Good Friday Agreement recognized "the birthright of all the people of Northern Ireland to identify themselves and be accepted as Irish or British, or both, as they may so choose."[37] So, in a country where national identity already is a hard-earned "choice," asking people to make yet another choice to subordinate one or both of those identities to a broader superordinate national identity is a tall task. Some, however, see it as a necessary one. As commentator Malachi O'Doherty argues: "When I tick a box that says I am Northern Irish, I am saying that my strongest identification is with this region and its people and that I want political stability here in a Northern Ireland that is connected to Ireland, Britain and Europe. . . . I am saying that where two large communal camps here obsess about identity over practical politics, I prefer politics to work and can compromise further on identity to achieve that."[38]

It is debatable how many of O'Doherty's fellow citizens are willing to make that same cross-community identity compromise. "Northern Irish" was first given as a national identity option on surveys in the late 1980s. In the most recent 2011 census, 39.89% of respondents saw themselves as "British only," 25.26% as "Irish only," and 20.94% as "Northern Irish only." In terms of religious breakdown, a higher percentage of those who were or had been brought up as Catholics were willing to identify as "Northern Irish only" (27%) compared to Protestants (15%). Across both communities, far fewer were willing to pair "British" or "Irish" with "Northern Irish": only 6.17% saw themselves as "British and Northern Irish only" (87% of whom were Protestant) and only 1.06% as "Irish and Northern Irish only" (86% of whom were Catholic).[39] In the more recent 2019 Northern Ireland Life and Times survey, 39% of respondents saw themselves as "British," 25% as "Irish," and 27% as "Northern Irish." After age 54, the percentage of those willing to see themselves as "Northern Irish" fell off considerably, with only 21% of those older than 65 willing to do so. A roughly similar number of Catholics (26%) and Protestants (23%) were willing to self-identify as "Northern Irish."[40]

It is unclear, however, how respondents to both surveys were interpreting the ambiguity of "Northern Irish" as a national identity label. Research suggests some may have chosen it is a political statement or cross-community identity claim—membership in an inclusive, superordinate, shared, common in-group. For others, it might have been a banal indicator of place—Catholics using the term to indicate their regional belonging to the northern part of Ireland or Protestants using it as an affirmation of belonging to a particular part of the UK. For still others, it simply could have been a safe identity label to disguise their background.[41] Given that uncertainty, the degree to which "Northern Irish" can become a superordinate unifying national identity that can override the subordinate binary we-identities that divide Northern Ireland remains to be seen.

Prior Genocides or Politicides

In terms of risk factors, a particularly notable indicator related to conflict history comes from whether or not the country in question has experienced a genocide (destruction of a communal group) or politicide (destruction of a political group) in its prior history. As defined in Article 2 of the UN Genocide Convention, "genocide means any of the following acts committed with intent to destroy, in whole or in part, a national, ethnical, racial or religious group, as such: (a) killing members of the group, (b) causing serious bodily or mental harm to members of the group, (c) deliberately inflicting on the group conditions of life calculated to bring about its physical destruction in whole or in part, (d) imposing measures intended to prevent births within the group, or (e) forcibly transferring children of the group to another group."[42] Recognizing that political groups can be an especially vulnerable population, political scientist Barbara Harff coined the term "politicide" to refer to victims of mass destruction defined in regard to their political opposition to the regime or dominant group.[43] The reality of overlapping identities, however, makes it difficult to clearly differentiate "genocide" from "politicide" since national, ethnical, racial, or religious victims of genocide are also often politically active. For this reason, most risk forecasting researchers use the term "genocide" to represent both genocide and politicide.

This risk factor predicts that countries with past experiences of genocide are at a substantially higher risk of experiencing future cases of genocide (likely due to resulting social and political instability, a habituation to violence, and legacies of vengeance or group grievance). This factor appeared in Harff's original 2003 assessments of risk and has remained throughout. As she writes: "The risks of new episodes (of genocide or politicide) were more than three times greater when state failures occurred in countries that had prior geno-/politicides."[44] Similarly, the Atrocity Forecasting Project found years since a previous genocide or politicide to be one of the six most potent predictive factors for the onset of genocide. In their list of states at a high risk of genocide, there was a cluster of states at the top with a comparatively short time interval since their last genocide.[45] Other forecasting models also have found that a history of genocide increases the predictive power for future genocides.[46]

To understand the impact of this particular risk factor on contemporary Northern Ireland requires unpacking the degree to which events in Irish or Northern Irish history can be couched within the frame of genocide. Certainly, as researcher Robbie McVeigh argues, "the idea and accusation of genocide is a routine part of Irish political discourse," regardless of its accuracy.[47] For instance, "genocide" is often used by Catholics to describe both the premise of British settler colonialism as well as its devastating consequence on the native Irish Catholic population. In truth, an argument can be made that the structural processes of settler colonialism—embodied in the Plantation of Ulster—is, in itself, inherently genocidal.[48] (Moreover, it could be argued that the violence intrinsic in settler colonialism directly sowed the seeds for what would become the Troubles more than three centuries later.[49]) On the other side of the coin, Protestants also evoke the term "genocide" to describe their victimization in massacres during the native Irish Catholic uprising of 1641.[50]

Most frequently, however, "genocide" is invoked as a descriptor for the Great Hunger ("An Gorta Mor" in Irish) of 1845–1852 and the suffering of the Irish people (the starvation of more than 1 million and emigration of up to 2 million more). While the potato blight may have been a natural disaster, many in the nationalist community see the British government's response, or lack thereof, as responsible for the famine itself. In these communities, there is widespread consensus that Irish people were not just starving—rather, they were being starved by the apathy and active neglect of the British government. In the Ballymurphy neighborhood of West Belfast, for instance, a timeworn memorial (Figure 3.1) dedicated to the men, women, and children who died of starvation during the Great Hunger says simply: "It was genocide." The accompanying mural, taking up the full end of a gable wall, is topped with "British Government Genocide in Ireland." Another mural in the neighborhood speaks of "Britain's Genocide by Starvation" and "Ireland's Holocaust."[51]

More than a century later, "genocide" returned in contemporaneous descriptions of the Troubles. In 1972, the bloodiest year of the conflict, John Lennon and Yoko Ono released "The Luck of the Irish," a folk medley with the following verse:

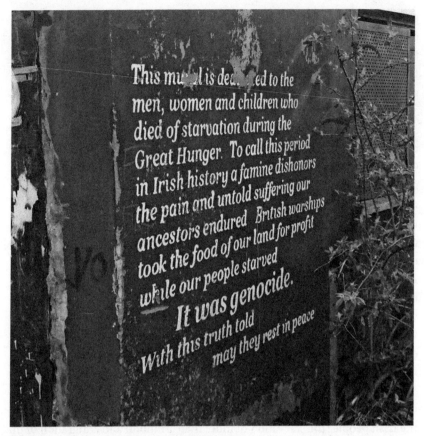

Figure 3.1 Memorial to the Great Hunger, from the Ballymurphy neighborhood in West Belfast.
Photo by author, February 4, 2017.

> *Why the hell are the English there anyway?*
> *As they kill with God on their side*
> *Blame it all on the kids the IRA*
> *As the bastards commit genocide! Aye! Aye! Genocide!*[52]

In contemporary Northern Ireland, in nationalist and republican communities, the use of the term "genocide" persists as a continuing portrayal of British colonial oppression and persecution. As one example, the Bloody Sunday March for Justice, held every January in Derry, draws a large parade of socialist and republican activists, dissidents, and bands from around the island. In 2017, one of the groups marched behind a banner proclaiming "The

British Army: Committing Genocide for Generations." Not to be outdone, unionists and loyalists draw on the language of "genocide" to describe ongoing attacks against Protestants living in the border areas between Northern Ireland and the Republic of Ireland—and as an object lesson to warn of how Protestants would be treated in a united Ireland.[53]

To be sure, the politics of victimhood is a well-practiced polemic in Northern Ireland, and politicizing one's suffering as "genocide" is a tough moniker to top. In this discourse, the "g-word" often is used by both sides of the sectarian divide for its emotive power, particularly employed in accusatorial tones to dramatize the plight of their persecuted group. Even when the "g-word" itself is not used, allusions to it are frequent and suggest that it has particularly found a home in the ideological mindset of the nationalist and republican communities. In early 2017, for instance, I interviewed a former republican political prisoner who described the British persecution of Catholics in Northern Ireland as "extermination" and referred to his time in a British prison as being in a "concentration camp," replete with "barbed wire and vicious dogs just like WWII." Later that same day, outside the Sinn Fein offices in West Belfast, I happened upon a ceremony memorializing the death of three people killed in those offices by an off-duty Royal Ulster Constabulary (RUC) police officer in 1992. Gerry Adams, then president of Sinn Fein, keynoted the ceremony and, in his speech, he repeatedly used the phrase "never again," resonantly evocative of the Holocaust, in stressing the importance of an agreed upon narrative for going forward.

Despite its frequent use, however, the degree to which the Troubles can be understood as "genocide" is markedly limited. This has less to do with numbers (even a small number of victims could constitute the crime of genocide) and more to do with intent. There is little evidence, beyond political rhetoric, that any of the parties involved in the Troubles had the "intent to destroy, in whole or in part" members of the other group. Before the violence reached the precipice of genocide in Northern Ireland, political elites, pushed by a robust and active civil society and reinforced by international actors, realized the necessity of moving from governing by monopolizing force to governing by inclusive consent.[54] Not being classified as "genocide," however, does not mean that the Troubles had any less residual impact. There are two significant ways in which the impact of the violence is still directly felt and relevant in understanding risk and resilience in contemporary Northern Ireland.

First, the most commonly agreed definitional threshold of "war" is any state-based conflict or dyad resulting in more than 1,000 deaths in a specific calendar year.[55] By that measure, despite the IRA's repeated and continuing attempts to legitimize it as such, the three decades of violence in Northern Ireland never met the threshold of "war." The years of bloodshed were also, though, far beyond what could constitute, in the minimizing and calloused words of one British government official, "an acceptable level of violence."[56] Falling short of war, but well past any specious concept of an "acceptable level of violence" or simply an aggravated crime wave, the Troubles are most commonly referred to as "low-intensity conflict." This is an irresponsible and misleadingly benign stamp for a society torn apart by internal conflict. It is insensitive to the realities of everyday civilian life lived in the no-man's land between the violent and sometimes indiscriminate anti-state terrorism of the IRA and the overreactive and often equally indiscriminate state-sponsored terrorism of the British government and its allies. Even if people did not choose conflict, the conflict could choose them. The suffering of the Troubles was multidirectional.

As we will see in reviewing the next risk factor ("Past Cultural Trauma"), in addition to the 3,532 deaths, thousands upon thousands of people were scarred—physically, psychologically and emotionally—by the violence. Everyone in a conflict society is a victim of a collective traumatization. As journalist Eamon Lynch remembers: "The threat of violence was more pervasive than the violence itself, metastasizing into every aspect of everyday life."[57] Similarly, George Mitchell recounted in a recent interview: "It's not just the number of deaths, 3,500 people killed during the Troubles. Not much attention is given to the tens of thousands who were permanently maimed through violence. You had kneecapping, where people were shot through the knees and ankles, and savage beatings that left people maimed for life. So indiscriminate was the violence, it created widespread fear."[58]

Second, there is a glorification of and even habituation to violence—both intergroup and interpersonal—in which violence is justified as a legitimate and strategic response to conflict. The lesson many children have learned in Northern Ireland is the power of the gun and the bomb to effect change; that you deal with difference through violence. In many unionist and nationalist neighborhoods, children "go to school" on the neighborhood murals glorifying the fallen loyalist and republican heroes and community protectors. Many former paramilitaries are now gatekeepers of their communities. Particularly in nationalist communities, to walk the streets with a "former" IRA volunteer is to see the nods of appreciation and respect afforded by passersby. Darach MacDonald, a writer and journalist based in Derry, even sees, particularly in bored urban youths too young to have experienced them, a disconcerting romanticized nostalgia for the Troubles, a "loss of memory of harm."[59] Placing it in the context of a folk ritual, MacDonald says: "It [the Troubles] would be something that they would see on news reels. A large part of the youth subculture in Derry is now a reenactment of the past . . . a nostalgia for a period when people in the outside world took heed of what happened here."[60]

On an interpersonal level, several people I interviewed believed that the habituation to violence, born of the Troubles and leaving its fingerprints on generations following, even helps explain the continuing rise of domestic abuse in Northern Ireland. In 2019, the Police Service of Northern Ireland (PSNI) recorded 18,033 domestic abuse crimes in total (about 16% of all recorded crime in Northern Ireland), the single highest 12-month period recorded since the start of data collection in 2004–2005.[61] This habituation to violence also can be seen in more innocuous everyday rhythms of life. In the city center, for example, most shops still close at 6:00 PM (except for Thursdays, when they remain open until 9:00 PM). As one local told me, "there's absolutely no security or economic reason for this, it's just something shops did during the Troubles since no one would dare come to the city centre in the evening and, over the years, we just all got used to it."

Past Cultural Trauma

Histories of identity-related tension and prior violent conflict leave their indelible mark in the legacies of trauma. As political scientist Jens Meierhenrich points out, we can think of two trauma types when studying the impacts of these legacies.[62] *Psychological trauma*, at an individual level, stems from a threat to our life or the lives of those close to us. Our assumptive world is challenged as the certainties of our "old" life are shaken or broken and our ability to make meaning of the predictability and stability of our "new" life is called into question. For some, such traumatic events may trigger natural, transitory, adaptive responses of the mind and body which dissipate when the event is over, allowing them to return to a normal level of functioning. In fact, most people exposed to trauma will suffer no or minimal long-term mental health disorders.

For others, however, the effects of traumatic events are so serious and persistent that they lead to a pathological reaction—the widely cited diagnostic category of *posttraumatic stress disorder* (PTSD). People who have PTSD suffer from symptoms of intrusive reexperiencing rather than remembering (including flashbacks or recurrent dreams related to the event), avoidance (staying away from distressing reminders of the event), negative cognitions and mood (persistent negative emotional state or markedly diminished interest in significant activities), and alterations in arousal (irritable behavior, exaggerated startle response, sleep disturbances, or constantly on guard).[63] PTSD takes us back to the moment of the traumatic event, even if it occurred years before. The threat becomes a clear and present one, not a past one. Work by Stanford's Research Group on Collective Trauma and Healing suggests that traumatic stress can even damage an individual's DNA and DNA repair mechanisms, leading to an increased risk for numerous diseases.[64] Similarly, psychiatrist Bessel van der Kolk's research has demonstrated how trauma reshapes both body and brain.[65]

While the clinical presentation of PTSD varies, the "disorder may be especially severe or long-lasting when the stressor is interpersonal and intentional."[66] As philosopher Susan Brison describes in her gripping personal narrative of trauma: "When the trauma is of human origin and is intentionally inflicted . . . it not only shatters one's fundamental assumptions about the world and one's safety in it, but it also severs the sustaining connection between the self and the rest of humanity. Victims of human-inflicted trauma are reduced to mere objects by their tormenters: their subjectivity is rendered useless and viewed as worthless."[67] As a point of fact, the highest rates of PTSD (ranging from one-third to more than one-half of those exposed) are found among survivors of "rape, military combat and captivity, and ethnically and politically motivated internment and genocide."[68]

In Northern Ireland, as Belfast-based mental health expert Peter McBride describes, some individuals (visible victims) were directly impacted psychologically by the Troubles and others (hidden victims) were indirectly impacted, though they may not necessarily identify themselves as victims or survivors of the conflict.[69] Both groups, however, bear the continuing psychological scars of living in a society dominated by conflict for 30 years; conflict that has a population-level impact. As theater director Paula McFetridge says: "Trauma is like water, it will always find its way through."[70] In contemporary Northern Ireland, an estimated 39% of the population have experienced a conflict-related traumatic event, with around 213,000 adults having mental health difficulties directly related to the Troubles.[71] A 2011 report based on World Health Organization (WHO) criteria concluded: "Northern

Ireland has the highest level of 12-month and lifetime PTSD among all comparable studies undertaken across the world including other areas of conflict."[72] Mental health expert David Bolton contends that at least 34,000 people in Northern Ireland suffer from PTSD and estimates that as many as 210,000 could be suffering from a litany of anxiety disorders that can be traced to Troubles-related trauma.[73] A former IRA member suggested to me that "Northern Ireland has the highest rate of PTSD in the world because, in part, there was no time to grieve during the Troubles. So, the unresolved grief has been passed on generationally through collective memory." Another nationalist politician described to me the "dark cloud of trauma" that still hung over contemporary Northern Ireland.

Suggesting a compromised level of psychological resilience, a 2012 WHO study found the lifetime prevalence of mental health problems among the general population in Northern Ireland to be 48.6%, higher than any other part of the UK.[74] Suicide remains a door ajar, a major public health issue exacerbated by the negative stigma tied to seeking preventive mental health care. Since the conflict ended, there has been an almost doubling of the suicide rate, meaning more people have died by suicide in Northern Ireland during the 20 years of peace than were killed in the 30 years of conflict. Nearly a fifth of those suicides were younger than 25.[75] A 2020 report found that young people in Northern Ireland aged 15–24 were more than twice as likely to take their own lives compared to young people in England.[76] Prescription rates, alcohol abuse, and pathology incidences (including the prevalence of PTSD) remain among the highest in the Western world.[77] People look older than they are, weathered by the grind of lives lived in less than ordinary times. As one former republican political prisoner admitted to me: "We have a big population with buried issues."

The individual costs of living through or with the effects of trauma are significant, particularly given the duration and scale of exposure to violence during the Troubles. There also are, however, trans-generational impacts—sociological, psychological, and biological—for those who come after. As a 2015 report by Ulster University prepared for Northern Ireland's Commission for Victims and Survivors states: "These impacts can include epigenetic risks (where the parents of the child transmit stress triggered and stress adapting genes to their children), developmental impairment, relationship and attachment problems, increased risk of mental health problems and the carrying forward of all or some of these problems in adulthood and then into parenthood."[78] The report concluded that the cumulative consequences

of the trans-generational impacts of the Troubles "on subsequent generations are a distinctive and significant factor associated with mental illness,
substance dependency and other problems for young people and their families."[79] In fact, more than 20% of young people in Northern Ireland suffer
"significant mental health problems" by the time they reach 18.[80] Finally, the
report cited early toxic stress as particularly acute among "children of victims
and survivors, ex-paramilitaries and police officers . . . impacted directly as a
result of their parents' experiences."[81]

In considering risk factors related to violent conflict, however, of even
more relevance is a second type of trauma described by Meierhenrich—
cultural trauma. The concept of cultural trauma is not meant to pathol-
ogize an entire population. Rather, it is meant to capture the collective
manifestations of what a society has experienced in conflict; to move from
the individual level to the whole of society. Cultural trauma is the residual
impact of conflict that enters into the core of the social group's sense of its
own identity. As sociologist Jeffrey Alexander writes: "Cultural trauma
occurs when members of a collectivity feel they have been subjected to a horrendous event that leaves indelible marks upon their group consciousness,
marking their memories forever and changing their future identity in fundamental and irrevocable ways."[82] The cultural trauma birthed by conflict
becomes crystallized and embedded in the structure of society.[83] The world
looks different when viewed through the lens of trauma. Cultural trauma
changes people's definition of "normal"; there is a normalization of the abnormal. Peter McBride: "Individuals and societies that live with ongoing violence, and the threat of violence, over extended periods . . . develop coping
mechanisms, defence mechanisms, to manage the threat. These societal psychological defences become normalized over time, and do not disappear
when peace arrives. A society that has adapted to cope with war, does not
necessarily easily adapt to peace when it comes."[84]

Cultural trauma is socially constructed. So, rather than trauma emerging from the traumatic events themselves, trauma comes from the social
reconstruction of those events. As Alexander writes: "Events are not inherently traumatic. Trauma is a socially mediated attribution. . . . Events are one
thing, representations of these events quite another."[85] Cultural trauma is
historically made, not born. Sometimes, cultural trauma is even constructed
on imagined events that can "be as traumatizing as events that have actually occurred."[86] So, even when imagined, the impact of cultural trauma is
real. As a Commission for Victims and Survivors report concluded: "The

transmission of narratives derived from memories of conflict and violence can also impact adversely on identity in the social sphere and convey or amplify perceptions of threat, fear and exclusion."[87]

Since cultural trauma is socially constructed, people do not even have to live through the traumatic event itself to be victimized by it. In June 2014, I was visiting Sanski Most, Bosnia-Herzegovina, at the time of their worst floods in more than 120 years. It was Bosnia's largest humanitarian disaster since the war in the 1990s, and many of the town residents, most of whom were survivors of mass atrocities committed during the war, lost everything—for the second time in two decades. I was struck, though, by how teenagers in the community, not alive at the time of the war, had the same sense of revictimization as their elders—the cultural trauma in the region ran so deep that this first loss in their young lives felt like the second.

As a social construction, past cultural trauma can lead to a redefinition of collective social identity that becomes reified in memorials, museums, school textbooks, rituals, performances, commemorations, sacred routines, and popular culture. In contemporary Northern Ireland, such community efforts to keep memory "alive" are particularly reinforced by the emotionally loaded imagery of political murals. As one interviewee told me: "The past screams at us from every gabled wall." The foremost documentarian of those murals is Bill Rolston, emeritus professor of sociology at Ulster University.[88] According to Rolston, the tradition of mural painting, particularly in loyalist communities, was well-established before the birth of the Northern Ireland in 1921. Beginning around 1908, many of those murals were, and still are today, painted to coincide with the annual Twelfth of July commemoration of the 1690 Battle of the Boyne in which Protestant King William of Orange defeated Catholic King James II. Over the course of the Troubles, loyalist muralists moved to flags (the Union Jack, Ulster flag, Scottish flag, and the flag of St. Andrew) and Red Hand of Ulster motifs as badges of communal identity. Many of the murals became highly militaristic, replete with guns and paramilitaries masked in balaclavas, with dominant anti-nationalist and anti-Catholic themes. As Rolston writes: "The sinister images [in these murals] are threatening, and are meant to be."[89] Perhaps the most threatening, and certainly one of the most well-known, political murals can be found on Mount Vernon Road at the entrance to a loyalist housing estate in North Belfast. Depicting two armed and masked loyalists from the Ulster Volunteer Force, the large mural (Figure 3.2) on the gable-end of a building reads "Prepared for Peace, Ready for War."

Figure 3.2 UVF mural found on Mount Vernon Road at the entrance to a loyalist housing estate in North Belfast.
Photo by author, March 3, 2017.

Initially, republicans were less likely to paint murals. It was not an element of communal identification in marginalized nationalist enclaves in large part because it would have been heavily censored and even legally prosecuted by the unionist state. That changed, however, as a result of the 1981 republican hunger strikes. "In the spring and summer of 1981," Rolston writes, "hundreds of murals were painted [in nationalist communities] . . ." with the two main themes being "the hunger strike itself and the armed struggle of the IRA" (Figure 3.3).[90] Once the political murals began to appear, they proliferated in nationalist communities related to a wide range of connected themes: "military action, protest against repression, prison conditions, media censorship or Britain's continued hold on Ireland in general, historical events and figures in Ireland, and murals identifying with anti-imperialist struggles taking place elsewhere in the world."[91] On Falls Road in Catholic West Belfast, for instance, on what is called the "International Peace Wall," you can see murals honoring Nelson Mandela and abolitionist Frederick Douglass alongside murals protesting the treatment of Palestinian political prisoners and the continuing imprisonment of Native American activist Leonard Peltier.

EVERYONE
REPUBLICAN
OR OTHERWISE
HAS THEIR OWN
PARTICULAR
ROLE TO PLAY

...OUR
REVENGE
WILL BE THE
LAUGHTER
OF OUR
CHILDREN

Bobby Sands MP
POET, GAEILGEOIR, REVOLUTIONARY, IRA VOLUNTEER.

Figure 3.3 Republican mural memorializing hunger striker Bobby Sands, from just off the Falls Road in West Belfast.
Photo by author, January 23, 2016.

Throughout nationalist communities around Northern Ireland, however, the prevailing political theme of many murals remains liberation: "Brits Out," "Free Ireland," "End British Collusion," "800 Years of Resistance," "PSNI Not Welcome," "Smash Stormont," "End British Rule," etc. The Ardoyne area of North Belfast, a working-class nationalist district, is frequent home to murals glorifying the role violence has played in the Irish liberation movement. Saoradh, for instance, a far-left republican party formed by dissidents in 2016, maintains a mural depicting Irish leaders from the 1916 Easter Rising flanked by an armed male and female figure. The border running at the bottom of the mural reads: "Salute the men and women of violence."

Northern Ireland has the oldest continuing tradition of political murals in the world and they persist as a dominant part of the cityscape, as many as 300 to 400 existing at any time—iconic ones standing pat, old ones changing, and new ones emerging constantly. Black taxi tours of the political murals, particularly in Belfast, have become a tourist must-do. On one hand, it can be argued that these murals play a vital propaganda role in political education and communal identification on both sides of the sectarian divide. On the other hand, however, it can be argued many of the murals are, for some, sources of secondary traumatization. They reflect, sustain, and renew past cultural trauma. The long-standing "Prepared for Peace, Ready for War" mural, for instance, reinforces the hypervigilant sense of "on guard" that enters into the core of what it means to be Protestant, unionist, or loyalist in contemporary Northern Ireland. Similarly, the continuing protest against British occupation and repression depicted in many Catholic, nationalist, or republican murals cements the besieged narrative of a perpetually oppressed people.

Rather than legislating murals out of existence, government-sponsored projects and community-led initiatives have attempted to reframe murals with more moderate and peaceful imagery as constructive and transformative elements in the ongoing peace process. That effort, however, has been only marginally successful at best. A few years ago, for instance, loyalists were given a cash grant to replace a threatening mural with one dedicated to George Best, an international soccer star and son of East Belfast. A few weeks after the mural was completed, however, it was painted over and the paramilitary mural, complete with guns and balaclavas, was restored.[92] As Belfast muralist Mark Ervine said: "You can't force them to paint birds and flowers if they still are afraid of crossing a road in the Catholic quarter."[93] Even in public housing, the Northern Ireland Housing Executive (NIHE) cannot find contractors willing to go into a housing estate and remove the murals because so many of them have been run off or attacked in past efforts to do so. As one person familiar with their office told me, "the best NIHE can do is work with community activists, who often are paramilitary leaders wearing a different hat, to try and reduce the violence in some of the images." In truth, the majority of political murals in contemporary Northern Ireland remain, unfortunately, less concerned with promoting trauma recovery and social cohesion and more concerned with transmitting past cultural trauma and social fragmentation. In so doing, the murals restrict broader and more inclusive definitions of identity by visually—and sometimes viscerally—reinforcing conceptions of "us" and "them."

As a risk factor, past cultural trauma can hand down unhealed psychological and social wounds that leave a post-conflict society acutely vulnerable to future outbreaks of violent conflict. Feelings of loss, displacement, injustice, and a possible desire for revenge can motivate or incentivize individuals or groups to resort to large-scale violence as a way to achieve "justice" or respond to real or perceived threats.[94] For Staub, past victimization can leave a deep mistrust of other people that, coupled with fear, makes "it difficult to resolve new conflict or to respond to a new threat in a manner commensurate with the actual threat. Believing that they need to defend themselves, members of the group may strike out in the face of new conflict or threat, even when forceful self-defense is not necessary."[95] The fragmenting influence of unresolved past cultural trauma can even come into play for perpetrator groups who continue to blame the victims for their own victimization and, as a result, may engage in new episodes of violence.

A Belfast mental health expert I interviewed said: "What we require to make peace in Northern Ireland is compromised by traumas of the past. We are stuck in trauma and the dysfunction of it has become normalized." To be sure, time does not necessarily heal; sometimes it entrenches, leading to a progressive accumulation of risk. Any peace agreement or political settlement that does not address the psychological legacy of conflict risks the return of future hostilities. Addressing the psychological legacy of conflict is a prerequisite to creating a healthy, fully functioning post-conflict society. Survivors of conflict cannot also become victims of peace, abandoned, in the words of David Bolton, in a "no-man's land between the past and the emerging future with nowhere to go back to yet feeling unable to go forward."[96] At an individual level, this means the development of trauma-informed clinical services. At a societal level, past cultural trauma, as a social reconstruction, can be repackaged as a unifying rather than dividing influence within society. As Alexander argues, "however tortuous the trauma process, it allows collectivities to define new forms of moral responsibility and to redirect the course of political action."[97] Moreover, as policy analysts at the World Bank have argued, "investing in mental wellbeing among post-conflict populations contributes to strengthening social capital . . . [and the] ability to form relations of trust, cooperation and mobilization for collective action."[98] As McBride contends, "the qualities of trust, forgiveness, compromise, generosity, empathy, understanding and friendliness are all required to construct a meaningful peace" in a post-conflict society.[99]

Legacy of Vengeance or Group Grievance

Birthed in histories of identity-related tension, some of which may have led to large-scale violence as well as past cultural trauma, it is common for there to be a legacy of vengeance or group grievance pervading a post-conflict society. While it may be true that every generation must know its own suffering, the legacies of those sufferings, particularly when politicized, become potent as a risk factor. Such legacies leave a society with deep cleavages, putting some societies at risk for violent retribution by vigilantes, militias, and extremists who are motivated by these legacies of vengeance or group grievance. At times, diaspora communities prove to be a major actor in the sustaining and animating of such legacies through memory, funds, and supplies.

Legacies of vengeance built on injustices of the past can go back decades or even centuries. Serb national mythology, for example, was built on a legacy of vengeance dating back to the 1389 martyrdom of Prince Lazar. Lazar's death, representing the death of the Serb nation, was the beginning of five centuries of humiliating rule by the Ottoman Turks—a traumatic event resonating through generations of Serb "victims." In this passion play, with Lazar as an explicit Christ figure, Slavic Muslims were reimagined as Christ killers. It would not be until they were purged from the Serbian people that the nation of Serbia could be resurrected again.[100] This legacy of—even call to—vengeance was enshrined as a key piece of Serb nationalist tradition and genocidal ideology during the violent collapse of Yugoslavia.

Group grievances are born in the painful legacies of groups who have been denied autonomy, self-determination, or political independence; subjected to institutionalized persecution, repression, oppression, or political exclusion; victimized by nationalist political rhetoric or scapegoating.[101] Such experiences—real or imagined—leave aggrieved groups feeling as the "other," outside of the nation, voiceless and powerless in the face of their imposed marginalization. Of particular import for group grievances is an absence of dispute resolution or transitional justice mechanisms—either through legislative frameworks, judicial systems, or community-based structures—to which aggrieved groups can turn for recourse. When there are no mechanisms for peaceful conciliation of different group interests, group grievances are left to fester as truth, reparation, reconciliation, and reintegration are held hostage.

To deal with legacies of vengeance or group grievance is to deal with the past. The present, and future, of dealing with the past is a matter of constant debate in contemporary Northern Ireland. Some advocate for drawing a line under the past or "disremembering," similar to Spain's unspoken *pacto del olvido* (pact of forgetting) regarding the repressive legacy of Francoism

(1939–1975).[102] Others have suggested a "Day of Atonement" as a way to begin a process of reconciliation.[103] Still others want to introduce a conditional amnesty or statute of limitations, while others demand continued and dogged pursuit of those who killed and committed crimes during the Troubles.[104] And yet others call for a non-legally binding truth commission that will bring a collective acknowledgment of past wrongs, while others simply will settle for knowing where the remains of their loved ones are located.

The reality, as one academic said to me, is that "there is a piecemeal approach, usually top-down initiatives with little community buy-in, to the past in Northern Ireland." As a result, by and large, the past remains undealt with in any constructive sense. When the past is dealt with, it most often is done so to weaponize and justify and blame rather than to explain and redress and move forward. "The problem, of course, is that most people don't want the past explained," columnist Alex Kane writes. "They want evidence from the past to sustain and justify their present prejudices, beliefs and political positions. In other words, the past is of no use to them unless it allows them to conclude every debate, letter to the editor, tweet, or call to a 'phone-in programme, with the words: 'See, I told you it was the fault of themuns all along. They started it.' For them, the past is an old weapon—always to hand—rather than an escape route."[105]

Dealing with the past is particularly problematized when the past becomes politicized, when legacies of vengeance or group grievance sustain and justify current political exigencies. As columnist and former Social Democratic and Labour Party (SDLP) councilor Brian Feeney describes the current political situation in Northern Ireland: "For the DUP [Democratic Unionist Party], the aim [of addressing the past] is to ensure that republicans are blamed for everything that happened whereas the RUC, the British army and their local proxies, the UDR [Ulster Defence Regiment], are recognised as heroes defending 'our wee country' against an evil conspiracy. For Sinn Fein the aim is to demonstrate that the British state engaged in illegal activity to support unionism, British forces and police conspiring with pseudo-gangs, the UVF [Ulster Volunteer Force] and UDA [Ulster Defence Association], supplying them with weapons to kill not only IRA members but innocent nationalist civilians."[106]

Indeed, both sides are afraid history will be rewritten in ways that depict their side as terrorists and villains rather than the freedom fighters and heroes they depict themselves to be. This was driven home to me following an interview with a former republican political prisoner early in my research. During our conversation, he recounted his experiences as a self-described "prisoner of war" and the negative impact his time in prison had on his subsequent life opportunities. At one point, he asked about my work and I briefly described my research on the psychology of perpetrator behavior. I used the word "perpetrator," a word I have lived with for much of my academic career, as a self-evident reference to both state and non-state actors. Later that evening, however, I returned home to an email from him with a reminder that what is self-evident to me is much less so to those in a contested and divided post-conflict society: "Please accept in spirit this is offered," he wrote. "It would maybe be a good idea to take care with the use of 'perpetrator' when speaking with Republicans. Language, as you know, is loaded and especially here via the decades of media onslaught on us. So, when we hear 'perpetrator' we know who/what is meant (whether the neutral speaker means it or not!)—certainly not the state or its forces. But us. Raises the hackles a bit but I opted not to comment."

Perhaps nowhere is the politicization of the past captured—and the hackles raised—as much as in the machinations, and implications, of defining who is and is not a "victim" in Northern Ireland. There is a complexity and multiplicity of voices in post-conflict societies, and the exercise of those voices, particularly related to victimhood, is part of acknowledging that reality. At an individual level, the term "victim" makes some feel frozen at the point of trauma "in a specific moment when they experienced loss and it reduces their identification to that experience."[107] In its place, and resisting definition based on what was done to them by others, many prefer to exercise agency with the more active and self-empowering term "survivor." Still others opt for "victim-survivor."

At the communal and political level, however, the "victim" card plays very well. Victimhood, manipulated for gain in the "politics of pain," becomes another way to secure an advantage for "us" at the expense of "them." Victimhood justifies the historical and perhaps even contemporary recourse to violence. Victimhood, and the dozens of funded victims groups that support it, offers sympathy, attention, credit, resources, political currency, and even validation for their suffering or the suffering they imposed on others. Victimhood is legitimized by connecting one's experience to that of other victimized peoples, as is apparent with the ubiquitous presence of Palestinian flags in many nationalist neighborhoods throughout Northern Ireland. As one political figure frustratingly told me: "The only way to win the Olympics of suffering in Northern Ireland is to be declared as the one and only 'real' victim of the Troubles."

Recognizing this, the Good Friday Agreement chose to remain noticeably silent on the definition of "victim," getting no more precise than "victims of violence" (even though there were well-established legal definitions of "victim" in international law from which the framers of the agreement could have drawn). Eight years later, it would fall to the Victims and Survivors (Northern Ireland) Order 2006 to define "victim and survivor" as any of the following: "(a) someone who is or has been physically or psychologically injured as a result of or in consequence of a conflict-related incident; (b) someone who provides a substantial amount of care on a regular basis for an individual mentioned in paragraph (a) or; (c) someone who has been bereaved as a result of or in consequence of a conflict-related incident." Conflict-related incidents were understood to be "violent" incidents occurring in or after 1966 in connection with the affairs of Northern Ireland.[108]

The Order's definition of "victim and survivor" is inclusive in that it makes no distinction between paramilitaries who were killed or injured and their victims. This is particularly galling for unionist politicians who repeatedly demand that perpetrators of violence—regardless of whose side they were on—not be redefined as victims. In 2009, for instance, DUP assembly member Jeffrey Donaldson argued: "It is about how we deal with the past, and what we are not prepared to countenance is a rewriting of the Troubles where the perpetrators, whoever they are, who carried out acts of terrorism are placed on a par with the thousands of people they killed and maimed."[109] More recently, in 2019, DUP leader Arlene Foster claimed: "The 2006 definition of a victim and survivor is indefensible. There is a clear distinction in law between a terrorist perpetrator and their innocent victim. To equate the two is morally indefensible. A perpetrator of an unlawful act cannot at the same time be a victim of the act they have perpetrated."[110] In response, republican politicians continue to counter there should be no false distinctions between "deserving" and "undeserving" victims or "innocent" and "guilty" victims.

The definition of "victims," and victimhood, is more than a semantic issue. It also has financial implications for who can and cannot seek compensation for their victimization. Following the 2006 Order establishing a Commission for Victims and Survivors, it would not be until the 2014 Stormont House Agreement that the Northern Ireland government and the five main political parties agreed "to find an acceptable way forward on the proposal for a pension for severely physically injured victims."[111] Five years later, in May 2019, Judith Thompson, Commissioner for Victims and Survivors, proposed a Victims and Survivors Pension Arrangement in which those "severely and permanently physically or psychologically injured as a consequence of a conflict-related incident" would be eligible for a pension (in a tiered approach according to the severity of injury with the option of a lump sum payment or regular payment).[112] The proposal still included as "victims" those who were injured while carrying out attacks. In response, in July 2019, the family of Grant Weir, a former UDR soldier left brain-damaged by an IRA bomb 40 years ago, declared they would not accept a Troubles-related pension if ex-paramilitaries were also eligible. "As a family," they said, "we would never accept a payment if it meant that the people who went out to destroy lives, destroy families, were to be put into the same category . . . as Grant, whose life they have destroyed."[113]

Finally, six years after the initial agreement "to find an acceptable way forward," Julian Smith, then Secretary of State for Northern Ireland, signed new legislation creating a victims' payments plan on January 31, 2020. The plan, called the Troubles Permanent Disablement Payment Scheme, provides for annual lifetime payments of between £2,000 and £10,000 for those who suffered physical or psychological injury "through no fault of their own" during the Troubles (covering January 1, 1966 through April 12, 2010). The payments will not be distributed to those who were injured due to their own actions (such as bombers caught up in their own explosions), who committed serious criminal offenses, or who served more than two-and-a-half years in prison. Unionists welcomed the fact that money would "not be awarded to victim makers" while nationalists claimed the legislation created a "hierarchy of victims."[114]

Sinn Fein, believing the plan discriminated against some former prisoners by intentionally subverting the legal definition of a victim established in the 2006 Order, initially refused to nominate a Stormont department to run the scheme until the list of who was eligible could be revisited. In August 2020, victims and survivors filed a legal challenge against the Northern Ireland Executive Office (TEO) for unlawfully delaying the introduction of the scheme. The court ruled in favor of the plaintiffs and the TEO then designated the Department of Justice to administer the scheme. As of this writing, however, politicians continue to wrangle over whether Stormont or Westminster should foot the bill, estimated to be on the order of at least £100 million over the first three years.[115] Once application for payments opens, tentatively set for March 2021, an independent judge-led panel will decide who will and will not receive payments. It is expected that there will be approximately 2,000 applications to consider.[116]

In Northern Ireland, as we have seen, there is a problem for every solution; once one matter is settled, another one (or dozen) quickly takes its place. On May 13, 2020, the UK Supreme Court dramatically overturned Gerry Adams's two convictions for attempting to escape from lawful custody in the 1970s on the basis that he was, in reality, imprisoned unlawfully because his detention was not "personally considered" by a senior government minister. In other words, his internment papers were signed by someone not authorized to decide against him. Because he won his appeal, the legal costs for his hearing likely will be met by the Secretary of State for Northern Ireland, and, if he chooses to pursue a compensation case, Adams could be in line for a six-figure payment. As a result of this judgment, it is expected that as many as 600 similar republican—and even a few loyalist—internment cases also will be quashed, with many resulting in substantial compensation.[117] To many victims of Troubles-related violence who still await compensation for their victimization, fortune continues to favor the "victim makers" over the victims. Jim Allister, leader of the Traditional Unionist Voice political party, voiced the frustration of many in the unionist community: "In contrast with the countless innocent victims of the IRA, who never enjoyed a right of appeal against the summary decision of the IRA to murder them, Gerry Adams benefits from appeal to the British legal system whose judges the Provos brutally murdered. No right to life for IRA victims, but a right of appeal for Adams."[118]

Often, legacies of vengeance or group grievances are exacerbated by celebrations of historical events recalling victories of one group over another. In contemporary Northern Ireland, these types of performative legacy are most evident in parades and bonfires. Parades are performative declarations of political, cultural, and religious loyalties. In 2018, there were 2,537 parades in Northern Ireland designated as Protestant, unionist, or loyalist (PUL), with another 117 designated as Catholic, nationalist, or republic (CNR). Of those, 130 of the PUL parades were considered as contentious by the Commission and had conditions imposed on them to ensure their legality, compared to 3 of the CNR parades.[119] Each of the parades, however, is an irrefutable statement of presence in the most public, and sometimes most contested, of spaces—including the space of collective memory. Loyalist parades, for instance, include banners, songs, flags, regalia, and imagery that recall a series of historical events reaching back to the seventeenth century in which Protestantism and Britishness have triumphed over Catholicism and Irishness. The parades, sometimes stretching miles, simply reenact the past rather than deal with it. In that sense, they become a source of community avoidance and entrenchment rather than mutual understanding and a shared future. They reinforce the dividing lines between "us" and "them." The parades often lead to counter-protests and, sometimes, civil disorder. In fact, to visit Northern Ireland in July, the peak of the loyalist parading season ("better than Christmas" as one marcher told me), is to find many shops and restaurants shuttered and away on holiday rather than running the risk of remaining open in the threat of violence.

Of particular concern in recent years has been the proliferation of contentious bonfires on both sides of the sectarian divide. Bonfires have a long history birthed from European "fire festivals" of worship or cleansing.[120] While most commonly associated with loyalist celebrations of the "Eleventh Night" of July before the following day's parades, bonfires also are a part of Catholic, nationalist, and republican communal life. On August 15 of each year, for instance, many nationalist neighborhoods throughout Northern Ireland light bonfires to mark the Catholic Feast of the Assumption. Bonfires in republican neighborhoods to mark the anniversary of the introduction of the policy of internment without trial also are increasingly common, and some lead to civil disorder. Most recently, in August 2019, the attempted removal of a bonfire in a nationalist north Belfast neighborhood, built to commemorate the 48th anniversary of internment, led to prolonged rioting and violence—including a number of stabbing incidents and one man even being shot with a crossbow. In response, editors of the *Belfast Telegraph* opined: "No one wants this kind of behaviour where others seize, almost as of right, opportunities to create mayhem on the anniversaries of certain events. Unfortunately, there are enough memories of contentious periods in our joint and shared history to give excuses for demonstrations on almost every day of the year. What is needed is a whole new mindset about the past, which will take a long time to manifest itself."[121]

The path to a new mindset about the past in any post-conflict society is a long one, and it is littered with legacies of vengeance and group grievance. To address those legacies means having in place functioning, open, and transparent dispute resolution or transitional justice mechanisms. Victims, however defined, should have free expression to advocate for the redress of their grievances, whether through individual criminal accountability, reparation, truth-seeking, or reconciliation processes. As political psychologist Neil Ferguson and colleagues suggest in their analysis of victimhood experiences in post-agreement Northern Ireland: "official public approaches need to be supplemented with activities (e.g., counselling, story telling, story sharing, restorative justice) to promote individual recovery, to provide closure, and to enhance reintegration into a postconflict society."[122] At the community level, women—often sidelined in these processes—can play an important leadership role in addressing legacies of vengeance and group grievance. Comprehensive reform measures in the security and judicial sectors, complemented by a strong civil society presence, may be necessary to ensure the safe practice of this voice and advocacy.[123]

One of the conditions of the January 2020 "New Decade, New Approach" deal was a commitment on the part of the UK government to deliver, within 100 days, legislation to address Northern Ireland's legacy issues. As an initial step, on March 18, 2020, the Secretary of State for Northern Ireland—with little to no consultation with victims' groups—released a set of core proposals calling for (a) a new independent body focused on providing information to families and swift examinations of all unresolved deaths from the Troubles, (b) an end to the cycle of reinvestigations that has failed victims and veterans for too long, and (c) assurances that Northern Ireland veterans receive equal treatment to their counterparts who served overseas. These new proposals will now be reviewed in "an intensive period of engagement with the Northern Ireland political parties, and the Irish government."[124]

With the timeline for implementation extended indefinitely due to the COVID-19 pandemic, many fear the proposals, like so many before them, are doomed to failure. Given that the proposals seem driven by a desire to ensure that British soldiers do not go to prison for Troubles-related offenses, some even see the failure of these proposals as absolutely necessary. Grainne Teggart, for instance, Amnesty International's Northern Ireland campaign manager, said: "The UK Government's latest proposals on how it will deal with the legacy of the conflict in Northern Ireland are simply not compatible with the European Convention on Human Rights."[125] Similarly, a joint report prepared by the Committee on the Administration of Justice in collaboration with academics from Queen's University Belfast found the proposals "are not only incompatible with the European Convention on Human Rights and the Good Friday Agreement, but are also incompatible with the Stormont House Agreement."[126]

In the meantime, awaiting implementation of any of these legacy proposals, the work of dealing with the past slogs on. Currently, legacy investigations route through three offices. The Legacy Investigation Branch (LIB) of the PSNI, formed in January 2015 to replace the Historical Enquiries Team (HET), investigates homicide and security forces-related deaths arising from the Troubles between 1969 and 2004 as well as unsolved "non-Troubles" related deaths from that same time period. As of this writing, the LIB—much smaller (about 55 detectives) and with far fewer resources than its HET predecessor—is dealing with more than 1,000 unresolved cases. The LIB's work is complemented by the Historical Investigations Directorate (HID) of the Office of the Police Ombudsman for Northern Ireland. HID, with a staff of around 25 people, looks at matters in which members of the RUC may have been responsible for deaths or serious criminality in the past, and in particular between 1968 until 1998. It also receives complaints of a grave or exceptional nature from members of the public about police conduct during this period, including allegations of police involvement in murder and attempted murder, as well as conspiracy and incitement to murder. As of this writing, HID's caseload is around 400 cases and growing. Finally, the Coroners Service for Northern Ireland is available to deal with matters relating to deaths that may require further investigation to establish the cause of death. The majority of deaths that occurred during the Troubles will have had a Coroner's inquest soon after the death occurred. Where there were shortcomings in the original inquest, the Attorney General for Northern Ireland can order a fresh inquest. There are currently more than 50 legacy inquests relating to almost 100 deaths proceeding through the Northern Ireland Coroners' courts on this basis.[127]

The work of these units in easing the tensions of a deeply divided society, as well as the pending discussions of legacy mechanisms or new proposals, remains as contested as the past with which they are trying to deal. While opening old wounds may be necessary for healing to take place, dealing with legacies of vengeance or group grievance often drives deeper divisions between victims' groups, politicians, and sectarian communities. Perhaps acknowledging this, respondents in a February 2020 online poll, on both sides of the border, ranked legacy issues among the lowest of their priorities. In Northern Ireland, legacy issues were considered most important among a list of priorities by only 2.8% of respondents; that figure rose to only 3.2% of respondents in the Republic of Ireland. Both groups placed much higher priority on a peaceful society, human rights, free healthcare, the economy, and education.[128] So, despite the dominance of legacy issues in the political narrative and among victim groups, the general population seems to recognize that becoming overly immersed in dealing with a divided past cannot take complete precedence over the construction of a shared future.

Record of Serious Violations of International Human Rights and Laws

A final risk factor related to conflict history is a cross-cutting issue threaded throughout the previous four risk factors—a record of serious violations of international human rights and laws. On December 10, 1948, the United Nations adopted the nonbinding Universal Declaration of Human Rights (UDHR), a milestone document in the history of human rights. The UDHR, for the first time in human history, spelled out the basic civil, political, economic, social, and cultural rights that all human beings should enjoy—the right to life, liberty, and security of person; equality before the law; no subjection to torture, arbitrary arrest, detention, or exile; the rights to freedom of movements, thought, conscience, religion, and nationality; etc.[129] These are the inherent entitlements which belong to every person as a consequence of being human.

Since the passage of the UDHR and its elaboration in the 1966 International Human Rights Covenants, a body of international human rights law has developed to legally ensure the respect, protection, and fulfillment of those universal human rights. International human rights law applies at all times, in peace and in war. That body of law is complemented by a body of international humanitarian law (also known as the law of war or the law of armed conflict) that specifically seeks to regulate and limit the use of violence in armed conflict. A society with a record of serious violations of these internationally recognized human rights and laws suggests an at-risk society markedly indifferent to the protection of its civilians. Research has found that countries with recent human rights abuses have a more than twofold increase in the risk of civil war in the subsequent year than do countries with a strong history of respect for human rights.[130]

In addition to UN treaties stemming from the UDHR, the European Convention on Human Rights (ECHR) is binding for the UK.[131] Originally drawn up in 1950 by the newly formed Council of Europe, the ECHR, since 1966, has allowed people from the UK to take cases to the European Court of Human Rights if they believe the UK government has failed to uphold their human rights. Since 1966, relatively few cases from Northern Ireland resulted in a judgment by the Court. Westminster's Human Rights Act of 1988, however, made the ECHR part of the law of all countries in the UK. The act came into full effect on October 2, 2000, and made the ECHR binding at the national level, meaning that people in Northern Ireland can appeal to the local courts about a failure to uphold their human rights. If dissatisfied with that decision, complainants still have the opportunity to take their case to the European Court of Human Rights.

As a risk factor, a record of serious violations of international human rights and laws is particularly pronounced when such violations have not been punished or adequately addressed. In the aftermath of serious and massive human rights violations, as occurred in the Troubles, the failure to provide justice to people and communities—a "justice gap"—is a perilous threat to lasting peace and guarantees of nonrecurrence.[132] Reducing the justice gap for both state and non-state actors is a necessary part of dealing with the past. To do so requires assessing judicial efforts over decades to determine what has been addressed and what is yet to be addressed. Unfortunately, as a UN Special Rapporteur found in 2016, there is no such comprehensive data on the prosecution of non-state or state actors related to the Troubles.[133] In the absence of such data, bias and mistrust step in as various sides make competing claims about a justice gap that unfairly victimizes their side.

In terms of non-state actors, a justice gap in Northern Ireland, on the surface, appears to be minimal. A 2012 report, for instance, estimated that up to 30,000 people, mostly young men, were imprisoned for offenses related to the Troubles, many with multiple life sentences for their crimes.[134] Other data suggest that number could be as high as 40,000, meaning that ex-prisoners make up around 23.6% of the Northern Irish male cohort 50–59 years of age and around 6.8% of the 60–69 years age cohort.[135] The vast majority of those imprisoned for conflict-related offenses and affiliated with organizations on ceasefire have been released under the Good Friday Agreement. The release was not a total amnesty, pardon, or gesture of impunity; rather it was conditional, with each prisoner receiving a license which could be revoked if they rejoined a proscribed organization or supported terrorist activity of any sort. Between 1998 and 2007, 449 prisoners qualified for release under the Sentence Review Commission and only 16 had their license revoked—a remarkably low recidivism rate.[136] Of those 449 prisoners, all had served between 67% and 72% of the time they would have served without early release.[137]

Many ex-prisoners have gone on to productive careers in government, education, or community work. Many, however, remain, in the words of one interviewee, "caught up in the struggle" and "unable to cope with peace." They are perpetually tagged as "ex-prisoners" or "former combatants," unable to redefine a life defined by that one identity. One former loyalist political prisoner told me: "If I ever cure cancer, the headline would still read 'Ex-Prisoner Cures Cancer.'" Ex-prisoners are crippled by policies and practices barring them from public-sector jobs, insurance, borrowing money from banks, or even travel to foreign countries. I learned early, for instance, that invitations to former political prisoners to participate in international conferences or as guest speakers on international university campuses were empty gestures—most would never receive the necessary security clearance to travel to those events. In some instances, the children, or even grandchildren, of former political prisoners are blocked from certain jobs. For example, Tom Roberts, director of a loyalist ex-prisoners center in Belfast, said: "We have people who cannot join the British Army because of something their grandfather did 40 years ago."[138] Similarly, republican ex-prisoners have difficulty passing the security checks required for many employment opportunities.

As a result, an estimated 40% of republican ex-prisoners and 30% of loyalist ex-prisoners are unemployed, about four times the rate of general unemployment in Northern Ireland.[139] Many take on the nebulous moniker of "community activist," making important contributions to peace and fostering mutual understanding through community organizations. These community organizations are particularly strong in Catholic neighborhoods where, historically, such organizations were necessary due to the lack of state involvement in those areas. Conversely, in Protestant neighborhoods, community organizations are relatively immature and are still evolving because Protestants could always assume the state would protect their areas. Others return to their community intent on reinforcing the deep identity divisions that were at the heart of the conflict, and some even find their way back into criminal activity, often through the conduit of clandestinely rejoining a paramilitary organization. As one unionist politician told me, the return to paramilitary activity is particularly enticing for loyalist ex-prisoners "because the paramilitary groups provide a place for esteem and affirmation that the ex-prisoners do not get from their local community, or elected officials, who most often treat them with disgust and disdain." This is in direct contrast to the heroic and warm reception generally received by republican ex-prisoners in nationalist communities and accorded them by nationalist politicians.

Despite the relatively high numbers of non-state actors prosecuted for crimes during the Troubles, however, there still remain people and communities anxiously waiting for justice to be delivered. For many, it still galls that, from 1999 on, former UK Prime Minister Tony Blair, to secure the ongoing peace process, gave about 200 IRA fugitives (colloquially known as "on the runs") written assurances they would not be arrested based on "evidence currently available."[140] Still today, anyone, on either side, convicted of a Troubles-related offense that occurred between 1973 and 1998, even if the offense includes multiple murders, will, under the Northern Ireland (Sentences) Act 1998, only serve a maximum of two years in prison. "A sentence so disproportionate to the crime," writes columnist Fintan O'Toole, "that it may be seen as devaluing, rather than honouring, the life of the victim."[141]

The threat of conviction for some of the most notorious offenses is not exactly a looming one. No one has ever been arrested or convicted, for instance, for the loyalist paramilitary bombings in Dublin and Monaghan in the Republic of Ireland on May 17, 1974. Similarly, no one has been brought to justice for the 1998 Real IRA attack in Omagh. In May 2019, counsel for one of the Omagh victim's families—believing enough intelligence existed from British security agents, MI5, and RUC officers to have prevented the bombing—appeared in the High Court of Northern Ireland to challenge the British government's refusal to hold a public inquiry. The counsel is requesting a public inquiry under Article 2 ("everyone's right to life shall be protected by law") of the ECHR. As of this writing, the case continues. September 2019 saw unionists renewing calls to extradite former priest Patrick Ryan, having publicly confessed to having a senior role in the IRA and providing financing for weapons and explosives, from Ireland to the UK to face justice. In February 2020, Alan Black, the sole survivor of the 1976 Kingsmill massacre in which 10 Protestant workmen were gunned down by suspected IRA men, rued he had "no confidence in the process" of justice as, 44 years on, no one had been convicted of the murders. Black said: "We were promised back in the day openness and transparency. It has become just the opposite. I am sick about it."[142] Most recently, in November 2020, the British government announced it would not be granting a public inquiry into the killing of Patrick Finucane, a high-profile Belfast human rights lawyer murdered by UDA gunmen in 1989.

In addition, there are 16 known cases of individuals who are thought to have been abducted, tortured, murdered, and secretly buried by republican paramilitary groups during the Troubles. Most were accused of being informers, stealing weapons, or being undercover British agents. Known as the "Disappeared," the remains of 13 victims have been recovered to date. Three men—Joseph Lynskey, British solider Robert Nairac, and Columba McVeigh—remain missing.[143] While the IRA have admitted to responsibility for 13 of the victims, and the Irish National Liberation Army (INLA) have accepted responsibility for one, families of the victims "have received no apology for the murders of their loved ones, no account of what happened to them, no opportunity to clear their names and certainly no justice."[144] Indeed, the confidential tips given to the Independent Commission for the Location of Victims Remains, leading to the discovery of most of the Disappeared, are not admissible in criminal prosecutions. As a result, this grants a de facto amnesty for those who carried out the killings.

In terms of state actors, the justice gap related to the Troubles is noticeably more pronounced. As one republican interviewee asserted: "They want to prosecute ours but you can't prosecute theirs." In truth, since 1998, only four former British soldiers have been convicted of illegally killing civilians while on duty. Originally given life sentences, all four were freed after just five years through the use of the "Royal Prerogative of Mercy." Upon release, all were allowed to rejoin the British Army.[145] The long-running inquest into the 1971 Ballymurphy massacre has yet to yield any prosecutions of security forces. To date, the only relief, albeit a darkly comic one, for families of the Ballymurphy victims has been General Sir Mike Jackson's insistence that the British Army "don't do conspiracies."[146] The few inquiries that are held "tend to centre on soldiers at the bottom of the chain of military command; they have concentrated on uniformed soldiers rather than plain clothes operations; killings carried out by British agents and informers within paramilitary groups are likely to be blocked by 'security considerations.'"[147] Clearly, impunity for security forces remains the rule rather than the exception.

The focal point of the justice gap for state actors remains the prosecution, or relative lack thereof, of security forces involved in Bloody Sunday. In 1972, the day after the killings, a tribunal was appointed by the UK government to hold an inquiry into the "loss of life in connection with the procession in Londonderry." The subsequent report, known as the Widgery Report, fully exonerated British soldiers and held those who organized the "illegal march" as responsible for creating a "highly dangerous situation" in which violence "was almost inevitable."[148] The scant 36-page report, refusing to take evidence from the vast majority of civilian eyewitnesses and hurriedly published 11 weeks after Bloody Sunday, was immediately denounced by nationalists and republicans as an utter whitewash. Families of the victims, undeterred, began the Sisyphean task of pursuing justice and accountability for those who had murdered their loved ones. Finally, in 2010, 38 years after Bloody Sunday, a 5,000-page 10-volume report from a 12-year tribunal conducted by Lord Saville (commonly referred to as the Bloody Sunday Inquiry), fully exonerated the victims and unequivocally concluded the shootings were "unjustified."[149] In a landmark moment, televised live and aired to a large crowd at Derry's Guildhall Square, including families of those who were killed and wounded on Bloody Sunday, Prime Minister David Cameron issued a formal state apology without qualification: "There is no doubt, there is nothing equivocal, there are no ambiguities. What happened on Bloody Sunday was both unjustified and unjustifiable. It was wrong."[150]

The Bloody Sunday Inquiry did not make any recommendations about prosecutions, and Cameron sidestepped the issue by saying that any decision regarding prosecution should be made independent of the report.[151] So, while the facts were now established, accountability would be and still is slow in coming. In 2017, seven years after the inquiry, the Public Prosecution Service (PPS) for Northern Ireland began considering whether to bring charges against 18 soldiers of the Parachute Regiment over their involvement in Bloody Sunday (four other soldiers under criminal consideration already had died) as well as two members of the Official IRA. The various charges included murder and attempted murder, wounding, perjury, and joint enterprise (meaning an offense where two or more people are involved).[152]

In March 2019, the PPS finally announced that only one former British soldier—Soldier F—would be prosecuted in connection with Bloody Sunday. Soldier F, now in his sixties, stands to be prosecuted for the murder of James Wray and William McKinney and for the attempted murders of Joseph Friel, Michael Quinn, Joe Mahon, Patrick O'Donnell, and a person or persons unknown. Other than that, however, the PPS could find no reasonable prospect of criminal conviction for the other 16 soldiers still alive (Soldier N died in January 2019) nor for the two members of the Official IRA.[153] Lawyers for the Bloody Sunday families, many of whom were broken with disappointment over the announcement, asked for a formal review of the PPS decision not to prosecute other former soldiers. On September 29, 2020, the PPS upheld its

March 2019 decision that only Soldier F would be prosecuted in connection with Bloody Sunday. As of this writing, families of the victims are considering applying for a judicial review in the High Court of Northern Ireland. As one family member told me: "We'll never be whole until the truth is told."

Since the announcement of his prosecution, t-shirts expressing solidarity with Soldier F have been sold on Amazon, Parachute Regiment flags and banners reading "Our Soldiers Are Heroes Not Criminals" have appeared in towns throughout Northern Ireland, and Parachute Regiment emblems have been displayed in parades—including a highly publicized, and politicized, August 2019 Apprentice Boys parade in Derry where one flute band displayed Parachute Regiment insignias on their sleeves. In response, a bonfire in a nationalist neighborhood of Derry was festooned with loyalist and unionist flags and Parachute Regiment regalia, including a sign reading "Burn in Hell Soldier F and All Loyalist Scum that Support Him." In counter-response, veteran advocacy groups such as the Northern Ireland Crown Forces Veterans for Justice, Paras Fight Back, and the Justice for Northern Ireland Veterans Original have ramped up their efforts to stop historical investigations against security force veterans of Northern Ireland.

In June 2020, the committal hearing for Soldier F was adjourned due to the ongoing COVID-19 pandemic. Once the case is listed again, it is expected, due to security concerns, that the eventual trial would be held in Belfast. In response, Mickey McKinney, whose brother William was shot dead, said: "What happened on Bloody Sunday happened here 200 yards from where we now stand and Soldier F should be appearing at this courthouse."[154] When, and wherever, he is tried, the UK government has pledged to offer full legal support to Soldier F, including bearing the costs of his defense.

Soldier F's case, as well as ongoing cases against other former soldiers, highlights the deep cleavages over the degree to which former security force personnel (including soldiers and police) who served during the Troubles should be held responsible for any criminal action.[155] In the foreword of the document launching the "Addressing the Legacy of Northern Ireland's Past" consultation process, MP Karen Bradley, then Secretary of State for Northern Ireland, made clear her government's long-standing position of not drawing equivalence between "terrorists" and state security forces: "This Government will never forget the huge debt of gratitude we owe to our Armed Forces and Police Officers. Over 250,000 people served in Northern Ireland during Operation Banner, the longest continuous military deployment in our country's history, the vast majority with great distinction. More than 3,500 people lost their lives during the Troubles, including over 1,000 members of the security forces. We will always salute the heroism and courage they displayed in upholding democracy and the rule of law in Northern Ireland. A Conservative Government will reject any attempts to rewrite the history of the past that seeks to justify or legitimise republican or loyalist terrorism or which seeks to displace responsibility from the people who perpetrated acts of terrorism."[156] Though she later issued a full apology, Bradley publicly stated that killings by the security forces during the Troubles cannot be classified as crimes. This belief was echoed by former head of the British Army, General Lord Dannatt: "Soldiers did their duty, got up in the morning, sometimes they came under attack. They returned fire. They didn't set out to murder people. Terrorists set out every morning to murder people and successfully did so. There is a huge distinction to be drawn."[157]

Humming the same tune, other senior government figures at Westminster have argued for, if not a statute of limitations or outright amnesty, at least legal protection from "witch hunts" against former security forces personnel involved in Troubles-related matters. Former British Defence Secretary Penny Mordaunt, for instance, wanted to create a "statutory presumption against prosecution" of current or former military personnel for alleged offenses committed in the course of duty abroad more than 10 years ago since, in her opinion, such prosecutions are not in the public interest unless there are "exceptional circumstances." Originally intended to cover wars in Iraq and Afghanistan, Mordaunt publicly stated that she also supported extending coverage to Northern Ireland.[158] Supporters of such legislation point out that, in the peace process, concessions were given to paramilitaries, such as early release from prison and letters of comfort to "on the run" fugitives assuring them they would not face prosecution. A bit unconvincingly, they maintain that halting or ending legal cases involving former security forces would help Northern Ireland move forward rather than get pulled back into the past. On the first full day following his appointment as UK Prime Minister in late July 2019, Boris Johnson agreed that the prosecution of veterans over their conduct during the Troubles has "got to stop" unless there was "compelling evidence" that criminal offenses had been committed.[159] This position was later affirmed by the new British Defence Secretary, Ben Wallace, himself a former soldier in the north of Ireland: "We've got to treat our veterans properly. We're not going to have this endless fishing inquest circle that's gone round and round in circles and not actually fixed the problem."[160] Most recently, one of the core tenets of the UK Secretary of State's legacy proposals focused on ensuring that ex-soldiers in Northern Ireland "receive equal treatment to their counterparts who served overseas."[161]

In contrast, nationalist politicians and human rights activists counter that a uniform should be no shield from prosecution for criminal acts. No one should be above, beyond, or past the rule of law and that to do so is to give a blank check to security forces for crimes they might commit. A clear majority of the respondents in the 2018 "Addressing the Legacy of Northern Ireland's Past" consultation opposed amnesty for crimes committed by former security force personnel during the Troubles. "Many were clear that victims, survivors and families are entitled to pursue criminal justice outcomes and such a move [allowing a statute of limitations or amnesty for former security forces] could risk progress towards reconciliation."[162] Similarly, Colonel John Wilson, in reviewing the book *Lost Lives* for the *British Army Review*, argued that there can only be one response for those soldiers who acted unlawfully during the Troubles: "punishment after due process of law." "To act otherwise," he continued, "is at best a grotesquely misplaced sense of loyalty and at worst it is complicit and criminal."[163] Taking a slightly different tack, but ending at the same place, some organizations representing former security forces in the 2018 consultation "argued against any type of statute of limitations or amnesty for former soldiers and police—they felt those they represented would have no difficulty in answering for their actions and would wish to see terrorist organisations and their members being held accountable. In addition, they felt that granting blanket immunity from prosecution could create a misleading impression of moral equivalence between security forces and terrorists."[164]

A family member of an IRA man killed by state security forces told me: "Justice is not about going after the soldiers, but about the system. Holding the state accountable for what they allowed." She is absolutely right in recognizing that the proactive duty and accountability to protect all human rights without discrimination and implement related laws lies first and foremost with states. This includes the translation of human rights treaties and the enactment of them in national legislation, training judicial and security sector personnel in human rights and laws, the dissemination of human rights texts and information, and engagement with regional and international organizations to promote and protect human rights.[165] In addition, however, there also is a need for accountability for collusion between British state institutions in Northern Ireland and loyalist paramilitaries. As historian Ugur Umit Ungor writes, much of this "collusion was more insidious, and included such actions as passing on security information, diverting law enforcement away from loyalist crimes, failing to provide protection to threatened persons, failing to investigate loyalist killings, and providing firearms to loyalists." [166] Its direct impact on the conflict, though, was anything but insidious and must be addressed as part of the contemporary urgency of attending to a conflicted past.

Conclusion

In an 1882 lecture titled "What Is a Nation," French historian Ernest Renan said: "The essence of a nation is that all of its individual members have a great deal in common and also that they have forgotten many things. . . . Forgetting, I would even say historical error, is an essential factor in the creation of a nation. . . . A nation is a soul, a spiritual principle. Two things which, properly speaking, are really one and the same constitute this soul, this spiritual principle. One is the past, the other is the present. One is the possession in common of a rich legacy of memories; the other is present consent, the desire to live together, the desire to continue to invest in the heritage that we have jointly received."[167]

Ninety years later, Renan's concern with the legacy of memory would be echoed in the work of an iconoclastic Belfast born-and-bred poet. The opening stanza of John Hewitt's oft-cited "Neither an Elegy nor a Manifesto," written in 1972, is a powerful reminder that memory and the word "remember" carries a barbed pain in the context of Northern Ireland's Troubles.

> *Bear in mind these dead:*
> *I can find no plainer words.*
> *I dare not risk using*
> *That loaded word, Remember . . .*[168]

That loaded word. Remember. Nearly 50 years after Hewitt penned that poem for the people of his province, "remember" remains a loaded word in contemporary Northern Ireland. "Remember" is a transitive verb; an action with a direct object. In Northern Ireland, as a friend told me on a late-night bus ride from Derry to Belfast through the Sperrin Mountains, you remember "at" someone. When "remember" is wielded, it is done so to wound and, perhaps, even to maim. To remember is not to forget. And while it is debatable how much the two sides of the sectarian divide in contemporary Northern Ireland realize they have in common, there is no debate over the fact that they have not forgotten many things. They remember very well. In fact, things are never forgotten because they are always being remembered. And it is those contested acts of remembering that have always interfered, and continued to interfere, in Renan's words, with the "present consent" to live together in a heritage "jointly received."

In a post-conflict society, the legacy of memory is a palpable part of the lived experience. To be sure, a post-conflict society can have the weight of too much memory. As one local told me with a note of exhaustion in her voice: "I wish I could live in a place with no memory. History is always dragging us back here." Such tyranny of memory nurtures persistent beliefs of victimization and injustice that leave a post-conflict society hostage to its past. In cults of remembrance, the past is wielded in ways that entrench the deep divisions of "us" and "them." If slights are buried, they are buried under very shallow layers of memory and can easily be disinterred. Similar to what James Baldwin described in his 1953 essay recounting his experiencing of being black in an all-white Swiss village, "people are trapped in history and history is trapped in them."[169] Memories of difference and division are destructive and deformative seeds that can be sown for future conflict and, as former UN High Commissioner for Human Rights Zeid Ra'ad Al Hussein warned, are "vulnerable to any misguided individual with charisma and leadership skills able to exploit and abuse lingering historical grievances for political ends in a way that revives historical hatreds to create new challenges to international peace and security."[170] Similarly, in her reflections on communism, Croatian writer Slavenka Drakulic wrote: "I came to the conclusion that we did not have 'too much history,' as it is often said about this part of the world. Rather we had too much memory and too many myths. And, in my life experience, this is a dangerous combination that has often resulted in ideology and manipulation leading to conflict and terrible suffering."[171]

The crushing weight of having too much memory, however, should not be taken as an argument for forgetting or collective amnesia. Contrary to journalist David Rieff's assertion, there is no "ethical imperative of forgetting" in a post-conflict society.[172] Nor, as essayist Lewis Hyde more recently argues, is forgetting some type of magical balm that leads to collective peace and reconciliation.[173] Rather, a post-conflict society leaves itself at risk by having too little memory. In Vladimir Putin's Russia, for example, things have not been forgotten because they have never been remembered in the first place.[174] Forgetting is not an acceptable, or even possible, response to violent intergroup conflict. Forced amnesia, however secure it appears on the surface, leaves a deep societal insecurity. The push and pull of memory remain potent, even when spoken of only in whispers. In this assault of organized forgetting, wounds left untended and unacknowledged can prove crippling with time.

We know, however, that there is a middle road between memory as debilitatingly divisive or paralyzingly avoided. Memory can be used constructively rather than destructively. Social solidarities can be extended rather than bounded; they can be reconfigured in ways to reduce, rather than exacerbate, the historical tensions and the resulting ideologies of antagonism behind them. Memory can promote a sense of community and social cohesion. A "healthy memory environment" allows for a right to truth in order to understand history, a space for contestation of differing interpretations of memory, the recognition of memory as both a public and private phenomenon, and an acknowledgment that memory is intrinsic to the formation of community and identity. Such an environment, recognizing the impossibility of many different people sharing a common mind, embraces strategies that can "shift a population towards deeper understanding, and potentially reconciliation, in both private and public spheres" of memory.[175] In April 2020, a group of Catholic bishops in Northern Ireland, challenging the UK Secretary of State on his recently released legacy proposals, wrote: "Real reconciliation means that we cannot forget the past. We must face the past, no matter how costly or painful that encounter may be, before real reconciliation can flourish."[176]

Indeed, dealing with the past means risking costly or painful vulnerability at both the individual and collective and institutional levels. As individuals, the work of memory is questioning ourselves as human beings, not just reflecting on an entangled past. As collectives, memory can aid in the building of resilience; the returning to a prior, or even better, form. As institutions, memory can help us adapt, debate, innovate, and try new approaches as we reconstruct a society torn apart by conflict. The violent past and present does not have to be visited on the children's future; their tomorrows do not have to be echoes of our yesterdays.

In contemporary Northern Ireland, ironically, perhaps it is in the very ashes of the conflict itself, a shared experience, where resilience and hope can be found. As Eamon McCann, a socialist civil rights activist from die-hard republican Derry, admits, he has discovered "an acceptance of

Northern Irishness. It's an acceptance of the fact that I think that we in Northern Ireland have shared an experience. We shared an experience which we're well aware people in the South did not share with us and don't understand."[177]

Notes

1. David Robson, "The Blessing and the Curse of the People Who Never Forget," *BBC Future* (January 26, 2016), accessed on January 30, 2020, at https://www.bbc.com/future/article/20160125-the-blessing-and-curse-of-the-people-who-never-forget

2. Jonathan Bardon, *A History of Ulster* (Belfast: Blackstaff Press, new updated edition, 2005), xiii.

3. "The past is a foreign country: they do things differently there" is the opening line of L. P. Hartley's *The Go-Between*, first published in 1953.

4. Alex Kane, "The Past Is Where We Go When There Is No Agreement on the Present or Future," *The Irish News* (December 1, 2017), accessed on June 7, 2019, at http://www.irishnews.com/opinion/columnists/2017/12/01/news/alex-kane-the-past-is-where-we-go-when-there-is-no-agreement-on-the-present-or-future-1199829/

5. Paul Nolan, *The Northern Ireland Peace Monitoring Report, Number Two* (Belfast: Community Relations Council, 2013), 166.

6. Jonathan Safran Foer, *Everything Is Illuminated* (New York: Harper Perennial, 2002), 198.

7. Dan Stone, "Genocide and Memory," in Donald Bloxham and A. Dirk Moses (eds.), *The Oxford Handbook of Genocide Studies* (New York: Oxford University Press, 2010), 118.

8. The defining characteristics of an assumptive world are taken from Joan Beder, "Loss of the Assumptive World—How We Deal with Death and Loss," *Omega* 50 (2004–2005), 255–265; quoted material comes from Ron Eyerman, *Cultural Trauma: Slavery and the Formation of African American Identity* (New York: Cambridge University Press, 2002), 2.

9. Eyerman, *Cultural Trauma*, 6.

10. David Lowenthal, "Fabricating Heritage," *History and Memory* 10 (1) (1998), 7–8.

11. Victor Roudometof, *Collective Memory, National Identity, and Ethnic Conflict: Greece, Bulgaria, and the Macedonian Question* (Westport, CT: Praeger, 2002), 7.

12. Accessed at https://valis79.wordpress.com/2013/05/20/andreas-huyssen-twilight-memories-pt-1/ on January 24, 2020. See also Huyssen's *Twilight Memories: Marking Time in a Culture of Amnesia* (London: Routledge, 2012).

13. Lowenthal, "Fabricating Heritage," 8.

14. Pierre Nora, "Between Memory and History: Les Lieux de Mémoire," *Representations* 26 (1989), 8.

15. Ronald J. Berger, *The Holocaust, Religion, and the Politics of Collective Memory* (New Brunswick, NJ: Transaction, 2012), 22.

16. George Orwell, *1984*, accessed on June 22, 2015, at http://www.planetebook.com/ebooks/1984.pdf, 44.
17. Michael Kammen, *Mystic Chords of Memory: The Transformation of Tradition in American Culture* (New York: Vintage Books, 1991), 3.
18. Quoted material comes from James E. Young, *The Texture of Memory: Holocaust Memorials and Meaning* (New Haven, CT: Yale University Press, 1993), 2.
19. Katherine Conway, "The Role of Memory in Post-Genocide Rwanda," accessed on June 22, 2015, at http://www.insightonconflict.org/2013/08/the-role-of-memory-in-post-genocide-rwanda/
20. Peter Novick, *The Holocaust in American Life* (New York: Houghton Mifflin, 1999), 261.
21. Jill Lepore, *This America: The Case for the Nation* (New York: Liveright, 2019), 15, 19–20.
22. Peter Winn, "'Without Yesterday There Is No Tomorrow': Ricardo Lagos and Chile's Democratic Transition," accessed on June 21, 2015, at http://www.asanet.org/footnotes/feb07/indexone.html
23. Quoted material in this paragraph from Ervin Staub, "The Psychology of Bystanders, Perpetrators, and Heroic Helpers," in Leonard S. Newman and Ralph Erber (eds.), *Understanding Genocide: The Social Psychology of the Holocaust* (New York: Oxford University Press, 2002), 30.
24. Walter G. Stephan, Oscar Ybarra, and Kimberly Rios Morrison, "Intergroup Threat Theory," in Todd D. Nelson (ed.), *Handbook of Prejudice, Stereotyping, and Discrimination* (New York: Psychology Press, 2009), 43.
25. Walter G. Stephan and Cookie White Stephan, "Intergroup Threat Theory," in Young Yun Kim (ed.), *The International Encyclopedia of Intercultural Communication* (Hoboken, NJ: John Wiley & Sons, 2018), 1499.
26. For an interesting review of intergroup threat from a neuroscience perspective, see Linda W. Chang, Amy R. Krosch, and Mina Cikara, "Effects of Intergroup Threat on Mind, Brain, and Behavior," *Current Opinion in Psychology* (2016), 69–73.
27. Stephan, Ybarra, and Morrison, "Intergroup Threat Theory," 54.
28. "They haven't gone away you know" is a well-known phrase taken from a 1995 speech by Gerry Adams at a large republican rally outside Belfast City Hall. Adams used the phrase in response to a heckler who said: "Bring back the IRA."
29. Walter G. Stephan and C. Lausanne Renfro, "The Role of Threat in Intergroup Relations," in D. M. Mackie and E. R. Smith (eds.), *From Prejudice to Inter-Group Emotions: Differentiated Reactions to Social Groups* (London: Psychology Press, 2016), 198.
30. Miriam Berger, "Israel's Hugely Controversial 'Nation-State' Law, Explained" (July 31, 2018), accessed on July 12, 2019, at https://www.vox.com/world/2018/7/31/17623978/israel-jewish-nation-state-law-bill-explained-apartheid-netanyahu-democracy
31. *News Letter*, "Irish Language Phone Service Has Never Been Used in 11 Years" (October 1, 2017), accessed on April 7, 2020, at https://www.newsletter.co.uk/news/irish-language-phone-service-has-never-been-used-11-years-1077323
32. "Sinn Fein to Continue Campaign for Irish Language Act During Stormont Talks," *Belfast Telegraph* (May 31, 2019), accessed on July 14, 2019, at https://www.belfasttelegraph.co.uk/news/northern-ireland/sinn-fein-to-continue-campaign-for-irish-language-act-during-stormont-talks-38168054.html

33. The "New Decade, New Approach" deal was accessed on June 5, 2020, at https://assets.publishing.service.gov.uk/government/uploads/system/uploads/attachment_data/file/856998/2020-01-08_a_new_decade__a_new_approach.pdf Quoted material is taken from p. 15.

34. Stephan, Ybarra, and Morrison, "Intergroup Threat Theory," 43.

35. Cited in Marc Lacey, "A Decade After Massacres, Rwanda Outlaws Ethnicity," *The New York Times* (April 9, 2004), accessed on July 15, 2019, at https://www.nytimes.com/2004/04/09/world/a-decade-after-massacres-rwanda-outlaws-ethnicity.html

36. See, for instance, Helen Hintjens, "Post-Genocide Identity Politics in Rwanda," *Ethnicities* 8 (2008), 5–41.

37. The full text of the Good Friday Agreement is accessible at https://www.gov.uk/government/publications/the-belfast-agreement

38. Cited in Mark Carruthers, *Alternative Ulsters: Conversations on Identity* (Dublin: Liberties Press, 2013), 9–10.

39. All 2011 census data in this paragraph taken from https://www.nisra.gov.uk/publications/2011-census-detailed-characteristics-northern-ireland-identity-religion-and-health, accessed on March 31, 2019.

40. Accessed on June 18, 2020, at https://www.ark.ac.uk/nilt/2019/Community_Relations/NINATID.html

41. See Kevin McNicholl, Clifford Stevenson, and John Garry, "How the 'Northern Irish' National Identity Is Understood and Used by Young People and Politicians," *Political Psychology* (2018), 1–19.

42. James Waller, *Confronting Evil: Engaging Our Responsibility to Prevent Genocide* (New York: Oxford University Press, 2016), 21–22.

43. Barbara Harff and T. R. Gurr, "Toward Empirical Theory of Genocides and Politicides: Identification and Measurement of Cases Since 1945," *International Studies Quarterly* 37 (1988), 357–371.

44. Barbara Harff, "No Lessons Learned from the Holocaust?: Assessing Risks of Genocide and Political Mass Murder since 1955," *American Political Science Review* 97 (2003), 66.

45. Charles R. Butcher et al., "Understanding and Forecasting Political Instability and Genocide for Early Warning" (2012), 15; accessed on July 16, 2019, at http://politicsir.cass.anu.edu.au/research/projects/atrocity-forecasting/publications.   See   also the more recent piece by Benjamin E. Goldsmith and Charles Butcher, "Genocide Forecasting: Past Accuracy and New Forecasts to 2020," *Journal of Genocide Research* 20 (2018), 90–107.

46. See, for instance, Nicolas Rost, "Will It Happen Again? On the Possibility of Forecasting the Risk of Genocide," *Journal of Genocide Research* 15 (2013), 50.

47. Robbie McVeigh, " 'The Balance of Cruelty:' Ireland, Britain and the Logic of Genocide," *Journal of Genocide Research* (2008), 543.

48. See, for instance, Roxanne Dunbar-Ortiz, *An Indigenous People's History of the United States* (Boston: Beacon Press, 2014), 6–10.

49. See, for instance, Hannah Arendt's conception of the "boomerang thesis" in her classic *The Origins of Totalitarianism* (New York: Schocken Books, 1951).

50. McVeigh, " 'The Balance of Cruelty,' " 550–551.

51. For competing perspectives on the question of whether the Great Hunger was a case of genocide, see Tim Pat Coogan's *The Famine Plot: England's Role in Ireland's Greatest Tragedy* (New York: St. Martin's Press, 2012) and Mark G. McGowan's "*The Famine Plot* Revisited: A Reassessment of the Great Irish Famine as Genocide," *Genocide Studies International* (2017), 87–104. In addition, genocide claims have more recently made news in Ireland following the discovery of a mass grave of some of the nearly 800 "illegitimate" children who died at the former Bon Secours (aka St. Mary's) Mother and Baby Home (1925–1961) in Tuam, County Galway.

52. Lyrics taken from https://songmeanings.com/songs/view/3530822107858491828/, accessed on August 5, 2019.

53. McVeigh, "'The Balance of Cruelty,'" 551–552.

54. See Max Koch, "Preventing Genocide in Chile and Northern Ireland: The Role of the Elites," *International Journal of Contemporary Sociology* 39 (2002), 283–298.

55. See Uppsala Conflict Data Program (UCDP) at https://www.pcr.uu.se/research/ucdp/definitions/#Warring_party_2, accessed on July 16, 2019.

56. Cited in Eamon Lynch, *Golfweek* (July 16, 2019), accessed on July 22, 2019, at https://golfweek.com/2019/07/15/golf-open-championship-portrush-northern-ireland/

57. Ibid.

58. Ian O'Connor, "Rory McIlroy, Two Irelands and a Complicated Homecoming" (July 16, 2019), accessed on July 16, 2019, at https://www.espn.com/golf/story/_/id/27194734/rory-mcilroy-two-irelands-complicated-open-homecoming

59. The phrase "loss of memory of harm" is taken from Mark Daly, Pat Dolan, and Mark Brennan, "Northern Ireland Returning to Violence" (2019), 23, accessible at https://senatormarkdaly.files.wordpress.com/2019/02/unesco-chairs-report-brexit-return-to-violence.pdf

60. Ed O'Loughlin and Richard Perez-Pena, "Lyra McKee, Northern Ireland Journalist, Is Killed in 'Terrorist Incident,' Police Say," *The New York Times* (April 19, 2019), accessed on July 17, 2019, at https://www.nytimes.com/2019/04/19/world/europe/lyra-mckee-northern-ireland-violence.html

61. Data taken from Police Service of Northern Ireland, "Domestic Abuse Incidents and Crimes Recorded by the Police in Northern Ireland: Update to 31 December 2019" (February 27, 2020).

62. Jens Meierhenrich, "The Trauma of Genocide," *Journal of Genocide Research* 9 (2007), 549–573.

63. See American Psychiatric Association, *Diagnostic and Statistical Manual of Mental Disorders* 5th ed. (Washington, DC: American Psychiatric Publishing, 2013), 271–272.

64. Summaries of the group's research can be found at https://traumaandhealing.stanford.edu, accessed on February 5, 2015.

65. Bessel van der Kolk, *The Body Keeps the Score: Brain, Mind, and Body in the Healing of Trauma* (New York: Penguin Books, 2015).

66. American Psychiatric Association, *Diagnostic and Statistical Manual of Mental Disorders*, 275.

67. Susan J. Brison, *Aftermath: Violence and the Remaking of a Self* (Princeton, NJ: Princeton University Press, 2002), 40.

68. American Psychiatric Association, *Diagnostic and Statistical Manual of Mental Disorders*, 276.

69. Peter McBride, "Prepared for Peace. Ready for War?," paper presented at a seminar hosted by the Auschwitz Institute for Peace and Reconciliation (November, 2018).

70. Quote taken from Vicky Cosstick, *Belfast: Toward a City Without Walls* (Belfast: Colourpoint, 2015), 97.

71. The first statistic comes from Brendan Bunting, Finola Ferry, Sam Murphy, Siobhan O'Neill, Gerard Leavey, and David Bolton, "Troubled Consequences: A Report on the Mental Health Impact of the Civil Conflict in Northern Ireland" (2011), prepared for the Commission for Victims and Survivors by the Bamford Centre for Mental Health and Wellbeing at the University of Ulster in partnership with the Northern Ireland Centre for Trauma and Transformation and Compass, accessed on June 1, 2020, at https://www.cvsni.org/media/1435/troubled-consequences-october-2011.pdf; the second statistic is taken from Siobhan O' Neill, Cherie Armour, David Bolton, Brendan Bunting, Colette Corry, Barney Devine, Edel Ennis, Finola Ferry, Aine McKenna, Margaret McLafferty, and Sam Murphy, "Towards a Better Future: The Trans-Generational Impact of the Troubles on Mental Health" (March 2015), prepared for the Commission for Victims and Survivors by Ulster University, accessed on June 1, 2020, at https://www.cvsni.org/media/1171/towards-a-better-future-march-2015.pdf

72. "Post Traumatic Stress Disorder Highest in Northern Ireland," *BBC News* (December 5, 2011), accessed on July 23, 2019, at https://www.bbc.com/news/uk-northern-ireland-16028713

73. David Bolton, *Conflict, Peace and Mental Health: Addressing the Consequences of Conflict and Trauma in Northern Ireland* (Manchester: Manchester University Press, 2017).

74. Jennifer Betts and Janice Thompson, "Mental Health in Northern Ireland: Overviews, Strategies, Policies, Care Pathways, CAMHS and Barriers to Accessing Services" (January 2017), accessed on July 22, 2019, at http://www.niassembly.gov.uk/globalassets/documents/raise/publications/2016-2021/2017/health/0817.pdf

75. Lyra McKee, "Suicide Among the Ceasefire Babies," *The Atlantic* (January 20, 2016), accessed on July 23, 2019, at https://www.theatlantic.com/health/archive/2016/01/conflict-mental-health-northern-ireland-suicide/424683/

76. Claire Simpson, "Suicide Rate for Young People in Northern Ireland More than Twice That of England," *The Irish News* (March 5, 2020), accessed on March 29, 2020, at http://www.irishnews.com/news/northernirelandnews/2020/03/05/news/suicide-rate-for-young-people-in-northern-ireland-more-than-twice-that-of-england-1858622

77. Prescription rate information comes from comments made by criminologist Gillian McNaull on March 8, 2017, during a panel presentation at Queen's University Belfast. See also "Northern Ireland 'One of World's Highest Rates for Anti-Depressants,'" *BBC News* (November 16, 2014), accessed on July 23, 2019, at https://www.bbc.com/news/uk-northern-ireland-30073669. The 2011 report for the Commission for Victims and Survivors, "Troubled Consequences: A Report on the Mental Health Impact of the Civil Conflict in Northern Ireland," held that Northern Ireland had the highest rates of PTSD in the world.

78. Commission for Victims and Survivors, "Towards a Better Future," 105.

79. Ibid., 15.

80. Cited in Betts and Thompson, "Mental Health in Northern Ireland," 10.

81. Commission for Victims and Survivors, "Towards a Better Future," 13.

82. Jeffrey C. Alexander, "Toward a Theory of Cultural Trauma," in Jeffrey C. Alexander, Ron Eyerman, Bernard Giesen, Neil J. Smelser, and Piotr Sztompka (eds.), *Cultural Trauma and Collective Identity* (Berkeley: University of California Press, 2004), 1.

83. Meierhenrich, "The Trauma of Genocide," 554.

84. Peter McBride, "Northern Ireland: The Mental Health Legacy" (2017), unpublished paper.

85. Alexander, "Toward a Theory of Cultural Trauma," 8, 10.

86. Ibid., 8.

87. Commission for Victims and Survivors, "Towards a Better Future," 105.

88. Bill Rolston has published four volumes of his political mural photographs (many of the murals are no longer in existence) under the main title *Drawing Support* and each volume (1992, 1988, 2003, and 2013) has been published by Beyond the Pale in Belfast. More information can be found at www.billrolston.weebly.com.

89. Bill Rolston, *Drawing Support: Murals in the North of Ireland* (Belfast: Beyond the Pale, 1992, reprinted in 2010), ii.

90. Ibid., iv.

91. Ibid.

92. Brian Feeney, "Travel Guide Got It Right on Loyalist Murals," *The Irish News* (June 19, 2019), accessed on July 23, 2019, at http://www.irishnews.com/opinion/columnists/2019/06/19/news/brian-feeney-travel-guide-got-it-right-on-loyalist-murals-1643994

93. Quoted in Maximilian Rapp and Markus Rhomberg, "Seeking a Neutral Identity in Northern Ireland's Political Wall Paintings," *Peace Review: A Journal of Social Justice* 24 (2012), 475.

94. United Nations, "Framework of Analysis for Atrocity Crimes," 13. English, French, and Spanish texts of the framework can be accessed at https://www.un.org/en/genocideprevention/publications-and-resources.shtml

95. Ervin Staub, *Overcoming Evil: Genocide, Violent Conflict, and Terrorism* (New York: Oxford University Press, 2011), 218–219.

96. Quote taken from Gerry Moriarty, "How the Trauma of the Troubles Risks Being 'Passed On,'" *The Irish Times* (August 7, 2017), accessed on July 23, 2019, at https://www.irishtimes.com/news/ireland/irish-news/how-the-trauma-of-the-troubles-risks-being-passed-on-1.3178681

97. Alexander, "Toward a Theory of Cultural Trauma," 27.

98. Florence Baingana, Ian Bannon, and Rachel Thomas, *Mental Health and Conflict: Conceptual Framework and Approaches* (Washington, DC: World Bank, 2005), 10.

99. McBride, "Northern Ireland: The Mental Health Legacy."

100. See Michael A. Sells, *The Bridge Betrayed: Religion and Genocide in Bosnia* (Berkeley: University of California Press, 1998).

101. Fund for Peace, "CAST: Conflict Assessment Framework" (2014), 7. CAST can be accessed at https://fundforpeace.org/tag/cast.

102. Madeleine Davis, "Is Spain Recovering Its Memory?: Breaking the *Pacto del Olvido*," *Human Rights Quarterly* 27 (2005), 858–880.

103. See, for instance, Sean Brennan, "Sean Brennan Argues for 'Day of Atonement' in Addressing the Past" (November 24, 2013), accessed on August 7, 2019, at http://eamonnmallie.com/2013/11/how-can-we-construct-a-context-in-which-the-truth-can-emerge-in-a-way-that-does-not-build-false-hope-for-the-victims-and-survivors-asks-sean-brennan/

104. For the most recent example of a proposal for a conditional amnesty, see written evidence submitted by John Green and Padraig Yeates to the House of Commons Select Committee on Northern Ireland on May 28, 2020, and available at https://committees.parliament.uk/writtenevidence/5708/pdf/, accessed on June 16, 2020.

105. Kane, "The Past Is Where We Go."

106. Brian Feeney, "We Need to Draw a Line Under the Past, Though Many Won't Agree," *The Irish News* (May 23, 2018), accessed on August 7, 2019, at http://www.irishnews.com/opinion/columnists/2018/05/23/brian-feeney-we-need-to-draw-a-line-under-the-past-though-many-won-t-agree-1335375

107. Dorte Kulle and Brandon Hamber, "Introduction," in Brandon Hamber, Dorte Kulle, and Robin Wilson (eds.), *Future Policies for the Past* (Belfast: Democratic Dialogue, 2001), 10.

108. A copy of the statutory instrument can be found at https://cain.ulster.ac.uk/hmso/vsniorder141106.pdf, accessed on August 5, 2019.

109. BBC News, "DUP Seek Victim Definition Change" (September 15, 2009), accessed on August 5, 2019, at http://news.bbc.co.uk/2/hi/uk_news/northern_ireland/8256468.stm

110. Gareth Cross and David Young, "Foster Demands New Definition of Victim to Exclude Terrorists," *Belfast Telegraph* (March 2, 2019), accessed on August 5, 2019, at https://www.belfasttelegraph.co.uk/news/northern-ireland/foster-demands-new-definition-of-victim-to-exclude-terrorists-37870236.html

111. The 2014 Stormont House Agreement can be accessed at https://www.gov.uk/government/publications/the-stormont-house-agreement

112. The Commission for Victims & Survivors, "Victims and Survivors Pension Arrangement (VASPA) Advice Paper" (May 2019), 7, accessed on August 5, 2019, at https://www.cvsni.org/media/1981/2019-vaspa-advice.pdf

113. Julian Fowler and Jayne McCormack, "Victims' Pension: Troubles Fund 'Rejected if Paramilitaries Eligible,'" (July 17, 2019), accessed on August 5, 2019, at https://www.bbc.com/news/uk-northern-ireland-49009064

114. Quotes taken from "Troubles Victims' Pensions: New Board to Decide Who Qualifies," *BBC News* (January 31, 2020), accessed on February 13, 2020, at https://www.bbc.com/news/uk-northern-ireland-51318297

115. Editor's Viewpoint, "Delay Over Troubles Pension Shames Us," *Belfast Telegraph* (May 22, 2020), accessed on May 26, 2020, at https://www.belfasttelegraph.co.uk/opinion/editors-viewpoint/delay-over-troubles-pension-shames-us-39224909.html

116. The complete text of "The Victims' Payments Regulations 2020" can be found at http://www.legislation.gov.uk/uksi/2020/103/pdfs/uksi_20200103_en.pdf, accessed on February 13, 2020.

117. Allison Morris, "Hundreds of Former Internees Could Get Payouts," *The Irish News* (May 14, 2020), accessed on May 14, 2020, at https://www.irishnews.com/news/2020/05/14/news/hundreds-of-internment-cases-set-to-be-quashed-following-supreme-court-ruling-1937988

118. Allan Preston, "Gerry Adams Court Ruling Will Cause 'Anger and Bewilderment' to IRA's Victims, Says Unionist Politicians," *Belfast Telegraph* (May 14, 2020), accessed on May 15, 2020, at https://www.belfasttelegraph.co.uk/news/northern-ireland/gerry-adams-court-ruling-will-cause-anger-and-bewilderment-to-iras-victims-say-unionist-politicians-39204904.html

119. Data on the Parades Commission can be found at https://www.paradescommission.org.

120. See John Duncan, *Bonfires* (Belfast: Belfast Exposed Photography, 2008).

121. Editor's Viewpoint, "Contentious Bonfires Are Blight on Society," *Belfast Telegraph* (August 9, 2019), accessed on August 9, 2019, at https://www.belfasttelegraph.co.uk/opinion/editors-viewpoint/editors-viewpoint-contentious-bonfires-are-blight-on-society-38387729.html

122. Neil Ferguson, Mark Burgess, and Ian Hollywood, "Who Are the Victims?: Victimhood Experiences in Postagreement Northern Ireland," *Political Psychology* 31 (2010), 881–882.

123. United Nations, "Framework of Analysis," 11.

124. See https://www.gov.uk/government/news/uk-government-sets-out-way-forward-on-the-legacy-of-the-past-in-northern-ireland, accessed on June 5, 2020.

125. Yasmin Ayyad, "With MPs Set to Examine New Legacy Proposals for Northern Ireland, We Hear a Palestinian Perspective," *The Detail* (May 1, 2020), accessed on June 5, 2020, at https://www.thedetail.tv/articles/with-mps-set-to-examine-new-legacy-proposals-for-northern-ireland-we-hear-a-palestinian-perspective?

126. See https://caj.org.uk/2020/04/09/drive-to-achieve-impunity-for-soldiers-risks-legacy-process-in-northern-ireland-according-to-new-report/ (April 9, 2020), accessed on June 5, 2020.

127. Descriptions of the remits of these three offices are taken from Part One of "Addressing the Legacy of Northern Ireland's Past" (May 2018), accessed on April 1, 2020, at https://assets.publishing.service.gov.uk/government/uploads/system/uploads/attachment_data/file/709091/Consultation_Paper_Addressing_the_Legacy_of_Northern_Irelands_Past.pdf

128. Sinead Ingoldsby, "Legacy Issues Not a Priority for People North or South of the Border," *The Detail* (February 25, 2020), accessed on May 22, 2020, at https://www.thedetail.tv/articles/legacy-issues-not-a-priority-for-people-north-or-south-of-the-border?

129. A total of 440 different translations of the UDHR can be found at http://www.ohchr.org/EN/UDHR/Pages/Introduction.aspx, accessed on February 8, 2015.

130. The World Bank, *World Development Report 2011: Conflict, Security, and Development* (Washington, DC: The World Bank, 2011), 82.

131. The degree to which the ECHR remains binding for the UK after its departure from the European Union remains, as of this writing, a point of contestation—despite the Conservative Party's belief that Brexit means a divorce from the ECHR as well as the European Court of Human Rights.

132. The phrase "justice gap" is taken from the International Center for Transitional Justice, *On Solid Ground: Building Sustainable Peace and Development after Massive Human Rights Violations* (May 2019), 1.

133. "Report of the Special Rapporteur on the Promotion of Truth, Justice, Reparation and Guarantees of Non-Recurrence on His Mission to the United Kingdom of Great Britain and Northern Ireland" (November 17, 2017), UN Document A/HRC/34/62/Add.1, 10.

134. See "Employers' Guidance on Recruiting People with Conflict-Related Convictions" (March 2012), accessed on August 9, 2019, at https://www.executiveoffice-ni.gov.uk/publications/employers-guidance-recruiting-people-conflict-related-convictions

135. Ruth Jamison, Peter Shirlow, and Adrian Grounds, *Ageing and Social Exclusion among Former Politically Motivated Prisoners in Northern Ireland* (Belfast: Changing Ageing Partnership, 2010), accessed on June 16, 2020, at https://irishcriminologyresearchnetwork.files.wordpress.com/2010/09/cap-reportfinal-jamieson-et-al.pdf

136. Democratic Progress Institute, "The Good Friday Agreement—Prisoner Release Processes" (London: Democratic Progress Institute, 2013).

137. "Report of the Special Rapporteur," 12.

138. Quote taken from Peter Geoghagen, "Legacy of the Troubles Still Haunts Northern Ireland," accessed on August 7, 2019, at https://www.politico.eu/article/northern-ireland-troubles-legacy-good-friday-agreement/

139. Peter Shirlow, *The State They Are In* (Ulster: University of Ulster, Social Exclusion Unit, 2001).

140. One of the interviewees showed me a copy of their so-called *comfort letter*. They, nearly 20 years after receipt, still kept it in a small safe and checked it every night before bed just so they could sleep peacefully.

141. Fintan O'Toole, "Investigating the Troubles Requires a Hard-Headed Exchange: Truth for Amnesty," *The Irish Times* (June 16, 2020), accessed on June 16, 2020, at https://www.irishtimes.com/opinion/fintan-o-toole-investigating-the-troubles-requires-a-hard-headed-exchange-truth-for-amnesty-1.4279721

142. Mark Edwards, "Sole Survivor of Kingsmill Massacre Alan Black 'Has Lost Confidence' in Inquest Process," *Belfast Telegraph* (February 26, 2020), accessed on March 29, 2020, at https://www.belfasttelegraph.co.uk/news/northern-ireland/sole-survivor-of-kingsmill-massacre-alan-black-has-lost-confidence-in-inquest-process-38993629.html

143. The most publicized case of the Disappeared is that of Jean McConville, a widowed mother of 10 from West Belfast. Patrick Radden Keefe provides a compelling and accessible account of her case in *Say Nothing: A True Story of Murder and Memory in Northern Ireland* (New York: Doubleday, 2019).

144. Martin Fletcher, "The Disappeared: Finding the Truth Behind the IRA's Lost Victims," *The Telegraph* (January 22, 2016), accessed on September 2, 2019, at https://www.telegraph.co.uk/news/uknews/northernireland/12110758/The-Disappeared-finding-the-truth-behind-the-IRAs-lost-victims.html

145. See https://www.patfinucanecentre.org/q-there-witch-hunt-against-ex-british-soldiers#_ftn3, accessed on September 2, 2019.

146. Rebecca Black, "Ballymurphy: British Army 'Don't Do Conspiracies,' Ex-Chief Says," *The Irish Times* (May 30, 2019), accessed on August 18, 2019, at https://www.irishtimes.com/news/crime-and-law/courts/coroner-s-court/ballymurphy-british-army-don-t-do-conspiracies-ex-chief-says-1.3909612

147. Patrick Murphy, "Reality Is We Will Never Know the Truth About Most Troubles Killings," *The Irish News* (February 4, 2017), accessed on June 8, 2020, at http://www.irishnews.com/opinion/columnists/2017/02/04/news/patrick-murphy-reality-is-we-will-never-know-the-truth-about-most-troubles-killings-917265/

148. The full text of the Widgery report can be found at https://cain.ulster.ac.uk/hmso/widgery.htm, accessed on August 18, 2019.

149. For a summary of the key findings of the report, see BBC News, "Key Findings" (June 15, 2010), accessed on August 14, 2019, at https://www.bbc.com/news/10319881. I also recommend Julieann Campbell's *Setting the Truth Free: The Inside Story of the Bloody Sunday Justice Campaign* (Dublin: Liberties Press, 2012).

150. A transcript of the full statement can be found at https://www.bbc.com/news/10322295, accessed on August 18, 2019.

151. Henry McDonald, Owen Bowcott, and Helene Mulholland, "Bloody Sunday Report: David Cameron Apologises for 'Unjustifiable' Shootings," *The Guardian* (June 15, 2010), accessed on August 18, 2019, at https://www.theguardian.com/uk/2010/jun/15/bloody-sunday-report-saville-inquiry

152. BBC News, "Bloody Sunday Paratrooper Soldier N Dies" (January 5, 2019), accessed on August 14, 2019, at https://www.bbc.com/news/uk-northern-ireland-46995647

153. Gerry Moriarty, "Why Soldier F Will Be Charged Over Bloody Sunday but Other Soldiers Will Not Be," *The Irish News* (March 14, 2019), accessed on August 14, 2019, at https://www.irishtimes.com/news/ireland/irish-news/why-soldier-f-will-be-charged-over-bloody-sunday-but-other-soldiers-will-not-be-1.3825921

154. Quote taken from https://www.irishtimes.com/news/crime-and-law/bloody-sunday-soldier-f-hearing-set-to-be-held-in-belfast-amid-security-fears-1.4142988, accessed on January 24, 2020.

155. The three most notable ongoing cases include the prosecution of two former paratroopers in the April 1972 murder of Joe McCann, the prosecution of former army major Dennis Hutchings for attempted murder and attempted grievous bodily harm in connection with the 1974 fatal shooting of John Pat Cunningham, and the prosecution of David Jonathan Holden for manslaughter over the killing of Aidan McAnespie in 1988.

156. Northern Ireland Office, "Addressing the Legacy of Northern Ireland's Past" (May 2018), 5.

157. John Manley, "Nationalists Critical of 'Amnesty' Plans for British Troops," *The Irish News* (May 16, 2019), accessed on August 14, 2019, at http://www.irishnews.com/news/northernirelandnews/2019/05/16/news/nationalists-critical-of-amnesty-plans-for-british-troops-1621021

158. Ibid.

159. John Manley, "Boris Johnson Says Prosecution of British Army Veterans Must End," *The Irish News* (July 25, 2019), accessed on July 25, 2019,' at https://www.irishnews.com/news/northernirelandnews/2019/07/25/news/boris-johnson-says-prosecution-of-british-army-veterans-must-end-1670146

160. Paul Ainsworth, "Defence Secretary: No Soldier Prosecutions Without 'New Evidence,'" *The Irish News* (August 15, 2019), accessed on August 18, 2019, at http://www.irishnews.com/news/northernirelandnews/2019/08/15/news/defence-secretary-no-soldier-prosecutions-without-new-evidence--1685227

161. See https://www.gov.uk/government/news/uk-government-sets-out-way-forward-on-the-legacy-of-the-past-in-northern-ireland, accessed on June 5, 2020.

162. Northern Ireland Office, "Addressing the Legacy of Northern Ireland's Past: Analysis of the Consultation Responses" (July 2019), 21, accessed on December 16, 2020 at https://assets.publishing.service.gov.uk/government/uploads/system/uploads/attachment_data/file/836991/Addressing_the_Legacy_of_the_Past_-_Analysis_of_the_consultation_responses__2_.pdf

163. John Wilson, book review of *Lost Lives*, *British Army Review* 149 (Summer 2010), 29.

164. Northern Ireland Office, "Addressing the Legacy of Northern Ireland's Past," 21.

165. International Committee of the Red Cross, "International Humanitarian Law and International Human Rights Law: Similarities and Differences" (January 2003).

166. Ugur Umit Ungor, "Political Violence and the Deep State . . . Paramilitarism Now a Global Phenomenon," *Belfast Telegraph* (June 11, 2020), accessed on June 12, 2020, at https://www.belfasttelegraph.co.uk/tablet/comment/political-violence-and-the-deep-state-paramilitarism-now-a-global-phenomenon-39276636.html

167. The complete text of Ernest Renan's speech can be found at http://ucparis.fr/files/9313/6549/9943/What_is_a_Nation.pdf, accessed on September 2, 2019.

168. John Hewitt, "Neither an Elegy nor a Manifesto," *Collected Poems*, edited by Frank Ormsby (Belfast: Blackstaff, 1991), 188–190.

169. Baldwin quote taken from Teju Cole, "Black Body: Rereading James Baldwin's 'Stranger in the Village,'" *The New Yorker* (August 19, 2014), accessed on December 18, 2018, at https://www.newyorker.com/books/page-turner/black-body-re-reading-james-baldwins-stranger-village

170. UN Document S/2014/30 (January 17, 2014), 2.

171. Slavenka Drakulic, *A Guided Tour Through the Museum of Communism* (New York: Penguin, 2011), xiii.

172. David Rieff, *In Praise of Forgetting: Historical Memory and Its Ironies* (New Haven, CT: Princeton University Press, 2016), 144.

173. Lewis Hyde, *A Primer for Forgetting: Getting Past the Past* (New York: Farrar, Straus and Giroux, 2019).

174. See, for instance, Masha Gessan and Misha Friedman, *Never Remember: Searching for Stalin's Gulags in Putin's Russia* (New York: Columbia Global Reports, 2018).

175. Conway, "The Role of Memory in Post-Genocide Rwanda."

176. Allison Morris, "Catholic Bishops Challenge Secretary of State on Legacy Proposals," *The Irish News* (April 9, 2020), accessed on June 8, 2020, at http://www.irishnews.com/news/northernirelandnews/2020/04/09/news/catholic-bishops-challenge-secretary-of-state-on-legacy-proposals-1896184

177. Carruthers, *Alternative Ulsters*, 231.

4

"With Deep Regret and Reluctance"

Governance in a Deeply Divided Society

On January 9, 2017, with the collars of his shirt comfortably tucked under a light brown V-neck sweater, a visibly frail Martin McGuinness, the former Irish Republican Army (IRA) commander and current deputy First Minister of Northern Ireland, sat at a desk and signed a resignation letter reading, in part: "Over ten difficult and testing years, in the role of deputy First Minister, I have sought with all my energy and determination to serve all the people of the north and the island of Ireland by making the power-sharing government work. . . . Over this period successive British governments have undermined the process of change by refusing to honour agreements, refusing to resolve the issues of the past while imposing austerity and Brexit against the wishes and best interests of people here. . . . Therefore, it is with deep regret and reluctance, that I am tendering my resignation as deputy First Minister with effect from 5 PM on Monday, 9th January, 2017. In the available period Sinn Fein will not nominate to the position of deputy First Minister."[1]

McGuinness's letter of resignation, warmly addressed with a hand-written "Robin a chara" (Irish for "my friend"), was tendered to Robin Newton, speaker of the Northern Ireland Assembly and member of the rival Democratic Unionist Party (DUP). Under the complex rules of power-sharing in Northern Ireland's government structure, the First Minister, Arlene Foster of the DUP, could not continue in her role without a deputy First Minister. The two offices are a joint office, with equal power, and both roles need the other to exist. So, with Sinn Fein's refusal to nominate a replacement for deputy First Minister, McGuinness's resignation brought an end to the most recent iteration of the power-sharing government in Stormont.

In the twilight of his life, the man whom former US President Bill Clinton later hailed as someone who "believed in a shared future, and refused to live in the past" was no longer able to believe in a shared future.[2] While it can be argued McGuinness came late to the realization that politics, rather than violence, was the way forward, his contributions to the peace process and

A Troubled Sleep. James Waller, Oxford University Press (2021). © Oxford University Press.
DOI: 10.1093/oso/9780190095574.003.0005

to the reestablishment of democratization in Northern Ireland are inarguable. Often criticized by his own party for a conciliatory disposition derisively called "Project Martin," McGuinness's resignation signaled the end of his personal project of reconciliation after 10 years as deputy First Minister.[3] Following his resignation, McGuinness's "deep regret and reluctance" would soon become Northern Ireland's deeper regret and reluctance.

* * *

In 1921, Northern Ireland became a country within a country (though some preferred, and still do so, to refer to Northern Ireland as a "province" or "region") when it was subsumed into what would come to be called the United Kingdom of Great Britain and Northern Ireland. At its birth, the devolved Parliament of Northern Ireland had a unique system of limited self-government in terms of controlling most domestic affairs and aspects of daily life while London retained responsibility for matters such as the making of peace or war, armed forces, treaties, titles of honor, currency, foreign trade, etc.[4] That changed, however, in 1972, with the implementation of direct rule from Westminster. In response to the escalating violence in Northern Ireland, the new post of the Secretary of State for Northern Ireland took over the functions of Stormont and assumed the day-to-day administration of the country. Originally viewed as a temporary measure, the intention of the British government was to restore some form of devolved government to Northern Ireland. Despite several attempts over the years to restore self-government to Northern Ireland, however, direct rule for Northern Ireland would remain in place for more than 26 years. It would not be until the establishment of the Northern Ireland Assembly under the terms of the Good Friday Agreement in 1998 that a devolved government would return to the region.

The core legislative vehicle that gives legal force to the Good Friday Agreement and subsequent agreements is the UK Parliament's Northern Ireland Act 1998. This act transferred legislative and executive powers over most local affairs to a power-sharing Northern Ireland Assembly (run by Members of the Legislative Assembly or MLAs) and Executive (10 ministers chaired by the First Minister and deputy First Minister, one unionist and the other nationalist). Devolution settlements also are in place, albeit structured differently, for Scotland and Wales. In Northern Ireland's case, "transferred" powers—effectively the end of direct rule—enabled the country to govern itself by making its own laws and taking decisions on such public matters as healthcare, education, roads, transport, policing, justice, agriculture, economic development, social security, and housing. Other powers related to "national importance"—such as international relations and treaties, nuclear energy, currency, elections, and defense and armed forces—were "excepted matters" and remained under the control of Westminster. Still other matters were "reserved" and also dealt with by Westminster unless it was decided by the Secretary of State that some of these matters should be devolved to the Northern Ireland Assembly.[5]

Since 1998, direct rule from Westminster has been temporarily reimposed when the Northern Ireland Assembly was suspended in 2000, 2001 (twice for 24 hours each time), and, amidst allegations of republican political espionage, from 2002 to 2007. On May 8, 2007, building on the St. Andrew's Agreement of the previous year, the longest post-Good Friday Agreement period of direct rule ended when the power-sharing government was restored with Ian Paisley (DUP, the largest unionist party) elected as First Minister and Martin McGuinness (Sinn Fein, the largest nationalist party) as deputy First Minister. That power-sharing government would function until McGuinness's resignation on January 9, 2017.

Fresh elections were called in March 2017, and, for the first time, even though the Assembly was still suspended, unionists no longer held an overall majority. Talks to restore the power-sharing government slogged on. The hung parliament resulting from the UK general election of June 2017, however, opened an unexpected window of influence for the DUP as the kingmakers in a "confidence and supply" agreement that propped up (albeit temporarily) Theresa May's prime ministership by ensuring a Conservative parliamentary majority. While the DUP's newfound power at Westminster ensured a very welcome fiscal transfer of a billion pounds to fund infrastructure developments in Northern Ireland, the political polarization and entrenchment in the country only deepened.

Both Sinn Fein and DUP held veto power over the restoration of any devolved government and, over the next three years, their mutually exclusive political interests meant that all attempts to restore power-sharing failed. As one interviewee told me: "It's not in the interests of nationalists to make Northern Ireland work and it's not in the interests of unionists to work with nationalists." The impasse left civil servants making day-to-day decisions on maintaining public services, but there was no sitting executive to approve major decisions or make significant funding allocations. On the street, people on both sides of the divide felt they had no say whatsoever in their own government. Political discourse became so sharply oppositional and uncompromising—a wilderness of lies and unstated truths—that it devolved into even greater depths of intransigence. Sinn Fein remained steadfast on the necessity for a stand-alone Irish Language Act to restore Stormont along with progressive national legislation on abortion and same-sex marriage. The DUP's social conservatism remained equally steadfast in its opposition to all of the above and, while twists and turns in UK politics meant the DUP eventually lost its 26-month period of leverage at Westminster, it still had little incentive to reenter a power-sharing agreement with Sinn Fein at Stormont. As an Alliance Party member told me: "In Northern Ireland, the working definition of politics is impasse." Another interviewee put it more bluntly: "Watching dumb smart people govern is our national hobby."

In the dramatic December 2019 UK general election, however, the DUP and Sinn Fein both saw a notable drop in their share of the Northern Irish vote, with the DUP falling 5.39% compared to 2017 and Sinn Fein plummeting 6.62%. These percentages translated into tens of thousands of votes lost by the two main parties. Conversely, the liberal and centrist Alliance Party, enjoying an unprecedented surge of support from former Ulster Unionist Party (UUP) supporters and younger voters from pro-union backgrounds, claimed a whopping 8.85% more voting share than in 2017, with the nationalist Socialist Democratic and Labour Party (SDLP, +3.15%) and unionist UUP (+1.5%) also rising slightly in the polls. Of Northern Ireland's 18 seats at Westminster (from the 650 seats representing parliamentary constituencies in the UK), the DUP lost two of its 10 seats (losing its outsized influence and returning to its status as a minor backbench party), Sinn Fein retained its seven seats (though, consistent with its abstentionist platform, still refusing to occupy them), the Alliance Party gained one seat, and the SDLP picked up two seats (neither the Alliance Party nor the SDLP held a seat in the previous election).[6] So, for the first time in Northern Ireland's history, there were more nationalist than unionist MPs elected to Westminster.[7]

In the UK general election, both the DUP and Sinn Fein, while remaining Northern Ireland's largest unionist and nationalist political parties (30.6% and 22.8% of the vote, respectively) clearly paid a price for the public's frustration over crises in health, education, public services, and, particularly, the lack of a functioning government and the nearly three-year deadlock in Northern Ireland politics. For the first time in years, the extremist positions of both parties appeared increasingly out of touch with Northern Irish voters as more centrist and accommodationist parties gained political momentum.

Julian Smith, then Secretary of State for Northern Ireland, set January 13, 2020 as the date by which the political parties had to reach an agreement to restore the Northern Ireland Executive. If the executive was not restored by that date, he would call for new elections for the Northern Ireland Assembly. Certainly, the DUP and Sinn Fein did not want to face an angry electorate again that soon and risk any further losses in power. Hardline unionism was now a minority in the Assembly (the March 2017 elections left the DUP with only a one-seat advantage over Sinn Fein), Belfast City Council, and Westminster for the first time in the history of Northern Ireland. Sinn Fein also had taken electoral dives in three consecutive northern elections. And, just as certainly, none of the parties wanted the return of direct rule if an Executive could not be restored. So, hearing the voters' message loud and clear, spaces for compromise were now open. Leaders of the five main Northern Ireland political parties, in discussions chaired by the UK and Irish governments, opened talks to restore a devolved government to Northern Ireland.

On January 9, 2020, three years to the day after McGuinness's resignation, their "New Decade, New Approach" deal was unveiled. The 62-page compromise agreement promised "a fair and balanced basis upon which to restore the institutions" of Northern Ireland's government.[8] It included a range of ambitious measures to restore public services, boost the economy, tackle paramilitarism, address legacy issues, respond to matters of language and national and cultural identity, and improve the sustainability of the Executive. Backed by the conditional promise of a major UK-government funded financial package (the need estimated by one economist was at least £5 billion for essential investment), as well as a pledge from the Republic of Ireland for significant cross-border investment, the deal allowed for devolution to be restored and the government of Northern Ireland to resume operations.[9] While neither side saw the deal as perfect, both the DUP and Sinn Fein could claim some wins over the other, with neither one emerging as the obvious victor or loser in the deal. Not all of their constituents, particularly those with more extremist tendencies, welcomed the deal with open arms, however. Mervyn Gibson, the grand secretary of the Orange Order, said there was "a lot of frustration and anger from the [loyalist] community at large" over the deal.[10] Dissident republicans, standing by their long-established mantra of "Smash Stormont," continued to oppose any form of an internal solution proposed by an illegitimate state whose existence they fundamentally reject.

Despite it all, on January 11, 2020, a new decade and new approach in Northern Ireland governance was christened when a new coalition Executive was formed with both of the top posts for the first time held by women: Arlene Foster of the DUP was reappointed as First Minister and Michelle O'Neill of Sinn Fein assumed the position of deputy First Minister. Based on their party's share of seats in the Assembly, eight other departmental ministers also were appointed, with three going to the DUP, two to Sinn Fein, one each to the UUP and SDLP, and Naomi Long, the leader of the Alliance Party, appointed as head of the Department of Justice through a cross-community vote in the Assembly. Less than three months later, and in the midst of an economically devastating global pandemic, the new government, for the first time since 2015, passed a one-year budget for current and capital spending.

Since devolved powers were formally granted to it in December 1999, the Northern Ireland Assembly has been suspended for more than 3,200 days of the nearly 7,000 days it was supposed to have been sitting. That is almost half its existence.[11] In the latest suspension, lasting more than three years, Northern Ireland earned the ignoble world record for the longest peacetime period without a sitting government, which it passed after 589 days.[12] Giving a new meaning to the term "understatement," Arlene Foster said the three years of suspended governance were "bad for Northern Ireland politics."[13] Indeed, while a return to direct rule was avoided, at least for this time, the three years of suspended governance severely eroded the cooperation and mutual trust underlying the spirit of the Good Friday Agreement. Little was done over that time to prepare for the government's return and the backlog of decisions that would await. The fundamental fragility and deep divisions of governance in Northern Ireland were not swept away with the new decade and the new approach. It remains to be seen if listening will be replaced by hearing, nodding by understanding, dysfunction by function.

As a result, cynicism—even with a functioning government now in place—is anything but undue. Indeed, even as Stormont resumed its duties, columnist Eilis O'Hanlon lamented the possibility of another false dawn: " 'New Decade, New Approach' looks more like a catchy soundbite dreamed up by media gurus in London and Dublin than a message which those who are expected to put it into action have taken to heart . . . those who dared to dream of the possibility of something different and something better emerging from the wreckage of the past three years have had a rude awakening."[14] Columnist Alex Kane: "We've all been here before and we've all been let down before. It will take a lot—and I really do mean a lot—to persuade us that it will be different this time."[15] Despite the well-earned skepticism and even more well-earned public apathy regarding sustainable power-sharing, the deal at least offered a new start to another vision of what good governance could be in a country sorely in need of one.

* * *

"Governance" refers, broadly, to the ways in which authority in a country is exercised. How are governments selected, monitored, and replaced? What is the capacity of the government to develop and implement sound policies? To what degree do the citizens respect the state and the institutions that govern them?[16] Nearly all early warning systems for violent conflict include various traits of governance as risk factors. In contemporary Northern Ireland, where politics is now the weapon of choice, we will consider five specific risk factors related to the practice of governance: (1) regime type, (2) state legitimacy deficit, (3) weakness of state structures, (4) identity-based polar factionalism, and (5) systematic state-led discrimination.

Regime Type

Autocracy and democracy define opposite poles of a theoretical governance scale. *Autocracies*—including absolutist monarchies and authoritarian, dictatorial, or military regimes—are repressive one-party states with an absence of effective contestation for political leadership and sharp restrictions on citizens' participation in the political process. Democracies have open and competitive elections with well-institutionalized political participation. Between these two ends of the governance scale lie "anocracies"—governments who are "neither fully democratic nor fully autocratic but, rather, combine an incoherent mix of democratic and autocratic traits and practices."[17] Anocracies "raise expectations for political participation but are not able to accommodate them."[18] Anocracies often appear in the transition from autocracy to democracy or, conversely, when emerging democratic institutions are undermined and a state becomes susceptible to "autocratic backsliding."

What is the relation of these three regimes types to the risk of violent conflict? Research has shown that, over the past 50 years, anocracies are 10 times more likely to experience intrastate conflict than democracies and two times more likely than autocracies.[19] These findings suggest a rough "inverted U" relationship between regime type and risk of violent conflict. In other words, full democracies and full autocracies are fairly stable and low-risk; it is anocratic mixed regimes, particularly those in transition, that are most volatilely instable and high-risk. As political scientist Ian Bremmer argues, "for a country that is 'stable because it's closed' to become a country that is 'stable because it's open,' it must go through a transitional period of dangerous instability."[20] Empirically, sociologist Jack Goldstone and colleagues found anocracies to have "markedly higher relative odds of future instability than full democracies or full autocracies."[21] Most particularly, they found the relative odds of future instability for partial democracies with factionalism (i.e., a pattern of sharply polarized and uncompromising competition between political blocs) were more than 30 times greater than for full autocracies. This is especially concerning given the fact that, from 1989 to 2013, the number of anocracies in the world increased from 30 to 53.[22]

So, while the path to democracy is a stony one, a diverse set of research does suggest that states with a lower degree of democratization and a higher degree of factionalism are at greater risk for the onset of violent conflict. In this light, the establishment of fully functioning democratic institutions in deeply divided societies like Northern Ireland is particularly important even as it is markedly difficult. As we have seen from the birth of Northern Ireland on, trust between the two sides of the divide is elusive, and looking forward is less important than wallowing in the past. So, a key provision of the Good Friday Agreement would be what, exactly, would Northern Ireland's government look like once direct rule was removed? How would a new constitution be designed? How would democratic institutions be constructed? What type of special mechanisms would be needed for democracy to take root again in a deeply divided society roiled by three decades of violent intergroup conflict?

Answers to many of these questions would be found in the work of Arend Lijphart, a Dutch political scientist who has spent the majority of his very productive academic career in the United States. For Lijphart, the most basic typological contrast in the patterns of Western democratic institutions is between majoritarian and consensus (nonmajoritarian) models of democracy. *Majoritarian models* (i.e., "government by the majority and in accordance with the majority's wishes") often result in permanent majorities and permanent minorities, the latter of whom have an indefinite exclusion from political power with little prospect for participation in governance.[23] Moreover, the exclusive, competitive, and adversarial nature of a majority government means that, in the words of Adrian Guelke, a professor of comparative politics at Queen's University Belfast, the majority government has "little reason to pay attention to minority interests and every reason to focus on those of the majority group, since the most serious political challenge such a government was likely to face was from within the majority group."[24] Locked out of governing and pitted against the majority, the minority group's only recourse in the face of real or perceived mistreatment may be mobilizing and agitating in ways that bring about social instability. For Lijphart, while there is a wide spectrum of practice in countries designated as "democratic," the only relatively pure majoritarian democracies are in parts of the United Kingdom, New Zealand, and Barbados.

In place of a majoritarian democracy where competing parties alternate in government, Lijphart advocates for a *consensus*, or *nonmajoritarian, model* in which political power is shared, dispersed, and limited in a variety of ways. Such a model, constraining certain forms of democratic competition and including as many groups as possible in the political process, "is characterized by inclusiveness, bargaining, and compromise."[25] Rather than waiting for today's minority to become tomorrow's majority, the heart of a consensus model of democracy is power-sharing, or an attempt to limit the domination of one party over another by ensuring the participation of minority groups in the political process. Though the data are much more tentative than he lets on, Lijphart asserts "consensus democracies do clearly outperform the majoritarian democracies with regard to the quality of democracy and democratic representation as well as with regard to what I have called the kindness and gentleness of their public policy orientations . . . they are more likely to be welfare states; they have a better record with regard to the protection of the environment; they put fewer people in prison and are less likely to use the death penalty; and the consensus democracies in the developed world are more generous with their economic assistance to the developing nations."[26] Lijphart cites Switzerland, Belgium, and the European Union as the purest cases of consensus democracy.

For deeply divided societies emerging from conflict or with the potential for conflict, however, Lijphart recognized the need for a specific and stronger form of consensus democracy to achieve and maintain political and social stability, a model he earlier termed "consociational democracy."[27] "Majority rule," Lijphart argued, "does not suffice in times of grave crisis in even the most homogenous and consensual of democracies."[28] In its place, consociational democracy, a form of power-sharing government, is better "designed to turn a fragmented political culture into a stable democracy."[29] Other research agrees that violent conflict prevention is enhanced when political institutions elevate inclusion, representativeness, power-sharing, and cross-identity group coalition building over winner-take-all majority rule.[30] Over time, Lijphart believed, politics based on divided identities could transform into politics based on shared interests. Mandatory coalitions could become voluntary coalitions. While he did not invent the term "consociational," Lijphart did develop a theoretical conception that has shaped the design of political settlements in deeply divided societies around the world, including Northern Ireland.

Lijphart believes consociational democracy in plural societies with deep cleavages requires two primary characteristics to foster democratic stability: (1) constitutional provisions for sharing of executive power between representatives of all significant communal groups (i.e., a multiparty coalition government) and (2) group autonomy in which the groups have authority to run their own internal affairs (especially in the areas of education and culture). In addition, two important secondary characteristics of a consociational democracy are (3) proportionality, with representation based on population, especially in legislative elections but also in cabinets, parliament, civil service, budgetary allocations, etc. and (4) some form of minority veto power.[31] In deeply divided societies such as Northern Ireland, Lijphart argues, "the interests and demands of communal groups can be accommodated only by the establishment of power sharing . . . power sharing has proven to be the only democratic model that appears to have much chance of being adopted in divided societies."[32] Indeed, he argues, the strength of the power-sharing model as the optimal form of democracy for deeply divided societies—either generated internally by political elites or externally by third-party intervention as a tool of conflict management—has been confirmed by its frequent and successful historical practical applications in Austria, Canada, Colombia, Cyprus, India, Lebanon, Malaysia, the Netherlands, and Switzerland.[33]

Nowhere, however, is governed quite like Northern Ireland. While neither word—"consensus" or "consociational"—appears in the Good Friday Agreement in respect to the structure of democratic institutions, it is clear that conceptual notions of power-sharing and multiple balances of power in the political decision-making process deeply inform the agreement. Specifically, Strand One of the agreement proposes "a democratically elected Assembly in Northern Ireland which is inclusive in its membership, capable of exercising executive and legislative authority, and subject to safeguards to protect the rights and interests of all sides of the community."[34] In Northern

Ireland, the two primary characteristics of Lijphart's consociational democracy are met in (1) cross-community power-sharing at the executive level, with the proportion of unionist and nationalist representation based on the number of seats a party wins in the election and (2) cultural equality for the two main traditions. The two secondary characteristics are met in (3) a proportional representation electoral system to elect MLAs and allocate positions of power (based on a single transferable vote in which voters can rank order individual candidates) and (4) special voting arrangements giving veto rights to the minority, with some Assembly decisions requiring cross-community support and not simply majority support.

Despite Lijphart's unfailing advocacy (one academic I spoke with called him, with equal parts derision and admiration, "Mr. Consociational"), the concept and practice of consociational democracy is not without its critics and their frequently pointed critiques.[35] And the embodiment of some of those critiques find easy display in the specific case of Northern Ireland, described by one academic as "the brightest star in the new consociational universe."[36] Three specific concerns, each with notably adverse impact on the degree of democratization, follow.

First, consociational frameworks for deeply divided societies emerging from conflict can, over time, actually end up institutionalizing the very ethnonational identities they are seeking to reconcile. For social anthropologist Rob Aitken, international policymakers too often assume identity divisions in a post-conflict society are permanent. This assumption "then defines post-conflict societies as ethnically divided societies and representative government as being the representation of ethnic groups [i.e., consociational democracy]."[37] Politicians win office by appealing exclusively to their own community. Voting becomes an ethnonational census headcount with little to no incentive for reaching across communal divides. Politics becomes a zero-sum game in which one person's or party's gain is another person's or party's equivalent loss. In this way, the focus on cross-community power-sharing can become a systematic organization of division built on divergent and competing ethnonational identities rather than on the integration of common and cooperative cross-cutting identities.

In contemporary Northern Ireland, party competition is incentivized *within*, rather than *across*, unionist and nationalist constituencies. The middle ground between the two sides, if it has not already left the station, has one foot on the platform. While power-sharing among elected community representatives in a jointly run government framework is assumed to be the tool then used to "smooth" the divisions between communities, ideally moving from adversarial to cooperative governance, it seldom outpaces the divisions on which it was built. As one "other" designated politician told me: "The Good Friday Agreement set up a system of government designed to rigidify sectarian identities and, ultimately, collapse under the very weight of those identities."

Second, even the best of consociational power-sharing frameworks inevitably have exclusion issues in which diverse political identities are sacrificed due to a very narrow conception of political inclusion. In Bosnia-Herzegovina, for instance, the tripartite state presidency is restricted to Bosniaks, Bosnian Serbs, and Bosnian Croats. Excluded from consideration for the presidency is anyone outside these three groups—meaning that Jews, Roma, and others cannot stand for election. Political scientists Timofey Agarin and colleagues have termed this systematic exclusion of others in consociational power-sharing as the "exclusion-amid-inclusion" (EAI) dilemma. Consociational power-sharing arrangements, by their nature, lead to the institutional inclusion of the dominant political groups in the divide (in Northern Ireland's case, the unionist and the nationalists) and to the institutional exclusion of other political groups (e.g., groups based on gender, sexuality, environmentalism, socialism, etc.). As they summarize the implications of the EAI dilemma: "Non-dominant groups—Others—may find themselves systemically side-lined from participating in and contributing to the development of a shared polity, calling into question the democratic legitimacy and stability of the new constitutional order."[38]

In contemporary Northern Ireland, the "exclusion-amid-inclusion" issue is embedded in the first day that the Assembly meets after an election. On that day, MLAs must sign the Register as "nationalist," "unionist," or "other" (a negative, seldom-used designation). Meant to facilitate cross-community voting, it most often means that political discussions become entrenched in dominant ethnonational identities ("nationalist" or "unionist") and that "other" categories of political identity, centrist or otherwise, are marginalized or excluded. Over time, power-sharing agreements may become "vulnerable to spoiling action" from those marginalized or excluded parties.[39]

Third, the power-sharing that lies at the heart of consociational frameworks can lead to political gridlock as interactions become less about power-sharing and more about power-grabbing. As politicians on both sides are fond of saying: "What we have we hold." The propensity for paralysis becomes more pronounced when each competing group is cohesive and has strong leadership. Moreover, while adding a large number of veto players to the political process may, in theory, help protect minorities, it also can be a death knell to meaningful political initiatives. The institutional design of veto power matters; to ignore such a design is to run the risk of abusive and disruptive use of veto power.[40]

In contemporary Northern Ireland, minority veto power was institutionalized by the Good Friday Agreement in the form of a "petition of concern" (PoC). Such a petition, expressing "concern" about a motion before the Assembly and requiring the support of 30 MLAs, can request that any decision be taken on a cross-community basis. Cross-community support on proposed legislation could be achieved by parallel consent (the support of more than 50% of all those voting, including more than 50% of unionists and nationalists) or by weighted majority (60% of all those voting, including at least 40% of unionists and nationalists). While designed to protect minority rights, both the DUP and Sinn Fein have weaponized PoCs to veto policy proposals they did not support. No reason has to be given to deploy a PoC, and there is no limit to the number of times it can be deployed. From 2011 to 2016 alone, it was used (or abused) as a form of veto more than 100 times (most often by the DUP to veto same-sex marriage proposals despite the proposals having the backing of a majority of Assembly members). As a result of this disruptive use, the "New Decade, New Approach" deal agreed that PoCs should only be used in the most exceptional circumstances and as a last resort. Keeping the threshold at 30 MLAs, it is now required that a PoC be triggered by members of two or more parties. These reforms, though not as far-ranging as many hoped, aim to restore some degree of policymaking efficiency to Stormont.

Despite these critiques, it may still be that some form of consociational democracy is necessary as a transitional step from the deeply divided society of Northern Ireland to a fully functioning democracy. In theory, the movement from identity politics to interest politics in consociationalism should eventually make it possible to do without its power-sharing mechanisms, particularly when forums are in place for continued (re)negotiation and dispute resolution between conflict parties.[41] In practice, however, the "cases in which consociationalism has ended because of its success are few and far between."[42] Current research affirms that power-sharing "can be an effective means to prompt parties to sign an agreement and cease hostilities in the short run, but it can create long-term obstacles for peace consolidation and reconciliation."[43] In this light, it must be remembered that consociation-alism is not, as Lijphart argues, "the only feasible solution" for a deeply divided society.[44] As political scientist John Fuh-sheng Hsieh has documented, Taiwan, a society deeply divided along ethnic and national identity lines, was able to achieve democratic stability without significant power-sharing arrangements.[45] In Taiwan, a majoritarian political structure, premised on a two-party or quasi-two-party system, actually diluted the divisive nature of political competition rather than enhancing it. Similarly, Guelke argues: "Power-sharing is only one of a number of different ways in which stability, peace, good governance, fairness and democracy can be promoted in a deeply divided society."[46]

Even if power-sharing is the way forward for contemporary Northern Ireland, there are alternative arrangements of power sharing, in which, for instance, political moderates are strengthened, that may emerge as relevant. Such an arrangement could be combined with an electoral system that requires or encourages candidates to reach out for votes from all communities rather than just their own. This could possibly even lead to a conventional single-person executive with a president who transcends ethnonational identity or, at least, can remain moderate on divisive issues.[47] In terms of the incorporation of minority rights in democratic institutions, we must also acknowledge that even majoritarian systems have developed effective means of protection. Hsieh: "In the contemporary world, as many majoritarian democracies have demonstrated, minority rights also can be protected by many other means. Civil society, free press, new forms of communication (e.g., social media), outside intervention, and so forth, may expose or directly help relieve the plight of the minority or minorities."[48]

State Legitimacy Deficit

To what degree is the state perceived by its citizens to be a legitimate actor representative of the people as a whole? Is there respect for the constitution, the national authorities, and representatives of the government? How transparent and accountable are state institutions and processes? Are there strong oversight mechanisms for the state? Is the state perceived as criminal? Does the state have the confidence of its people? These are questions of state legitimacy, and any perceived deficit in that legitimacy can leave a governance system at risk.

Endemic levels of corruption—entrusted public power exercised for private gain—are particularly damaging to state legitimacy. Corruption implies that the state has been "captured" by elites and private or corporate interests.[49] Corruption, both internal and transnational, leads to a jungle of personal empires.[50] The integrity of people in positions of authority cannot be assumed, and, as a result, the state's legitimacy is called into question. Each year, the independent nongovernmental organization Transparency International issues a "Corruption Perceptions Index" scoring countries on a scale from 0 (highly corrupt) to 100 (very clean). Their 2019 analysis of 180 countries found more than two-thirds of countries scoring below 50 on this measure of the perceived level of public-sector corruption—from children denied an education to elections decided by money not votes to counterfeit medication to public procurement contracts—leading the organization to conclude: "Corruption chips away at democracy to produce a vicious cycle, where corruption undermines democratic institutions and, in turn, weak institutions are less able to control corruption."[51] In situations where corruption is skewed along identity lines, it serves as a fuel for identity-based conflict.[52] In terms of state legitimacy, corruption is a corrosive agent that erodes public trust in governance.

Unfortunately, the "Corruption Perceptions Index" treats the United Kingdom as one country rather than a collection of four countries. Were contemporary Northern Ireland considered separately, the perception of corruption would be clear in impressions of improper patronage and conflict of interest. In fact, McGuinness's January 2017 resignation was due, in part, to a political scandal that erupted in November 2016. The Renewable Heat Incentive (RHI) scandal, or the "Cash for Ash" scandal, was born in a government scheme launched in November 2012 in which businesses and the public sector were offered generous subsidies to switch from fossil fuels to renewable heating sources (such as biomass heating systems, mostly burning wood pellets, as well as solar thermal and heat pumps). RHI was run by Northern Ireland's Department of Enterprise, Trade and Investment, a ministry then headed by Arlene Foster of the DUP. The plan effectively paid people to heat their properties, covering the cost of their new renewable energy heating system and the fuel used to power it for 20 years. RHI was extended to the domestic sector of Northern Ireland in late 2014.

Beginning in 2013, concerns about abuse of the clean energy scheme were expressed to Arlene Foster. The RHI scheme paid out more in subsidies than the costs of the fuels, and there was no cap on the subsidy payments, effectively meaning users could earn more money by burning more fuel. The more they heated, the more money they made—regardless of what, exactly, they were heating. One farmer allegedly stood to collect more than £1 million over the next 20 years for heating an empty shed. When senior civil servants, facing costs spiraling out of control, suggested closing the scheme in September 2015, DUP advisors resisted it. In addition, these same advisors allegedly tried to remove the name of Arlene Foster, now the leader of the DUP, from any documents associated with RHI. Finally, recognizing the inevitable financial calamity of the burn-to-earn abuse, the RHI scheme was closed to new applications on February 29, 2016. Successful applicants prior to that date, however, will continue to receive contractual payments for the 20-year lifetime of the scheme, amounting to more than £1 billion of public money.

By December 2016, allegations of the abuse of the scheme had come under the media spotlight through the BBC Radio Ulster's "Nolan Show," the most widely listened to radio show in Northern Ireland, as well as an exposé in the BBC's "Spotlight" regional news program. After surviving a vote of no confidence in the Assembly on December 19, calls for Foster to step down over the scandal, or at least recuse herself from the investigation, were staunchly resisted, replete with rebuttals from Foster that such calls were misogynistic. In response, McGuinness submitted his letter of resignation the following month, effectively shutting the doors of Stormont. "The DUP leader [Arlene Foster] has a clear conflict of interest," McGuinness wrote in his resignation letter. "She was the Minister responsible for the RHI scheme at its inception. No cost controls were put in place and warnings were ignored. This has led to an enormously damaging pressure on our public finances and a crisis of confidence in the political institutions."[53] Foster denounced his resignation and Sinn Fein's support of it as "political, not principled."[54]

So, a well-intentioned scheme to reduce carbon emissions resulted in opening a Pandora's box of political pollution and public condemnation. Beginning on November 7, 2017 and concluding on December 14, 2018, 114 days of public inquiry into the RHI scandal were held at Stormont, at a cost of almost £13 million. On March 13, 2020, the final report of the oral evidence collected at the inquiry, along with more than 1 million pieces of documentary evidence collected before the inquiry began, was released. Running to 656 pages published in three volumes comprising 276,000 words, the report was carefully measured. Relying only on mentions of "instances of unacceptable behaviour," the report is silent on the issue of corruption but makes clear that the RHI was a "project too far" for a beleaguered Stormont and that the scandal came from "an accumulation and compounding of errors and omissions over time and a failure of attention."[55] Two months after the report's release, as disciplinary proceedings into potential misconduct by civil servants began, Finance Minister Conor Murphy confirmed that those who chose to retire would escape discipline over RHI.[56] As of this writing, only one member of the civil service has been disciplined as a result of the findings of the inquiry.

Rather than bringing closure, the aftermath of the scandal has only heightened the public perception of a state legitimacy deficit and the dysfunctional workings of devolution. The "crisis of confidence in the political institutions" to which McGuinness referred in his resignation letter struck at the heart of the public's belief in the legitimacy of Northern Ireland's democracy and of its leadership. This was reaffirmed in a June 2020 review of Northern Ireland's planning system that found poor levels of public trust, including concerns that decision-making councilors were "too close" to developers.[57]

For states that have a notable legitimacy deficit, we often see the manifestation in rallies, peaceful demonstrations, mass protests against state authority or policies, uprisings, or even riots. As researchers Monty Marshall and Benjamin Cole write: "Mass protest should not be viewed as an exercise in democracy, but, rather, as a signal that the political process, whether democratic or autocratic, is failing to adequately recognize the levels of discontent and dissent and properly address an important and valued issue in public policy."[58] The mass mobilizations central to the Civil Rights Movement in the United States, for instance, were clear and compelling reflections of discontent that signaled widespread perceptions of a state delegitimized by de facto and de jure racial segregation, discrimination, and exclusion. Similarly, following Museveni's disputed election to a fourth term in 2011, thousands of Ugandans expressed their concerns with the legitimacy of the state—its electoral process, corruption, and economic policies—by engaging in peaceful "walk-to-work" protest demonstrations. Deadly crackdowns by government security forces only added to the perceived state legitimacy deficit. The October 2014 ouster of Burkina Faso's Blaise Compaore followed national protests over a controversial parliamentary vote to change the constitution in a way that would have extended his 27 years in power. In that particular case, civilians' protest over a perceived state legitimacy deficit led to a peaceful political transition during which the country's constitution, though temporarily suspended, ultimately would be respected.

In the long history of mass protests against state authority or policies in Northern Ireland, the most recent to reveal the deep sectarian divisions still at play in the country were triggered on December 3, 2012, following the Belfast City Council's decision to change its policy and practice of flying the Union Flag, the official flag of the United Kingdom. Prior to that decision, the Union Flag, for many years, had been flown at Belfast City Hall 365 days a year. While some nationalist councilors wanted the flag removed permanently, a compromise motion passed to fly the flag only on 18 designated days (mainly royal birthdays).[59] On the days the Union Flag does not fly, there is no flag above Belfast City Hall. Similar policies of only flying the Union Flag on designated days already were in place at Stormont, many public buildings throughout the UK, and even in some unionist-controlled councils in Northern Ireland.[60]

The Belfast City Council's decision, however, struck a chord of vulnerability in a city coming off a summer of heightened tensions between Protestant and Catholic communities. Within minutes after the Council's vote, seeing the changes as an attack on their cultural and national identity of "Britishness," loyalist protesters descended on City Hall and a riot ensued. Fifteen police officers were injured as well as two security guards and a press photographer. Over the next several days, loyalist protests continued in Belfast and spread throughout Northern Ireland, often accompanied by violence allegedly organized by loyalist paramilitaries such as the Ulster Volunteer Force (UVF) and Ulster Defence Association (UDA). Members of the Alliance Party, who had brokered the compromise motion, were frequent targets of the violence, even being subjected to death threats. Tensions were ratcheted up with loyalists putting up thousands of Union Flags in public places. Some loyalists even planned to travel to Dublin to "sarcastically" ask for the Irish flag to be taken down. In the words of the late loyalist activist Willie Frazier: "It's to give Irish people a sense of how we feel. I would be very offended if I was living in Ireland and someone came and asked me to take the flag down. That's exactly how we feel in Belfast. People keep telling us we're still part of the UK, yet here we are without a flag."[61]

In the nine weeks following the Council's decision, the Police Service of Northern Ireland estimated policing costs totaled greater than £15 million with another £15 million estimated lost in trade because of the protests and rioting.[62] Nationwide, the street protests and violence, varying in intensity, would continue through most of 2013, with economists estimating about £50 million in lost revenues.[63] As of this writing, every Saturday, a small group of loyalist protestors still gather at the gates of Belfast's City Hall, with a larger number commemorating the anniversary of the protests each year. At one such commemoration, in 2019, Billy Dickson, a member of the DUP and former Royal Ulster Constabulary (RUC) reservist, said: "I have been asked many times if the protests will continue and I can assure you they will. This protest began because unionist people felt the erosion of their identity had gone too far."[64]

Indeed, many in the Protestant, unionist, and loyalist communities saw the Belfast City Council's decision as yet another governmental attempt to dilute their Britishness. Several people I interviewed cited the flag protests as a significant factor in these communities' deepening mistrust of the legitimacy of the state institutions in Northern Ireland. Loyalist communities were particularly quick to pull back from civic engagement following the flag protests and focus their attention instead on mobilizing to protect their identity from further erosion. One civil service officer I interviewed said: "Loyalists have a decreased passion and energy for working with us. It's not apathy or problem fatigue; rather they have gone into an active recruitment of young boys into the paramilitaries . . . often behind the guise of a community development organization with lines and lines of lads out back waiting to join." The flag protests also significantly deepened the divide between the Protestant-unionist-loyalist and Catholic-nationalist-republican communities. One republican activist I interviewed described the flag protests as "a huge turning point that heightened some of the psychological and social barriers that were going down a bit." He went on to say that, the week before the flag protests, he had been invited to speak as part of a reconciliation panel in a loyalist community. After the flag protests, however, the invitation was rescinded and has not been reissued since.

Only time will tell if the "New Decade, New Approach" agreement can reinstate—or, for some communities, begin to build—public trust in the legitimacy of Northern Ireland's state institutions. Certainly, the agreement sees as one of its aspirational responsibilities the restoration of public confidence in government through increased transparency and accountability. While, as of this writing, the implementation of many of the details for that ambitious restoration are yet to be put in practice, all parties recognize that increasing the legitimacy with which the state is viewed by its people, as well as by the international community, is necessary for the return of good governance. Building citizens' robust acceptance of the state's "right to rule" means addressing issues related to process legitimacy (observance of agreed or customary rules of procedure) as well as output legitimacy (perceptions about state performance and the provision of services).[65] In practice, attending to those two sources of legitimacy entails removing public-sector corruption (including the provision of appropriate remuneration for public officials to disincentivize engaging in corruption), following written constitutional policies and norms, and increasing the level of transparency and accountability for state institutions and processes.

Weakness of State Structures

To what degree can the state provide basic public services and answer people's needs? How effective are state structures—hospitals, schools, police departments, courts systems, sanitation, public transportation, etc.? To what degree does the state follow the rule of law? Can the state protect its citizens, or do crime and violence threaten to overrun the state? All of these indicate the relative strength or weakness of state structures, and, as state structures weaken, political and social instability rises.

In Northern Ireland, in the absence of a functioning government from 2017 to 2020, the basic public services of the country were managed by civil servants with frustratingly limited powers in regard to major (or even minor) policy decisions, even more severely limited resources, and little public accountability. Decisions, when made, proceeded at a glacial pace, most often related only to the continuation of existing policies and seldom instituting any new ones. As a result, the quality of provision of basic public services, already in steep decline before Stormont closed, suffered deeply. The everyday realities of the here and now in contemporary Northern Ireland reflect a state fundamentally too weak to provide an acceptable quality of basic public services. The weakness of these state structures tears at the social and economic fabric of an already deeply divided society.

The quality of provision of basic public services in both rural and urban areas can be measured through several quantitative cairns of services, goods, and infrastructure: housing costs; education enrollment and literacy rates (including gender differences in both areas); fuel supply; access to medicine, number of clinics and hospitals, number of physicians; potable water; safe roads; adequate sanitation; and number of airports and railroads for sustainable development.[66] The "New Decade, New Approach" agreement recognized the need for priority actions in many of these areas, including affordable housing, a more efficient education system, high-quality provision of early education and childcare initiatives, welfare reform, resources for policing in the community, the transformation of health services, and providing living wages and employment rights.

Among those priority actions, of particularly pressing concern was the country's health and social care system. A long-standing funding gap, coupled with the mounting demographic pressures of an aging population, had led to inconceivably long waiting lists for treatment. Some patients had been waiting years for hospital appointments and surgical procedures. Even those needing emergency room visits found no beds, a full waiting room, exhausted nurses and doctors, and lines of people waiting for crisis treatment—some for longer than 13 hours. With the workload and backlog so demanding, many general practitioners left their jobs or took early retirement. A 2018 audit warned "that the health and social care system, as currently configured, is simply unable to cope with the demands being placed on it. . . . As the . . . system faces mounting pressures and rising demand for care, the costs of maintaining existing service models are increasing at a pace that cannot be sustained within available budgets."[67]

By late 2019, the situation had deteriorated to the degree that hospital trade unions in the country went on strike over pay and staffing levels. The strikes led to the cancellation of outpatient appointments and scheduled surgeries, further exacerbating the waiting list crisis. While the Northern Ireland Executive, once restored in January 2020, was able to settle the ongoing pay dispute, what they may never be able to settle is the waiting list crisis. Health Minister Robin Swann (Ulster Unionist Party; UUP) has been told that some patients who have an urgent referral for a painful and debilitating condition can expect to wait between two and three years for their first hospital appointment. In Belfast alone, for instance, the waiting time for an *urgent* urology appointment was 196 weeks as of November 2019. Thousands more patients with routine referrals may never be seen. One hospital doctor said: "As it stands, there are actually people who are being referred who will simply never get an appointment. They will continually be bumped down the list by people being added on who need to be seen more urgently."[68]

After a mere month in his ministerial position, and just weeks before the tsunami wave of the COVID-19 pandemic, Swann acknowledged the near impossibility of the task ahead: "There are . . . deep-seated problems across the health and social care system that will take years to put right. . . . In terms of waiting lists, it [the 2020/2021 budget] would allow a focus on red flag and urgent cases such as suspected cancer but overall the current totally unacceptable waiting list position would be unlikely to improve."[69] Swann estimated that, in addition to £492 million to maintain existing services, another £169 million would be necessary to meet the very ambitious "New Decade, New Approach" targets to reduce waiting lists. Unfortunately, all of these fissures in the health and social care system would be further stressed and exacerbated by the 2020 coronavirus pandemic.

Another priority action highlighted in the agreement involves an increase in resources, both human and financial, for policing. The agreement sets a specific target of increasing police numbers from 6,700 to 7,500. This need is particularly pronounced in the face of the high rate of officer absenteeism for stress, anxiety, or depression resulting from the severe and daily threat of terrorist-related violence.[70] Certainly more challenging, however, is developing effective approaches and mechanisms for policing in the community—especially with a police force carrying the weight of its historical role in a deeply divided society. Policing in Northern Ireland mirrors a societal habituation to violence as, in several parts of the country, one seldom sees a police officer in normal uniform doing normal community policing; rather, the police are militarized—replete with riot gear, armored vehicles, assault rifles, and a reliance on a military operational tactics. As journalist Allison Morris argues: "This militarised style of policing makes transforming hearts and minds an impossibility."[71]

Beyond the approaches and mechanisms, however, the heart of effective policing is the question of how well the force represents and is trusted by the communities it polices. From its establishment in June 1922 until its rebranding in November 2001, the police force in Northern Ireland was the RUC. From its inception, the personnel of the RUC were predominately Protestant, with Catholic representation peaking at 23% in 1923, falling to 17% by 1927, and diminishing to around 10% or less by the late 1960s.[72] In many areas, particularly during the Troubles, the RUC had become a heavily militarized force, complete with its own specialized and entirely Protestant paramilitary wing—the Ulster Special Constabulary, or B Specials. While the RUC was distrusted in Catholic neighborhoods throughout Northern Ireland, the B Specials—notorious for a lack of proper discipline, especially in the use of firearms—were feared. When the B Specials were stood down on April 30, 1970, they were replaced by the Ulster Defence Regiment (UDR), a locally recruited regiment of the British Army. The UDR hoped to attract more cross-community support (it did have up to 18% Catholic membership early on) but many nationalists grew leery of it when it began to absorb too many former B Specials. Allegations of links between the UDR and loyalist paramilitaries only deepened nationalist mistrust. Over the years of the Troubles, and by whatever name they were called (RUC, B Specials, or the UDR), these partisan security forces compromised the rule of law by being, at best, armed wings of unionism and, at worst, loyalists with guns that made violence possible and permissible.

As the most visible manifestation of state authority, the Good Friday Agreement recognized the importance of a police force that could attract and sustain support from both sides of the sectarian divide. To do so, however, would require significant police reform on multiple levels. One year after the Good Friday Agreement, the Independent Commission on Policing for Northern Ireland, chaired by Lord Patten, published a report with 175 specific recommendations for comprehensive police reform.[73] Among these were a renaming of the force to the Police Service of Northern Ireland (PSNI) and, most importantly for cross-community buy-in, a 50/50 recruitment policy for Catholics and Protestants with an eventual target of at least 30% of the force being Catholic officers within 10 years after implementation of the policy. From the beginning, the 50/50 recruitment policy raised hackles on both sides. Unionists resentfully saw it as reverse discrimination. More problematically, nationalists remained suspicious of Northern Ireland policing, and the few Catholics who did step forward to join the PSNI often were the subject of abuse and even death threats from their own communities. So, from the outset of the policy's implementation in 2001, the number of Catholics entering the force remained low.

On January 28, 2007, however, Sinn Fein, overturning a century of opposition to any UK policing presence in Ireland, finally gave their backing to the PSNI with a pledge to "participate in local policing structures in the interests of justice" once devolution was restored.[74] In Gerry Adams words: "We cannot leave policing to the unionist parties or the SDLP or the Irish government. We certainly cannot leave it to the British government."[75] While about 900 party members at the Sinn Fein Ard Fheis in Dublin voted overwhelmingly in support of the motion (opposed only by Sinn Fein's youth wing), one interviewee told me there was a lot of behind-the-scenes work beforehand to get buy-in from a very reluctant IRA and, particularly, the families of victims who had been killed by security forces. He recounted the emotional difficulty of those conversations but also his pride at the level of trust victims' families placed in Sinn Fein leadership to make the right decision. He also recalled the relational cost it entailed when, in a phone call with a friend later that evening, the friend asked if he had voted "yes" to support policing. When he indicated he had, he said they were no longer comrades and hung up with a goodbye that has lasted until this day. By June 2007, Sinn Fein MLAs had joined the policing board, and Catholic enrollment in the PSNI began to steadily increase.

When the 50/50 recruitment policy went into effect in 2001, only 8% of the PSNI identified as Catholic. By the time the policy ended in 2011, four years after Sinn Fein's vote to support policing, the PSNI had become significantly more diversified with about 30% of its officers identifying as Catholic. Unfortunately, recent years have seen a notable plateauing of that diversification. The 2018–2019 annual report of the Northern Ireland Policing Board demonstrated that, even as Catholics continue to increase as a share of the population in Northern Ireland, the 70/30 ratio of Protestant to Catholic officers remains status quo as 32.2% of PSNI officers identified as Catholic.[76] Moreover, those Catholics who do join tend to be overrepresented from middle-class families and underrepresented from working-class families. Going up the ladder of ranks in the PSNI, the disproportionate representation becomes even more pronounced. Of the 68 officers above the rank of superintendent, for example, 57 are Protestant.[77] As one nationalist politician told me: "The PSNI is becoming, once again, a cold house for Catholics." In the near future, given a decreased intake rate of Catholic applicants, there is concern that Catholic representation in the PSNI will begin to decline substantially unless there are fundamental policy and culture changes.

In December 2019, Archbishop Eamon Martin, head of the Catholic Church in Ireland, advocated for a return to the 50/50 recruitment policy in the PSNI: "Because if we do not have a police service which is representative of the society that it polices, you immediately begin to run into accusations that the police service is not friendly to Catholic people, or you allow a vacuum to be created which allows others to exploit intimidation and fear in communities."[78] In response, PSNI Chief Constable Simon Byrne, while not ruling out a return of the policy, expressed his belief that the timing was not ideal for its reintroduction. So, the PSNI is yet to, and likely never will, become an organization representative of Northern Ireland's society (also painfully true in reference to gender and ethnic minorities). As an important and visible state structure, this lack of representation is a weakness that perilously intersects with questions of state legitimacy. As analysts Mariana Caparini and Juneso Hwang summarize in their 2019 report for the Stockholm International Peace Research Institute: "Perhaps most fundamentally, the challenges of consolidating trust in and the legitimacy of the police in the eyes of society as a whole are linked to lingering challenges of political legitimacy of the post-conflict state."[79]

As a state structure, the legitimacy of policing becomes increasingly important as levels of violence and crime rise in a state. In contemporary Northern Ireland, much of those social ills fall at the feet of republican and loyalist paramilitaries whose ranks still include thousands of sworn members who became increasingly mobilized with the political paralysis and economic stagnation plaguing the country. Brexit, and resulting debates over the potential return of a border, have only heightened recruitment efforts and paramilitary activity on both sides. While operating in smaller and less sophisticated groupings, the paramilitaries continue to pose a challenge to effective policing in communities. This threat is especially pronounced in working-class communities that may already suffer from high rates of unemployment and an intersection of other oppressions.

Anthony Harbinson, a member of Northern Ireland's Tackling Paramilitarism, Criminality, and Organised Crime Programme Board, describes the unique challenge: "These paramilitaries style themselves as protectors of communities. They would like to see themselves as a second police force, dealing with individuals within their communities, who have stepped outside the law."[80] In communities that may see the PSNI as agents of persecution rather than protection, paramilitaries fill a void as defenders of their communities, inflicting "by appointment" punishment beatings and shootings (often in kneecaps) to alleged drug dealers, spouse and child abusers, and other petty criminals. Many residents perceive such "paramilitary peacekeeping" and its corresponding level of "acceptable violence" as an effective deterrent to criminality and anti-social behavior in their communities. As a matter of fact, 35% of people interviewed by the Board believed these forms of paramilitary violence were justified as a way to sort out local problems and criminality (such community beliefs, and the fear or retaliation that comes from openly opposing them, go a long way toward understanding why only 3% of paramilitary-style attacks end in a criminal conviction).[81]

I spoke with people on both sides of the sectarian divide who were quick to say they would put word out to local paramilitary actors to address a community grievance long before they would think about calling the PSNI. The data bear out those remarks. Between July 2018 and June 2019 alone, for instance, 81 people in Northern Ireland were victims of paramilitary-style punishment attacks, with 17 shot and 64 assaulted. That compares to 79 such attacks in the previous year, with 20 shooting and 59 assaults. In November 2019, in its second annual report on progress towards ending paramilitary activity, the Independent Reporting Commission (IRC), established jointly by the British and Irish governments as part of the 2015 Fresh Start Agreement, confirmed that while there had been a downward trend in paramilitary violence over the past 10 years, the number of deaths linked to paramilitary organizations and the number of paramilitary-style attacks carried out since the commission's first report in October of 2018 had increased.[82] While the 2020 IRC annual report noted "some reduction in reported paramilitary-related incidents," likely attributable to movement restrictions resulting from the COVID-19 pandemic, it did conclude that "the overall threat remains a serious concern."[83] Some even suggest paramilitary-style assaults and shootings can be directly linked to increasingly high suicide rates through both the fear they instill in a community as well as their traumatic impact on the families of the victims.[84]

Peter Sheridan, a former police officer, maintains that the activities of paramilitaries in contemporary Northern Ireland have little to nothing to do with the former conflict. "It is about turf wars," he argues, "it is about internal feuding, it is about ordinary criminality—it is nothing to do with the conflict that they are involved in. Yet we continue to separate out these two things as if they are somehow different."[85] Indeed, more than protectors of their communities, many paramilitaries also have become involved in a broader variety of criminal activities, sometimes in concert with organized crime groups (of the 88 organized crime groups in Northern Ireland, 22 have paramilitary links). The organized crime activities with which some paramilitaries are involved include extorting small businesses, illegal money lending, cybercrime such as ransomware attacks and sextortion, illegal drugs, fuel and cigarette smuggling, money laundering, armed robbery, prostitution, counterfeiting, violent housing intimidation (primarily based on sectarianism but also racism and homophobia), human trafficking, and slavery. Indeed, for columnist Tom Kelly, "[p]aramilitarism in Northern Ireland has morphed into pure and unadulterated organised criminality." [86]The 2020

IRC report affirmed that while there is a broad spectrum of people involved in paramilitarism for a wide variety of reasons, some "use paramilitarism as a cover for criminality." The framers of the report warn that paramilitarism remains "a reality of Northern Ireland life in 2020" and presents a "clear and present danger," particularly in light of the impending impact of Brexit.[87]

Responses to the problem of paramilitaries in contemporary Northern Ireland, however ineffectual they have been to this point, have not been slow in coming. In addition to the annual reports from the IRC, the Paramilitary Crime Task force (including the PSNI, the National Crime Agency, and Her Majesty's Revenue and Customs) continues its law enforcement efforts to tackle criminal activity by paramilitary groups. Their work is complemented by Northern Ireland's Department of Justice and, in particular, its Tackling Paramilitarism Programme. The program's work includes building confidence in the justice system, creating and maximizing strategies and powers to tackle criminal activity and the harm it causes, building capacity to support transition away from paramilitary activity and structures, and ensuring long-term prevention of paramilitary influence. To date, they estimate that more than 10,000 people have taken part in initiatives to tackle paramilitarism through more than 50 organizations (including seven government departments, more than 20 public and statutory bodies, and more than 22 voluntary and community organizations). One of its most recent notable initiatives is their "Ending the Harm Campaign," an innovative multimedia campaign with the accompanying slogan "Paramilitaries don't protect you. They control you."[88] The "New Decade, New Approach" deal calls, however abstractly, for a strategic priority of "a targeted and specific focus across government to tackle paramilitarism."[89] Most recently, Justice Minister Naomi Long has announced plans to pursue legislation, called "unexplained wealth orders," to target family members or friends who are used to hide paramilitary assets.[90]

In conclusion, many state structures in contemporary Northern Ireland have eroded to a point of destructive impact. A dysfunctional health and social care system and a lack of public trust in and support of the rule of law stand as two of the more notable examples. The challenge facing Stormont is to find ways in which those state structures can be developed and administered to ensure fair and equitable provision of basic public services. Building public confidence and trust in state structures, particularly after a prolonged period of political paralysis, is a vital step in promoting resilience in a deeply divided society.

Identity-Based Polar Factionalism

As we discussed in Chapter 1, there is widespread agreement that social identity groups and organizations claiming to represent such groups lie at the core of many contemporary violent conflicts. State institutions fragmented among identity lines—national, racial, ethnic, religious, class, clan, or tribe—often lead to a high level of political contentiousness and identity-based factionalism. Marshall and Cole define factionalism as "polities with parochial or ethnic-based political factions that regularly compete for political influence in order to promote particularist agendas and favor group members to the detriment of common, secular, or cross-cutting agendas."[91] Such factionalism can become so sharply oppositional and uncompromising that it becomes a winner-take-all approach to politics and "lead[s] the political process toward greater levels of confrontation and greater depths of intransigence, placing it at the gateway to political instability and regime change."[92] Goldstone et al. have offered additional empirical support that "a polarized politics of exclusive identities or ideologies, in conjunction with partially democratic institutions" form the most exceptionally unstable type of regime.[93] Similarly, Marshall and Cole's summary of their research found "that countries with [polar] factionalism are twice as fragile on average as those without factionalism."[94]

Identity-based polar factionalism is fueled by exclusionary and harmful ideologies, often nationalistic in intent and propagated by extremist rhetoric in politics, education, hate radio, and media. These ideologies—rooted in the "us" and "them" binaries of the in-group bias—are based on the supremacy of a certain identity or on extremist versions of identity. These ideologies also often include themes of communal irredentism or communal solidarity.[95] For instance, Slobodan Milosevic's call to unite all Serbs into one state—a "Greater Serbia"—was based on the grounds of an extremist nationalist ideology rooted in Serbian identity. As journalist Ed Vulliamy describes: "On this land [a Greater Serbia], wherever lived a Serb, Serbs and only Serbs were to live, with others removed by death or deportation."[96] In Rwanda, the theme of communal solidarity and identity-based exclusion was broadcast on radio. During the 1994 genocide, one particular broadcast was repeated several times over: "The *inyenzi* [a Kinyarwanda word meaning 'cockroach'] have always been Tutsi. We will exterminate them. One can identify them because they are of one race. You can identify them by their height and their small nose. When you see that small nose, break it."[97]

Clearly, legitimate and effective governance is compromised by the rise of identity-based polar factionalism and the ideological and political exploitation of such differences. The military and judicial systems become more polarized and less representative of the population. Equal access to political activity and participative decision-making becomes more restricted. The legitimacy of the state is called into question as nonrepresentative of the citizenry. Minorities find themselves outside the concept of the "nation" or the "people." Resource accumulation and distribution is unfairly distributed on the basis of identity. Cross-identity respect dissolves in the face of identity-based polar factionalism.

As we saw in Chapter 2, the entire history of the north of Ireland following British colonization is a history of identity-based polar factionalism. Today, in contemporary Northern Ireland, it remains part and parcel of all phases of life. It is a cross-cutting risk factor that intersects with and underlies every other risk factor. Particularly in governance, cross-identity respect lost out long ago to identity-based polar factionalism. Martin McGuinness, for instance, spoke frequently of the lack of respect he felt from DUP politicians regarding Irish identity and culture. One republican activist I interviewed recalled McGuinness sharing the story of a Sinn Fein politician walking into an elevator at Stormont and having DUP politicians march out of the elevator holding their noses as if affronted by the stench. In turn, Arlene Foster has spoken just as often of Sinn Fein's need to respect British identity and culture. "For too long," she said, "they [Sinn Fein] have shown nothing but disdain and disrespect for the national flag, the royal family, the armed forces, British symbols, the constitutional reality and the very name of this country."[98] Here, politics becomes a vocabulary of insult with voices and behaviors drenched in a pool of reproach. Reflecting the political stagnation resulting from such animosity, another unionist politician told me: "Our government doesn't talk policy; half of them are suing each other!"

In the Good Friday Agreement, the price of peace was to bring the extremists from both sides (DUP and Sinn Fein) into the center of governance. As we have seen, however, that center quickly became a storm. Flying in the face of power-sharing, both parties fought to define the state in reference to a dominant social identity. They outflanked the more moderate voices of unionism (the UUP) and nationalism (the SDLP), pushing them to the obscurity of the political and social margins. History was used as political currency and tragedy for political capital. And for years, voters gravitated to those identity-based polar positions. They voted for either of the two communities embedded in the Good Friday Agreement, Orange (unionist) or Green (nationalist), for no reason other than social identity. "They [the voters] know and they've accepted," Alex Kane wrote, "that the chances of constructing a credible, genuine, power-sharing government here are remote. So they'll back the party which, from their perspective, is most likely to protect and promote their constitutional position. Whether or not they voted Yes/No in 1998 is irrelevant: they know that the Good Friday Agreement is now incapable of delivering reconciliation and inter-community cooperation."[99]

In governance systems rife with such identity-based factionalism, there is limited freedom of political expression, especially from those voices proposing compromise. In late 2017, Kane concluded: "I'm not convinced there is an actual middle ground here, because I'm not convinced you can create a middle ground between the polar opposites of unionism and republicanism. . . . The middle ground didn't win between 1921 and 1972. It didn't win in 1998. It didn't win between 2007 and 2016. . . . It's never going to win. A terrible conclusion, I know; yet, for the life of me, I'm unable to draw another one."[100]

Recent council and European election results, along with the December 2019 UK general election, offered some challenge to Kane's "terrible conclusion," however, as those elections revealed a rising support for the Alliance party, a liberal middle ground party whose vision statements focus on a "shared" society, neither unionist nor nationalist. As former Northern Ireland Office advisor Tom Kelly optimistically noted following the 2019 UK general election: "In Northern Ireland pessimism is always easy. Cynicism is bred in the bones—and with good reason. But this election has shown that change can happen. That there are now limits to the polarising effect of the two traditions and that there is a viable centre ground tradition which is neither Orange or Green."[101]

The possibility of a viable center ground slowly emerging between the two polar opposites of unionism and nationalism was, however, questioned by results from the 2019 Northern Ireland Life and Times Survey (NILT). In that face-to-face survey, 39% of respondents identified as "neither" unionist nor nationalist. While "neither" was the most preferred of the three categories of political identity, it was dramatically lower than the 50% of respondents who identified as "neither" from the previous year and was, in fact, the lowest figure in the past 15 years of NILT surveys. There was, as would be expected from the decrease in "neithers," an increase in those claiming a unionist identity (up from 26% in 2018 to 33% in 2019) as well as in those claiming

a nationalist identity (up from 21% in 2018 to 23% in 2019). Of those identifying as unionist, 67% described themselves as fairly or very strongly so,
up from 64% the previous year. Of those identifying as nationalist, 71%
described themselves as fairly or very strongly so, up significantly from 61%
the previous year and the highest figure seen since the surveys began in 1998.
This increase in the intensity of nationalist identity is particularly striking in
light of the fact that the survey organizers admit Sinn Fein supporters are underrepresented in their sample.[102]

While the fact remains that more people identify as "neither" than as either
unionist or nationalist, the reality of the here and now in Northern Ireland
remains that the vast majority of those who vote continue to do so for parties
steeped in identity-based polar factionalism. The higher, though recently declining, percentage of "neithers" seems to have little impact on the lived reality of governance in contemporary Northern Ireland. As Cathal McManus,
a political sociologist at Queen's University Belfast, contends: "The vast
majority of neithers say that they do not feel close to any of the political
parties. . . . It seems that a political apathy may have set in within the neithers
section of the population which, of course, both limits its political impact
and ensures that the traditional nationalist/unionist narrative continues to
define our political culture."[103]

In other words, most "neithers" support no specific political party. Rather,
their unwillingness to embrace unionism or nationalism is simply a statement of rejection of the dominant political parties rather than an embrace
of any strong alternative; statements of who they are not rather than who
they are. As such, as McManus concludes with colleague Katy Hayward, this
disengagement makes the emergence of any "third-way" type of politics in
Northern Ireland difficult to envisage. Neithers, they argue, are "not translating into a significant force in terms of party or electoral politics . . . [nor
offering a] clear coherent expression of an alternative way forward."[104] Kane's
"terrible conclusion" regarding the absence of a middle ground between the
two communities may, indeed, be terrible precisely because of its truth.

In contemporary Northern Ireland, it remains a major challenge of governance to be inclusive and representative of the multiplicity and plurality of
overlapping identities in its population. With only 6% of MLAs not members
of the governing parties, the legislature is almost indistinguishable from the
Executive, leaving little official opposition to scrutinize the Executive.[105]
As a result, managing governance in constructive ways that reduce susceptibility to identity-based polar factionalism and ensure equal access to

political activity and participative decision-making at all levels of the political structure remains difficult. Identity still reigns over policymaking, and the winner-take-all approach to politics still rules over compromise. For political scientist Kal Holsti, a common characteristic of politically stable countries "is an inclusive political system and political parties that transcend ethnic and language groups and that focus instead on policy differences."[106] Unfortunately, despite the promise of a "New Decade, New Approach," the intransigence of identity-based polar factionalism in Northern Ireland's governance augurs that political instability remains far more likely than political stability for its near-term future.

Systematic State-Led Discrimination

A final risk factor related to the practice of governance concerns the degree of systematic state-led discrimination. Does the state have a legal framework for civilian protection—including ratification and domestication of relevant international human rights and humanitarian law treaties? Does it have the resources, training, and independent institutions to enforce such frameworks? When such frameworks or institutions are inadequate or simply do not exist, "populations are left vulnerable to those who may take advantage of the limitations of the dysfunction of State machinery, or to those that may opt for violence to respond to real or perceived threats."[107]

Systematic state-led discrimination against a minority group—including removal of civil liberties, restricting educational access, arbitrary detention or imprisonment, torture as state policy, large-scale illegal round-ups of civilians, the revocation of the right to citizenship, expropriation or destruction of property (including cultural religious and sacred sites), etc.—is a governance risk factor that weighs heavily as a concern for the protection of civilians. Such systematic state-led discrimination is a clear signal of a lack of respect for fundamental human rights and a dark portent of what may escalate with the onset and continuance of state instability. Goldstone et al. affirmed that "countries with high levels of state-led discrimination against at least one minority group . . . faced roughly triple the relative odds of future civil war onsets than those without such discriminations."[108]

Recognizing the importance of institutionalizing the promotion and protection of human rights, particularly in a deeply divided society, the Good Friday Agreement called for the creation of an independent Northern Ireland

Human Rights Commission (NIHRC) that would affirm "the mutual respect, the civil rights and religious liberties of everyone in the community."[109] The new Commission, brought into being by the Northern Ireland Act 1998 and established in 1999, would become the first national human rights institution in the UK. While funded by the UK government and answerable to Westminster, NIHRC works as a quasi-independent public body to promote and protect human rights. The NIHRC promotes awareness of human rights through education, training, and research; advises Westminster, the Northern Ireland Executive and Assembly, and other key agencies on legislation and compliance with human rights frameworks; monitors international treaties; and operates an advice clinic for legal cases.[110]

Most importantly, it was hoped that the NIHRC would develop a Bill of Rights for Northern Ireland reflecting "mutual respect for the identity and ethos of both communities and a parity of esteem."[111] By institutionalizing human rights in this way, Northern Ireland could implement safeguards against the recurrence of violence by building a fairer, more inclusive society. The hope for a Bill of Rights for Northern Ireland predated the Good Friday Agreement by more than three decades. The idea for a human rights instrument had first been proposed at Stormont in 1964, and again at Westminster in 1971, but neither proposal resulted in the passage of legislation. Proposals continued through the 1970s and 1980s, but no bill made its way successfully through Stormont or Westminster. The idea was still floated by academics, activists, and politicians through the early 1990s, but it was never seriously considered by the Northern Ireland Office.[112]

After nearly a decade of intensive outreach measures and consultations, and following through on its mandate from the Good Friday Agreement, the NIHRC finally presented initial recommendations for a human rights bill to the Secretary of State in December 2008. Their report recommended that a Bill of Rights for Northern Ireland should include various rights supplementary to the European Convention on Human Rights, with the majority of those drawn from international human rights treaties to which the UK was already legally bound. The Northern Ireland Office then conducted a months-long public consultation in response to those recommendations before eventually rejecting the majority of them since they were not specific to the "particular circumstances" of Northern Ireland.[113] Months later, an NIHRC response paper noted that "the tone and content of the NIO consultation paper is disappointing . . . [in its] lack of understanding of the purpose and function of a Bill of Rights, [its failure] to take appropriate account of international human rights standards, [its suggestion to lower] existing human rights standards in Northern Ireland, [its failure] to satisfy the minimum common law consultation requirements, and [its misrepresentation of] the advice given by the Commission."[114]

As of this writing, despite years of back-and-forth debate and consultations, the process of developing a Bill of Rights in Northern Ireland is at a standstill; an unfinished work of the peace process. Annual budget and staffing cuts to the NIHRC, combined with three years of paralyzed governance, have gutted its ability to fulfill its mission, let alone regain momentum on a Bill of Rights. Regardless of political and economic circumstances, the NIHRC's 2020 annual statement reemphasized that "the need for overarching rights protections that provide safeguards for everyone in Northern Ireland remains one of the essential tools for a durable, peaceful society moving forward."[115] The "New Decade, New Approach" deal acknowledges the importance of the NIHRC and proposes an Ad-Hoc Assembly Committee be established to consider the creation of a Bill of Rights in light of Northern Ireland's "particular circumstances."[116] Unfortunately, such work remains low on the priority list as legislators deal with more pressing issues to get Stormont—and the country—up and running again.

The Northern Ireland Act 1998 also created another complementary human rights body titled the Equality Commission for Northern Ireland (ECNI). Like the NIHRC, the ECNI was set up as a quasi-independent public body sponsored by the Northern Ireland Executive Office, with a specific charge for "providing protection against discrimination on the grounds of age, disability, race, religion and political opinion, sex and sexual orientation."[117] The ECNI took over the work of previously separate bodies dealing with anti-discrimination and equality laws. With much more robust staffing and support than the NIHRC, the ECNI works to ensure that equality of opportunity is mainstreamed by public authorities in their policymaking, policy implementation, and policy review. This watchdog work also places them in the crosshairs of some very divisive political, social, and religious issues related to policies of systematic state-led discrimination—particularly in the areas of same-sex marriage and abortion rights.

Historically, and out of step with the rest of the UK, Northern Ireland has been traditionally conservative in respect to both issues, with same-sex marriage not legal and abortion allowed only when a woman's life was at risk (rape, incest, and fatal fetal abnormality were not sufficient reasons for an abortion). In 2017–2018, termination of pregnancy statistics from Northern

Ireland's Department of Health revealed only 12 terminations nation-wide, one less than the previous year. In 2018, then vice-chair of the United Nations Committee on the Elimination of Discrimination Against Women, Ruth Halperin-Kaddari, said Northern Ireland's abortion laws, the violation of which were potentially punishable by life imprisonment, constituted "violence against women that may amount to torture or cruel, inhuman or degrading treatment."[118] Like many other social issues in Northern Ireland, marriage equality and abortion rights became weaponized in the perpetual political war between the DUP and Sinn Fein. The socially conservative DUP maintained a hardline stance with its support of a traditional definition of marriage between one man and one woman and its family values and pro-life commitment through one of the world's most restrictive and punitive abortion laws. Sinn Fein, despite its Catholic heritage, stood up a human rights-based party platform of support for marriage equality and pro-choice abortion rights.

Over time, there has been growing—if grudging from some quarters—public support for more progressive perspectives on both issues. The 2013 NILT survey, for instance, revealed that 59% of respondents believed same-sex marriages should be recognized by the law as valid. In the next survey in which NILT asked the question, in 2018, that figure had risen to 68%, with 81% of Catholic respondents agreeing compared to 53% of Protestant respondents.[119] Similarly encouraging trends have emerged for abortion rights. In 2016, 71% of respondents "agreed" or "strongly agreed" that abortion should be a matter for medical regulation and not criminal law. In 2018, that figure had increased to 82% (with nearly identical rates of agreement for Catholic and Protestant respondents), with "strongly agree" moving from 23% to 44%.[120]

For years, the DUP had the political weight at Stormont to wield the PoC to block any attempts at reform related to same-sex marriage or abortion rights. In July 2019, however, in the absence of a sitting government at Stormont, MPs at Westminster overwhelmingly passed a momentous amendment to a routine bill on governance of Northern Ireland. The amendment mandated the introduction of same-sex marriage legislation in Northern Ireland as well as the liberalizing of abortion rights. While the votes did not automatically change law in Northern Ireland, they did compel the UK government to make the changes if Stormont was not restored by October 21, 2019.

When devolution was not restored by that date, same-sex marriage in Northern Ireland became legal as of midnight on Monday, October 21, 2019.

On February 11, 2020, after changes in the law had been formally approved, Robyn Peoples and Sharni Edwards made history by becoming the first couple to finalize a same-sex civil marriage wedding in Northern Ireland (it would be another 10 months before the first same-sex religious marriage wedding in Northern Ireland would take place). Echoing the views of many who had long fought for marriage equality, Peoples said: "Our love is personal, but the law which said we couldn't marry was political . . . we can now say that those days are over."[121] The Court of Appeal in Belfast would later rule that the preexisting ban on same-sex marriage was unjustified discrimination. Lord Chief Justice Sir Declan Morgan concluded: "We are satisfied that it was clear by the time of the delivery of the first instance judgment in this case in August 2017 that the absence of same-sex marriage in this jurisdiction discriminated against same-sex couples, that a fair balance between tradition and personal rights had not been struck and that therefore the discrimination was not justified."[122]

On March 25, 2020, a new legal framework for lawful access to abortion services in Northern Ireland, in alignment with the United Nations' Convention on the Elimination of Discrimination Against Women, was rolled out by the Northern Ireland Office. With First Minister Arlene Foster (DUP) describing it as "a very sad day for Northern Ireland" and Deputy First Minister Michelle O'Neill (Sinn Fein) hailing it as "welcomed progress," the legislation, from March 31 on, allows for abortion on request for the first 12 weeks of pregnancy and abortion up to 24 weeks on the grounds that continuance of the pregnancy would involve risk of injury to the physical or mental health of the pregnant woman. Abortion will also be available in cases of severe and fatal fetal anomalies, with no gestational limit.[123]

In response to these sweeping reforms, Arlene Foster contends, now that Stormont is up and running again, the Northern Ireland Assembly need to have their voice heard on same-sex marriage and abortion rights since they are, in her opinion, devolved matters. She maintains "it will be a very different voice to what has been imposed on us from Westminster."[124] The DUP is particularly adamant about legal protections for religious organizations or individuals who refuse to marry same-sex couples on the grounds of religious belief (a legal position also supported by the ECNI, though it insists "that any exception to the law must be narrowly defined and objectively justifiable . . . [and] in compliance with human rights law").[125] The DUP also see the decriminalization of abortion as extremely too liberalizing, particularly compared to the rest of Europe, and have doubled-down on their standing as Northern Ireland's only pro-life party. In June 2020, a DUP motion calling for the rejection of the abortion law enacted by Westminster passed the Assembly by 46 votes to 40. Its passage, however, does not have the power itself to override the Westminster legislation and actually change the law. Rather, it was a purely symbolic message to the British government about Stormont's views on the "constitutional indignity" of Westminster unilaterally imposing the legislation on Northern Ireland.[126]

Despite these recent advances in the specific areas of same-sex marriage and abortion rights, the general human rights situation in Northern Ireland remains discouragingly stagnant over recent years. As described by Northern Irish academics Colin Harvey and Anne Smith in March 2018: "The human rights and equality promises of the peace process have not been delivered."[127] In early 2019, Liam Kennedy, professor emeritus of economic history from Queen's University Belfast, similarly bemoaned "Northern Ireland is still the black spot in Western Europe for the most serious human rights abuses."[128] Likewise, in its 2019 annual statement, NIHRC's Chief Commissioner Les Allamby lamented "that not one human rights concern has been effectively resolved in 2019. . . . The [human rights] issues making no progress are substantial, lengthy, and broad based."[129]

Why do human rights still have such a difficult time gaining purchase in contemporary Northern Ireland? Some of this is due to the widespread perception that organizations such as the NIHRC and ECNI are "dominated by nationalists and leftists."[130] Indeed, unionists have long held that these organizations are biased—in outlook, membership, and action—against the pro-Union community. As became apparent time and again in my interviews, unionist and loyalist communities see the vocabulary of "human rights" as a continuation of the civil rights agitation by nationalists and republicans that, in their view, started the Troubles. As a result, many see Sinn Fein's push for "human rights" and its corresponding focus on state abuses of those rights as a revisionist cover for an agenda that has, at its heart, the desire for a united Ireland. As one community activist, a former loyalist political prisoner, told me: "Sinn Fein just uses 'human rights' [fingers used as air quotes for emphasis] as a lever for what they really want—the death of our British identity." Similarly, an interviewee in a study by Maggie Beirne and Colin Knox stated: "Protestants are culturally happy with principles such as being good to one's neighbour, but feel that the language of equality and rights is being superimposed on society."[131]

Some in the unionist and loyalist community point to an even deeper, philosophical difference between Catholics and Protestants on the issue of individual rights. "Protestants can see rights as selfish," said John Kyle, a Councilor on Belfast City Council and a member of the Progressive Unionist Party. "They can lead," he continued, "to legal conflict and can heighten the role of un-elected judges, which may undermine the democratic process."[132] Through this lens, the "human rights" vocabulary is seen "as too legalistic, too state-centric, and too focused on international principles to successfully affect local realities and divisions."[133] So, the top-down human rights approach, with its focus on outcomes related to state accountability and international standards, can be portrayed as oppositional to the grassroots work of local community relations and the process of reconciliation. While the two approaches can and should work in a more interdependent, complementary, and synergistic fashion, their perceived tension (and the false dichotomy it implies) helps explain why most unionist and loyalist voices have disengaged from any discussion about a Bill of Rights. From their viewpoint, the expansive proposals put forth to date for such a bill have gone far beyond what was called for in the Good Friday Agreement. Moreover, the international and European legal conventions regarding human rights to which the UK government already has subscribed are, in their minds, more than sufficient tools for Northern Ireland.

Unfortunately, however, Brexit may threaten the relevance of at least some of those conventions. Part of the UK's process of withdrawing from the European Union (EU) included a commitment to ensure that there is no diminution of rights, safeguards, and equality of opportunity as outlined in the Good Friday Agreement. In an early version of its EU withdrawal deal, the UK government, in order to protect human rights and equality legislation in Northern Ireland, committed to allocate special oversight and enforcement powers to the NIHRC and ECNI. The final version of the 599-page withdrawal agreement, signed on January 24, 2020, affirmed the UK's commitment to facilitating "the related work of the Northern Ireland Human Rights Commission [and] the Equality Commission for Northern Ireland."[134] The extent of post-Brexit oversight and enforcement granted to the NIHRC and ECNI, however, has not yet been detailed. Nor has the financial resources for adhering to the no-diminution commitment. The transition period for the withdrawal agreement extends until December 31, 2020, so these specific details of the NIHRC's and ECNI's future work in Northern Ireland remain up to negotiation. Should, however, no long-term deal be reached by the end of the transition period, the human rights safeguards ensured by the Charter of Fundamental Rights of the European Union will no longer be applicable in Northern Ireland. This could be particularly destructive if Northern Ireland fails to make any movement on the creation of a Bill of Rights, one reflective both of international standards as well as the particular circumstances of the society for which it is developed, as a backstop alternative.

Conclusion

The "New Decade, New Approach" deal represented a renewed effort to breathe life into the systems of governance in Northern Ireland. In signing it, the five main political parties of Northern Ireland committed to coming together to govern in the best interests of everyone in their country. To do so will require far-reaching acts of political generosity and courage by political leaders, acts that may well draw condemnation from more short-sighted constituents with a range of vested interests—emotional, historic, constitutional, economic, political, geographic, national, psychological, physical, and social—in maintaining the status quo of a deeply divided society.[135]

Such political generosity and courage are not unheard of in Northern Ireland. At a charity event in Belfast, on a Wednesday morning in June 2012, Martin McGuinness, then deputy First Minister of Northern Ireland, shook hands with Queen Elizabeth. He did not bow his head, as others did, but the handshake was firm and sustained as McGuinness greeted the Queen in Irish. The public moment, with McGuinness wearing a green tie and the Queen an "apple green" outfit and hat, was captured by photographer Paul Faith of the *Press Association* and made the front pages of newspapers around the world.[136] As BBC columnist John Simpson wrote: "In 1972, it would have seemed like the most absurd fantasy that the Queen would ever shake hands with a leading figure from the Provisional IRA."[137] Particularly poignant was the fact that the Queen lost her cousin, Lord Louis Mountbatten, to an IRA bomb that blew up his fishing boat in County Sligo in 1979—when McGuinness was the IRA's Chief of Staff.

The handshake was viewed by many as an iconic mark of progress and reconciliation. Former US Secretary of State Hillary Clinton described it as "the most remarkable sign of change yet" in the Northern Ireland peace process. Similarly, former UK Prime Minister David Cameron described the moment as "the most transformative bit of diplomacy I have seen. It was amazing."[138] Later, in a speech at Westminster, McGuinness said the handshake "was in a very pointed, deliberate and symbolic way offering the hand of friendship to unionists through the person of Queen Elizabeth for which many unionists have a deep affinity. It is an offer I hope many will accept in the same spirit it was offered."[139] Gerry Adams, then President of Sinn Fein, agreed: "I think the vast majority of unionists will be pleased this happened because they know it was essentially a real gesture towards their sense of identity and their sense of allegiance."[140] He later affirmed it was "the right decision at the right time and for the right reasons."[141]

The political generosity exhibited on both sides was certainly not without its risk. It was a step, and a handshake, too far for some. Some unionists saw the handshake as an overly choreographed sellout that was leagues beneath the Queen's stature as the symbol of British rule in Ulster. Others aimed their frustrations at Sinn Fein for hijacking the Queen's Diamond Jubilee visit to Northern Ireland marking her 60-year reign. Then First Minister Peter Robinson of the DUP parsed that concern carefully: "I know for many in the media, the focus has been on a handshake and a photograph, but for most people in Northern Ireland it is not about one moment of history but the opportunity to celebrate and give thanks for 60 very full years of Your Majesty's service to this nation."[142]

On the other side of the divide, McGuinness's action was a moment of stark betrayal for some republicans, a rejection of a life oath he took when he joined the IRA. The day before the scheduled handshake, dissident republicans had installed a large protest sign on Belfast's Black Mountain reading "Eriu [an Irish Celtic warrior queen] is Our Queen," with a massive Irish tricolor below it. Just after the handshake, one journalist yelled: "Martin, are you still true to your convictions?" McGuinness's quick reply, "I'm still a republican," fell on deaf ears for some.[143] In his hometown of Derry, for instance, I interviewed one dissident republican, a former political prisoner, who said: "That was the day McGuinness became dead to us in the true republican movement. You don't shake the hand of an imperialist murderess and expect to still be respected by the people you claim to represent and lead." McGuinness would later be the target of a death threat from the Continuity IRA.

Despite the sporadic grumblings on both sides, the handshake stood, and still stands, as an exemplar of the political generosity and courage necessary for effective governance in a post-conflict society. Unfortunately, it does not equally stand as a lesson learned. As I write these words, even in the midst of a COVID-19 pandemic that calls for resolute unity, the deep political fissures in Northern Ireland's governance are still apparent. In selfish pursuit of sectarian point-scoring, the DUP and Sinn Fein have clashed over when to close schools, which businesses were to be deemed "essential," how much temporary power to grant police over discouraging people from crowding in public places, to what degree the Health Minister (Robin Swann of the UUP) or Finance Minister (Conor Murphy of Sinn Fein) is responsible for the slow response to the pandemic, whether the British Army should be called in for assistance with the crisis, and when to reopen recycling centers, parks, and cemeteries. Sinn Fein has been openly challenging the UK's approach for tackling coronavirus and is advocating, instead, for an all-Ireland approach that takes geographical rather than political ties into account and is tied to recommendations from the World Health Organization and the EU's European Centre for Disease Prevention and Control. The DUP, conversely, blindly carries on in taking its lead on crisis response from London which continues to drag its feet and mindlessly ignore the mitigation and containment recommendations of relevant international bodies. All of these fissures where deepened when, on June 30, 2020, Michelle O'Neill contravened the very social distancing guidelines she helped set for the pandemic by attending, along with almost 2,000 other mourners, the funeral of prominent republican Bobby Storey in west Belfast. As of this writing, an investigation into any potential breaches of public health regulations has been submitted to the Public Prosecution Service.

Clearly, the erosion of mutual trust and respect among those in governance, assuming it has ever been there to begin with, has not been counteracted by a momentary public health crisis—and likely will not be, no matter how significant that crisis may become. The politicized self-interests are deepening divisions within the newly restored and still fragile Northern Ireland Executive and, by working against a common response strategy, having deadly implications for the people of Northern Ireland. There is, once again, Orange and Green and a blank political canvas in between. For Eilis O'Hanlon, "'We're all in this together' is just a slogan, not a blueprint that ministers at Stormont think applies to them, too."[144] Recognizing the same reality, Alex Kane implored of the political leadership: "COVID-19 isn't going to give a damn about where the border begins and ends; and nor will it give a damn about national identities or voting habits in Northern Ireland. Every one of us, every single one, is a target for the virus and every one of us, every single one—irrespective of political beliefs—must be on the same side until this crisis is over."[145]

Being "on the same side" in contemporary Northern Ireland remains a tall task. Too many people remain caught in the vise-grip of the tyranny of divided memories discussed in the previous chapter. Politics in Northern Ireland is existential; frightfully, but understandably, representative of that divided reality. The Good Friday Agreement, for all its noble intentions, has sewn those deep divisions into the very fabric of governance. Identity has become entrenched and reified rather than expanded and reconciled. To enable the "New Decade, New Approach" deal to bring good governance back to Northern Ireland will require levels of political generosity and courage that bow to the past but do not bend to it. Whether the political leadership emerges to extend that generosity and enact that courage remains to be seen.

Notes

1. The full text of Martin McGuinness's resignation letter can be found at https://www.belfasttelegraph.co.uk/news/northern-ireland/martin-mcguinness-resignation-letter-in-full-35353349.html, accessed on September 5, 2019.
2. Clinton quote taken from *Belfast Telegraph* (March 21, 2017), accessed on September 5, 2019, at https://www.belfasttelegraph.co.uk/news/northern-ireland/martin-mcguinness-death-thousands-pay-tribute-to-sinn-fein-veteran-in-west-belfast-candlelight-vigil-35553585.html
3. See Colin Coulter and Peter Shirlow, "From the 'Long War' to the 'Long Peace': An Introduction to the Special Edition," *Capital & Class* 43 (2019), 16–17.
4. The exact legislative powers for the Parliament of Northern Ireland and those retained for Westminster were laid out in the Government of Ireland Act of 1920. The complete text of the act can be accessed at http://www.legislation.gov.uk/ukpga/1920/67/pdfs/ukpga_19200067_en.pdf.
5. For more complete details, see https://www.gov.uk/guidance/devolution-settlement-northern-ireland, accessed on September 5, 2018.
6. This upholds Sinn Fein's long-standing tradition of nationalist abstentionism in which those elected as Members of Parliament refuse to take their seats because they do not recognize the Parliament's right to legislate for any part of the island of Ireland.
7. Voting data in this paragraph taken from https://www.belfasttelegraph.co.uk/news/politics/general-election-2019/, accessed on January 27, 2020.
8. "New Decade, New Approach" (January 2020), accessed on January 27, 2020, at https://static.rasset.ie/documents/news/2020/01/new-decade-new-approach.pdf
9. See Ralph Hewitt, "It Will Take £5bn to Get Northern Ireland Running Again," *The Belfast Telegraph* (January 13, 2020), accessed on January 27, 2020, at https://www.belfasttelegraph.co.uk/news/northern-ireland/it-will-take-5bn-to-get-northern-ireland-running-again-boris-johnson-warned-by-economist-birnie-38859221.html

10. Andrew Madden, "Orange Order Chief Mervyn Gibson: Community 'Frustrated and Angry' Over Stormont Deal," *The Belfast Telegraph* (January 31, 2020), accessed on February 3, 2020, at https://www.belfasttelegraph.co.uk/news/politics/orange-order-chief-mervyn-gibson-community-frustrated-and-angry-over-stormont-deal-38913189.html

11. Jon Tonge, "Power-Sharing Agreement May Be On the Horizon . . . But It Has to Stick," *The Belfast Telegraph* (January 2, 2020), accessed on January 28, 2020, at https://www.belfasttelegraph.co.uk/opinion/news-analysis/power- sharing-agreement- may-be-on-the-horizon-but-it-has-to-stick-38830498.html

12. The suspension of the Northern Ireland Assembly from 2002 to 2007 led to the return of direct rule from the UK government; so, technically, there was a sitting government in Northern Ireland over that period. The previous record for longest period without a functioning government in a democracy was held by Belgium in 2010–2011, when the opposing Flemish and Walloons were unable to form a governing coalition following national elections.

13. John Manley, "Big Two Give Green Light to Restoration of the Stormont Institutions," *The Belfast Telegraph* (January 11, 2020), accessed on January 28, 2020, at http://www.irishnews.com/news/northernirelandnews/2020/01/11/news/big-two-give-green-light-to-restoration-of-the-stormont-institutions-1811362/

14. Eilis O'Hanlon," "Is That It?," *The Belfast Telegraph* (January 13, 2020), accessed on January 27, 2020, at https://www.belfasttelegraph.co.uk/opinion/columnists/eilis-o-hanlon/is-that-it-long-awaited-stormont-could-have-been-a-fresh-start-but-its-just-a-case-of-deja-vu-38856188.html

15. Alex Kane, "Speed of Return Shows Just How Much SF and DUP Wanted to Avoid an Election," *The Irish News* (January 17, 2020), accessed on February 11, 2020, at http://www.irishnews.com/opinion/columnists/2020/01/17/news/alex-kane-speed-of-return-shows-just-how-much-sf-and-dup-wanted-to-avoid-an-election-1815400

16. These defining features of governance are taken from the "Worldwide Governance Indicators" project, accessed on January 16, 2015, at http://info.worldbank.org/governance/wgi

17. Monty G. Marshall and Benjamin R. Cole, *Global Report 2014: Conflict, Governance, and State Fragility* (Vienna, VA: Center for Systemic Peace, 2014), 21.

18. Nicolas Rost, "Will It Happen Again? On the Possibility of Forecasting the Risk of Genocide," *Journal of Genocide Research* 15 (2013), 49.

19. Maarten Gehem, Philipp Marten, Matthijs Maas, and Menno Schellekens, *Balancing on the Brink: Vulnerability of States in the Middle East and North Africa* (The Hague: Centre for Strategic Studies, 2014), 12.

20. Ian Bremmer, *The J Curve: A New Way to Understand Why Nations Rise and Fall* (New York: Simon & Schuster, 2006), 5.

21. Jack A. Goldstone, Robert H. Bates, David L. Epstein, Ted Robert Gurr, Michael B. Lustik, Monty G. Marshall, Jay Ulfelder, and Mark Woodward, "A Global Model for Forecasting Political Instability," *American Journal of Political Science* 54 (2010), 197.

22. See http://www.systemicpeace.org/polity/polity4.htm, accessed on February 23, 2015.

23. Arend Lijphart, *Patterns of Democracy: Government Forms and Performance in Thirty-Six Countries,* 2nd ed. (New Haven, CT: Yale University Press, 2012), 12. The first edition of the book was published in 1999.

24. Adrian Guelke, *Politics in Deeply Divided Societies* (London: Polity, 2012), 114.

25. Lijphart, *Patterns of Democracy,* 12.

26. Ibid., 144, 135.

27. See Arend Ljiphart, *Democracy in Plural Societies: A Comparative Exploration* (New Haven, CT: Yale University Press, 1977) as well as his "Consociational Democracy," *World Politics* 21 (January 1969), 207–225.

28. Arend Lijphart, "Consociational Democracy," *World Politics* 21 (January 1969), 214.

29. Ibid., 216.

30. David J. Simon, "Building State Capacity to Prevent Atrocity Crimes: Implementing Pillars One and Two of the R2P Framework," *Policy Analysis Brief* (The Stanley Foundation, September 2012), 3.

31. See Arend Lijphart, "Constitutional Design for Divided Societies," *Journal of Democracy* 15 (April 2004), 96–109.

32. Ibid., 96, 99.

33. Ibid., 97.

34. The full text of the Good Friday Agreement can be found at https://assets.publishing. service.gov.uk/government/uploads/system/uploads/attachment_data/file/136652/ agreement.pdf

35. For a technical summary of these critiques, see Ian S. Lustick, "Lijphart, Lakatos, and Consociationalism," *World Politics* 50 (October 1997), 88–117.

36. Rubert Taylor, "Introduction: The Promise of Consociational Theory," in Rupert Taylor (ed.), *Consociational Theory: McGarry and O'Leary and the Northern Ireland Conflict* (London: Routledge, 2009), 7.

37. Rob Aitken, "Cementing Divisions? An Assessment of the Impact of International Interventions and Peace-Building Policies on Ethnic Identities and Divisions," *Policy Studies* 28 (2007), 262.

38. Timofey Agarin, Allison McCulloch, and Cera Murtagh, "Others in Deeply Divided Societies: A Research Agenda," *Nationalism and Ethnic Politics* 24 (2018), 300.

39. David Lanz, Laurie Nathan, and Alexandre Raffoul, "Negotiations, Continued: Ensuring the Positive Performance of Power-Sharing Arrangements," *United States Institute of Peace* (September 2019), 5.

40. See, for instance, Allison McCulloch and Stef Vandeginste, "Veto Power and Power-Sharing: Insights from Burundi (2000–2018)," *Democratization* 26 (2019), 1176–1193.

41. Lanz et al., "Negotiations, Continued."

42. Guelke, *Politics in Deeply Divided Societies,* 122.

43. Lanz et al., "Negotiations, Continued," 4.

44. Arend Lijphart, "The Wave of Power-Sharing Democracy," in Andrew Reynolds (ed.), *The Architecture of Democracy: Constitutional Design, Conflict Management, and Democracy* (New York: Oxford University Press, 2002), 37.

45. John Fuh-sheng Hsieh, "Arend Lijphart and Consociationalism," *Taiwan Journal of Democracy* Special Issue (2013), 87–101.

46. Adrian Guelke, "Institutionalized Power-Sharing: The International Dimension," *Ethnopolitics* (2019), accessed on September 17, 2019, at https://doi.org/10.1080/17449057.2019.1569860

47. For an application of some of these approaches in Cyprus, see John McGarry, "Centripedalism, Consociationalism and Cyprus: The 'Adoptability' Question," *Political Studies* 65 (2017), 512–529.

48. Hsieh, "Arend Lijphart and Consociationalism," 93.

49. See World Bank, "Worldwide Governance Indicators," accessed on December 16, 2020 at http://info.worldbank.org/governance/wgi/

50. See the Organisation for Economic Co-operation and Development's "Foreign Bribery Report" of 2014, accessed on January 26, 2015, at http://www.oecd.org/corruption/launch-foreign-bribery-report.htm/

51. See http://www.transparency.org, accessed on February 11, 2020.

52. I. William Zartman, *Preventing Identity Conflicts Leading to Genocide and Mass Killings* (New York: International Peace Institute, 2010), 12.

53. The full text of Martin McGuinness's resignation letter can be found at https://www.belfasttelegraph.co.uk/news/northern-ireland/martin-mcguinness-resignation-letter-in-full-35353349.html, accessed on September 5, 2019.

54. Quote taken from https://www.bbc.com/news/uk-northern-ireland-38301428, accessed on September 24, 2019.

55. Complete information about the Renewable Heat Incentive Inquiry can be found at https://www.rhiinquiry.org/, accessed on March 17, 2020.

56. Sam McBride, "Stormont Civil Servants Who Retire Will Escape Discipline Over RHI," *Belfast News Letter* (May 13, 2020), accessed on May 14, 2020, at https://www.newsletter.co.uk/news/politics/stormont-civil-servants-who-retire-will-escape-discipline-over-rhi-2851043

57. Conor Maccauley, "NI Planning System Has Low Levels of Public Trust, Research Finds," *BBC News* (June 26, 2020), accessed on July 28, 2020, at https://www.bbc.com/news/uk-northern-ireland-53179484

58. Marshall and Cole, *Global Report 2014*, 21.

59. After Brexit, Europe Day was removed, leaving only 17 designated days. As part of the "New Decade, New Approach" agreement, however, designated days are set to be increased to 20.

60. The Flags (Northern Ireland) Order 2000 and its associated regulations set out the position of the flying of the Union Flag on specific government buildings and courthouses on specified days.

61. Una Bradley, "Loyalists to Request Lowering of Tricolour," *The Irish Times* (January 5, 2013), accessed on February 11, 2020, at https://www.irishtimes.com/news/loyalists-to-request-lowering-of-tricolour-1.954313

62. Data taken from https://cain.ulster.ac.uk/issues/identity/flag-2012.htm, accessed on February 11, 2020.

63. See Julian O'Neill, "Loyalist Flag Protests 'Factor' in £50m Economic Losses," *BBC News*, September 9, 2013, accessed on February 11, 2020, at https://www.bbc.com/news/uk-northern-ireland-24144378

64. John Toner, "Loyalists March on Belfast City Hall for Union Flag Protests Anniversary," *Belfast Telegraph* (November 30, 2019), accessed on February 11, 2020, at https://www.belfasttelegraph.co.uk/sunday-life/loyalists-march-on-belfast-city-hall-for-union-flag-protests-anniversary-38741197.html

65. OECD, *Supporting Statebuilding in Situations of Conflict and Fragility: Policy Guidance* (Paris: OECD Publishing, 2011), 37–38.

66. See Fund for Peace, "CAST: Conflict Assessment Framework Manual" (2014), 12, accessed on December 16, 2020 at https://fundforpeace.org/wp-content/uploads/2018/08/cfsir1418-castmanual2014-english-03a.pdf

67. Michael McHugh, "Health Service Reform Needed Urgently Says Auditor General," *The Irish News* (December 18, 2018), accessed on February 15, 2020, at https://www.irishnews.com/news/healthcarenews/2018/12/18/news/health-service-reform-needed-urgently-says-auditor-general-1510849/

68. Lisa Smyth, "'Some Will Never Be Seen': Shock Extent of Waiting List Crisis Facing Robin Swann," *Belfast Telegraph* (January 16, 2020), accessed on February 15, 2020, at https://www.belfasttelegraph.co.uk/news/northern-ireland/some-will-never-be-seen-shock-extent-of-waiting-list-crisis-facing-robin-swann-38869045.html

69. See Northern Ireland Department of Health statement of February 11, 2020, accessed on February 15, 2020, at https://www.health-ni.gov.uk/news/health-budget-202021-will-be-crucial-swann

70. See Lauren Harte, "Over 500 Police Officers Off Work with Stress in Northern Ireland During the Past Year," *Belfast Telegraph* (May 4, 2020), accessed on June 8, 2020, at https://www.belfasttelegraph.co.uk/news/northern-ireland/over-500-police-officers-off-work-with-stress-in-northern-ireland-during-the-past-year-39177707.html

71. Allison Morris, "Policing in Northern Ireland Is Still Far from Normal," *The Irish News* (February 6, 2020), accessed on February 14, 2020, at http://www.irishnews.com/opinion/columnists/2020/02/06/news/allison-morris-militarised-policing-has-an-impact-on-transforming-hearts-and-minds-1834757/

72. Cited in Brendan O'Leary, *A Treatise on Northern Ireland,* Volume 2 (London: Oxford University Press, 2019), 36–37.

73. The full text of the report, titled *A New Beginning: Policing in Northern Ireland* and released in September 1999, can be accessed at https://cain.ulster.ac.uk/issues/police/patten/patten99.pdf

74. Steve James, "Sinn Fein Endorse Police Service of Northern Ireland and MI5 Operations," *World Socialist Web Site* (February 7, 2007), accessed on February 15, 2020, at https://www.wsws.org/en/articles/2007/02/irel-f07.html

75. Owen Bowcott, "Historic Vote Ends Sinn Fein's Long Battle with the Police Service in Northern Ireland," *The Guardian* (January 29, 2007), accessed on February 16, 2020, at https://www.theguardian.com/politics/2007/jan/29/uk.northernireland

76. See *Northern Ireland Policing Board Annual Report and Accounts* (1 April 2018–31 March 2019), accessed on February 15, 2020, at https://www.nipolicingboard.org.uk/sites/nipb/files/publications/Northern%20Ireland%20Policing%20Board%20Annual%20Report%20and%20Accounts%201%20April%202018%20-%2031%20March%202019.PDF

77. BBC News, "Catholics 'Must Be Encouraged to Join PSNI,' says George Hamilton" (June 7, 2019), accessed on February 15, 2020, at https://www.bbc.com/news/uk-northern-ireland-48550423

78. BBC News, "PSNI Recruitment: Catholic Primate Encourages Return to 50:50 Recruitment" (December 15, 2019), accessed on February 15, 2020, at https://www.bbc.com/news/uk-northern-ireland-50793205

79. Marina Caparini and Juneseo Hwang, "Police Reform in Northern Ireland: Achievements and Future Challenges" (October 28, 2019), accessed on February 15, 2020, at https://www.sipri.org/commentary/topical-backgrounder/2019/police-reform-northern-ireland-achievements-and-future-challenges

80. Emma Vardy, "Adverts Bid to End Paramilitary-Style Attacks in NI," *BBC News* (October 8, 2018), accessed on February 16, 2020, at https://www.bbc.com/news/education-45881781

81. The criminal conviction statistic comes from Allison Morris, "Links Between Suicide and Paramilitary Attacks 'Needs Addressed.'" *The Irish News* (February 17, 2020), accessed on February 17, 2020, at http://www.irishnews.com/news/northernirelandnews/2020/02/17/news/links-between-suicide-and-paramilitary-attacks-needs-addressed-1844189

82. The complete text of the second annual Independent Reporting Commission (IRC) report can be accessed at https://www.ircommission.org/publications/irc-second-report, accessed on February 16, 2020.

83. The complete text of the third annual IRC report can be accessed at https://www.ircommission.org/sites/irc/files/media-files/IRC%20Third%20Report.pdf. Accessed on December 16, 2020. Quoted material is taken from p. 17 of that report.

84. See Morris, "Links Between Suicide and Paramilitary Attacks 'Needs Addressed.'"

85. BBC News, "NI Paramilitaries 'Just Organised Criminals'" (October 2, 2018), accessed on February 16, 2020, at https://www.bbc.com/news/uk-northern-ireland-45712438

86. Tom Kelly, "Paramilitary Gangs Are Choking Northern Ireland's Chance of Shared Future," *The Irish News* (November 30, 2020), accessed on December 21, 2020 at https://www.irishnews.com/opinion/columnists/2020/11/30/news/tom-kelly-paramilitary-gangs-are-choking-northern-ireland-s-chance-of-a-shared-future-2144435/

87. The complete text of the third annual IRC report, from which quoted material in this paragraph is drawn (see pp. 18,7, 8 of the report), can be accessed at https://www.ircommission.org/sites/irc/files/media-files/IRC%20Third%20Report.pdf. Accessed on December 16, 2020.

88. A summary of the program's activities can be found at https://www.northernireland.gov.uk/articles/executive-programme-tackling-paramilitary-activity-and-organised-crime-0. The "Ending the Harm Campaign" can be viewed at https://www.endingtheharm.com/. Both sites were accessed on February 16, 2020.

89. Quoted material taken from p. 40 in "New Decade, New Approach" (January 2020), accessed on January 27, 2020, at https://static.rasset.ie/documents/news/2020/01/new-decade-new-approach.pdf

90. Suzanne Breen, "NI Justice Minister Naomi Long to Use New Powers to Go After Paramilitary and Crime Gang Assets," *Belfast Telegraph* (June 19, 2020), accessed on June 20, 2020, at https://www.belfasttelegraph.co.uk/news/northern-ireland/ni-justice-minister-naomi-long-to-use-new-powers-to-go-after-paramilitary-and-crime-gang-assets-39297891.html

91. Marshall and Cole, *Global Report 2014*, 5.

92. Ibid.

93. Goldstone et al., "A Global Model," 198.

94. Marshall and Cole, *Global Report 2014*, 6.

95. Fund for Peace, "CAST: Conflict Assessment Framework," 15.

96. Ed Vulliamy, *The War Is Dead, Long Live the War* (London: Vintage Books, 2012), xxvi.

97. Linda Melvern, *Conspiracy to Murder: The Rwanda Genocide* (London: Verso, 2006), 210.

98. Fiona Kelly, ""Arlene Foster Has Said Sinn Fein Need to 'Respect British Culture,'" (November 25, 2017), accessed on March 22, 2020, at https://www.buzz.ie/news/arlene-foster-sinn-fein-need-respect-british-culture-263205

99. Alex Kane, "As Talks Collapse, We Are Moving into the Political Endgame," *The Irish News* (February 16, 2018), accessed on September 17, 2019, at http://www.irishnews.com/opinion/columnists/2018/02/16/news/alex-kane-as-talks-collapse-we-are-moving-into-the-political-endgame-1256523/

100. Alex Kane, "The Political Middle Ground Is Never Going to Win," *The Irish News* (October 27, 2017), accessed on September 17, 2019, at http://www.irishnews.com/opinion/columnists/2017/10/27/news/alex-kane-the-political-middle-ground-is-never-going-to-win-1172272/

101. Mark Edwards, "DUP and Sinn Fein Must Restore Power Sharing or Face Angry Voters," *The Belfast Telegraph* (January 6, 2020), accessed on January 27, 2020, at https://www.belfasttelegraph.co.uk/news/northern-ireland/dup-and-sinn-fein-must-restore-power-sharing-or-face-angry-voters-tom-kelly-38837248.html

102. Katy Hayward and Ben Rosher, "Research Updates: Political Attitudes at a Time of Flux" (June 2020), accessed on June 18, 2020, at https://www.ark.ac.uk/ARK/sites/default/files/2020-06/update133.pdf

103. Suzanne McGongle, "50 Per Cent Identify as 'Neither Unionist nor Nationalist' in North," *The Irish News* (June 20, 2019), accessed on March 22, 2020, at http://www.irishnews.com/news/northernirelandnews/2019/06/20/news/more-people-in-north-claim-to-be-neither-unionist-or-nationalist-according-to-new-research-1645657

104. Katy Hayward and Cathal McManus, "Neither/Nor: The Rejection of Unionist and Nationalist Identities in Post-Agreement Northern Ireland," *Capital & Class*, 43 (2019), 152.

105. Sam McBride, "Hints of Reformist DUP Wing Could Discomfit Arlene Foster but Help Her Party," *Belfast News Letter* (May 30, 2020), accessed on June 3, 2020, at https://www.newsletter.co.uk/news/politics/sam-mcbride-hints-reformist-dup-wing-could-discomfit-arlene-foster-help-her-party-2869443

106. Cited in Adam Jones, *Genocide: A Comprehensive Introduction*, 2nd ed. (New York: Routledge, 2011), 570.

107. United Nations, "Framework of Analysis," 12.

108. Goldstone et al., "A Global Model," 197.

109. The full text of the Good Friday Agreement was accessed on September 2, 2019, at https://www.gov.uk/government/publications/the-belfast-agreement

110. See https://www.nihrc.org/about-us, accessed on March 25, 2020.

111. The full text of the Good Friday Agreement was accessed on September 2, 2019, at https://www.gov.uk/government/publications/the-belfast-agreement

112. For a comprehensive review of this history, see Colin Harvey and Alex Schwartz, "Designing a Bill of Rights for Northern Ireland," *Northern Ireland Legal Quarterly* 60(2) (2009), 181–199.

113. The complete response of the Northern Ireland Office, dated November 30, 2009, can be found at https://cain.ulster.ac.uk/issues/law/bor/nio301109bor.pdf, accessed on March 31, 2020.

114. Northern Ireland Human Rights Commission, *A Bill of Rights for Northern Ireland: Next Steps* (Belfast: Author, February 2010), 5.

115. Northern Ireland Human Rights Commission, *The 2020 Annual Statement: Human Rights in Northern Ireland* (Belfast: Author, December 2020), quoted material taken from p. 8.

116. Quoted material taken from p. 37 in "New Decade, New Approach" (January 2020), accessed on January 27, 2020, at https://static.rasset.ie/documents/news/2020/01/new-decade-new-approach.pdf

117. See https://www.equalityni.org/AboutUs, accessed on March 25, 2020.

118. Rohan Naik, "Division over Abortion Exposed During COVID-19 Despite Change in Law," *The Detail* (May 6, 2020), accessed on June 4, 2020, at https://www.thedetail.tv/articles/abortion-northern-ireland-covid-19

119. See https://www.ark.ac.uk/nilt/2018/LGBT_Issues/SSEXMARR.html, accessed on March 25, 2020.

120. See https://www.ark.ac.uk/nilt/2018/Abortion/ABMEDCR.html, accessed on March 25, 2020.

121. BBC News, "Same-Sex Marriage: Couple Make History as First in NI" (February 11, 2020), accessed on March 30, 2020, at https://www.bbc.com/news/uk-northern-ireland-51466588

122. Belfast Telegraph, "Ban on Same Sex Marriage was 'Unjustified Discrimination,' Northern Ireland Court Rules," *Belfast Telegraph* (April 7, 2020), accessed on April 12, 2020, at https://www.belfasttelegraph.co.uk/news/northern-ireland/ban-on-same-sex-marriage-was-unjustified-discrimination-northern-ireland-court-rules-39110100.html

123. Rebecca Black, "NI's First and Deputy First Ministers Divided over New Abortion Regulations," *Belfast Telegraph* (March 25, 2020), accessed on March 30, 2020, at https://www.belfasttelegraph.co.uk/news/northern-ireland/nis-first-and-deputy-first-ministers-divided-over-new-abortion-regulations-39075971.html/

124. Peter Dunne, "Arlene Foster Says Same-Sex Marriage and Abortion Rights 'Were Imposed on Northern Ireland,'" *GCN* (January 23, 2020), accessed on March 30, 2020, at https://gcn.ie/arlene-foster-same-sex-marriage-imposed-northern-ireland/

125. Roisin Mallon, letter to Raphaela Thynne re: Proposed Regulations on same-sex religious marriage and conversion (February 23, 2020), 1.

126. Quoted material comes from Suzanne Breen, "Stormont May Still Say No to Abortion . . . But It Can't Turn Clock Back," *Belfast Telegraph* (June 2, 2020), accessed on June 4, 2020, at https://www.belfasttelegraph.co.uk/opinion/columnists/suzanne-breen/stormont-may-still-say-no-to-abortion-but-it-cant-turn-clock-back-39255540.html

127. Colin Harvey and Anne Smith, "Good Friday Agreement at 20: The Return of the Bill or Rights?" (March 29, 2018), accessed on September 2, 2019, at http://qpol.qub.ac.uk/return-bill-rights-ni/

128. Liam Kennedy, "Onus Is on Intelligence Services to Arrest These Vigilantes on Basis of Other Criminal Activities," *Belfast Telegraph* (January 1, 2019), accessed on March 25, 2020, at https://www.belfasttelegraph.co.uk/opinion/news-analysis/onus-is-on-intelligence-services-to-arrest-these-vigilantes-on-basis-of-other-criminal-activities-37671250.html

129. Northern Ireland Human Rights Commission, *The 2019 Annual Statement: Human Rights in Northern Ireland* (Belfast: Author, December 2019), quoted material taken from p. 6.

130. Ruth Dudley Edwards, "A Human Rights Sector That Is Interested Only in the Sins of the State Can Have Little Credibility," *Belfast Telegraph* (January 7, 2019), accessed on March 25, 2020, at https://www.belfasttelegraph.co.uk/opinion/columnists/ruth-dudley-edwards/ruth-dudley-edwards-a-human-rights-sector-that-is-interested-only-in-sins-of-the-state-can-have-little-credibility-37685390.html

131. Maggie Beirne and Colin Knox, "Reconciliation and Human Rights in Northern Ireland: A False Dichotomy?," *Journal of Human Right Practice* 6 (2014), 35.

132. Dan Keenan, "Catholics and Protestants 'See Human Rights Differently,'" *The Irish Times* (August 31, 2009), accessed on March 31, 2020, at https://www.irishtimes.com/news/catholics-and-protestants-see-human-rights-differently-1.728625

133. Beirne and Knox, "Reconciliation and Human Rights in Northern Ireland," 33.

134. Quoted material is taken from Article 2 of the EU-UK Withdrawal Agreement. The full legal text of the agreement can be found at https://ec.europa.eu/info/european-union-and-united-kingdom-forging-new-partnership/eu-uk-withdrawal-agreement_en, accessed on March 29, 2020.

135. The concept of "political generosity" is taken from Seamus Mallon, "Why a Simple Majority in Favour of United Ireland Will Not Deliver Future We Deserve," *Belfast Telegraph* (May 18, 2019), accessed on May 18, 2020, at https://www.belfasttelegraph.co.uk/opinion/news-analysis/seamus-mallon-why-a-simple-majority-in-favour-of-united-ireland-will-not-deliver-future-we-deserve-38122624.html

136. The public handshake had been preceded by a private one in an earlier meeting at Belfast's Lyric Theatre.

137. BBC News, "Queen and Martin McGuinness Shake Hands," (June 27, 2012), accessed on April 1, 2020, at https://www.bbc.com/news/uk-northern-ireland-18607911

138. Carly Read, "'What Was I Meant To Do?,' Queen's Handshake with Ex-IRA Leader McGuinness Revealed," *Express* (September 17, 2018), accessed on April 2, 2020, at https://www.express.co.uk/news/royal/1018603/the-queen-martin-mcguinness-IRA-handshake-bloody-sunday

139. The Clinton and McGuinness quotes are taken from Deborah McAleese, "Historic Moment Martin McGuinness Shook Hands with Queen Elizabeth," *The Irish News* (March 21, 2017), accessed on April 1, 2020, at https://www.irishnews.com/news/northernirelandnews/2017/03/21/news/historic-moment-martin-mcguinness-shook-hands-with-queen-elizabeth-971302/

140. BBC News, "Queen and Martin McGuinness Shake Hands."

141. PBS Newshour, "Despite Historic Handshake, Belfast Still Deeply Divided Society" (June 27, 2012), accessed on April 2, 2020, at https://www.pbs.org/newshour/world/ireland-handshake

142. BBC News, "Queen and Martin McGuinness Shake Hands."

143. This exchange comes from Caroline Davies, "The Belfast Handshake: After Years of Fiery Rhetoric Came Rapprochement," *The Guardian* (June 27, 2012), accessed on April 2, 2020, at https://www.theguardian.com/uk/2012/jun/27/queen-martin-mcguinness-handshake-troubles

144. Eilis O'Hanlon, "Why 'We're All in this Together' Is Just a Slogan, Not a Blueprint That Ministers at Stormont Think Applies to Them Too," *Belfast Telegraph* (March 29, 2020), accessed on April 2, 2020, at https://www.belfasttelegraph.co.uk/opinion/columnists/eilis-o-hanlon/why-were-all-in-this-together-is-just-a-slogan-not-a-blueprint-that-ministers-at-stormont-think-applies-to-them-too-39085627.html

145. Alex Kane, "With Sinn Fein Challenging UK's Coronavirus Tactics and Wanting an All-Ireland Strategy, Are We Really All Together in This?," *Belfast Telegraph* (April 1, 2020), accessed on April 2, 2020, at https://www.belfasttelegraph.co.uk/opinion/comment/with-sinn-fein-challenging-uks-coronavirus-tactics-and-wanting-an-all-ireland-strategy-are-we-really-all-together-in-this-39092853.html

5

"The Walls Entered into Our Souls"

Social Fragmentation in Everyday Life

During the winter and spring of 2017, I spent my sabbatical term as an honorary visiting research professor in the Senator George J. Mitchell Institute for Global Peace, Security and Justice at Queen's University Belfast (QUB). QUB is a public research university widely recognized as one of the top research universities in the world and certainly perceived as the most prestigious university in Northern Ireland. Its graduate student population draws students from around the world, while the majority of its undergraduate students are from Northern Ireland. While the university does not publish data on the religious affiliation of its students, there has been for the past several decades a growing share of Catholics in the undergraduate population (one staff member guesstimated the breakdown as 55% Catholic and 45% Protestant). Part of this comes from the fact that higher education is an elevated priority, even expectation, among Catholic families in Northern Ireland. Moreover, for those relatively fewer Protestants who do go on to pursue a university degree, most choose to do so in Great Britain rather than staying home in Northern Ireland. So, for many, QUB is now seen, in the words of a local, as a "cold house for Protestants."

During my sabbatical term at QUB, I would often speak with classes or groups of students about my fieldwork and research in deeply divided societies around the world. On those occasions, I would begin by asking if they could recall the first time they met someone from the "other side" (Protestant or Catholic). Inevitably, the overwhelming majority of those who responded said their initial meeting with someone from the other identity group was when they came to university. For nearly the first two decades of their lives, nearly all of them lived in complete segregation based on community identity—separated housing, schools, churches, and social lives. Particularly for those students born and bred in Belfast, it was typically only when shopping in the neutral space of the city center that they interacted with someone from the other community—and, even then, those were nominal, often

A Troubled Sleep. James Waller, Oxford University Press (2021). © Oxford University Press.
DOI: 10.1093/oso/9780190095574.003.0006

unknown interactions based simply on shopping proximity or a purchase in a store. For their friends who do not go on to university, meaningful contact with someone from the other community identity group was unlikely ever to happen. Even for those who found employment in a mixed workplace, there is "a presumption of avoidance of contentious issues, rather than any strong sense of integration and sharing."[1]

In 2017, this remarkable degree of lived and experiential social segregation was quantified in a new mapping project developed by software engineer and data analyst Mathew Doherty. Doherty drew on census data from 1971, 1981, 1991, 2001, and 2011 to show where Protestants and Catholics live in Northern Ireland. The color-coded maps he developed revealed a "greening" of Northern Ireland with a rapid increase in the Catholic population over those 40 years. In 2011, for the first time, Protestants no longer made up the majority of the population (48.36%) and Catholics had increased to 45.14% of Northern Ireland's population. The maps also reveal the degree to which cities or towns were predominately populated by one identity group as well as the degree to which some were divided between identity groups. The maps visually attest to a continuing and stunning pattern of social segregation across the country, with little, if any, positive change since the Good Friday Agreement.[2] As one unionist politician admitted to me, "we like the rigorous segregation of neighborhoods and communities because it gives us an easy and solid voting bloc . . . we don't have to contend with any issues of political diversity."

This stubbornly persistent pattern of social segregation—a visible apartheid—is particularly noticeable in social housing estates (public housing owned by the government and provided at a sliding scale). About 90% of these estates are home to single-identity working-class populations with limited social mobility.[3] Already separated by the invisible walls of social segregation, they are further separated from the "other side" by a series of physical barriers or so-called *peace walls*. As columnist Paul Nolan writes of these barriers, "there is nothing grand about the interrupted series of fences, corrugated metal and brick structures that stop and start in their zigzag progress through these depressed working-class neighbourhoods." It is a physical geography carved as brutally as the political geography discussed in the previous chapter (Figure 5.1). In the shadows of these stark dividing lines, social segregation is made viscerally visible; the walls are stark reminders of stagnant, entrenched division—not symbols of peace but structures of fear. Nolan: "The neighbourhoods on both sides of those walls are showrooms of

Figure 5.1 Section of peace wall in Belfast.
Photo by author, January 25, 2016.

ethnic antagonism: painted kerbs, flags, murals of paramilitary heroes, and walls festooned with slogans."[4]

In 2017, alongside a former loyalist political prisoner, I walked the length of one of these peace walls in north Belfast, where a patchwork of Catholic/nationalist/republican and Protestant/unionist/loyalist communities abut. (Such areas are often called "interfaces," though that word misleadingly implies linkages and connections that are seldom to be found.) Since his release under the Good Friday Agreement (he had been serving four life sentences for murder), he had become a well-known community activist with a focus on reintegrating other former loyalist political prisoners into the communities from which they had come. Despite being, very literally, a stone's throw from the Catholic side of the wall, it was not until just a few years ago, well into his mid-50s, that he had ever walked on that side of that divide. As we walked along the wall together, more time was spent in silence than in conversation; a silence born from a mixture of regret and little optimism for a common way forward. At one point, he stopped and, looking away at things I could not see, said, to himself more than to me: "We always thought the walls were for our protection. But, at the end of the day, the walls entered into our souls and just hardened our differences into divisions. All they have protected us from is hope."

* * *

The notion of "two communities" or, more coarsely, "two tribes," within Northern Ireland is a thesis commonly challenged by political elites as well as academics. In 1997, for instance, Lord John Alderdice, then leader of the centrist Alliance Party, questioned the "two communities" notion on the grounds that it ignored the many individual narratives in Northern Ireland that refused collective categorizations. "A considerable number of Protestants," he wrote, "have more in common with some Catholics in terms of their values and outlook on life than with some other Protestants and vice versa." For him, in the leadup to the peace agreement, the "two communities" language that was deeply ingrained in the discussions was "not only . . . inaccurate, but is fundamentally counterproductive to the future health of this society . . . [as] the recognition of parity of esteem for only two traditions, would not mark a healing of divisions but an institutionalising of them."[5] More recently, in 2019, Katy Hayward and Cathal McManus of QUB took the "two communities" thesis to task by pointing out that "at least 4 out of every 10 people in Northern Ireland tend to describe themselves as *Neither* Unionist *nor* Nationalist" [emphasis in original].[6]

Alderdice was certainly prescient in fearing how the peace agreement might institutionalize identity-based politics. Similarly, Hayward and McManus were spot-on in recognizing and calling our attention to the number of people in Northern Ireland who are attempting to break out of the binary boxes born from history and institutionalized by the Good Friday Agreement. As we discussed in Chapter 1, nuance is a necessary tool in understanding the complexity of Northern Ireland identities. I think it more than a few steps too far, however, to dismiss the "two communities" thesis as inaccurate, inadequate, or antiquated. In the hours and hours I spent in various homes and neighborhoods of Northern Ireland—with civil society leaders, community activists, students, former political prisoners, shopkeepers, and the unemployed—it became painfully apparent that the oft-proclaimed death of the "two communities" thesis is little more than an aspirational hope. On the ground, the notion of "two communities" is much more than a thesis in contemporary Northern Ireland: it is a lived reality. As one interviewee told me: "We are well and truly two separate communities. Always have been and always will be."

There is a yawning gap of social separation between these two communities that, as one interviewee described, "is institutionally constructed and reinforced at every level of Northern Ireland's society." It is in this isolated space of social separation that suspicion, mistrust, stereotypes, fears, stigmas, misunderstandings, and fearmongering grow unbridled. Social separation creates echo chambers in which difficult conversations are unspoken, assumptions unchallenged, and herd mentalities unchecked. Social separation births stand-alone islands subject to Balkanization rather than cooperation. And, as Christopher Moran, chair of the cross-border peacebuilding charity Co-operation Ireland, is fond of saying: "These islands [meaning the UK and Ireland] are small enough without making them any smaller."[7]

* * *

Negative trends among risk factors in the categories of memory (Chapter 3) and governance (Chapter 4) shackle a society in the bonds of fragility. This can lead to, as well as be the result of, an increased susceptibility to social disharmony and isolation. This state of disconnect between the larger society and the groupings of some members of that society is known as fragmentation. While fragmentation can manifest itself along economic, institutional, or geographic lines, this chapter focuses on risk factors related specifically to social fragmentation. *Social fragmentation* is defined "as a process in modern society by which different groups form parallel structures within society, which have little or no consistent interaction between them over the full spectrum of the social experience."[8] In the World Bank's view, "social fragmentation can permeate society, erupting, for example, as domestic violence in the household, rising crime and violence in the community, and massive corruption and civil conflict at the state level."[9] Where intergroup social cohesion can unite a people and strengthen a society, social fragmentation splinters a people, reduces the resiliency of a society, and places it at increased risk for violent conflict.

In everyday life in contemporary Northern Ireland, social fragmentation undeniably rules over the full spectrum of the lived experience. We will examine five specific risk factors related to social fragmentation: (1) identity-based social divisions, (2) demographic pressures, (3) unequal access to basic goods and services, (4) gender inequalities, and (5) political instability.

Identity-Based Social Divisions

Identity-based social divisions—particularly when intertwined with differential access to power, wealth, status, and resources—are a considerable source of risk for violent conflict. As we have seen in our discussion of the in-group bias in Chapter 1, social identity matters deeply as a source of intergroup conflict. Social identity can be manipulated by powerholders to create or deepen societal divisions and advance their own partisan interests. Powerholders recognize that reinforcing identity-based differences actually gains political, social, and even financial capital. The undermining impact of identity-based social divisions then reduces incentives for trust, cooperation, dialogue, and long-term social exposure to the "other." As a result, individuals prioritize divisive subordinate identities rather than being closely connected to the unifying superordinate identity of the state or nation.

Unstable political, social, and economic environments are particularly lethal brews for fostering intergroup tension among identity lines. In this vein, the "other" is perceived as an existential threat, or, in the words of Australian scholar Rhiannon Neilsen, a "toxification" considered collectively and fundamentally lethal to the in-group.[10] The reality of this threat is less important than its perception in the mind of the in-group. Moreover, the degree of existential threat perceived to be posed by the "other" increases as the powerholding capacities of the in-group decreases.

In contemporary Northern Ireland, the "other" as existential threat is most clearly captured in the corporeal reality of peace walls. These interface barriers are similar to border walls and fences that have been used or are still being used throughout the world as security measures to keep out migrants and refugees, curb smuggling, separate warring parties with a buffer zone, or protect trade routes. At the end of World War II, there were seven border walls and fences across the world. Today, in a time of rising nationalism and global disorder, there are at least 77 such barriers in countries as far ranging as Finland, France, Morocco, Spain, Saudi Arabia, Turkey, China, India, Israel, and the United States.[11]

In Northern Ireland, an interface area is defined as "the contested space where intercommunity tensions have the potential to lead to a confrontation between segregated Unionist and Nationalist communities."[12] The barriers in some interface areas are subtly embedded—vacant plots of land, car parks, or decorative steel fencing. In one area of east Belfast, the interface barrier creatively relies on space to create defensive architecture between a Protestant and Catholic neighborhood—a two-lane road, a sidewalk, some shrubbery, another sidewalk, and then housing. In most interface areas, however, the barriers scarify the landscape with their lurid obviousness—harsh concrete or cinderblock walls (often with mesh fencing above), tall green fencing, corrugated metal sheeting, razor wire, road closure barriers, or solid brick walls meant to stand the test of time. These walls are often marked with graffiti, loyalist slogans on one side and republican on the other. Some of these barriers can be seen through; most cannot. Some include lockable gates allowing for some level of pedestrian or motor access at certain times or days; others do not. Some are covered with hedges to make them look more innocuous; most are not. Most have been built and are owned by government agencies, some privately owned, and others have unknown ownership. Many have grown gradually over the years, being built higher and higher to thwart the creativity of those striving to launch projectiles over them.

Some maintain that the first peace wall in the north of Ireland dates to 1866, when Belfast city decided to open a cemetery and installed a nine-foot deep underground wall to separate Protestant graves from Catholic graves.[13] The use of barriers to wall off the living, however, dates back to Northern Ireland's birth pangs in 1920. In July of that year, Belfast was in turmoil after loyalists marched on the city's shipyards to expel thousands of "disloyal" workers—meaning Catholics and those assumed to not be sufficiently anti-Catholic (particularly left-wingers or socialists). "Some were kicked and beaten, others were pelted with rivets, and some were forced to swim for their lives."[14] In the Short Strand interface area of Belfast, where loyalists had attempted to burn Catholic homes and businesses out, railroad cars were stacked between Protestant and Catholic neighborhoods in hopes of stopping the ongoing rioting. Often referred to as "the first Troubles," sectarian violence in Belfast would continue for the next two years and lead to 416 deaths and more than 1,000 wounded.

Such makeshift barricades would reappear nearly 50 years later in the violent summer of 1969. August 14 of that year saw the deployment of British troops to Northern Ireland to restore security after a series of riots in Derry. Rioting then spread throughout the country, and August would bring the most sustained violence Northern Ireland had seen since the early 1920s. In Belfast, amid rising tensions in interface neighborhoods, residents on both sides of the divide attempted to protect themselves by building makeshift barricades from burnt-out cars, trees, telegraph poles, construction debris, or rubble from destroyed houses. These barricades were erected on both sides of Cuper Street, an unmarked dividing line between the Falls Road (Catholic) and Shankill Road (Protestant). A three-day period of unrest from August 14 to 16 in west and north Belfast left seven people dead and 179 homes destroyed, with a loyalist mob burning Bombay Street to the ground. About 1,820 families were displaced from their homes because of the violence; 1,505 were Catholic and 315 Protestant.[15] In response to the violence, on September 9, 1969, James Chichester-Clark, the Prime Minister of Northern Ireland, announced the "systematic removal" of the makeshift barricades between the Falls and Shankill area and their immediate replacement with a physical "peace line" that would be manned by British troops.[16] Construction on a five-foot-tall barbed wire fence began the next day.

The peace line—not celebrating peace but keeping the peace—was meant to be "a very, very temporary affair," probably gone by Christmas of 1969.[17] Instead of being removed, however, it was replaced with corrugated iron sheeting twice as high and bristling with barbed wire. Months later, the army put up a second wall in north Belfast, again meant to be temporary. The abnormal was quickly trending in a direction of normality as these walls become deeply embedded parts of everyday life in Northern Ireland. The barriers clearly identified the "other," the "threat," and, for some, the "targets." As criminologist Jonny Byrne of Ulster University explained: "The whole plan was to get the communities to talk and then to start taking the walls down, but then what happened was, we normalized the policy."[18] Over the next three decades, as the Troubles unfolded, the stock government, and sometimes private ownership or community, response was the installation of another wall. And then another. And then another. While data on dates when barriers are constructed are difficult to substantiate, the number of barriers increased steadily after 1969 and particularly during the course of the peace process. In fact, a large number were built *after* the ceasefires of

1994, and many of those were reinforced or extended *after* the peace agreement of 1998.[19]

There is inconsistency in defining what, exactly defines a peace wall or interface barrier or "boundary treatment." As a result, the actual counts vary. An exhaustive 2017 report by the Belfast Interface Project (BIP) identified 116 separate, independent barriers across Northern Ireland.[20] A less detailed 2019 report by the International Fund for Ireland estimated that "approximately 100 barriers remain in place as visible symbols of community segregation and division" in Northern Ireland.[21] In many of the interface areas separated by these barriers, former (or present) paramilitaries have a significant interest and wield correspondingly significant influence. Houses by these barriers, often found in urban, working-class neighborhoods stricken by poverty and contentious cultural issues, frequently have, as journalist Vicky Cosstick writes, "metal grilles over their windows, or perhaps almost no windows at all, or wire cages over back gardens, creating a sense of incarceration." She continues: "Interface areas often have further signs of blight: derelict houses, shops and factories; abandoned wasteland. Some interface areas have become dumping grounds for rubbish, and, some would say, for vulnerable people."[22]

Belfast is the undisputed capital of interface areas and barriers. Indeed, Belfast has become so proficient at barriers, one interviewee told me, that the Police Service of Northern Ireland (PSNI) have been invited to consult on their development and use in Iraq. The Belfast peace walls, including the only public park in Europe bisected by a wall, have become such a must-see dark tourism attraction they even have their own Flickr group.[23] Visitors are drawn not despite the history of conflict but because of it. In its 2017 report, BIP identified 97 barriers across Belfast, totaling about 21 kilometers in length, with the most recent new wall having been built in 2012. David Coyles, Brandon Hamber, and Adrian Grant of Ulster University maintain that number is even greater when one takes into account the "hidden barriers" embedded across Belfast's residential communities. Created during a little-known process of security planning between 1976 and 1985, these hidden barriers "take the form of everyday elements of the built environment. They vary in both type and scale, and include the use of infrastructure such as footpaths and roads, as well as the use of retail, office and industrial buildings, to control vehicular and pedestrian movement and to physically separate residential areas . . . [and they also include] the closing off of former thoroughfares, the dividing of through-streets into cul-de-sacs, and a proliferation of dead-end alleyways and courtyards with a single entry-exit point."[24]

Most residents who live along these interface barriers recognize that they have deleterious impacts individually and communally, as well as creating negative external perceptions about their neighborhoods. There is a ready admission that the barriers, dividing communities into single-identity areas, block normal social engagement and interaction. Most residents still, however, want the walls to remain. While politicians and academics and civil society activists often preach (at least publicly) for their removal, there was not a single resident in these interface neighborhoods, among the dozens I spoke with, who wanted the walls removed. If anything, most wanted the walls to be built even higher (though some are already so tall that to build them even taller would make them structurally unsound).

Interface residents have come to rely on the walls for protection and security; barriers of strength offering physical defense from bricks, stones, bottles, petrol and paint bombs, beatings, and shootings. One east Belfast resident interviewed by the *Irish Times* in 2019 captured well these beliefs: "The peace wall is better staying up. I don't want it taken down. We had a questionnaire coming around asking us how we'd feel if the peace wall came down. I'd be away because it'd just be murder on the street."[25] A 2019 survey of those living beside the barriers found that while 81% of respondents wanted their removal within the lifetime of their children or grandchildren, only 18% believed it was safe to take the barriers down now.[26] Similarly, the 2019 Northern Ireland Life and Times (NILT) survey found only 25% of respondents wanting the peace lines to come down now, with another 29% wanting them to come down in the future.[27] One police officer I interviewed said the PSNI were in full agreement about the ongoing necessity of the peace walls. "If those walls come down," he told me, "then the police have to step in and become the walls to separate these communities and none of us want that."

These attitudes, deeply entrenched on all sides, make removal of interface barriers—visible or hidden—particularly problematic since a successful removal depends upon locally led initiatives. In a real sense, the walls have entered into the souls of enough people in Northern Ireland to make their removal only an aspirational hope for far in the future. In 2013, under direct pressure from Westminster to make headway toward that aspiration, Northern Ireland's government leaders issued their most significant policy framework to date regarding community relations—a 116-page strategy document titled "Together: Building a United Community" (T:BUC).[28] Some criticized T:BUC for its "underlying assumption of the permanence of the two main community blocs and for its lack of ambition in terms of societal integration."[29] Where the document did not lack ambition, however, was in its 10-year plan to remove all interface barriers by 2023. It confined that focus to 59 interfaces under the ownership of the Department of Justice (who inherited them from the Northern Ireland Office following devolution of policing powers in 2007 and justice powers in 2010) and another 14 owned by the Northern Ireland Housing Executive. T:BUC aimed to accomplish this Herculean objective by "leafleting, door-to-door surveying, drop-in workshops and community engagement events to meet local people living in interface areas in order to discuss potential adjustments to interface structures, where an appetite exists locally to do so."[30] The strategy also called for a support package and accompanying budget to implement this engagement activity and, most importantly, find ways to ensure community safety in the absence of the barriers.

Unfortunately, few interface areas have had the "appetite" to engage this formidable, delicate, and expensive removal program. Moreover, the glacial pace of political progress on this initiative from its inception, exacerbated by three years of Stormont being closed and the uncertainty posed by Brexit, has led to virtually no progress toward the 2023 goal. The 2017 BIP report found only two fewer barriers in Belfast than noted in its 2012 report. In its most recent annual report, T:BUC maintains that the number of Department of Justice-owned interface barriers has reduced by 13 over the years, though, in many of those cases, they have been replaced by some other form of interface barrier. In January 2020, for instance, the Department of Justice demolished one of Belfast's oldest peace walls, only to replace it "with a lower structure which will have a brick bottom half and a fence on the upper half."[31] The Housing Executive's first removal of a peace wall would not come until 2016, after three years of tense negotiations between residents of the Catholic Ardoyne and Protestant Woodvale sections of Belfast.

As the International Fund for Ireland concluded in its 2019 report: "Failure to develop an Aftercare Package and a budget for its implementation at an earlier date has had a notable impact on the confidence of communities considering barrier removal, caused a loss of faith in the overall process and has hampered the capacity of those working with communities towards the eventual removal of the Peace Walls."[32] Similarly, Joe O'Donnell, the strategic director of BIP, laments: "There is no comprehensive plan, there is no champion to lead the regeneration."[33] Unfortunately, the "New Decade, New Approach" deal of 2020 just mentions the word "barriers" one time and only then in the context of the UK government's indeterminate commitment of "funding being made available for a range of projects aimed at supporting community and reconciliation initiatives."[34] For Jim Donnelly, a former republican political prisoner, the real work of removal is tearing down the walls in people's minds. "If we don't try to break them down," he says, "we won't break the bricks and mortar down."[35]

In contemporary Northern Ireland, not a day seemingly goes by without identity being manipulated in the most blatant of ways to exacerbate social divisions. In such a deeply, and physically, divided society, where people feel under constant threat from "them," symbols—even as they give a sense of self rooted in community—are particularly divisive. Indeed, "Northern Ireland's politico-military conflict has morphed into a politico-cultural one."[36] As we saw in the previous chapter's discussion of the 2012 protests over the Belfast City Council's decision to change its policy and practice of flying the Union Flag, flags in contemporary Northern Ireland can be particularly contentious flashpoints. As one interviewee told me: "Northern Ireland has a great affinity to flags. Once put up, we leave them up until they are in tatters." Indeed, flags—national (Union Jack or Irish tricolor) and paramilitary—serve as stark territorial markers of identity and, at times, even starker forms of sectarian intimidation. Police will only remove the flags if they pose substantial threat to public safety though, as one PSNI officer told me, "the real threat would be to our own safety if we ever tried to take them down."

The painting of curbstones (in Union Jack blue, red, and white in Protestant neighborhoods and Irish tricolor green, white, and orange in Catholic ones) is yet another territorial marker of identity. In some cases, these have been reported as sectarian hate crimes.[37] A recent specific incident treated as a sectarian hate crime involved a delivery driver convicted of deliberately flattening orange lilies planted outside an Orange Hall near Ballymoney.[38] In Country Antrim, a woman who put an Irish language sign on the garden fence of her property was threatened with prosecution for violating council advertising regulations.[39] Sport also often becomes a proxy stage for territorial markers of identity. In 2018, for instance, the Irish Football Association decided to play "God Save the Queen," the British national anthem, before the Irish Cup final pitting Cliftonville, a Belfast soccer club based in a predominately nationalist community, against Coleraine, from a predominately unionist community (but whose team also included players with a nationalist background). As the anthem was played (which had not been done in previous years when Cliftonville made the finals), Cliftonville players bowed their heads as a sign of renouncing the anthem.[40] A wide range of other forms of cultural expressions—bonfires, parades, murals, language, graffiti, and music—also contribute to marking out an area as single identity and exacerbating social fragmentation in everyday life.

On June 20, 2016, recognizing the need to address these issues, the government of Northern Ireland appointed a Commission on Flags, Identity, Culture, and Tradition (FICT).[41] The Commission was tasked to produce a report and recommendations on the way forward in regard to a range of symbols-related issues. Its findings were supposed to be released by December 2017. By June 2019, a year and a half after that due date and at a cost of £730,000, FICT had yet to release any findings. Particularly irksome for many was that more than half of the Commission's cost had been spent on remuneration paid for travel expenses of Commission members. Reflecting the complexity of their charge, particularly in the midst of three years of political paralysis, it would not be until July 2020 that FICT submitted its final report, including recommendations, to Stormont ministers. As of this writing, the final report has not yet been made public. In the meantime, the onus continues to fall on local bodies to address these contentious issues at a community level.

Stepping into the symbols fray with bureaucratic resolve, the "New Decade, New Approach" document called for the creation of an Office of Identity and Cultural Expression to "celebrate and support all aspects of Northern Ireland's rich cultural and linguistic heritage, recognizing the equal validity and importance of all identities and traditions."[42] This office, with a proposed budget of £28 million over the next three years, would work closely with FICT as well as a range of other stakeholders. For some, like commentator Dennis Kennedy, this new Office "arouses echoes of Orwell's *1984* and a Big Brother totalitarian approach telling us how we should think."[43] For others, conversely, it holds promise for a broader institutional and structural approach to the promotion of cultural pluralism.

Regardless of what commission or office deals with these issues going forward, it is important to recognize that all of these territorial markers of identity-based social divisions protect what anthropologists and political scientists refer to as *shatter zones*. A shatter zone is a borderland, or zone of refuge, where people feel safe from oppression or persecution.[44] That protective function and its alleged efficacy is counteracted by the myriad ways in which deeply ingrained identity-based social divisions slow a society from building resiliency or overcoming fragility, however. As international studies scholar Seth Kaplan argues: "Society becomes obsessed by the conflict between identity groups, not with generating wealth or increasing national prestige."[45] The results of such an obsession include a diversion of resources from promoting sustainable development and growth to simply managing the disabling impasse caused by intergroup tension. This can have life-and-death consequences in some societies. In sub-Saharan Africa, for instance, the least ethnically divided societies are able to spend five times more per capita than the most divided societies on HIV prevention and treatment programs.[46]

I saw this diversion of resources in Northern Ireland firsthand in January 2016, during a visit to an operational room in a police station in the city center of Belfast. There, preparations were in place to monitor, for yet another night, a recurring demonstration (typically drawing about 25 or so protestors) in the Protestant Twaddell section of north Belfast. First beginning in July 2013, following a Parades Commission decision to restrict a Protestant Orange Order march, the nightly protests would not end until October 2016. When a negotiated agreement finally ended the three-year dispute, its total cost to police and the country was estimated at more than $US 26 million.[47]

Contemporary Northern Ireland, to its credit, has invested much time, money, and effort in cross-community schemes to deconstruct the identity-based social divisions that dominate everyday life in a socially fragmented society. T:BUC's most recent annual report, for example, describes a range of initiatives meant to restore good relations and reconciliation. Among these are a Camps Programme that allows young people aged 11 to 19 come together, on a cross-community basis, to build long-term relationships. Since its inception, this program has hosted 442 camps involving more than 16,000 young people in Northern Ireland. According to T:BUC, 76% of participants had a positive attitudinal change toward people from the other religious/community background, with 83% evidencing an increased willingness to be more involved in peacebuilding activities. Another Shared Housing Programme has built 428 new homes in communities open to those who wish to live in a mixed area (defined as containing not more than 70% of one identity group).[48]

A wealth of similar cross-community good relations programs are happening at the grassroots local level through civil society organizations and people intent on improving relations between the two dominant we-identities.

Each summer, for example, through the international PeacePlayers program, Trevor Ringland, a former Irish rugby star and member of the Northern Ireland Conservatives party, brings together about 200 children from Catholic and Protestant neighborhoods to play youth sports. For more than 9 out of 10 of the participants, it will be the first time they have interacted with someone from a different religious/community background. "We have kids from North, South, East and West Belfast," Ringland said. "We have kids from either side of the wall playing together. It takes two minutes for those kids to be playing together. It's more than playing together, it's community relations. We focus on the common ground that is between them. We're a good example of what the future can be like."[49]

Unfortunately, however, the impact of such creative and inclusive programming seems discouragingly limited. As one interviewee cynically told me, only partly tongue-in-cheek: "You want to know what I took back from my time in a cross-community initiative? One strategically useful thing. 'I know where you live now.'" Another civil society leader I interviewed shared his frustration that too many organizations grabbed funding only to get cross-community people together in the same space, but with no real interest in or plans for meaningful engagement. After the flag protests of 2012 and the Brexit referendum of 2016, the initiative to bring people together in a shared space, let alone to engage each other in that space, continued to wane. The most recent NILT survey, for instance, found that 49% of respondents reported being unaware of cross-community schemes or projects operating in Northern Ireland over the past 5 years.[50] Such findings suggest a more limited participative impact of cross-community programming than would be desired.

Even when carried out, the potential efficacy of cross-community programming remains largely thwarted by the reality that most participants, once the camp or program or event is over, will return to be immersed in the deeply segregated neighborhoods, schools, churches, holidays, rituals, social activities, sporting events, and family socialization systems that gave birth to the identity-based social divisions in the first place. As one past participant of these programs told me, "the change that feels so right when I'm in the program, doesn't feel right at all when I go back home and am surrounded by murals glorifying violence, eat dinner by the Celtic cross sitting in my house made of matchsticks by a republican political prisoner, go to school with people who have no interest in living with them'uns." This sentiment was affirmed by recent research demonstrating that family socialization is predictive of intergroup bias and higher levels of adolescent participation in sectarian antisocial behavior.[51]

More problematically, existing cross-community programs, already confronted with austerity cuts, face perhaps insurmountable financial challenges with the upcoming end of the PEACE IV Programme. A unique initiative of the European Union, the PEACE Programme was initially created as a positive response to the paramilitary ceasefires of 1994. The most recent programming period runs from 2014 to 2020. Over that time, a €270 million commitment was made to Northern Ireland and the border counties of Ireland to support peace and reconciliation efforts. After 2020, particularly as EU ties go away with the implementation of Brexit and the economic consequences of the COVID-19 pandemic are tallied, many of the most important grassroots efforts to heal the identity-based social divisions in Northern Ireland will find themselves unable to continue their good work due to an absence of funding avenues.

Demographic Pressures

Social fragmentation can be escalated with demographic pressures that can be particularly taxing for already fragile societies. Some demographic pressures stem from population issues such as voluntary group resettlement patterns that may lead to border disputes, ownership or occupancy of land controversies, contested access to transportation outlets, or disputed control of religious or historical sites. Demographic pressures may also come from a "high population density relative to food supply, access to safe water, and other life-sustaining resources" or divergent rates of population growth among competing social identity groups. At times, infrastructure development and industrial projects may, while benefitting the state in general, have very particular stressor impacts (e.g., environmental hazards or agricultural failure) on a specific demographic population (typically, indigenous peoples).[52]

High population density is low on the scale of demographic pressures facing contemporary Northern Ireland. (Journalist Martin Fletcher has affectionately called Northern Ireland "just one huge farm."[53]) As of this writing, that farm's current population is 1.88 million spread out over a total land area of 14,130 square kilometers. Over the past decade, Northern Ireland had a slow, but consistent, annual growth rate of between 0.33% and 0.78% (adding around 6,100 to 14,500 people to the population each year). The population density is only about 133 people per square kilometer (mostly concentrated in the Belfast metropolitan area), about half of the number for the rest of the United Kingdom and about twice that of the much larger Republic of Ireland. For comparison's sake, the world's top five most densely populated countries (not including small island or isolated states) are Bangladesh (1,252 people per square kilometer), Lebanon (595), South Korea (528), the Netherlands (508), and Rwanda (495).[54]

Racially, Northern Ireland is strikingly non-diverse, with the 2011 census revealing 98.21% of the population reported as white, 1.06% as Asian, 0.2% as black, and 0.53% as other. Most international migration into Northern Ireland continues to come from residents of the Republic of Ireland. Since 2004, there also has been an increasing influx of Eastern European immigrants that has the potential to redefine the "two communities" antagonism that has long defined Northern Ireland. Among these have been significant numbers of Polish and Lithuanian Catholic immigrants. Generally such immigrants are not seen as contributing to the binary sectarian divide because, as one local resident told me, "they aren't agitating for Northern Ireland to become part of Poland or Lithuania." There is hope that the development of established immigrant communities will lead to "greater cultural and social diversity" and put Northern Ireland "on a trajectory towards a more pluralist society" with "significant opportunities for positive political and social change where Northern Ireland can move on from its older focus on the Catholic/Protestant divide."[55]

This is not to say, however, that all immigrants have received equally warm welcomes. As one mental health expert told me: "Northern Ireland has a boundless capacity for 'isms,' where sectarianism can easily become racism." While data from the 2019 NILT survey suggest that, in principle, respondents have broadly positive attitudes toward minority ethnic people, the reality remains that the Good Friday Agreement and Northern Ireland society is oriented toward two communities only.[56] Everyone else, as one immigrant interviewee told me, "falls through the gap." Even more disturbingly, some exclusionary—and incendiary—viewpoints have emerged with the changing faces of communities impacted by immigration. During the first week of my visiting position at QUB in January 2017, for example, Northern Ireland's most popular talk radio show, hosted by Stephen Nolan, was having a debate on Donald Trump's immigration ban (predominately targeted at Muslim countries). One Belfast caller, Janice, said Trump was "absolutely right in his actions" and, furthermore, she would rather "go home and die" than be treated by a Muslim doctor in a hospital. In a combative exchange, Nolan pressed: "Do you understand Muslims are born here? They are we." To which Janice tellingly replied: "They will never be we." Nolan went on to ask his audience: "How many Janices are there in Northern Ireland?"[57]

From the media's perspective, there are many Janices in Northern Ireland. Hate crimes against immigrant communities, particularly in the urban areas of Belfast and Derry, have been reported so frequently that Northern Ireland has been dubbed the "race hate capital of Europe." A 2018 review of survey data by sociologist Stefanie Doebler and colleagues found that educational and employment deprivation and a lack of contact opportunities with minorities, particularly among the young, were strong predictors of negativity toward immigrants and ethnic minorities in Northern Ireland (as they were across the UK and Europe). They also argued that negativity toward ethnic minorities is on the increase in Northern Ireland and remains a cause for concern, particularly in housing intimidation tactics (often by paramilitaries) that force minorities out of single-identity communities. They concluded, however, that: "Calling Northern Ireland the 'race hate capital' of the UK, let alone Europe, would be a gross over-generalization."[58]

Nevertheless, PSNI statistics show that hate crimes have overtaken sectarian crimes in Northern Ireland in recent years, with the true number of racially motivated attacks likely significantly higher than reported. One investigative report, for instance, suggested there could have been up to 10,000 racist incidents in Northern Ireland between June 2016 and December 2018, compared to the 2,093 reported by the PSNI over that time period.[59] Moreover, of those race hate incidents that are reported, fewer than 1 in 10 result in conviction. As Socialist Democratic and Labour Party (SDLP) policing spokesperson Dolores Kelly admitted in June 2020: "We absolutely need to do more to assure people from black and minority ethnic communities that they will be protected."[60] Unfortunately, the Racial Equality Strategy 2015–2025 prepared by the Northern Ireland Executive Office has yet to be fully implemented and, in many regards, already is outdated.

Many of the immigrants and ethnic minorities I spoke with during my time in Northern Ireland expressed a higher level of comfort living in Catholic and nationalist communities. One recent immigrant, living off the Falls Road in Catholic west Belfast, told me she simply "felt a greater amount of acceptance and tolerance and was perceived less like a threat" in that area as compared to a Protestant neighborhood in which she had previously lived. Her experience is consistent with research suggesting that Protestants and unionists do indeed report relatively more negative attitudes toward a range of immigrant and ethnic target groups than do Catholic or nationalist respondents.[61] Similarly, the PSNI reported that "most of the major race incidents that we have seen have occurred generally in loyalist areas."[62] Psychologist Samuel Pherson and colleagues argue that this difference is due to a higher level of perceived cultural threat in Protestant and unionist communities—a collective and self-protective zero-sum response to changes in contemporary Northern Ireland that have challenged the dominant status they have enjoyed in the past.[63]

The most significant demographic pressure faced in contemporary Northern Ireland, however, is the same as it ever was: divisions between unionist and nationalist populations. As mentioned at the beginning of this chapter, the 2011 census, following decades-long demographic trajectories, was the first time that "belonging to or brought up in Protestant or other Christian-related denominations" represented less than half (48.36%) of Northern Ireland's population. Those identifying as either Catholic or brought up as Catholic constituted 45.14% of those surveyed. Those reporting neither belonging to nor having been brought up in a religion represented 5.6% of the respondents.

Rather than being a blip on the demographic radar, the momentum of this trend away from a Protestant majority in Northern Ireland is very likely to continue for three intersecting reasons. First, the fact that, on average, Catholics are younger, naturally translates to higher birth rates and lower death rates relative to Protestants. Second, Protestants are more likely to migrate out of country than Catholics (this is particularly true for Protestants who pursue higher education in Great Britain and are relatively unlikely to return to Northern Ireland, further exacerbating the average age gap between the two communities). Finally, in terms of "switching behavior," Protestants are more likely to transfer to "none" for religious affiliation than are Catholics.[64] All of these trends are more pronounced in urban areas and in the east of Northern Ireland, with one researcher predicting in 2018 that "within a decade, Belfast will almost certainly have a Catholic majority."[65]

As we saw in Chapter 1, it is too simplistic to assume that Catholic always aligns with nationalist and Protestant with unionist; one can find Catholic unionists as well as Protestant nationalists in contemporary Northern

Ireland. As political scientist Duncan Morrow of Ulster University reminds us: "Translating statistics about religious background into clear consequences for politics and national identity is never straightforward."[66] Nevertheless, there is enough consistency between these religious and national social identities to warrant concern about how Northern Ireland will navigate the swells of these transitional demographic waters. As the demographics change, so will the distribution of power, or at least its perception. The deep divisions within Northern Irish society have not gone away with the passage of time, nor will they. Rather, they must be actively and constructively managed as the minority–majority structure of the country changes. This is particularly necessary, as we will discuss later in this chapter, in the climate of political and national uncertainty birthed by Brexit.

Such situations of instability can exacerbate already-stressed societies and activate tectonic shifts in demographic pressures that increase a state's or region's vulnerability to instability and conflict. Research demonstrates that identity polarization with two relatively large groups of approximately the same size, as we see in contemporary Northern Ireland, is a potent risk factor for violent conflict. As economist Paul Collier and his colleagues have demonstrated in their model of civil war onset: "A completely polarized society, divided into two equal groups, has a risk of civil war around six times higher than a homogenous society."[67]

Unequal Access to Basic Goods and Services

As we have seen, the intersection of social identities and inequalities is a volatile one. Inequalities between and among social identity groups—whether economic, social, political, or cultural—can leave one group feeling discriminated against and the other enjoying privileges which it fears to lose. Particularly relevant to social fragmentation are horizontal social inequalities—issues of identity-based unequal access to basic goods and services, including "health, education, water, sanitation, communications and infrastructure."[68] Having equal access to such basic goods and services is a common social expectation. For fragmented societies, however, this is an expectation often unmet as the ability to access these basic goods and services varies "within and across different social groups and geographic locations; rural communities and women and girls . . . are particularly vulnerable to being underserved."[69]

Access to education is a basic good and service that can be negatively impacted by social fragmentation. For example, political scientist Gudrun Ostby hypothesized that the higher the level of horizontal social inequality in a country—operationalized as differential access to educational opportunities—the higher the risk of civil conflict. Indeed, she found that for countries "with low levels of horizontal social inequality (5th percentile), the probability of onset of civil conflict is any given year is 1.75%." When horizontal social inequality between groups increases from the 5th to the 95th percentile, however, "the probability of conflict more than doubles, to 3.7%."[70] This is consistent with research suggesting that large cohorts of poorly educated youth, often reflecting horizontal social inequalities in educational access, increase the risk of conflict in societies.[71]

For the identity-based social divisions and demographic pressures wracking contemporary Northern Ireland, one of the most relevant and contested basic good and service is education. Here, the issue is less a lack of unequal access and more a question of whether educational delivery can be separate but remain equal. And, more pressing for a deeply divided society, if education remains separate, to what degree does it reinforce divisions rather than ameliorate them? Is education segregated by identity concretizing social fragmentation or promoting social cohesion?

The role of education in addressing social fragmentation becomes particularly pressing with the realization that, in a divided society, children develop a very early understanding of conflict-related social identities. In a 2019 study, for instance, psychologist Laura Taylor and colleagues used a novel testing approach to empirically measure how symbols (neighborhoods and flags, sports and activities, and community and religion) are associated with knowledge of national (British/Irish) and religious (Protestant/Catholic) social identities in children aged 5–11. The children were drawn from both state-controlled (de facto Protestant) and Catholic church-maintained schools in Northern Ireland. They found that children as young as five across both samples begin to differentiate "the other" on the basis of symbols related to these social identities. Children's awareness of and sensitivity to the in-group and out-group distinctions associated with the symbols only increased as they aged.[72] In light of this research, educational settings involving direct contact between identity groups can be seen as an essential intervention that can challenge and expand social identities before they become solidified or entrenched.

Responsibility for education in Northern Ireland is a devolved matter. There are three main categories of publicly funded schools (there are very few independent or private schools in Northern Ireland), categorized according to their management type:

- *State-controlled schools* were previously owned by the Protestant churches and transferred to local authorities beginning in the 1930s, but with guarantees that effectively left Protestants with control over the schools. As a result, these publicly funded schools are attended by mainly Protestant pupils. In its 2019–2020 report on enrollments in schools, Northern Ireland's Department of Education tallied 490 state-controlled schools.[73]
- *Voluntary schools* are publicly funded schools not under the ownership of the state (though their running and capital building costs come from the state). The majority of these schools are maintained by the Catholic church, which never entertained the idea of handing control of its schools over to the state, and are attended mainly by Catholic pupils. A 2019–2020 tally found 539 voluntary schools in Northern Ireland.
- *Integrated schools*, upheld by the Good Friday Agreement as an essential aspect of the reconciliation progress, are publicly funded schools required by law to maintain a reasonable balance of Protestant and Catholic pupils and staff. Churches have not been involved in the development of religiously integrated schools (though the schools do have a core principle of Christian ethos) and these schools, like their segregated counterparts, also receive full funding from the state.[74] In Northern Ireland, 65 integrated schools (25 of which were preexisting state-controlled or voluntary schools that changed their status to integrated) were in operation in 2019–2020.

The same 2019–2020 annual report counted 348,928 pupils across these three categories of publicly funded schools (as well as 54 special needs schools, hospital schools, or independent schools). Of those, 50.56% (176,408) were Catholic, 32.28% (112,637) Protestant, and 17.16% (59,883) designated as other Christians, non-Christians, or of no religion. More than 93% of these pupils are attending publicly funded schools in overwhelmingly segregated environments, a percentage that has held fairly consistently since the Good Friday Agreement. Only 6.6% of pupils attending state-controlled schools are Catholic, and less than 1% of pupils attending Catholic maintained schools

are Protestant.[75] In some schools, the pupil segregation is whole and complete. In 2012, for instance, 180 schools in Northern Ireland had no Protestant
students on their roster and 111 schools had no Catholic students.[76]

Segregation is reflected not only in pupil identity, however. It also is reflected in the formal curriculum (texts, films, and teaching materials).
A 2020 survey, for instance, of how Northern Ireland history is taught found
the overwhelming majority of Catholic schools teaching a more modern unit
(1965–1998) focusing on the civil rights movement and the Troubles, while
the majority of Protestant state-controlled schools studied an earlier period
(1920–1949) emphasizing the creation of the Northern Ireland state and its
role in fighting Nazism during World War II.[77] More subtly, segregation also
is reflected in the informal curriculum (co-curricular activities) and even the
hidden curriculum (the organizational design of the school as well as the unspoken or implicit messages communicated by teachers and administrators).
In this way, segregated schools form parallel systems of knowledge, often
based on rejecting the "other."[78]

This segregated educational system is a subject of continuing attention
and often contentious debate. In 2010, Owen Paterson, then Secretary of
State for Northern Ireland, attacked the educational system as a "criminal
waste of public money" and argued that "the British taxpayer should [not]
go on subsidising segregation."[79] Several days later, then First Minister and
Democratic Unionist Party (DUP) leader Peter Robinson decried the system
as a "benign form of apartheid which is fundamentally damaging to our society" and raised the question of why the state should fund church schools.[80]
Sinn Fein immediately responded by accusing Robinson of launching an attack on Catholic education. Bishop Donal McKeown, a prelate of the Roman
Catholic Church, joined the fray to insist that faith-based schools are a "hallmark of a stable and pluralist society."[81]

Integrated schools often find themselves caught in the maelstrom of these
controversies, depicted as either the ideal for which to strive or the target at
which to rail. The hallmark of integrated education is intergroup contact, with
a religious balance of pupils and staff who study and learn together every day
in the same school. The first planned integrated school, founded by a small
group of parents intent on a different way forward for their children, was
the establishment of the independent Lagan College secondary school on the
outskirts of Belfast in 1981. For the first eight years of its existence, the school
was not recognized by the government. It would not be until the Education
Reform Order of 1989 that integrated schooling was formally endorsed by

the state. Currently, fewer than 7% (24,261) of Northern Ireland students go to integrated schools. While this represents an increase of 637 pupils compared to the previous year—and a 2,305 pupil increase compared to five years ago—it is still, for many, a disappointingly low percentage and number of students whose families choose to have them attend an integrated school. For many, the reality of everyday life is that school choice is based more on locality than ideology. And, given the pronounced residential segregation, decisions based on locality mean that "children generally attend a school associated with their religious affiliation and/or community background."[82]

Today, despite public support for integrated education remaining extremely high (a 2019 NILT survey, for instance, revealed 61% of respondents indicating they would prefer their children go to a mixed-religion school) and decades of civil society campaigning for fully integrated education, political and policy discourse (with the exception of the Alliance Party) has shifted away from integrated education and toward the easier to digest compromise of "shared education."[83] Shared education programming attempts to mitigate the negative consequences of segregated education by emphasizing "the sharing of learning experiences by pupils across communal borders and the sharing of resources by schools" even while maintaining separate and segregated schools.[84] It differs from integrated education in that the focus is on periodic intergroup contact across partner schools rather than everyday contact in the same school. Shared education covers a broad network of collaborative engagement between those of different religious beliefs as well as those of differing socioeconomic status—joint curricular activities, joint extracurricular activities, and shared campuses. Shared education builds a network of Protestant, Catholic, and integrated schools in which pupils and teachers pool resources and move between schools to take classes and share experiences.[85]

Supporters of integrated education still advocate fiercely for its relevance, pointing to the fact that existing integrated schools are oversubscribed. In 2017, the Integrated Education Fund (IEF) launched the "Integrate My School" campaign, including a promotional advert from actor Liam Neeson of Ballymena, to work with parents and teachers to transform their segregated school into an integrated one.[86] By 2019, six additional schools, with an overwhelming majority of parental support built through the campaign, had voted to transform themselves from segregated to integrated. Such moves ring true for Belfast-based stand-up comedian Jake O'Kane: "If we are ever to have anything resembling normality, then the foundation on which that society is built will involve us educating our children together."[87] In further defense of integrated education, the IEF cite years of research suggesting "that integrated schooling has a significant and positive social influence on the lives of those who experience it, most notably in terms of fostering cross-community friendships, reducing prejudicial attitudes and promoting a sense of security in religious, racial, or ethnically diverse environments."[88]

Advocates of integrated education argue that shared education is a partisan means of preserving the status quo rather than transforming it. In their view, "shared education perpetuates division, with children being labelled according to the school they attend and the uniform they wear."[89] The IEF maintains that "shared facilities and shared campuses do not equate to shared education. They may facilitate the potential for collaboration between schools but it is the level of interaction and contact between pupils that counts the most."[90] As one post-primary pupil reflected: "Without full integration opinions aren't going to change. We still have our Protestant and Catholic schools; we mix for computers but we still go home to our Protestant and our Catholic schools."[91]

Proponents of shared education counter that, after years of decidedly low enrollment in integrated education, shared education is the best—and only—way forward for contemporary Northern Ireland. They contend, as some research suggests, that the everyday cross-contact of integrated education may actually reinforce community division and stereotypes rather than dismantling them.[92] Shared education, conversely, is "associated with: a reduction in in-group bias; greater out-group trust; reduced anxiety regarding the out-group; more positive feelings when in the company of out-group members; and more 'positive action' tendencies towards the other group (for example, desires to seek contact, help out, support and find out more)."[93] In 2015, the Council for Catholic Maintained Schools argued: "If after 30 years the sector [integrated schooling] has grown to the point where it commands only 6.89 per cent of the school age population in Northern Ireland, the department should evaluate the public appetite for 'integrated education' as a sectoral entity, reconsider the 'statutory duty' and look to the promotion of other 'initiatives' which have a greater chance of making more effective use of limited resources." Similarly, the Ulster Teachers' Union maintained: "Many schools already collaborate across all sectors ensuring that all children and young people have opportunities to learn together . . . we would agree that with continued support financially in this area we can continue to allow examples of good practice to be shown and modelled upon by other schools."[94]

In contemporary Northern Ireland, it certainly appears that integrated education remains a bridge too far for far too many. Since its launch in 2007, shared education—despite the substantial logistical challenges it entails and the relative lack of comparative research to validate its efficacy—seems to have won the day as a safer contact alternative more in line with the norms of this deeply divided society. Politically and culturally, shared education sidesteps the issue of whether contact should be institutionalized in segregated or integrated schools by allowing for an intersection of both worlds: "Collaboration between separate schools in which pupils and teachers moved between schools to take classes on a regular basis would allow for a degree of mixing and contact, while at the same time protecting the ethos and existence of separate schools."[95] Similarly, a 2013 report of a Ministerial Advisory Group stated that they did "not agree that integrated schools should be viewed and actively promoted as the 'preferred option' . . . [since] parents and children have the right to their religious, cultural and philosophical beliefs being respected."[96] The Shared Education Act (Northern Ireland) 2016 formally embedded shared education within the Northern Ireland education system. A May 2018 follow-up biennial report found "a significant increase in participation across the reporting period in the numbers of pupils, teachers, leaders, governors, and parents involved in Shared Education."[97] Currently, there almost 60,000 young people involved in some form of shared education in about 580 schools from preschool to post-primary, from across all sectors, in Northern Ireland.[98] Those figures account for about 17% of Northern Ireland's total pupils and involve about 51% of its schools, suggesting shared education is well on its way toward becoming mainstreamed in the country's education system.

It is clear, however, that while there may be growing appetite for shared education, there likewise remains a significant appetite for nonshared education in Northern Ireland. As one interviewee told me, "If Christ came back, he'd have to go to two different churches. So he might as well have to go to two different schools." Such sectarianism is blind to the significant economic consequences of a segregated system of education. Essentially, the state spends hundreds of millions of pounds each year administering two parallel education systems. As one example, Sir Robert Salisbury, in testimony before the House of Commons, described: "Omagh [Northern Ireland], where I live, has six post-primary schools with six principals, six building costs and six staffing costs. Retford in Nottinghamshire [England], with a similar population, has two. If you replicate that across the whole of Northern Ireland, you have your funding crisis in one view."[99] The subsequent 2019 report carefully addressed this inefficiency of too many schools while recognizing the identity-based sensitivities involved: "We saw there is a clear need to reduce duplication across the education sector and for consolidation of the school estate. Witnesses were clear that alongside the immediate funding pressures on education, the complicated structure of education in Northern Ireland meant that money was not being spent in the most efficient way. Achieving change will be challenging, and it is important that the wishes of communities and the demand that exists for different types of education in Northern Ireland are understood."[100]

Dismantling the parallel education system in Northern Ireland is not going to solve all of the society's problems related to social fragmentation. Its role in sustaining the identity-based social divisions that lie at the heart of such fragmentation, though, is clear. In the chasm of separate education, where we-identity is reinforced, division is spawned. Education becomes the avoidance of a threat to one's dominant identity, a haven in which to protect, rather than challenge, oneself and one's misconceptions about the "other."

Equally clear, however, is the potential, mostly untapped, for education reform to promote social cohesion in a deeply divided society by creating a shared future instead of repeating a divided past. Education, as a basic good and service, can shape, rather than simply reflect, the society in which it operates. In so doing, education is fundamentally tied to the rebuilding of a post-conflict society. As Karen Murphy, director of international strategy for Facing History and Ourselves, has argued: "Education as a sector is also uniquely positioned to make a substantive contribution to the repair, reconstruction, and redress of inequalities, divisions, and, in the spirit of transitional justice, political repression and human rights violations. . . . It is also the most appropriate medium for embodying and passing on the skills, dispositions, and behaviors that must be learned to nurture and protect democratic citizenship and human rights."[101]

Channeling the spirit of the parent-led movement that began integrated schooling in 1981, it may be that educational reform is sparked by a new generation of parents and even students who choose to no longer live with the status quo. An inspiring example of this comes from another deeply divided society, Bosnia and Herzegovina (BiH). With origins dating back to 1999, the educational system of BiH operates with a "two schools under one roof" system. Under this segregated system, children from different backgrounds (predominately Muslim Bosniaks and predominately Catholic Croats) attend the same school in the same building but have different ethnic curriculum, using different languages and different textbooks. Sometimes, they attend schools in staggered shifts or use different entrances or different stairwells or study on different floors or different sides of the building. While there are more than 50 schools around BiH operating under the "two schools under one roof" system, students in one school, in the central city of Jajce, rebelled against a proposal for a new segregated school in their community. "They began a battle with someone who is much stronger and richer than them. They did not want to be hostages of the manipulative politics that our government leads," a representative of the protesters said in a speech.[102] Eventually, in 2017, the education ministry capitulated and plans for the segregated school were dropped. After winning their demand to study together, rather than apart, the students continue to lead protests against segregated schools throughout BiH.

For widespread and lasting change, however, governance must be accountable for the vision to facilitate inclusive aspirational goals of educational reform. While short on specifics, the "New Decade, New Approach" deal of 2020 listed among its carefully worded priorities for the restored Executive: "To help build a shared and integrated society, the Executive will support educating children and young people of different backgrounds together in the classroom." Part of that process, recognizing that the current system "is not sustainable," includes reviewing "the prospects of moving towards a single education system."[103] As columnist Allison Morris has reflected: "Showing our children a better way should not have taken this long. . . . It need not be so. We have a chance to start again, a chance to show the next generation that we have their best interests at heart. Let's hope it isn't squandered."[104]

Gender Inequalities

The relationship between gender inequalities and conflict often focuses on how the consequences of conflict affect women and men differently. In a significant way, however, we also can understand gender inequalities as a driver of conflict. A 2013 Oxfam report describes several examples of gender inequalities fueling conflict: "In South Sudan, for example, high bride price fuels cattle raiding and conflict between tribal groups; in Gaza, patriarchal values create a sense that leadership is about self-interest rather than protecting the community; in Afghanistan, women may be 'given' or 'taken' to settle community disputes and conflicts."[105] In some cases, gender inequalities also may drive conflict by leading women and girls to become combatants. A 2010 Saferworld survey in Nepal, for instance, found that nearly 20% of Maoist female combatants cited the desire to challenge gender inequality and promote the empowerment of women as their main reason for joining the rebellion—with another 25% having joined in response to sexual abuse and rape by opposing state security forces.[106]

There is an increasingly widespread recognition among researchers of the role gender inequalities play as a risk factor in violent conflict. In one of the seminal studies, political scientist Mary Caprioli found that domestic gender inequality was correlated with a state's greater use of violent military solutions to resolve international disputes.[107] Looking more specifically at intrastate rather than international conflict, Erik Melander, deputy director of the Uppsala Conflict Data program in Sweden, also found that gender inequality was significantly predictive of higher levels of intrastate armed conflict (i.e., civil war).[108] A 2009 policy paper by the Organisation for Economic Cooperation and Development (OECD) included unequal gender relations among its list of key structural risk factors for armed violence.[109] Two years later, the Institute for Economics and Peace found a strong correlation between three separate measures of gender equality (in public, at work, and in private) and a general measure of state peacefulness (the Global Peace Index, or GPI). For each of the measures, as gender equality decreased, a country's ranking on the GPI decreased (particularly on the index's internal peace measure).[110] Focusing specifically on gender inequalities in family law and practice (including marriage, divorce, custody, inheritance, and other intimate family issues), international security expert Valerie Hudson and her colleagues discovered that levels of state peacefulness decreased as the level of inequities in family law and practice increased.[111]

In addition, gender inequalities have been shown to be a cross-cutting issue intersecting with other risk factors for violent conflict. For example, economist Daniel Kaufmann, in a study of 80 countries, found that corruption increased as women's social and economic rights decreased.[112] Political scientist Steven Fish, in looking at the connection between Islam and regime type, argues that the most significant driver of the low degree of democratization in Muslim societies is the subordination of women and girls. As he concludes: "The station of women, more than other factors that predominate in Western thinking about religious systems and politics, links Islam and the democratic deficit."[113] There are a range of other studies confirming strong cross-national linkages between the treatment of women and a wide array of economic and health variables.[114]

In contemporary Northern Ireland, the Equality Commission for Northern Ireland (ECNI) has been at the forefront of efforts to highlight and address gender inequalities. In a February 2019 meeting with the UN Committee on the Elimination of Discrimination Against Women (CEDAW), the ECNI urged it to "hold the UK government to account for its lack of progress in protecting and extending equality for women in Northern Ireland."[115] The ECNI's submitted report expressed concern about the weakness of institutional mechanisms for gender equality in Northern Ireland, the potential negative economic impact of Brexit on women's equality, and the legislative and policy gaps in equality protection for women in Northern Ireland. The report detailed women's frequent experiences of sexual discrimination and harassment in the workplace as well as the ongoing gender pay gap in favor of men across private and public sectors, industrial sectors, and occupational groups.[116] In its reply briefing, CEDAW noted "with particular concern the inadequacy of laws and policies to protect women in Northern Ireland" and recommended the state "revise its legislation in Northern Ireland to ensure that it affords protection to women on an equal footing with women" in the rest of the UK.[117]

ECNI's report also highlighted the myriad ways in which women in Northern Ireland remain underrepresented in all spheres of political life—at Westminster, in the Assembly (despite female leadership in three of the five major political parties), and in local government. Not only are women underrepresented in numbers, but, as one nationalist politician expressed to me, when they are present in the political structures "they generally are not in positions that can effect change." She continued: "While their presence improves the tone of discourse, they too often do not have the room to speak up in the culture of toxic masculinity that still pervades Northern Ireland politics, particularly at the local level of government." In fact, a September 2020 survey carried out by the *Belfast Telegraph* found that more than a quarter of female Members of the Legislative Assembly have been sexually harassed during their political life (with the majority having experienced it in local government) with three-quarters having been victims of sexism and abuse on social media.[118]

The underrepresentation of women continues in government public appointments, private-sector boards, and major employment sectors. Appointments to the FICT in 2016, for example, included only one female, conflict researcher Katy Radford, among its 15 appointed members (eight of whom were drawn from outside government and seven, all male, appointed by leaders of the five largest political parties). While the Commission is not technically a regulated body under public appointments legislation, the Commissioner of Public Appointments did note its composition was strikingly at odds with the gender equality targets set by the Northern Ireland Executive.[119] A 2018 analysis of 7,000 jobs across 10 employment sectors found only three of the *Belfast Telegraph*'s Top 100 Northern Ireland Companies were led by female chief executives. Despite women making up half of the working-age population in Northern Ireland, they occupied only 35% of the top jobs at universities, just 34% of the top jobs in the judiciary, only 27% of the PSNI's most senior ranks, and just 27% of councilor positions in local government across the country.[120] Overall, women tend to be concentrated in lower paid, part-time employment. In 2018, for instance, 39% of female employees worked part-time compared to only 9% of male employees. All told, 82% of part-time employees in Northern Ireland were women.[121]

When gender inequalities are deeply embedded within society, one of the clear indicators is a lack of physical security for women in a society—often manifest in physical, sexual, and/or psychological gender-based violence. "There is considerable evidence that gender inequality—in the form of social, economic, legal and political inequalities—is a root cause of violence against women."[122] Indeed, social epidemiologist Lori Heise found that the most consistent predictor of the use of violence by men against women and girls are the discriminatory attitudes and norms toward women and girls that underlie gender inequalities.[123] Political scientist Valerie Hudson and colleagues examined the level of physical security of women in a society—including the prevalence of domestic violence, rape, marital rape, and murder of women—in relationship to levels of peacefulness. They found that it is the physical security of women (even more so than levels of democracy, wealth, or prevalence of Islamic culture) that is most predictive of "which states would be the least peaceful or of the most concern to the international community or have the worst relations with their neighbors."[124] In short, there is a strong correlation between levels of gender-based violence and conflict. As a 2013 joint consultation report by the UN and Saferworld summarized: "There is emerging evidence that a high prevalence of violence against women within societies may be a structural cause or enabling factor for armed conflict and instability at the national level."[125]

Unfortunately, the rise of gender-based violence against women in Northern Ireland is clear. The number of rape offenses has shown an escalating annual trend, with the level reported in 2018–2019 (983 rapes) more than four times greater than that reported in 2000–2001 (similar trends hold true for sexual assault).[126] Conviction rates for these offenses are strikingly low. Of the 820 allegations of rape reported to police in 2016–2017, for instance, only 15 people were convicted of the crime by the courts.[127] The ECNI has highlighted an increase in the objectification and degradation of women in contemporary Northern Ireland, including in the media, as promoting an increasingly sexual and sexualized culture. In such an atmosphere, gender inequalities are reinforced and gender-based violence against women can become normalized. The PSNI certainly did not help cultural sensitivity to gender-based violence against women when, in February 2020, they mistakenly issued "victim blaming" rape leaflets at an event in North Belfast reading: "Alcohol is the number one rape drug. How much have you taken already?"

On the domestic front of gender-based violence, the figures are even more glaring, particularly in recognition that there is vast underreporting (especially related to domestic abuse and crimes allegedly committed by former political prisoners released on license who, if reported, may face reimprisonment). In 2019, the PSNI recorded 31,705 domestic abuse incidents, one of the highest 12-month periods since the start of data collection in 2004–2005. In 2019, 15,110 of those incidents involved one or more domestic abuse crimes. This amounted to 18,033 domestic abuse crimes in total (about 16% of all recorded crime in Northern Ireland), the single highest 12-month period recorded since 2004–2005. These figures translate to 17 domestic abuse incidents and 10 domestic abuse crimes per 1,000 population, with police responding to a domestic incident about every 18 minutes daily. For comparison's sake, since 2004–2005, that is about a 51% increase in domestic abuse incidents and a 68% increase in domestic abuse crimes.[128] The vast majority (upward of 70%) of those victimized in domestic abuse incidents and crimes are women. It is estimated that one in four women in Northern Ireland have, at some point in their life, been a victim of domestic abuse.[129]

In April 2020, Justice Minister Naomi Long (Alliance Party) intro-duced legislation in the Assembly that would see domestic abusers facing up to 14 years in prison for the most serious offenses. The legislation also criminalizes "coercive control," including psychologically or emotionally abusive behavior. In the isolation imposed by the COVID-19 lockdown, the legislation proved particularly timely as the PSNI reported 3,755 domestic abuse calls—including three domestic killings—from the time period of March 25 to May 5, 2020. This was an increase of 618 cases from the same time period during the previous year.[130]

Women can be recognized not only as victims of conflict but as a cor-rective to it. An October 2000 UN Security Council Resolution (UNSCR 1325) affirmed "the important role of women in the prevention and reso-lution of conflicts and in peace-building" and stressed "the importance of their equal participation and full involvement in all efforts for the mainte-nance and promotion of peace and security, and the need to increase their role in decision-making with regard to conflict prevention and resolu-tion."[131] Six years later, speaking on his last International Women's Day as UN Secretary-General, Kofi Annan reaffirmed "that no policy [referring to the empowerment of women and girls] is more important in preventing con-flict, or in achieving reconciliation after a conflict has ended."[132] As a post-conflict society, for example, Rwanda has taken seriously the contributions that women's skills and experiences can bring to public policy discussions. Gender rights and some of the most women-friendly policies in the world are now enshrined in Rwanda's constitution, along with a mandate that at least 30% of government positions be occupied by women. As of 2019, a remark-able 61% of Rwanda's parliamentarians were women, the highest proportion of any parliament in the world and the only one with a female majority.[133] Similarly, Guatemalan women are playing a key role as agents of change in their country's ongoing peacebuilding process.

States should remain diligent about increasing participation by women in decision-making and dialogue, including adopting national action plans on UNSCR 1325. Unfortunately, such plans have yet to be adopted in Northern Ireland. This omission was highlighted in a 2014 summary report by the Northern Ireland Women's European Platform that found "little evidence to show the effective implementation of these [UNSCR 1325's] commitments for women" in Northern Ireland. The report raised significant concerns about the lack of inclusion of women in peacebuilding and post-conflict recon-struction. In both republican and loyalist communities, the report argued, there was little space for women to speak out, either in critique or support of the peace process. T:BUC also was called to task for its lack of recognition for the work of women in peacebuilding and conflict resolution.[134]

In response, the ECNI's 2019 report again urged the implementation of UNSCR 1325 to advance the participation of women in public and political life as well as peacebuilding. The CEDAW's reply noted its continuing concern "about the underrepresentation of women in political and public life" in Northern Ireland while also reiterating a previous concern "where women [in Northern Ireland] continue to face intimidation by paramilitary groups and are underrepresented in post-conflict reconstruction and peacebuilding processes." The CEDAW strongly recommended that "concrete measures" be taken to redress these issues and guarantee the participation of women in the rebuilding of contemporary Northern Ireland.[135] As Oxfam summarizes: " 'Gender' is not the optional extra which we simply can't manage in fragile contexts, because we have more urgent things to do. Tackling gender inequality *must* be heart and centre of fragility programming, to both secure women's rights *and* promote peace and stability in such contexts."[136]

Political Instability

Social fragmentation is exacerbated in the face of political instability. Political instability intersects with many of the governance risk factors discussed in the previous chapter. The governance category was concerned with the ways in which a state's structure and authority is exercised and how that relates to risk of violent conflict. The risk factors in that category were fairly static elements that alert us to *where* violent conflict might be more likely. Our discussion of political instability, however, looks more closely at internal or external threats to a state's authority or legitimacy that can intensify social fragmentation. The fluid risk factors associated with political instability—what political scientist Matthew Krain has termed "openings in the political opportunity structure"—are a bridge from *where* to *when* violent conflict might be most likely.[137] In contemporary Northern Ireland, the opening in the political opportunity structure that posed, and still poses, the greatest risk in terms of political instability is the looming reality of Brexit and its implications for issues of national identity on both sides of the sectarian divide.

On June 23, 2016, 17.4 million people in the United Kingdom voted to leave the European Union. Proportionally, this translated to a slim majority of 51.9% voting "leave" with only 48.1% voting "remain." The UK's divorce from the EU, commonly known as Brexit, was the first time ever a nation had voted to leave the EU. "Leave" did not win in all regions of the UK, however. In Northern Ireland, though it had the lowest voter turnout of any region in the UK, the majority of voters (55.8%) preferred to remain in the EU (a figure that increased to 69% in a May 2018 survey). Of the 18 parliamentary constituencies, 11 voted "remain." Four of the five major political parties were pro-Remain; only the DUP was pro-Leave. The referendum also revealed the depth of divisions on the issue between Protestants and Catholics in Northern Ireland. Protestants voted to leave the EU by a proportion of 60 to 40, with Catholics, fearful of the return of a hard border between Northern Ireland and Ireland, overwhelmingly voting to stay by a proportion of 85 to 15.[138] Similarly, the 2016 NILT survey found that 46% of Protestants believed Northern Ireland would be definitely or probably better off outside the EU, while only 13% of Catholics believed so.[139] Those divisions only sharpened during the protracted and increasingly contentious Brexit negotiations. An October 2018 poll even found that a staggering 87% of Northern Ireland's leave voters "would see the collapse of the peace process as an acceptable price for Brexit."[140]

The three and a half years following the referendum was a tortured process full of twists and turns, elections and resignations, negotiations and counters, insults and recriminations, deadlines and extensions. It would not be until October 2019 that a Withdrawal Agreement, after several revisions, gained enough traction to be approved by the EU. While the Agreement would eventually be approved by the UK parliament in early January 2020 as a far better scenario than a no-deal exit, devolved governments in Scotland and Wales both rejected the Agreement. Northern Ireland's normally fractious political parties also found themselves standing together in opposition to the Withdrawal Agreement, even if for different reasons. For the largely pro-Brexit DUP, the potential for customs checks on goods traveling between the UK and Northern Ireland undermined the integrity of the union and led them to feel like "second class citizens . . . subject not to Westminster but subject to the EU." As one DUP politician bemoaned, the Agreement "makes me less British, less of a unionist."[141] In contrast, Sinn Fein's opposition to the Agreement was born of a political and economic desire to maintain European citizenship and out of a fear that cross-border trade and relations with the Republic of Ireland would be compromised.

On January 20, 2020, in one of its first substantive acts after restoration, the Northern Ireland Assembly voted overwhelmingly to reject the Agreement. There were no audible dissenters to the vote of rejection. Even without legislative consent of these devolved administrations, however, the UK's departure from the EU continued unimpeded. On January 29, 2020, the Brexit Withdrawal Agreement was formally ratified by the EU Parliament.[142] Two days later, on Friday, January 31, 2020, at 11:00 PM local time, the UK officially left the EU after 47 years of membership.

For the next 11 months, the UK entered a "transition period" where it would remain part of the single market and customs union for the EU, but powerless to shape any of the laws and regulations of that market and union. During that time, the UK and the 27 remaining Member States of the EU entered negotiations on what a new free trade agreement would look like as well as a number of other crosscutting areas where agreement was needed. Though not widely discussed in the run-up to the Brexit referendum, the "invisible" open land border that currently separates Northern Ireland from the Republic of Ireland, some 310 meandering miles with 208 border crossings, quickly became the single most difficult political question in the Brexit negotiations.

The border was first established in 1920 as a result of the Government of Ireland Act. Gerrymandered to ensure a unionist majority in the north of Ireland, the new border ran along centuries-old county lines that were often out of alignment with the contemporary growth of communities around them. As a result, "even individual farms and houses were divided by the border . . . [as it] runs along the middle of eleven roads while it also meets in the middle of at least three bridges and dissects two ferry crossings."[143] Former UK Prime Minister Margaret Thatcher infamously described the meandering complexity of the border as having "all those kinks and wiggles in it."[144] Customs control and tariffs at the border were implemented by the Irish Free State in April 1923. Since that time, customs posts were manned with varying degrees of strictness, with the British Army maintaining large military checkpoints at major crossings throughout most of Operation Banner (August 1969 to July 2007) to control the IRA's cross-border movement of arms and smuggling. The British Army "also used explosives to blow up unapproved roads, demolished border bridges over streams and rivers, and set concrete, metal and wire barricades on many of these local roads."[145]

Border custom checks ended with the introduction of the EU single market in January 1993, and the large military checkpoints began to be dismantled after the Good Friday Agreement in 1998. In journalist Roisin McAuley's words: "The single market had made the border invisible. The Good Friday Agreement meant it was no longer guarded by soldiers."[146]

When both Northern Ireland and the Republic of Ireland were within the EU, there was free movement between the two of trade, goods, people, and services. In map-maker Garrett Carr's description of the border, "No living thing would be impeded by it, it merely demarcates nations."[147] Today, about 30,000 people cross that soft land border unimpeded each day, living their lives on both sides of the borderlands.[148] An estimated 177,000 lorries, 208,000 light vans, and 1.85 million cars cross unimpeded every month.[149] A 2016 survey of Northern Ireland respondents found that 63% reported crossing the border several times a year or more.[150] In the 2016 Brexit referendum, every one of the six border constituencies, recognizing the cross-border realities of their everyday life, voted "remain" in large majorities. Were Brexit to lead to a hard land border between the two countries—with the Republic of Ireland remaining part of the EU and Northern Ireland not— Northern Ireland would have the only land border (aside from Gibraltar) between an EU country and the UK. Resulting bureaucratic and economic concerns regarding market disruptions would be compounded by heightened security concerns. Recognizing this, and in anticipation of a credible return of paramilitary violence with the border as a target for attacks, the PSNI abruptly pulled out of plans to sell three fortified police stations near the border and requested financial assurances from the UK to ensure they have the security personnel to patrol the border in the case that it was closed.[151] Many people I spoke with, however, said that ordinary folk on both sides of the border would tear the infrastructure down even before paramilitaries had a chance to attack it.

Throughout the negotiations, the EU, UK, Irish, and Northern Ireland governments made clear that they wanted to keep an open land border between Northern Ireland and Ireland, even though the former would now be outside the EU and the latter remains within it. None wished to see "any return to the borders of the past," meaning a hard, physical border, complete with checkpoints and customs controls, between the two countries.[152] Such a hard border would have violated the spirit of the Good Friday Agreement, a violation already creeping in as a rising number of passport and identity checks are being carried out on cross-border buses as of this writing.[153]

A June 2020 investigative report also found "disproportionately high levels of immigration checks" taking place in Belfast, almost four times higher than in London.[154] For political and logistical reasons, a hard border was also highly unpopular among the public in Northern Ireland and in the Republic of Ireland. A 2019 poll, for instance, found that, if they had to choose, an over-whelming 86% of Irish respondents would opt for a united Ireland, and all the economic and political challenges that might entail, over a hard border.[155]

Despite the desire not to return to borders of the past, however, some border of the future had to be determined by the end of the transition period. Under the terms of a protocol embedded in the Brexit Withdrawal Agreement, the pressure point was moved from a north–south land border to an east–west water border between the islands.[156] Specifically, the Agreement called for a customs and regulatory border in the Irish Sea between Northern Ireland and the rest of the UK in order to avoid one with the Republic of Ireland. In opposition to the DUP's wishes that it be treated like the rest of the UK, the Agreement gave Northern Ireland a type of special status, allowing it to stay in the UK's customs territory but operate under the EU's customs rules for its trade with the Republic of Ireland. Loyalists joined unionists in seeing this status as far less than special. As conflict specialist Eamonn O'Kane pointed out: "Culturally, loyalists fear a customs border dilutes their 'Britishness'—it makes Northern Ireland's terms of trade different from the rest of the UK."[157] In practice, this arrangement would leave, in the words of one disillusioned and infuriated loyalist activist I spoke with, "an economic united Ireland."

Throughout the negotiations, Johnson publicly and bombastically maintained a commitment to frictionless trade from the rest of the UK into Northern Ireland by insisting there would be no hard border across the Irish Sea and no checks on goods moving across it. Conversely, the EU maintained there would have be checks at the ports and airports in Northern Ireland on at least some types of goods, particularly those at risk of going on to the Republic of Ireland. By May 2020, the British government finally con-ceded that there would have to be post-Brexit checks on goods crossing the Irish Sea—in the form of physical border control posts at ports in Belfast, Warrenpoint, and Larne.[158] Once the inevitability of a sea border dawned on the DUP, they made a U-turn on their previous position that such a border would "destabilise Northern Ireland" and began actively promoting the benefits of a sea border in order to fashion a political "win" out of a clear-cut political loss.[159] Other rival unionists, however, did not following suit. For Traditional Unionist Voice (TUV) leader Jim Allister, for instance, the implementation of such control posts would be a "betrayal of the highest order, made all the worse by repeated assurances that it would not happen."[160] Indeed, many unionists and loyalists were left wondering why they remained so loyal to a British government and union that seemed to care so very little about their identity, citizenship, and constitutional future.

On December 17, 2020, the betrayal became reality as the UK and EU announced formal agreement on the workings of an Irish Sea border. The agreement will keep Northern Ireland in the EU single market for goods even as the rest of the UK leaves that market at the end of 2020. This means Ireland and Northern Ireland will be treated as a single market area in the EU's eyes, so there will be no necessity for customs checks at the Irish land border. It also means that the vast majority of goods being shipped from Great Britain to Northern Ireland will not have tariffs imposed, though there will be additional customs, safety, and security declarations enforced. If there is the possibility of any of those goods being shipped on to the Republic of Ireland, however, tariffs will be charged. While UK officials insist this new sea border is not a threat to the union of Great Britain and Northern Ireland, not all are so easily assuaged. Jim Allister bemoaned that there is now "partition down the Irish Sea" and that "the EU's gameplan has left Northern Ireland in a waiting room for Irish unity."[161]

Even with the question of the border resolved, however, there remain many details still to be negotiated between the UK and the EU on a myriad of issues related to healthcare, aviation, education, nuclear cooperation, security and law enforcement, driving, participation in EU programs, pensions, etc. Most pressing, given that the EU is the UK's biggest single trading partner, is a post-Brexit free trade agreement—including fishing rights, fair competition rules, mechanisms for resolving trade disputes, and a negotiated grace period to allow for implementation of the details surrounding the agreements. In the absence of a UK-EU free trade agreement, the UK and EU would trade under terms set by the World Trade Organization, the basic rules for countries without trade deals. This likely means that prices would go up for the goods the UK buys and sells from and to the EU. It also is very likely that the lack of a UK-EU free trade agreement would mean an even harder Irish Sea border.

Finalizing all of these agreements, a process that normally takes several years, must be done by the time the transition period ends on December 31, 2020 (the UK stubbornly rejected an option for an extension of the transition period, even in the face of the COVID-19 pandemic). Failure to reach an agreement by that date would lead to a "no-deal scenario" in which the UK crashes out of the EU. Not only resulting in calamitous political and economic instability, such a scenario, in the grip of crippling pandemic, would pose a threat to the vital supply chain of drugs and medical supplies for the UK.

Johnson proclaimed Brexit—with its pillars of isolationism, nationalism, and immigration restriction—"the dawn of a new era" for the UK.[162] The fears are, however, that the dawn of this new era will have very different, and darker, reverberations for a beleaguered Northern Ireland. There certainly were no signs of Brexit unity in the newly restored Stormont Executive. DUP First Minister Arlene Foster, pleased in theory about the UK's exit even while frustrated on the specifics of the Withdrawal Agreement, asserted that "there is not now any debate on whether the UK should or will leave the European Union" and that now is the time to look forward as "our economic wellbeing must be one of those issues upon which we can all unite."[163] Sinn Fein Deputy First Minister Michelle O'Neill, conversely, looked forward in a more southerly direction, reminding the people of Northern Ireland that Brexit was "entirely contrary to the democratically expressed wishes of a cross community majority of the electorate in the North" and calling for "mature and inclusive debate about new political arrangements which examine Ireland's future beyond Brexit."[164] Outside the halls of Stormont, Brexit day was met with Union Jack flags and bunting in some areas of Northern Ireland and signs and marches of protest in others.

A "democratic consent" mechanism within the Withdrawal Agreement does give the Northern Ireland Assembly an opportunity, beginning four years after the end of the transition period, to vote periodically on whether this arrangement should continue. As sociologist Katy Hayward of QUB cautions, however: "Given the nature of politics here, this debate will almost inevitably be framed less as a policy or economic matter than as a constitutional and identity one."[165] If the vote, based on a simple majority rather than a majority of both unionists and nationalists, is to discontinue the trade arrangement outlined in the Agreement, a hard land border is again back on the table.

Regardless of how Brexit is resolved politically, the seismic sectarian damage already has been done in Northern Ireland. In terms of social fragmentation, Brexit has compounded the psychological, social, and physical identity borders that already divide Northern Ireland. The cooperation and mutual trust fundamental to the Good Friday Agreement is now under greater threat than ever; concerns about self-determination and national allegiance are again front and center. As one local warned, "those are fragile bricks to be moving."[166] Brexit's immediate and sure consequence for Northern Ireland has been to take the never dormant divisive questions of national identity—pro-Irish Catholic nationalists and pro-British Protestant unionists—and accentuate them even more. As SDLP Member of Parliament Claire Hannah said: "For Northern Ireland in particular, Brexit has sharpened all of the lines that the Good Friday Agreement was designed to soften around identity, around borders, around sovereignty. Brexit . . . reopens old wounds and limits our horizon."[167] Likewise, historian Thomas Hennessey, also a member of FICT, says: "Identity is what it's all about here—and Brexit brings all of the issues around [identity] right back into the heart of things."[168]

Conclusion

In deeply divided societies, the focus often settles on managing social fragmentation rather than transforming it into social cohesion. Asserting social identity through community ties certainly can promote a sense of belonging; it also, though, can undermine social cohesion by reinforcing and entrenching fragmentation. And the costs of that undermining are significant. When the walls of division enter into the souls of a people, the social, political, and cultural costs are debilitating. The economic costs even are quantifiable. A 2007 report, for instance, put a heavy price on the toll of social fragmentation in Northern Ireland—including direct and indirect costs, duplicate services, community relations work, and the opportunity cost of lost tourism or investment—at £1.5 billion a year.[169] A more recent 2018–2019 State of the State report by Deloitte attested to the continuing costs of division as reflected in the fact that, compared to the rest of the UK, "NI spending is higher per head of population on public order and safety costs, housing and community amenities, recreation, culture and religion and social protection."[170] Even before the economic devastation associated with the COVID-19 public health crisis, the report concluded that Northern Ireland's pattern of spending rendered its financial situation unsustainable.

The unsustainably of social fragmentation is not, however, limited to economic considerations. Social fragmentation is a cross-cutting and intersecting liability that renders all segments in a deeply divided society unsustainable. Societal sustainability will only be found, ultimately, in the promotion of social cohesion. While social fragmentation and cohesion will always be in an ebb and flow pattern in deeply divided societies, the pursuit of social cohesion must be intentional, institutionalized, and intensive. This means continually renegotiating horizontal social cohesion between identity groups as well as vertical social cohesion between those groups and the state. As political scientists Fletcher Cox and Timothy Sisk argue: "Social cohesion is more likely to form over time where strong institutions cause groups to interact with one another under conditions of equality, and where an inclusive state provides basic services to all groups equally."[171] Kaplan lays out the far-ranging implications of strong social cohesion: "Countries whose citizens share common ideas about who they are and how they should work together are far more likely to enjoy the state legitimacy and good governance necessary to spur and sustain economic and political development."[172]

In light of this, governments and civil society in deeply divided societies have an essential responsibility to constructively manage diverse social identities in ways that move beyond binary social cleavages. A shared vision must be articulated and widely embraced, one that nurtures a more inclusive superordinate social identity of "us" rather than the more divisive subordinate social identities that leave antagonistic clusters of "thems." Reframing "us" by defining and promoting a common superordinate identity, accepted and valued by both groups, lies at the heart of promoting social cohesion. It is less about denying the subordinate identity and more about constructively holding that identity in the broader context of a common superordinate identity. It is a simple, but transformational, recognition that we are both similar to and different from members of other identity groups.

The notion that one can hold both identities means that the cognitive dissonance stirred by having to be either "us" or "them" is a false choice. Unfortunately, in deeply divided societies, there is a long history of opposition between social identities, including seeing "them" as a threat to the existence of "us," that makes the perception of finding any degree of commonality in a superordinate identity particularly demanding. If, however, the subgroup identity of "us" is secure enough to explore the possibility of finding some degree of commonality with "them" in a superordinate identity, the social cohesion benefits stand to be substantial. "When both subgroup and superordinate identities are maintained (referred to as *dual identities*)," writes management expert Marlene Fiol and colleagues, "one can anticipate greater acceptance of the opposing subgroup."[173] Indeed, research has suggested that "holding both the subgroup identity and the superordinate identity reduces intergroup bias by creating a sense of commonality."[174]

A common, superordinate identity—a more inclusive and unifying understanding of "us"—can promote resilience in a community victimized by deep divisions. "Prejudice can be reduced by increasing the salience of common superordinate memberships. . . . A shared common identity suggests that previous outgroup members are now ingroup members, receiving the rewards of ingroup favoritism."[175] The acceptance of a common, superordinate identity does not need to preclude also holding other subordinate identities; embracing a larger "us" need not mean the denial of other distinctive secondary identities (racial, ethnic, religious, national, etc.) that also are an important part of our complex self-definition.[176] Finding a common identity simply means we have a place, a foothold, a shared experience from which we can begin to climb away from conflict and toward relationship.

This dual identity approach, and the decreased intergroup biases to which it can lead, can pave the way for more substantive possibilities of social cohesion. The sense of commonality engendered by a dual identity approach can allow us to "develop the ability to let go of well-established patterns of perceiving and begin to see things anew."[177] This, in turn, can open windows for deep engagement and appreciation of the "other" through cross-cutting relations in education, sports, religion, cultural programs, and physical integration in housing, schools, and work.[178] Cote d'Ivoire's national football team, for instance, comes from both sides of their country's North–South divide but have stepped forward as an example of a unified national institution and have initiated peacebuilding and development initiatives throughout the troubled country. As social psychologist Ervin Staub preaches, "deep engagement between people belonging to different groups . . . especially in the framework of cooperation in joint projects in the service of shared goals . . . can lead to experiencing the humanity of the other."[179] Conversely, as Duncan Morrow warns, "failure to actually engage can only result in the decay of reconciliation into a sullen and deep-rooted resignation and resentment . . . and a risk of ongoing resort to violence."[180]

Decades of social psychological research testify to the fact that intergroup contact is a powerful tool for improving intergroup relations. Unfortunately, as we have seen in this chapter, social fragmentation, particularly in postconflict societies, makes scarce the opportunities for meaningful face-to-face interactions. Even when opportunities for intergroup contact arise, they are often characterized by the practice of " 'avoidance,' of not discussing political or potentially sensitive issues in 'mixed company' or with people whom one did not know well."[181] This can lead to intergroup anxiety that makes it even more psychologically difficult for individuals to engage in ways that reduce, rather than exacerbate, preexisting prejudices.

Fortunately, as psychologist Iris Zezelj and colleagues remind us, there are many alternative types of indirect intergroup contact that, while less preferable than face-to-face, may be tools for improving intergroup relations. One fairly impactful alternative is extended contact, "either in the form of extended friendships (having an in-group friend who has an out-group friend), or in the form of vicarious contact where one observes, listens to, or learns about the interaction of an in-group member with an out-group member."[182] In a meta-analytic review of the literature, psychologists Eleanor Miles and Richard Crisps also found imagined contact—that is, imagining a positive interaction with an out-group member—is another indirect contact strategy that can reduce prejudice and encourage positive intergroup behavior.[183] Basing their research in three post-conflict and deeply divided societies (Serbia, Cyprus, and Croatia), Zezelj et al. even suggest that online or internet contact can also lead to positive changes in intergroup relations.[184] So, in situations of social fragmentation where direct contact is not easily available or even desired, alternative interventions built on indirect contact can be utilized to prepare individuals for constructive face-to-face contact and, ultimately, promote social cohesion.

Unfortunately, in contemporary Northern Ireland, the threat of the "other" remains so embedded in everyday life that even indirect contact is a step too far for many. Threat leads to an exaggerated sense of belonging to one's own community and fear of the "other." People are conditioned to expect more, rather than less, threat in everyday life, resulting in a noticeable hypervigilance. Every former member of the security forces I interviewed, for example, would arrive early to the café or restaurant where we were meeting to ensure they could sit with their back to a wall rather than exposed to a window. What once was an occupational best practice has now become a reflexive hypervigilance, embarrassingly self-noted on many occasions but scrupulously practiced nonetheless.

I also saw this hypervigilance in action when I attended a commemorative panel in Derry in January 2019. During the discussion, as I took notes and jotted down observations, a republican organizer of the event kept eyeing me. There was no attempt to be subtle about it; I was under surveillance. As soon as the event was over, he made a beeline to me, backed up by a hefty security guard, to ensure that I was not a journalist or outside agitator since, in his words, I did not look "local." When he found out I was actually speaking at another memorial event in Derry the following day, suggesting I was more "us" than "them," there was no apology given. The expectation and perception of threat was its own reality.

Living in such conditions also brings with it a hypersensitivity—a persistent state of high reactivity in response to living in a deeply divided society—that manifests itself in constant offense-taking. As one interviewee told me in Armagh, "We have to get over ourselves." That is much more easily said than done. In May 2012, for example, Willie Frazier, the late loyalist activist, posted inflammatory remarks about a Donaghmore school that, to his eyes, was flying an Irish tricolor. In an online posting, he described the school as "the junior headquarters of SF/IRA youth . . . I wonder do they also train the children in how to use weapons?" As it turned out, however, the flag was an Italian one, flying alongside Turkish and Polish flags in honor of a European integration project. Frazier, whose father was killed by the IRA and who was a walking testament to the hypersensitivity such loss can engender, had mistook the red third of the Italian flag for the orange third of the Irish tricolor. While he obliquely apologized for what he termed a "genuine mistake," Frazier also added: "If they think I'm going to get down on my hands and knees, basically the answer is no."[185]

It is such "genuine mistakes," born from everyday lives lived under debilitating conditions of social fragmentation, that continue to breathe life into the deep divisions in contemporary Northern Ireland. The emotional, cognitive, and behavioral consequences are clear in patterns of avoidance, biases, stereotyping, prejudice, discrimination, competitiveness, fear, anxiety, stress reactions, intolerance, passive aggression, hatred, anger, mistrust, contempt, resentment, and, still, open intergroup conflict. For Northern Irish broadcaster Mark Carruthers, however, hope still resides in a rediscovery of a shared common, superordinate identity in the north of Ireland: "Ulster teems with apparent contradictions. It is Irish and it is British. Its inhabitants look to Dublin and they look to London. People speak English, Irish and maybe even Ulster-Scots. They are Protestant and they are Catholic. There is no dispute that a great deal divides these people, but arguably it is their Ulster inheritance that unites them."[186]

Notes

1. Neil Jarman and John Bell, "Routine Divisions: Segregation and Daily Life in Northern Ireland," in Cillian McGrattan and Elizabeth Meehan (eds.), *Everyday Life After the Irish Conflict: The Impact of Devolution and Cross-Border Cooperation* (Manchester: Manchester University Press, 2012), 48.

2. The maps were accessed on April 6, 2020, at https://www.irishtimes.com/news/politics/separate-lives-the-divided-north

3. The Northern Ireland Housing Executive defines single-identity estates as those housing more than 80% of one community or less than 20% of one community. See Ian Shuttleworth and Chris Lloyd, "Mapping Segregation in Northern Ireland," a report commissioned by the Northern Ireland Housing Executive (June 2009).

4. Quoted material in this paragraph taken from Paul Nolan, "Two Tribes: A Divided Northern Ireland," *The Irish Times* (April 1, 2017), accessed on April 6, 2020, at https://www.irishtimes.com/news/ireland/irish-news/two-tribes-a-divided-northern-ireland-1.3030921

5. Quoted material from Alderdice is taken from his "Attempting to Reshape a Deeply Divided Society," *The Irish Times* (October 30, 1997), accessed on April 6, 2020, at https://www.irishtimes.com/culture/attempting-to-reshape-a-deeply-divided-society-1.121005

6. Katy Hayward and Cathal McManus, "Neither/Nor: The Rejection of Unionist and Nationalist Identities in Post-Agreement Northern Ireland," *Capital & Class* 43 (2019), 140.

7. Quoted in Tom Kelly, "With Two Sides Trapped in Silos, We Are Facing a Gloomy Future," *The Irish News* (April 23, 2018), accessed on April 6, 2020, at http://www.irishnews.com/opinion/columnists/2018/04/23/news/tom-kelly-with-two-sides-trapped-in-silos-we-are-facing-a-gloomy-future-1308887

8. Eric Sean Williams, "The End of Society? Defining and Tracing the Development of Fragmentation Through the Modern and into the Post-Modern Era" (2010), 47. Accessed on February 20, 2015, at http://aladinrc.wrlc.org/bitstream/handle/1961/9237/Williams_cua_0043A_10094display.pdf

9. World Bank, "Social Fragmentation," p. 175, accessed on February 20, 2015, at http://siteresources.worldbank.org/INTPOVERTY/Resources/335642-1124115102975/1555199-1124115187705/ch6.pdf/

10. Rhiannon Neilsen, "Toxification as a More Indicative Early Warning Sign for Genocide," paper presented at the biennial meeting of the International Association of Genocide Scholars (Winnipeg, CA), July 19, 2014.

11. Data taken from Kim Hjelmgaard, "From 7 to 77: There's Been an Explosion in Building Border Walls Since World War II," *USA Today* (May 24, 2018), accessed on April 7, 2020, at https://www.usatoday.com/story/news/world/2018/05/24/border-walls-berlin-wall-donald-trump-wall/553250002/

12. Cited in Vicky Cosstick, *Belfast: Toward a City Without Walls* (Newtownards: Colourpoint Books, 2015), 31.

13. Paul Nolan, *Northern Ireland Peace Monitoring Report, Number Three* (Belfast: Community Relations Council, 2014), 67.

14. Jonathan Bardon, *A History of Ulster* (Belfast: Blackstaff Press, 2001, new updated edition), 471.

15. Figures cited in Ibid., 671.

16. Quoted material taken from *The New York Times*, "Barriers Will Go, Ulster Chief Says" (September 10, 1969).

17. Quoted material taken from Henry McDonald, "Belfast Park Opens Door to Peace," *The Guardian* (September 16, 2011), accessed on April 9, 2020, at https://www.theguardian.com/uk/2011/sep/16/belfast-park-door-peace-wall

18. Quote taken from a podcast titled "Peace Lines" on 99% Invisible (August 20, 2019), accessed on April 8, 2020, at https://99percentinvisible.org/episode/peace-lines/

19. See Belfast Interface Project, "Interface Barriers, Peacelines and Defensive Architecture" (2017), report accessed on December 17, 2020 at https://www.belfastinterfaceproject.org/sites/default/files/publications/Interfaces%20PDF.pdf

20. Ibid., Appendix 4.

21. International Fund for Ireland, "Peace Walls Programme Attitudinal Survey Summary of Results" (November 2019), report accessed on December 17, 2020 at https://www.internationalfundforireland.com/the-2019-community-attitudes-to-peace-walls-survey

22. Cosstick, *Belfast: Toward a City Without Walls*, 31–32.

23. See https://www.flickr.com/groups/belfastpeacewall/, accessed on April 7, 2020.

24. David Coyles, Brandon Hamber, and Adrian Grant, "Hidden Barriers and Divisive Architecture: The Case of Belfast," Knowledge Exchange Seminar Series (June 20, 2018), quoted material taken from pp. 1, 9.

25. Freya McClements, "Why Belfast Residents Want to Keep Their Peace Walls," *The Irish Times* (August 16, 2019), accessed on April 8, 2020, at https://www.irishtimes.com/news/politics/why-belfast-residents-want-to-keep-their-peace-walls-1.3987423

26. International Fund for Ireland, "Peace Walls Programme Attitudinal Survey Summary of Results."

27. See https://www.ark.ac.uk/nilt/2019/Community_Relations/PLINEREM.html, accessed on June 19, 2020.

28. The "Together: Building a United Community" strategy can be downloaded at https://www.executiveoffice-ni.gov.uk/articles/about-together-building-united-community-tbuc, accessed on April 9, 2020.

29. Ann Marie Gray, Jennifer Hamilton, Grainne Kelly, Brendan Lynn, Martin Melaugh, and Gillian Robinson, "Northern Ireland Peace Monitoring Report, Number Five" (October 2018), 170, report accessed on December 17, 2020 at https://www.community-relations.org.uk/publications/northern-ireland-peace-monitoring-report

30. Quoted material taken from T:BUC's Annual Update Report 2018/19, accessed on April 9, 2020, at https://www.executiveoffice-ni.gov.uk/articles/about-together-building-united-community-tbuc

31. Claire Simpson, "Peace Wall Demolished in North Belfast," *The Irish News* (January 30, 2020), accessed on April 10, 2020, at http://www.irishnews.com/news/northernirelandnews/2020/01/30/news/peace-wall-demolished-in-north-belfast-1828998

32. International Fund for Ireland, "Peace Walls Programme Attitudinal Survey Summary of Results," 10.

33. Quote taken from Cain Burdeau, "Will Northern Ireland's 'Peace Walls' Ever Come Down?," *Courthouse News Service* (June 28, 2019), accessed on April 8, 2020, at https://www.courthousenews.com/will-northern-irelands-peace-walls-ever-come-down/

34. The "New Decade, New Approach" deal was accessed on April 9, 2020, at https://assets.publishing.service.gov.uk/government/uploads/system/uploads/attachment_data/file/856998/2020-01-08_a_new_decade__a_new_approach.pdf. The quoted material is taken from p. 53.

35. David Blevins, "Belfast: A City Still Divided Two Decades After the Good Friday Agreement," *Sky News* (April 10, 2019), accessed on April 17, 2020, at https://news.sky.com/story/belfast-a-city-still-divided-two-decades-after-the-good-friday-agreement-11317515

36. Robin Wilson, "Northern Ireland Peace Monitoring Report, Number Four" (November 8, 2016), 123, report accessed on December 17, 2020 at https://www.community-relations.org.uk/publications/northern-ireland-peace-monitoring-report

37. Brendan Hughes, "Tricolour Painted Kerbs Treated as a Hate Crime," *The Irish News* (August 9, 2018), accessed on April 10, 2020, at https://www.irishnews.com/news/northernirelandnews/2018/08/09/news/why-are-kerbs-painted-green-white-and-orange-a-hate-crime--1403237/

38. "Driver Convicted of Flattening Orange Lilies Told Case Treated as 'Hate Crime," *The Irish News* (June 8, 2018), accessed on May 2, 2020, at https://www.irishnews.com/news/northernirelandnews/2018/06/08/news/driver-convicted-of-flattening-orange-lilies-told-case-treated-as-hate-crime--1350917/

39. Newton Emerson, "For Unionists, the Randalstown Irish Language Sign Is Just Like Putting a Flag Out," *The Irish News* (June 20, 2019), accessed on April 10, 2020, at http://www.irishnews.com/opinion/columnists/2019/06/20/news/newton-emerson-for-unionists-the-randalstown-irish-language-sign-is-just-like-putting-a-flag-out-1644929

40. Cahair O'Kane, "Anthem Debate Places Sport Back at the Heart of the Divide," *The Irish News* (May 8, 2018), accessed on April 10, 2020, at http://www.irishnews.com/sport/gaafootball/2018/05/08/news/kicking-out-anthem-debate-places-sport-back-at-the-heart-of-the-divide-1323886/

41. The website of the Commission can be found at https://www.fictcommission.org/en, accessed on April 10, 2020.

42. "New Decade, New Approach," 32.

43. Dennis Kennedy, "Why an Office of Identity and Cultural Expression Has Echoes of Orwell's 1984," *Belfast Telegraph* (February 5, 2020), accessed on April 10, 2020, at https://www.belfasttelegraph.co.uk/tablet/comment/why-an-office-of-identity-and-cultural-expression-has-echoes-of-orwells-1984-38929864.html

44. James Scott, *The Art of Not Being Governed. An Anarchist History of Upland Southeast Asia* (New Haven, CT: Yale University Press, 2009).

45. Seth Kaplan, "Identity in Fragile States: Social Cohesion and State Building," *Development* 52 (2009), 469.

46. Ibid., 467.

47. "Twaddell Camp Dismantled as Orange Parade Past Ardoyne Shops in North Belfast Passes Off Peacefully," *The Belfast Telegraph* (October 1, 2016), accessed on December 19, 2018, at https://www.belfasttelegraph.co.uk/news/northern-ireland/twaddell-camp-dismantled-as-orange-parade-past-ardoyne-shops-in-north-belfast-passes-off-peacefully-35092282.html

48. T:BUC's most recent annual report can be found at https://www.executiveoffice-ni.gov.uk/sites/default/files/publications/execoffice/tbuc-annual-report-2018-19_1.pdf, accessed on April 12, 2020.

49. Quoted material taken from Burdeau, "Will Northern Ireland's 'Peace Walls' Ever Come Down?"

50. See https://www.ark.ac.uk/nilt/2019/Community_Relations/NICCPRJ.html, accessed on June 19, 2020.

51. Laura Taylor and Shelley McKeown, "Does Violence Beget Violence? The Role of Family Ethnic Socialization and Intergroup Bias Among Youth in a Setting of Protracted Intergroup Conflict," *International Journal of Behavioral Development* 43(5) (2019).

52. Examples in this paragraph, as well as quoted material, come from Fund for Peace, "CAST: Conflict Assessment Framework Manual," 5.

53. Martin Fletcher, *Silver Linings: Travels Around Northern Ireland* (London: Abacus, 2000), p. 141.

54. Data taken from https://ourworldindata.org/most-densely-populated-countries, accessed on April 14, 2020.

55. Ian Shuttleworth and Chris Lloyd, "Moving Apart or Moving Together? A Snapshot of Residential Segregation from the 2011 Census," *Shared Space* (2013), 63, 64.

56. NILT data on attitudes toward ethnic minority people was accessed on June 19, 2020, at https://www.ark.ac.uk/nilt/2019/Minority_Ethnic_People

57. Quoted material related to this exchange taken from Jonathan Bell, "BBC's Nolan Says Northern Ireland Woman's 'Prejudice Is Scary,'" *Belfast Telegraph* (January 31, 2017), accessed on April 14, 2020, at https://www.belfasttelegraph.co.uk/news/northern-ireland/id-rather-die-than-be-treated-by-muslim-doctor-bbcs-nolan-says-northern-ireland-womans-prejudice-is-scary-35411634.html

58. Stefanie Doebler, Ruth McAreavey, and Sally Shortall, "Is Racism the New Sectarianism? Negativity Towards Immigrants and Ethnic Minorities in Northern Ireland from 2004 to 2015," *Ethnic and Racial Studies* (2018), 2438.

59. Barry McCaffrey, "Northern Ireland Unlikely to Suffer Brexit Rise in Race Hate Attacks Says Senior Police Chief," *The Detail* (January 18, 2019), accessed on June 8, 2020, at https://www.thedetail.tv/articles/race-hate-crime

60. Gillian Halliday, "Fewer than One in 10 NI Race Hate Incidents Results in Conviction," *Belfast Telegraph* (June 19, 2020), accessed on June 19, 2020, at https://

www.belfasttelegraph.co.uk/news/northern-ireland/fewer-than-one-in-10-ni-race-hate-incidents-results-in-conviction-39297488.html

61. See, for instance, Samuel Pehrson, Mirona A. Gheorghiu, and Tomas Ireland, "Cultural Threat and Anti-immigrant Prejudice: The Case of Protestants in Northern Ireland," *Journal of Community & Applied Social Psychology* (2012), 111–124.

62. McCaffrey, "Northern Ireland Unlikely to Suffer Brexit Rise in Race Hate Attacks."

63. Pehrson et al., "Cultural Threat and Anti-immigrant Prejudice."

64. See Ian Shuttleworth and Stefanie Doebler, "Religious Affiliation in Northern Ireland 2001–2011: A Longitudinal Perspective," accessed on April 14, 2020, at http://calls. ac.uk/wp-content/uploads/Filetoupload483256en.pdf

65. Duncan Morrow, "Sectarianism in Northern Ireland: A Review" (May 2019), 10. Accessed on April 14, 2020, at https://www.ulster.ac.uk/__data/assets/pdf_file/0016/ 410227/A-Review-Addressing-Sectarianism-in-Northern-Ireland_FINAL.pdf

66. Ibid., 12.

67. Paul Collier, V. L. Elliott, Haard Hegre, Anke Hoeffler, Marta Reynal-Querol, and Nicholas Sambanis, *Breaking the Conflict Trap: Civil War and Development Policy* (Washington, DC: The World Bank, 2003), 58.

68. OECD, *Supporting Statebuilding in Situations of Conflict and Fragility: Policy Guidance.* DAC Guidelines and Reference Series. (Paris: Author, 2011), 34.

69. Ibid.

70. Quoted material from Gudrun Ostby, "Polarization, Horizontal Inequalities and Violent Civil Conflict," *Journal of Peace Research* 45 (2008), 155.

71. See Henrik Urdal, "A Clash of Generations? Youth Bulges and Political Violence," *International Studies Quarterly* 50 (2006), 607–629.

72. Laura K. Taylor, Jocelyn Dautel, and Risa Rylander, "Symbols and Labels: Children's Awareness of Social Categories in a Divided Society," *Journal of Community Psychology* (2020), 1–15.

73. Data taken from Northern Ireland Statistics and Research Agency, "Annual Enrolments at Schools and in Funded Pre-School Education in Northern Ireland" (March 2020), accessed on April 15, 2020, at https://www.education-ni.gov. uk/sites/default/files/publications/education/Revised%203rd%20March%20 2020%20-%20Annual%20enrolments%20at%20schools%20and%20in%20pre-school%20....pdf

74. Information on school management type is taken from Laura Lundy, "Northern Ireland," in C. L. Glenn and J. De Groof (eds.), *Balancing Freedom, Autonomy and Accountability in Education: Volume 2* (Tilburg, NL: Wolf Legal Publishers, 2012), 363–382, and the Education Authority's website at https://www.eani.org.uk/parents/ types-of-school/management-types, accessed on April 16, 2020.

75. Data cited in Peter Weir, Margaret Topping, and Colm Cavanaugh, "Integrating Education in Northern Ireland: Celebrating Inclusiveness and Fostering Innovation in our Schools" (November 2016), 15. Accessed on April 17, 2020, at https://www. education-ni.gov.uk/sites/default/files/publications/education/Integrating%20 Education%20Report.pdf

76. Kathryn Torney, "How Integrated Are Schools Where You Live?," *The Detail* (November 23, 2012), accessed on April 16, 2020, at https://www.thedetail.tv/articles/how-integrated-are-schools-where-you-live

77. Suzanne Breen, "How Teaching in Northern Ireland Schools Divides on 'Conflict Lines,'" *Belfast Telegraph* (July 15, 2020), accessed on July 26, 2020, at https://www.belfasttelegraph.co.uk/news/education/how-teaching-in-ni-schools-divides-on-conflict-lines-39368683.html

78. For a more detailed discussion of schools used as tools for division, see the "Report of the Special Rapporteur on the Right to Education," United Nations A/74/243 (July 29, 2019), accessed on December 17, 2020 at http://undocs.org/A/74/243

79. Sam Lister and David Gordon, "Schools Strategy a Criminal Waste of Public Money, says Owen Paterson," *Belfast Telegraph* (October 6, 2010), accessed on April 15, 2020, at https://www.belfasttelegraph.co.uk/news/education/schools-strategy-a-criminal-waste-of-public-money-says-owen-paterson-28562962.html

80. Cited in *The Guardian*, "The Religious Divide in Northern Ireland's Schools" (November 24, 2012), accessed on April 15, 2020, at https://www.theguardian.com/news/datablog/2012/nov/24/religious-divide-northern-ireland-schools

81. BBC News, "Catholic Church Reacts to Robinson Remarks on Education" (October 16, 2010), accessed on April 15, 2020, at https://www.bbc.com/news/uk-northern-ireland-11558249

82. Jarman and Bell, "Routine Divisions," 49.

83. NILT data on school preferences was taken from https://www.ark.ac.uk/nilt/2019/Community_Relations/OWNMXSCH.html, accessed on June 19, 2020.

84. Karen Murphy, "Education Reform Through a Transitional Justice Lens: The Ambivalent Transitions of Bosnia and Northern Ireland," in Clara Ramirez-Barat and Roger Duthie (eds.), *Transitional Justice and Education: Learning Peace* (New York: Social Science Research Council, 2017), 84.

85. For a helpful review of shared education, see Tony Gallagher, "Shared Education in Northern Ireland: School Collaboration in Divided Societies," *Oxford Review of Education* (2016), 362–375.

86. See https://www.integratemyschool.com, accessed on April 16, 2020.

87. Jake O'Kane, "Separate Education: What Better Definition of Insanity Could There Be?," *The Irish News* (September 21, 2019), accessed on April 16, 2020, at http://www.irishnews.com/lifestyle/2019/09/21/news/jake-o-kane-separate-education-what-better-definition-of-insanity-could-we-have--1716906/

88. See Integrated Education Fund, https://www.ief.org.uk/about-us/what-we-do/achievements/, accessed on April 15, 2020. See also chapter 3 of Weir, Topping, and Cavanaugh, "Integrating Education in Northern Ireland."

89. *The Irish News*, "Shared Education vs Integrated Education" (January 5, 2015), accessed on April 15, 2020, at http://www.irishnews.com/news/2015/01/05/news/shared-education-vs-integrated-education-112130/

90. Ibid.

91. Caroline Perry and Barbara Love, "Young People's Views on Sharing and Integration in Education," *Research and Information Service Research Paper* (January 29, 2015), 17.

92. Research cited in Joanne Hughes and Caitlin Donnelly, "Promoting Good Relations: The Role of Schools in Northern Ireland," in McGrattan and Meehan (eds.), *Everyday Life After the Irish Conflict*, 55.

93. Ibid., 63–64.

94. *The Irish News*, "Shared Education vs Integrated Education."

95. Gallagher, "Shared Education in Northern Ireland," 368.

96. Paul Connolly, Dawn Purvis, and P. J. O'Grady, Report of the Ministerial Advisory Group, "Advancing Shared Education: Executive Summary" (March 2013), 14, accessed on December 17, 2020 at https://pureadmin.qub.ac.uk/ws/portalfiles/portal/14596498/Filetoupload_382123_en.pdf

97. Department of Education, "Advancing Shared Education: Report to the Northern Ireland Assembly" (May 2018), 3, reported accessed on December 17, 2020 at https://www.education-ni.gov.uk/publications/shared-education-0

98. Robbie Meredith, "60,000 Pupils in Shared Education in Northern Ireland," *BBC News* (October 12, 2018), accessed on April 16, 2020, at https://www.bbc.com/news/uk-northern-ireland-45826351

99. House of Commons, Northern Ireland Affairs Committee, "Education Funding in Northern Ireland" (Ninth Report of Session 2017–2019), published July 22, 2019, 34, accessed on December 17, 2020 at https://publications.parliament.uk/pa/cm201719/cmselect/cmniaf/1497/149702.htm

100. Ibid., 3.

101. Murphy, "Education Reform Through a Transitional Justice Lens," 65–66.

102. Igor Spaic, "Bosnian Pupils Rally Against Ethnic Segregation in Schools," *Balkan Transitional Justice* (June 20, 2017), accessed on April 17, 2020, at https://balkaninsight.com/2017/06/20/bosnian-pupils-rally-against-ethnic-segregation-in-schools-06-20-2017/

103. "New Decade, New Approach" (January 2020), quoted material taken from pp. 7, 43.

104. Allison Morris, "To Tackle Sectarianism We Must First Stop Paying Paramilitaries to Behave," *The Irish News* (May 16, 2019), accessed on April 16, 2020, at http://www.irishnews.com/opinion/columnists/2019/05/16/news/allison-morris-integrated-education-should-be-the-norm-1620674

105. Oxfam, "Governance and Fragility" (2013), accessed on February 21, 2015, at http://policy-practice.oxfam.org.uk/publications/governance-and-fragility-what-we-know-about-effective-governance-programming-in-306683

106. Saferworld, "Common Ground? Gendered Assessment of the Needs and Concerns of Maoist Army Combatants for Rehabilitation and Integration," (November 2010), accessed on February 22, 2015, at http://www.saferworld.org.uk/resources/view-resource/502-common-ground

107. Mary Caprioli, "Gendered Conflict," *Journal of Peace Research* 37 (2000), 51–68.

108. Erik Melander, "Gender Inequality and Intrastate Armed Conflict," *International Studies Quarterly* 49 (2005), 695–714.

109. OECD, "Armed Violence Reduction: Enabling Development" (2009), 33. Accessed on February 21, 2015, at http://www.poa-iss.org/kit/2009_OECD-DAC_Guidlines.pdf

110. Institute for Economics and Peace, "Structures of Peace" (2011), accessed on February 21, 2015, at http://economicsandpeace.org/wp-content/uploads/2011/09/Structures-of-Peace.pdf

111. Valerie M. Hudson, Bonnie Ballif-Spanvill, Mary Caprioli, and Chad F. Emmett, *Sex & World Peace* (New York: Columbia University Press, 2012).

112. Daniel Kaufmann, "Challenges in the Next Stage of Corruption," in Transparency International (ed.,) *New Perspectives on Combating Corruption* (Washington, DC: Transparency International and World Bank, 1998).

113. M. Steven Fish, "Islam and Authoritarianism," *World Politics* 55 (2002), 37.

114. See Valerie M. Hudson, Mary Caprioli Bonnie Ballif-Spanvill, Rose McDermott, and Chad F. Emmett, "The Heart of the Matter: The Security of Women and the Security of States," *International Security* 33 (2008/2009), 27.

115. Victoria Leonard, "Commission Urges United Nations to Take Government to Task on Equality," *Belfast Telegraph* (February 25, 2019), accessed on April 21, 2020, at https://www.belfasttelegraph.co.uk/news/northern-ireland/commission-urges-united-nations-to-take-government-to-task-on-equality-37848820.html

116. The complete report by the Equality Commission of Northern Ireland, Women in Northern Ireland (2019), was accessed at https://www.equalityni.org/ECNI/media/ECNI/Publications/Delivering%20Equality/CEDAW-ShadowReport2019.pdf on April 21, 2020.

117. Committee on the Elimination of Discrimination Against Women, "Concluding Observations on the Eight Periodic Report of United Kingdom of Great Britain and Northern Ireland," CEDAW/C/GBR/CO/8 (March 14, 2019), quoted material taken from pp. 7, 4.

118. Suzanne Breen, "NI Female MLAs Daily Battle with Sexism Revealed with Quarter Victim of Harassment," *Belfast Telegraph* (September 20, 2020), accessed on December 17, 2020 at https://www.belfasttelegraph.co.uk/news/politics/ni-female-mlas-daily-battle-with-sexism-revealed-with-quarter-victim-of-harassment-39546469.html

119. Gray et al., "Northern Ireland Peace Monitoring Report, Number Five" (October 2018), 199–200.

120. Data taken from Victoria Leonard, "Only Three of Northern Ireland's Top Firms Led by Women," *Belfast Telegraph* (February 25, 2019), accessed on April 21, 2020, at https://www.belfasttelegraph.co.uk/news/northern-ireland/only-three-of-northern-irelands-top-firms-led-by-women-37848734.html

121. Part-time employment data taken from Northern Ireland Statistics and Research Agency, "Women in Northern Ireland 2018" (December 18, 2018).

122. Henk-Jan Brinkman, Larry Attree, and Sasa Hezir, "Addressing Horizontal Inequalities as Drivers of Conflict in the Post-2015 Development Agenda" (2013), 13. Accessed on February 22, 2015, at http://www.saferworld.org.uk/resources/view-resource/725-addressing-horizontal-inequalities-as-drivers-of-conflict-in-the-post-2015-development-agenda

123. Lori L. Heise, "What Works to Prevent Partner Violence: An Evidence Overview" (September 2012), Expert Paper prepared for UN Women, accessed on February 22,

2015, at http://www.unwomen.org/~/media/headquarters/attachments/sections/csw/57/egm/egm-paper-lori-heisse%20pdf.pdf

124. Hudson et al., "The Heart of the Matter," 41.

125. Brinkman et al., "Addressing Horizontal Inequalities," 14.

126. Data taken from Police Service of Northern Ireland, "Trends in Police Recorded Crime in Northern Ireland 1998/99 to 2018/19" (November 8, 2019), 13–16.

127. Data taken from Gray et al., "Northern Ireland Peace Monitoring Report, Number Five" (October 2018), 103–104.

128. Data taken from Police Service of Northern Ireland, "Domestic Abuse Incidents and Crimes Recorded by the Police in Northern Ireland: Update to 31 December 2019" (February 27, 2020).

129. See http://www.womensaidni.org/domestic-violence/frequently-asked-questions/#1, accessed on April 21, 2020.

130. *Belfast Telegraph*, "More Than 3,700 Domestic Abuse Calls to PSNI During Coronavirus Lockdown in NI" (May 13, 2020), accessed on May 15, 2020, at https://www.belfasttelegraph.co.uk/news/health/coronavirus/more-than-3700-domestic-abuse-calls-to-psni-during-coronavirus-lockdown-in-ni-39202985.html

131. UN S/Res/1325 (October 31, 2000).

132. Accessed on February 28, 2015, at http://www.un.org/press/en/2006/sgsm10370.doc.htm

133. Rania Abouzeid, "How Women Are Stepping Up to Remake Rwanda," *National Geographic* (October 15, 2019), accessed on April 21, 2020, at https://www.nationalgeographic.com/culture/2019/10/how-women-are-remaking-rwanda-feature/

134. Northern Ireland Women's European Platform, "An Inquiry into the Position of Women in Northern Ireland Since the Peace Agreement: Summary Report" (2014), accessed on December 17, 2020 at https://tbinternet.ohchr.org/Treaties/CEDAW/Shared%20Documents/IRL/INT_CEDAW_LIP_IRL_26737_E.pdf

135. Quoted material taken from Committee on the Elimination of Discrimination against Women, "Concluding Observations on the Eight Periodic Report of United Kingdom of Great Britain and Northern Ireland," CEDAW/C/GBR/CO/8 (March 14, 2019), pp. 9–10.

136. Accessed on February 28, 2015, at http://policy-practice.oxfam.org.uk/blog/2014/03/gender-inequality-as-a-driver-of-conflict

137. See Matthew Krain, "State-Sponsored Mass Murder: The Onset and Severity of Genocides and Politicides," *The Journal of Conflict Resolution* 41 (1997), 331–360.

138. John Garry, "The EU Referendum Vote in Northern Ireland: Implications for Our Understanding of Citizens' Political Views and Behavior," Knowledge Exchange Seminar Series 2016–2017, accessed on December 17, 2020 at https://www.qub.ac.uk/brexit/Brexitfilestore/Filetoupload,728121,en.pdf

139. See https://www.ark.ac.uk/nilt/2016/Political_Attitudes/NIBREXIT.html, accessed on April 26, 2020.

140. Gareth Cross, "Shock Poll Finds 87% of Northern Ireland Leave Voters Say Peace Process Collapse Price Worth Paying for Brexit," *Belfast Telegraph* (October 8, 2018).

141. Quoted material in these two sentences comes from Weizhen Tan, "'Anger, Frustration' and 'Betrayal' in Northern Ireland after New Brexit Deal," *CNBC* (October 21, 2019), accessed at https://www.cnbc.com/2019/10/21/irish-backstop-what-new-brexit-deal-means-to-northern-ireland.html, on April 23, 2020.

142. A complete copy of the Withdrawal Agreement can be found at https://eur-lex.europa.eu/legal-content/EN/TXT/PDF/?uri=OJ:C:2019:384I:FULL&from=EN, accessed on April 23, 2020.

143. Diarmaid Ferriter, *The Border: The Legacy of a Century of Anglo-Irish Politics* (London: Profile Books, 2019), 10, 141.

144. Ibid., 106.

145. Gray et al, "Northern Ireland Peace Monitoring Report, Number Five," 54.

146. Cited in John Mair, "Borders ...," in John Mair and Steven McCabe (eds.), *Brexit and Northern Ireland: Bordering on Confusion?* (Online: Bite-Sized Books, 2019), 37.

147. Garrett Carr, *The Rule of the Land: Walking Ireland's Border* (London: Faber & Faber, 2017), 31. Also recommended in Colm Toibin's *Bad Blood: A Walk Along the Irish Border* (London: Picador, 1987).

148. Andrew Testa and Megan Specia, "Invisible Irish Border Carries the Scars of a Fractured Past," *The New York Times* (October 15, 2018), accessed on October 17, 2018, at https://www.nytimes.com/2018/10/15/world/europe/northern-ireland-brexit-border.html

149. Gray et al, "Northern Ireland Peace Monitoring Report, Number Five," 55.

150. See https://www.ark.ac.uk/nilt/2016/Political_Attitudes/CROSSBDR.html, accessed on April 26, 2020.

151. Ibid.; see also David Young, "Government Must Give Financial Assurances to PSNI in Event of a No Deal," *The Irish News* (November 29, 2018), accessed on December 17 2020 at https://www.irishnews.com/news/brexit/2018/11/29/news/government-must-give-financial-assurances-to-psni-in-event-of-a-no-deal-1496689/

152. John Manley, "In the Crazy World of Brexit, We're All Winners—and Losers," *The Irish News* (January 31, 2020), accessed on April 23, 2020 at http://www.irishnews.com/news/northernirelandnews/2020/01/31/news/in-the-crazy-world-of-brexit-we-re-all-winners-and-losers-1830080

153. Claire Simpson, "Rise in Passport Checks on Cross-Border Buses, Martina Anderson Says," *The Irish News* (March 5, 2020), accessed on May 13, 2020, at http://www.irishnews.com/news/northernirelandnews/2020/03/05/news/rise-in-passport-checks-on-cross-border-buses-martina-anderson-says-1859048/

154. Maresa Fagan and Luke Butterly, "Concerns Over 'Disproportionately High' Levels of Immigration Checks in Belfast," *The Detail* (June 8, 2020), accessed on June 8, 2020, at https://www.thedetail.tv/articles/concerns-over-disproportionately-high-levels-of-immigration-checks-in-belfast

155. Niall McCarthy, "Most Irish Want United Ireland Rather Than Hard Border" (January 29, 2019), accessed on April 24, 2020, at https://www.statista.com/chart/16828/survey-responses-in-ireland-regarding-a-united-ireland-and-hard-border/

156. A copy of the 64-page "Protocol on Ireland/Northern Ireland" included in the Withdrawal Agreement can be found at https://ec.europa.eu/commission/sites/

beta-political/files/revised_withdrawal_agreement_including_protocol_on_ire-land_and_nothern_ireland.pdf, accessed on April 23, 2020.

157. Quoted in Jonathan Gorvett, "Northern Ireland Is in a Culture War. Brexit Is Making It Worse," *Foreign Policy* (January 31, 2020), accessed on April 26, 2020, at https://foreignpolicy.com/2020/01/31/northern-ireland-culture-war-brexit/

158. *The Irish Times*, "Brexit: There Will Be Physical Border Posts at North Ports, Committee Told" (May 14, 2020), accessed on May 14, 2020, at https://www.irishtimes.com/news/world/uk/brexit-there-will-be-physical-border-posts-at-north-ports-committee-told-1.4252819

159. Newton Emerson, "The Real U-Turn on a Brexit Sea Border Has Been by the DUP," *The Irish Times* (May 21, 2020), accessed on May 24, 2020, at https://www.irishtimes.com/opinion/newton-emerson-the-real-u-turn-on-a-brexit-sea-border-has-been-by-the-dup-1.4258433

160. Gerry Moriarty, "DUP Leader Demands Gove's Key Brexit Commitments Be Honored," *The Irish Times* (May 20, 2020), accessed on May 24, 2020, at https://www.irishtimes.com/news/ireland/irish-news/dup-leader-demands-gove-s-key-brexit-commitments-be-honoured-1.4258489

161. Alban Maginess, "DUP Have Been the Authors of Their Own Misfortune on Brexit," *Belfast Telegraph* (December 16, 2020), accessed on December 17, 2020 at https://www.belfasttelegraph.co.uk/opinion/columnists/alban-maginness/dup-have-been-the-authors-of-their-own-misfortune-on-brexit-39868498.html

162. David Hughes, "No Signs of Brexit Unity in Northern Ireland as New Era Dawns," *Belfast Telegraph* (January 30, 2020), accessed on April 23, 2020, at https://www.belfasttelegraph.co.uk/news/brexit/no-signs-of-brexit-unity-in-northern-ireland-as-new-era-dawns-38912193.html

163. Arlene Foster, "We Must Work on Challenges We Face and Seize Opportunities," *Belfast Telegraph* (January 31, 2020), accessed on April 23, 2020, at https://www.belfasttelegraph.co.uk/opinion/comment/we-must-work-on-challenges-we-face-and-seize-opportunities-38912194.html

164. Michelle O'Neill, "Irish Unity Has Taken on a New Dynamic as a Result of Brexit," *Belfast Telegraph* (January 31, 2020), accessed on April 23, 2020, at https://www.belfasttelegraph.co.uk/opinion/comment/irish-unity-has-taken-on-a-new-dynamic-as-result-of-brexit-38912191.html

165. Katy Hayward, "Northern Ireland," in Anand Menon (ed.), *Brexit: What Next?* (February 2020), 39, accessed on December 18, 2020 at https://ukandeu.ac.uk/wp-content/uploads/2020/02/Brexit-what-next-report.pdf

166. Cited in Victoria Pope, "In Northern Ireland, a Fragile Peace Is Threatened," *National Geographic* (December 2017), accessed on October 21, 2018, at https://www.nationalgeographic.com/magazine/2017/12/irish-borderlands-brexit-northern-ireland-britain

167. Richard Wheeler, "Northern Ireland Brexit Concerns Dismissed by Those Who Won't Be Impacted, Claire Hanna Tells MPs," *Belfast Telegraph* (December 21, 2019), accessed on April 24, 2020, at https://www.belfasttelegraph.co.uk/news/brexit/northern-ireland-brexit-concerns-dismissed-by-those-who-wont-be-impacted-claire-hanna-tells-mps-38804599.html

168. Gorvett, "Northern Ireland Is in a Culture War."
169. Deloitte, "Research Into the Financial Cost of the Northern Ireland Divide" (April 2007), 24. The report was accessed on April 28, 2020, at https://cain.ulster.ac.uk/issues/segregat/docs/deloitte0407.pdf
170. Deloitte, "The State of the State 2018–2019 Northern Ireland: What Next" (2018), 13. The report was accessed on April 28, 2020, at https://www2.deloitte.com/content/dam/Deloitte/uk/Documents/public-sector/deloitte-uk-state-of-the-state-northern-ireland.pdf
171. Fletcher D. Cox and Timothy D. Sisk, "'Social Cohesion' in Deeply Divided Societies: Five Findings for Peacebuilding" (August 30, 2016), accessed on April 28, 2020, at https://politicalviolenceataglance.org/2016/08/30/social-cohesion-in-deeply-divided-societies-five-findings-for-peacebuilding/
172. Kaplan, "Identity in Fragile States," 466.
173. C. Marlene Fiol, Michael G. Pratt, and Edward J. O'Connor, "Managing Intractable Conflicts," *Academy of Management Review* (2009), 40. Emphasis in the original.
174. See Sebastian Uhrich and Johannes Berendt, "Acknowledging Versus Ignoring the Identity-Relevance of Rivalry: Why Endorsing Dual Identities Decreases Spectator Aggression and Downplaying Makes Things Worse," *Advances in Consumer Research* (2018), 924.
175. Sheri R. Levy and Julie Milligan Hughes, "Development of Racial and Ethnic Prejudice Among Children," in Todd D. Nelson (ed.), *Handbook of Prejudice, Stereotyping, and Discrimination* (London: Psychology Press, 2009), 60.
176. For an interesting series of field experiments testing this hypothesis in the German soccer league Bundesliga, see Johannes Berendt and Sebastian Uhrich, "Rivalry and Fan Aggression: Why Acknowledging Conflict Reduces Tension Between Rival Fans and Downplaying Makes Things Worse," *European Sport Management Quarterly* (2018), 517–540.
177. Fiol et al., "Managing Intractable Conflicts," 44.
178. Pauline H. Baker, "Getting Along: Managing Diversity for Atrocity Prevention in Socially Divided Societies," *Policy Analysis Brief* (Stanley Foundation, September 2012), accessed on December 18, 2020 at https://stanleycenter.org/publications/getting-along-managing-diversity-for-atrocity-prevention-in-socially-divided-societies/
179. Ervin Staub, *Overcoming Evil: Genocide, Violent Conflict, and Terrorism* (New York: Oxford University Press, 2011), 330, 341.
180. Duncan Morrow, "The Rocky Road from Enmity," in McGrattan and Meehan (eds.), *Everyday Life After the Irish Conflict*, 36.
181. Jarman and Bell, "Routine Divisions," 41.
182. Iris L. Zezelj, Maria Ioannou, Renata Franc, Charis Psaltis, and Borja Martinovic, "The Role of Inter-Ethnic Online Friendships in Prejudice Reduction in Post-Conflict Societies: Evidence from Serbia, Croatia and Cyprus," *Computers in Human Behavior* (2017), 387.
183. Eleanor Miles and Richard J. Crisp, "A Meta-Analytic Test of the Imagined Contact Hypothesis," *Group Processes & Intergroup Relations* (2014), 3–26.

184. Zezelj et al., "The Role of Inter-Ethnic Online Friendships in Prejudice Reduction in Post-Conflict Societies," 386–395.

185. Quoted material in this paragraph taken from Anna Maguire, "School Demands Direct Apology for Frazier's Flag Slur," *Belfast Telegraph* (May 18, 2012), accessed on April 28, 2020, at https://www.belfasttelegraph.co.uk/news/northern-ireland/school-demands-direct-apology-for-frazers-flag-slur-28750993.html

186. Mark Carruthers, *Alternative Ulsters: Conversations on Identity* (Dublin: Liberties Press, 2014), 9.

PART III

A TROUBLED SLEEP

In 1970, the *Belfast Telegraph*, to mark its centenary as a newspaper, ran a competition called "The Kind of Ulster I Want." Young people were invited to submit essays describing their hopes and dreams for the future of Northern Ireland. One of the winners of the competition, Jeffrey Nelson, wrote: "I would like to see an Ulster where there were no riots. I would like to see an Ulster where all people live together in peace without fighting. I would like to see all children no matter what religion going to the same school. This way they could grow up together and understand each other, understand that there is no difference between them. The children would become friends and when they left school would continue their friendship. . . I hope I don't have too long to wait for the Ulster I would like to see."[1]

Fifty years after Jeffrey penned that letter, has Ulster become what he longed to see? To answer that question, Part II of the book reviewed risk and resilience in contemporary Northern Ireland related to issues of memory, governance, and social fragmentation. Comparative research has given us a good handle on the longer term quantitative and qualitative information we need to identify the structural risk factors that leave a society vulnerable to violent conflict. The "black swan" metaphor, in this case the notion that violent conflict is unpredictable and comes as a surprise, is demonstrably false. Risk is not unforeseeable nor is it only visible in hindsight. The better metaphor, strategist Michele Wucker argues, is the "gray rhino." She writes: "The gray rhino is the massive two-ton thing with its horn pointed at you, stomping the ground and getting ready to charge—and, most important, giving you the chance to act."[2] If we pay attention, risk and vulnerabilities can be analyzed and weighed. And, fortunately, comparative research also provides insight into the chances we have to act on that risk and vulnerability—the mitigating points of resiliency that can head off the things we see in front of us and help inoculate against the recurrence of violent conflict.

It is clear that the risk factors discussed in the previous three chapters are a creeping, erosive rot that continue to undermine the structural integrity and stability of Northern Irish society. If left unaddressed, they can drag this deeply divided "post-conflict" society back into the abyss of violent conflict. To return to an analogy used in the introduction to Part II, risk assessment helps us identify countries where the "wood is stacked" for risk of violent conflict. To understand the "matches" that may be struck to set that wood afire requires an analysis of accelerating factors that lead to an escalation of crisis and the triggering factors that spark the onset of conflict itself. An at-risk society with accelerants is like a stack of dry wood doused in gasoline; the outbreak of a fire is likely and unavoidable unless preventive measures are taken. Accelerants multiply risk by increasing incentives for, or the feasibility of, violent conflict. Arson investigators use the term "flashover" to describe the point at which radiant heat causes a fire in a room to become a room on fire.[3] Similarly, triggers are those flashover points at which a society at risk for violent conflict becomes a society caught in the lethal grip of that conflict.

Part III of this book reviews the internal and external accelerants, some of which could metastasize into triggers, that further threaten the stability of peace in contemporary Northern Ireland and increase the risk of violent conflict. Among these are acute economic deteriorioation, outbreaks of limited paramilitary violence, and a vote on a united Ireland.

The book concludes with the recognition that, despite the escalating risk and fading resilience, a return to violent conflict in Northern Ireland need not be inevitable. While hope is hard-won in contemporary Northern Ireland, it resides nevertheless. To hold the strained filiments of the peace process together will require renewed commitments to developing a shared memory, governing by compromise rather than by identity, and birthing a more inclusive sense of social cohesion.

Notes

1. *Belfast Telegraph*, "'The Kind of Ulster I Want:' Children's Hopes for the Future . . . in 1970" (August 25, 2020), accessed on December 21, 2020 at https://www.belfasttelegraph.co.uk/belfast-telegraph-at-150/the-kind-of-ulster-i-want-childrens-hopes-for-the-future-in-1970-39474319.html
2. Michele Wucker, "No, the Coronavirus Pandemic Wasn't An 'Unforeseen Problem,'" *The Washington Post* (March 17, 2020), accessed on May 20, 2020, at https://www.washingtonpost.com/outlook/2020/03/17/no-coronavirus-pandemic-wasnt-an-unforseen-problem/
3. David Grann, *The Devil & Sherlock Holmes: Tales of Murder, Madness, and Obsession* (New York: Vintage Books, 2011), 84.

6

"A Farewell to Peace?"

Escalating Risk and Fading Resilience

In our risk and resilience audit of contemporary Northern Ireland, I have argued that the former is outpacing the latter by a fair amount. Risk is accreting in a rising tide and resilience is rapidly receding. The peace delivered by the Good Friday Agreement is a peace defined more by the absence of armed violence than by progress toward the structural transformations that create and sustain a stable and enduring peaceful society. As a 2019 UN report argued: "Peace cannot . . . be reduced to an absence of violence; it also implies social or societal peace—the building of strong solidarity and relationships of mutual understanding."[1] That type of peace is in short supply in contemporary Northern Ireland. In fact, the majority of locals scoff when Northern Ireland is described as a "post-conflict" society. If it is post-anything, they argue, it is "post-peace agreement" or "post-ceasefire" and even those are debatable. Some would maintain that contemporary Northern Ireland is not even "post-violence" since the violence has just moved from armed confrontation to political and social and cultural confrontation.

Deeply divided societies with contested memory, flawed governance, and profound social fragmentation, have preexisting conditions of structural risk that leave them vulnerable to events that may accelerate, or even trigger, the onset of violent conflict. Accelerants and triggers help us understand the transformation of possibilities into probabilities; where into when.

Generally, accelerants are identifiable and, to some degree, modifiable. Accelerants may unfold slowly or, in some cases, very rapidly. Accelerants can be internal to the state (e.g., post-conflict peace stabilization programs that are poorly designed or implemented, major governance or legal reforms, release of political prisoners, failed ceasefires or peace agreements, or actual outbreaks of limited violence) or external (e.g., the impact of externally imposed structural reforms, illicit trade, an international financial crisis, or climate change). Accelerants, whether internal or external to the state in

A Troubled Sleep. James Waller, Oxford University Press (2021). © Oxford University Press.
DOI: 10.1093/oso/9780190095574.003.0007

question, aggravate preexisting conditions of structural risk and open windows in which triggers can instigate the onset of violent conflict.

The range of triggers is broad and diverse but, generally, they are discrete events or chains of events that transition a tense situation into a crisis. Triggers are the dynamic, real-time stressors, often the outgrowth of one or more accelerants, that can make the outbreak of violent conflict likely or imminent. In situations of underlying structural vulnerability exacerbated by internal or external accelerants, triggers are the spark that precipitates violent conflict. Triggers push an at-risk state over the brink; they are the "intervening variables between the existence of conditions necessary for the occurrence of conflict and the outbreak of conflicts."[2] Some triggers are difficult to predict or identify in advance (e.g., coups, political assassinations, natural disasters, contested succession or secession, social media attacks, closure or liquidation of large employers, epidemics, acts of incitement, or terrorist attacks). Other triggers are more easily predictable and identifiable (e.g., the taking of a census, legal judgments, anniversaries of highly traumatic and disputed historical events, or elections).

Once we have identified countries as at-risk for violent conflict, understanding the role of accelerants and triggers allows us to have a better idea of which countries are more likely to experience the onset of violence at a certain moment in time. Sensitivity to the accelerating or triggering events—the environmental stressors—that could lead to the onset of violent conflict gives us an advocacy tool to provide relevant actors with significantly more lead time to take preventive structural action before conflicts actually erupt.

Brexit was, and will continue to be, a high-impact event exerting tremendous influence on how the accelerants and potential triggers in contemporary Northern Ireland will unfold. "Orange" and "green," always dominant in the color landscape of Northern Ireland, are, once again, definitory. The COVID-19 pandemic of 2020 brought yet another high-impact event to Northern Ireland, and its ramifications also will be felt in the myriad ways—many yet unknown—that will compound the structural risk conditions and multiply the threat of accelerants and potential triggers. Together, these conjoined extreme events will rattle an already fragile and deeply divided society.

In early 2019, I was speaking about the role of accelerants and triggers for violent conflict in deeply divided societies during a public lecture in Belfast. In the question-and-answer period that followed, a woman in the audience expressed her frustration at what she saw as a peace process protracted for political and even entrepreneurial gain over more than two decades. Referring to it derisively as the "peace-processing industry," she recognized that its inefficacy had left contemporary Northern Ireland in a very vulnerable spot. Her eyes welled with tears of frustration about a society destroyed, made partially whole, and now on the precipice of being destroyed again. In her words: "These are dangerous times to be wasting on peace-processing. I worry that we've taken a wrong turning and it's time to say a farewell to peace."

Embedded in her vexation and fear is a recognition that, as political scientist Duncan Morrow of the University of Ulster has argued, contemporary Northern Ireland has achieved "truce rather than a transformation." He writes: "In a truce, the requirement for vigilance and suspicion remains and the threat of a return to violence, however *sotto voce*, remains as an ever-present risk."[3] Truce, rather than transformation, leaves the country in a state of fragility, easily vulnerable to the multiplication of threat posed by Brexit and the COVID-19 pandemic. There are a range of internal and external accelerants, some of which could metastasize into triggers, that further threaten the stability of peace in contemporary Northern Ireland and increase the risk of violent conflict. Among these are (1) acute economic deterioration, (2) outbreaks of limited paramilitary violence, and (3) a vote on a united Ireland.

Acute Economic Deterioration

Comparative research suggests substantial evidence of a relationship between low levels of economic development and state fragility.[4] As the Fund for Peace argues, a "sharp decline with high inflation and low GDP [gross domestic product]" is a key economic indicator for state collapse.[5] This economic deterioration is often chronic and progressive but can manifest in acute and sudden drops in commodity prices, trade revenue, and foreign investment or in the collapse, hyperinflation, or devaluation of the national currency.[6] The Russian currency, for instance, went down by well over half after Vladimir Putin's decision to invade Ukraine.[7] Violent conflict destroys the accumulated physical, social, and human capital that are essential to improving economic development, inclusiveness, stability, and resiliency in a post-conflict society.[8] One study, for instance, suggests that an average of 30 years of economic growth is lost through a civil war and that the country's international trade takes on average 20 years to recover.[9] Given the prolonged

30-year period of the Troubles, many believed that any hope for a sharp and timely economic recovery was, at best, a delusional optimism.

Following the Good Friday Peace Agreement in 1998, however, the Northern Ireland economy grew rapidly, even ahead of the UK rate. Unemployment decreased, employment increased, and the economy began to rebalance with focused growth in the private sector (about 70% of the Northern Ireland workforce either works in the public sector, part of the economy concerned with providing various governmental services, or in a field dependent on the public sector). With a boost in tourism and substantial fintech development, macroeconomic diversity and stability deepened and foreign direct investment increased.

The 2008 global recession, however, took a devastating toll on these decade-old peace dividends. Since then, growth has lagged behind the UK rate and has yet to rebound to pre-2008 recession levels. In February 2020, for instance, the Northern Ireland Composite Economic Index (a proxy for Northern Ireland's GDP), found that, while economic output was growing, it still remained significantly below pre-2008 recession levels.[10] In the words of business columnist Francess McDonnell, "the much-heralded prospects of a peace dividend have simply evaporated following the meltdown of global financial markets. Negative equity, job fears and the cost of living dominate the domestic economic horizon."[11] Similarly, Dr. Caoimhe Archibald, Social Democratic and Labour Party (SDLP) Member of the Legislative Assembly (MLA) and Chairperson of the Assembly's Committee for the Economy, summarized: "In the so-called recovery since 2008, insecure, exploitative and low-paid employment replaced more stable and better-paid jobs, as businesses sought to get back on their feet with cheaper labour costs."[12] Beyond the 2008 recession, Northern Ireland's continuing economic struggles reveal a legacy of chronic structural weaknesses and fragility. The resultant challenges, as pointed out by economists Richard Johnston and Jordan Buchanan of Ulster University's Economic Policy Centre, "include relatively lower income levels per capita and employment rates, higher levels of economic inactivity, weaker productivity and as a result, a sizeable annual fiscal transfer from Westminster."[13]

In terms of economic output per capita (i.e., level of income per person), Northern Ireland has the third lowest of the 13 UK regions, is 25% below the UK average, and almost 55% lower than London and Ireland. While unemployment in Northern Ireland has been reduced, the country still retains the lowest employment rate (69.7%) of all UK regions.[14] Almost one in three of Northern Ireland's working-age adults do not have a job, and around one in five live in poverty.[15] In social housing estates, most of which are single-identity and several of which I visited during my research, 75% of the tenants are unemployed or underemployed. Moreover, for 94 of the last 104 quarters, Northern Ireland had the highest economic inactivity rate (i.e., people not involved in the labor market—students, early retirees, and the long-term sick) of the UK regions. With so much of the post-peace investment Belfast-centered, other areas of the country have proved particularly vulnerable to economic fragility, with the highest levels of deprivation concentrated in the west of the country.[16] After the 2016 Brexit referendum, a weakened exchange rate led to rising levels of inflation that squeezed household budgets as wage growth did not keep pace. The structural vulnerabilities also are revealed in the prevalence of small companies, with 9 in 10 local businesses in Northern Ireland having fewer than 10 employees.[17]

Reflecting the widespread concern over these realities, a September 2019 survey by Ulster Bank suggested Northern Ireland's economy "has entered or is entering recession" based on a sizeable decline in private sector output.[18] Similarly, an October 2019 survey by the Northern Ireland Chamber of Commerce found that 77% of respondents believed an economic recession was likely in the next 6–12 months. Northern Ireland chamber chief executive Ann McGregor said: "These figures are tangible warning signs about current economic conditions in Northern Ireland, with this quarter's performance being arguably the weakest in almost a decade."[19] The end of 2019 found an increasing number of retail shop vacancies and a sharp decline in retail footfall, leading to one drastic news headline reading: "Tumbleweed Continues to Blow Through North's Shopping Centres and High Streets."[20] In January 2020, Northern Ireland chamber president John Healy implored the government to "move fast" to "reinvigorate our stagnant economy, build new infrastructure, boost skills and lower the cost of doing business in 2020."[21]

The uncertainty generated by Brexit, coupled with the three-year absence of economic leadership in policymaking from Stormont, negatively impacted consumer confidence and contributed to these significant slowdowns in the country's economic growth and job creation. Losing EU membership compounds this economic stress with the loss of billions of Euro in EU funding previously used for cross-community relations schemes, infrastructure and agricultural projects, cultural development, and cross-border initiatives. In fact, Northern Ireland "receives the second largest amount of

EU funding in terms of percentage of regional GDP."[22] Brexit also will have damaging implications for Northern Ireland's labor market which, in recent years, has become increasingly dependent on the migrant workforce.

Even more perilously, as of this writing, the very real cliff edge of a no-deal scenario remains on the table. If that were to eventuate, England, Scotland, and Wales would face tariffs on some goods and services and other trade barriers with the EU, while Northern Ireland would not since the Withdrawal Agreement allows them to operate under the EU's customs rules for its trade with the Republic of Ireland and, by extension, with other EU countries. The disruption of Northern Ireland's trade with the rest of the UK, however, would be very harmful to their economy since much of it is built on those profitable east–west trade routes. A July 2019 paper, released by Northern Ireland's Department for the Economy, found that a no-deal Brexit could put at least 40,000 jobs at risk in the country.[23] As Lucinda Creighton, Ireland's former Minister for European Affairs, summarized: "There is no doubt that the harder the Brexit, the harder the impact on Northern Ireland and the border counties in the Republic of Ireland."[24]

Recognizing these challenges, the January 2020 "New Decade, New Approach" deal called for the development of a "regionally-balanced economy" as a top priority for the newly restored Executive.[25] Even before that work could begin, however, March 2020 would find Northern Ireland's economic resilience facing an even greater test with the arrival of a second high-impact event: the COVID-19 pandemic. Governments around the world told their people to stay home and effectively shut down global economic activity. While the economic toll has yet to be tallied, it is a near-certainty that the pandemic will throw the world, and Northern Ireland, back into another recession, undoubtedly much more severe than 2008. Given that Northern Ireland still had not completed its recovery from the 2008 recession, Ulster University economists project the pandemic will have an outsized effect and shrink the north's economy by nearly 13% in 2020 (the equivalent of £5.4 billion in economic output in one year). They also project 249,500 Northern Irish workers (almost half of private-sector jobs) likely to be at least temporarily laid off, if not permanently released, by the end of the year.[26] As a result, Danske Bank expects Northern Ireland's unemployment rate to double due to "a staggering decline in economic activity."[27] The region's economic collapse in activity from March to April was the steepest in the whole of the UK.[28] Even with immediate relief action (e.g., tax cuts, social pensions, unemployment insurance, job creation, relief or social welfare plans, microcredit, etc.), it may take a generation for Northern Ireland to re-cover economically.

Acute economic deterioration, however, serves as an accelerant for insta-bility and violent conflict beyond simply the economic costs. As political sci-entist Adam Jones points out, a severe economic crisis throws the material base of people's lives into question, "may undermine the legitimacy and ad-ministrative capacity of state authorities . . . and may encourage rebellious, revolutionary, and secessionist movements."[29] Similarly, social psychologist Ervin Staub writes: "economic deterioration frustrates both material needs and the psychological needs of whole groups of people for security, effective-ness, and identity. People worry that they will be unable to take care of them-selves and their families."[30]

In contemporary Northern Ireland, these worries and disaffections will be acutely felt in working-class communities who already wake up on the wrong side of capitalism every morning. Youth in these communities, who have little in the way of other viable options, may be left particularly suscep-tible to targeted recruitment by paramilitaries. As Allison Morris, a colum-nist with *The Irish News*, warns: "Those without that opportunity stay and can be dragged into violence, because the status and power that comes with membership of any organisation is more attractive when there are few other options."[31]

Outbreaks of Limited Paramilitary Violence

Outbreaks of limited or low-level violence against a targeted group are accelerants that can transform the risk of widespread violence into reality. In his work on mass atrocities and armed conflict, international security expert Alex Bellamy refers to such outbreaks as "trial massacres" and sees them as indicative of the potential for a broader campaign of violent con-flict. "Typically," he writes, "these [trial massacres] target the victim group in relatively small numbers and are sometimes conducted as a test for negative repercussions in the form of arrests or substantive international engagement."[32] If the perpetrators are not held to account by state or in-ternational authorities, this may be taken as validation to escalate the vi-olence since future acts are likely to go unpunished. Counter-violence by the victim group further facilitates the escalation of violence. In contem-porary Northern Ireland, outbreaks of limited violence have, and will likely

continue to, come from both the republican and loyalist sides of the paramilitary divide.

In November 2020, the Independent Reporting Commission released
its third annual report on progress towards ending paramilitary activity in
Northern Ireland. The report concluded: "There are still too many communities in Northern Ireland and many individuals and families in local communities who remain under the coercive control of paramilitary groups and
that is simply unacceptable." The report recognized "there is a level of risk involved for society as a whole by the continuation of paramilitarism."[33] As we
have seen in Chapter 4, the threats that paramilitaries pose to communities
which they "protect and defend," as well as to state security forces charged
with maintaining public order, are significant.

Paramilitaries in Northern Ireland are listed as proscribed organizations under the Terrorism Act 2000 of the UK government.[34] While technically illegal, their presence remains a grim reality of everyday life in
contemporary Northern Ireland. While all sides say they have "stood
down" and decommissioned all arms, nearly every former political prisoner
I interviewed readily admitted the command structures of most paramilitaries were still in place (organized along militaristic lines), members were
still being actively recruited, and arms, even if limited, were still accessible
(including rifles, machine guns, pistols, detonators, and Semtex, a commercial high explosive). Though precise numbers of enrolled or active members
are impossible to come by, it is estimated that there are thousands of sworn
members of paramilitary organizations across Northern Ireland.[35] Since
2007, official Police Service of Northern Ireland (PSNI) security situation statistics suggest that, due to increased recruitment, the paramilitary presence
in Northern Ireland has been on the rise.[36] Stormont's three-year closure left
a vacuum that paramilitaries exploited to further entrench their influence
in communities abandoned by their politicians. As columnist Alex Kane
reflects: "If the key political parties are in positions of almost constant stalemate and open disrespect then don't be surprised if certain on-the-ground
elements choose to exploit those schisms, usually by promotion of the absurd
and spurious logic that 'we are still needed, there's still a role for us.' "[37]

While none of these organizations has complete control over the activities of its members, paramilitaries still wield outsized effect on everyday life
in contemporary Northern Ireland. Communities are marred by their flags,
graffiti tags, murals, and intimidating posturing. Their ubiquitous presence
creates the impression that the rule of law is limited. They are particularly at

home in communities with serious social and economic deprivation. In these communities, there is a tyranny of low expectations—reinforced by poverty, high rates of unemployment and underemployment (especially among urban male youth), educational underattainment, drug and alcohol abuse and addiction, and poor mental health—that makes for a ready and supportive audience for the exhibitionism of paramilitary strength.[38] The COVID-19 pandemic has only compounded these deprivations and increased the pool of people in these communities who see paramilitary involvement as their only viable option for connection, escape from boredom, social identity, income, empowerment, glory, and, even, revenge.

In many communities, "former" paramilitary members have created an unhealthy dependency by using the peace process as a funding opportunity. Drawing on resources meant to advance peace initiatives, they instead use the funds to further identity-based entrenchment in their communities. "While I have reported on numerous groups who do sterling work in their community," Allison Morris writes, "for every good project there are 20 dud ones run by men of violence who see the peace process as a career opportunity. People who any normal society would have sidelined become people of power and influence in highly paid jobs that achieve nothing other than the further segregation of their own community. For the threat of mayhem has to be just in eyesight for them to remain relevant. They must retain the ability to turn street disorder on and off in order to maintain their grip. Young people from families who do not share their ideology or who stand up to their bullying are excluded from the heavily funded programmes that bring endless benefits to those in the know."[39]

On the republican side, both the Provisional Irish Republican Army (PIRA, more commonly known as the IRA) and the Irish National Liberation Army (INLA) still exist and maintain a relatively public profile. Security analysts believe the IRA's command structure, including the Army Council, remains in place, though in a much reduced form. They do not believe the group is actively recruiting, but, despite taking part in decommissioning and being on ceasefire, it is believed the IRA does still have access to some weapons (Figure 6.1). Overall, however, there is a recognition that the IRA "remains committed to the peace process and its aim of achieving a united Ireland by political means." The INLA also has command structures still in existence but little evidence of centralized control of those structures (Figure 6.2). The INLA likewise took part in decommissioning and remains on ceasefire, though there are indications that it is active in recruiting new

Figure 6.1 IRA graffiti on gable end of building in Derry.
Photo by author, January 29, 2017.

members and continues to have access to some weapons. They are "heavily involved in criminality including extortion, drug dealing, distribution of stolen goods and fraud."[40]

The most significant republican paramilitary threats in contemporary Northern Ireland, however, come from a range of dissident groups that reject the Good Friday Agreement, all subsequent ceasefires, and the decommissioning of weapons.[41] These groups see the Provisional IRA and its political arm of Sinn Fein as a "sellout" and "betrayer" of true republicanism. Steeped in the tradition of physical force republicanism, dissidents still see violence as the best route to a united Ireland and are believed by security analysts to "pose a severe threat to NI's security and stability."[42] According to one senior PSNI officer, dissident republicans are "immersed in a constant campaign to kill police."[43]

Dissident republican groups include Oglaigh na hEirann (ONH or "Soldiers of Ireland," also the Irish term for the official Irish Defence Forces), the Continuity IRA, and the New IRA. The ONH, formed in late 2005 or early 2006 following a split from the Continuity IRA and later reinforced in

Figure 6.2 Sign for the Irish National Liberation Army (INLA), a republican paramilitary group, in West Belfast.
Photo by author, January 31, 2017.

2009 with defections from the now-defunct Real IRA, suspended "all armed actions against the British State" with immediate effect in January 2018.[44] The ceasefire only applied to the "British State," and ONH did not say what would happen to weapons still under its control. Since the ceasefire, ONH has divided into two rival factions, both fighting for control over the organization.

The reach of the Continuity IRA, in existence since 1986 following a split with the Provisional IRA, was damaged by a 2014 MI5 bugging operation that eventually led to the November 2020 sentencing of seven defendants.

Each pled guilty of belonging to a proscribed organization, with several also pleading guilty to providing weapons and explosives training with intent to endanger life.[45] None of the men were sentenced to longer than five years and several could walk free in as few as three years. As of this writing, the Continuity IRA remains a significant threat as evidenced by the 2020 planting of a "Brexit day" bomb timed to coincide with the UK's departure from the EU (PSNI eventually found the bomb attached to a heavy goods vehicle in a commercial yard and disabled it).

Today, however, security analysts believe the greatest republican paramilitary threat comes from the New IRA, formed in 2012 after a collection of smaller dissident republican groups (including the Real IRA and Republican Action Against Drugs) joined under one command structure. As journalist Gerry Moriarty describes: "It [the New IRA] is the most dangerous of the dissident republican groups, made up of young inexperienced members and those old enough to have been involved in violence during the days of the Provisional IRA."[46] I witnessed the New IRA's capacity for violence firsthand when, on Saturday evening, January 19, 2019, they detonated a car bomb on Bishop Street by the courthouse in Derry, just next to the hotel where I was staying. Two months later, the New IRA were blamed for delivering packages containing explosives to several targets in England and Scotland.[47] The following month, in April, the New IRA also would claim responsibility for the murder of journalist Lyra McKee, offering "full and sincere apologies" while also accusing police of provoking the riot during which the shooting occurred.[48] Six weeks later, the New IRA was responsible for a car bomb murder attempt on a high-profile PSNI officer. Despite the arrests of the group's alleged leadership as a result of a sting operation in August 2020, security analysts still see the threat posed by the New IRA as "severe" and believe that future attacks by the dissident group are "highly likely."[49] It is suspected that the New IRA, having forged connections with radical groups in the Middle East, have begun importing arms to replenish their depleted supplies.[50]

On the loyalist side, paramilitary groups include the Ulster Volunteer Force (UVF), Red Hand Commando (RHC), Ulster Defence Association (UDA), South East Antrim UDA (SEA UDA), Ulster Freedom Fighters (UFF), and the Loyalist Volunteer Force (LVF). The UVF (formed in 1966, adopting the name and symbols of an original group founded in 1912) and the closely linked RHC (formed in 1972) still have command structures in place, have some indications of recruitment, and access to some weapons.

While many UVF members "are extensively involved in organized crime including drug dealing, extortion and smuggling" as well as punishment attacks "on those they accuse of anti-social behaviour," some have taken active roles in politics, usually within the Progressive Unionist Party.[51] The structures of the UDA (formed in 1971) are very fragmented, with individual units in discrete geographic areas (Figure 6.3). Some of these units focus on

Figure 6.3 Graffiti tags in loyalist area of Derry, with curbstones painted red, white, and blue in honor of the Union Jack. UDA is the Ulster Defence Association, a loyalist paramilitary group. KAT stands for "Kill All Taigs," with "Taig" being a derogatory term for Catholics.
Photo by author, January 28, 2017.

positive community-based activism, but most have remained active in crim- inality and violence. The SEA UDA, who split from the UDA in 2006, con- trol turf stretching 20 miles from Larne to north Belfast and also continue to engage predominantly in criminal and violent activity. The UFF, seen as the military wing and a cover name for the UDA, no longer exists. The LVF, formed following a split in the UVF in 1996, was the first paramilitary orga- nization to decommission some of its weapons and today is largely inactive and exists only as a criminal group in Antrim and mid-Ulster. More so than the various strands of republican paramilitaries, loyalist paramilitaries have engaged in ongoing bouts of infighting—including internal disputes, feuds, violence, and counter-violence.

Security analysts see the UVF and the UDA as representing the most sig- nificant loyalist paramilitary threats in contemporary Northern Ireland. A December 2020 leaked security assessment revealed that there are about 7,500 current "card carrying" members of the UVF and 5,000 in the UDA.[52] Those numbers translate to about £250,000 a month in dues and payments funneled to loyalist paramilitary groups.[53] In the communities these groups hold, they recruit significant numbers of young people to their gang-like cultures, replete with widespread drug and alcohol abuse, toxic mascu- linity, and violent rites of initiation. Once involved, "it's effectively a life sen- tence . . . virtually impossible to get out." Some join voluntarily but others join to settle a drug debt or debt for money that has been borrowed or services rendered. "Once you fall in debt to these organisations," the PSNI's Bobby Singleton said, "they determine how they want to see that repaid. In many instances that can involve you becoming actively involved in activity on be- half of those paramilitary groups. It could be holding weapons for them, it could be being involved in targeting or even the distribution of drugs."[54]

* * *

As the Independent Reporting Commission concluded in 2019, while Brexit may not "be the direct cause of a renewal of violence," it will "add fuel to the fire of continued paramilitarism."[55] Indeed, Brexit has fueled unrest on both sides of the paramilitary divide: dissident republicans and loyalists alike have a new edge that may very well manifest itself in outbreaks of limited violence.

For dissident republican groups, that fuel has, in the words of one New IRA member, "forced the IRA to refocus and has underlined how Ireland remains partitioned. It would be remiss of us not to capitalize on the op- portunity."[56] Even in the midst of the COVID-19 pandemic, the New IRA, seeing themselves as the true standard bearer of the republican cause and rehashing common dissident tropes, stayed focused on Brexit and its implications: "While we face an unprecedented health crisis, it won't be long until Brexit and its continuing difficulties for Britain re-emerges," it said in a public Easter statement. "They [the British establishment] listen to one thing and one thing only—physical force. Faced with this reality we remain committed to bringing the British government's undemocratic rule of the occupied part of our country to an end."[57]

If Brexit negotiations had led to the return of a hard border between Northern Ireland and the Republic of Ireland, complete with physical infrastructure as well as checks and controls, it was a near-certainty that dissident republican groups would heighten recruitment efforts as well as engage in outbreaks of—at the very least—limited violence. As a February 2019 report succinctly concluded: "There will be a return to violence in Northern Ireland in the event of the installation of infrastructure, custom checks and security on the Irish border as a result of a no deal Brexit. The only issue is the scale of the violence."[58] In fact, every person I interviewed affirmed the reality that the return of a hard border would bring with it a return to violence in Northern Ireland. As one former republican political prisoner told me: "It would be a shooting gallery with the targets being whatever eejit is dumb enough to be constructing or working at the checkpoints." In October 2019, the New IRA, in a rare on-camera interview, similarly warned "any infrastructure would be a legitimate target for attack and armed actions against those infrastructures and against the people who are manning them."[59] It also was very likely that a hard border, replete with tariffs on imports and exports, would have led to a rise in criminal activities by dissident groups, particularly since the smuggling of diesel and other goods and products would be further incentivized.

The fuel of Brexit, however, remains especially stark and worrisome for its accelerating impact on the voice and actions of loyalist paramilitaries. A deep part of the unionist psyche, particularly reflected in loyalism, is the prevailing assumption that someone is going to betray them. As one unionist politician told me: "Unionists are clairvoyant and its always bad news." Unionist politicians have made high art of portraying themselves as "publicly maligned" and "an insecure majority," both of which stoke loyalism's sense of standing alone in a struggle to prevent the loss of rights that have always been theirs. These feelings were exacerbated after the Good Friday Agreement in which the majority privileges of Protestants, held since the founding of Northern Ireland, were no longer guaranteed. The Democratic Unionist Party (DUP), which opposed the Agreement, were particularly adept at depicting unionism and, by extension, loyalism as victims and losers of the peace process—even though, for many unionists and loyalists, the Agreement still left them with what they wanted: a British identity. This discourse was easily sold when their opponents, particularly Sinn Fein, seemed so publicly pleased with the Agreement.

Mainstream unionism, in the words of one interviewee, "has never given a damn about working class loyalism." While elites within unionism privately supported loyalist violence, they kept their hands clean by never doing so publicly. As one interviewee told me, "the DUP just keep them [loyalists] in a cupboard until they are needed." Nevertheless, their fear-mongering messages still resonated as deeply as a Lambeg drum within those communities. As more than one loyalist interviewee reflected, "we were told the GFA [Good Friday Agreement] really meant we 'Got Fuck All' and since then we've simply had to fight to hold what we have." Through a zero-sum lens, loyalist insecurities see Sinn Fein on an ascendant and threatening trajectory: even with the DUP holding a seat at the table of power-sharing, loyalists still end up losing. The PSNI are seen as puppets of Sinn Fein's agenda, a position conspicuous in graffiti tags throughout loyalist neighborhoods reading: "PSNIRA." This is coupled with loyalist perceptions that the DUP has become too moderate and accepting of the peace process, abandoning their voice of dissent and opposition. Loyalists, with a lack of narrative relative to republicans and with far fewer idealized books and movies and songs and poems devoted to them, already had a deep feeling of marginalization. Even the accusations of loyalist collusion with British security forces minimizes their sense of agency. "Why do people think we couldn't commit the same violence the IRA did," one former loyalist political prisoner asked me, "but do it by ourselves? Why do they just assume we had to have the British soldiers backing us?" It is little wonder that loyalism has a besieged mentality and a sense of betrayal and isolation as their culture and country is being taking from them without permission (Figure 6.4). As elections expert Nicholas Whyte describes contemporary loyalist sentiment: "There's a perception the other side is winning, a feeling of left-behindness."[60]

Moreover, loyalists have long had to live with a feeling of unrequited love and loyalty from Britain, the very place that holds such deep identity meaning for them. Several loyalists I spoke with called themselves

Figure 6.4 Loyalist mural in Derry illustrating the siege mentality, with curbstones painted red, white, and blue in honor of the Union Jack.
Photo by author, January 28, 2017.

"the forgotten people" and refused to even accept the name of "Northern Ireland"—in their minds, they live in Ulster. There is an old-style artwork mural in Crimea Street and Shankill Road in East Belfast, commonly known as the "Ulster Girl," depicting this yearning relationship to be remembered and recognized by Britain: "Ulster to England: Thou mayest find another daughter with a fairer face than mine, with a gayer voice and sweeter, and a softer eye than mine; but thou canst not find another that will love thee half so well!"[61] A similar sentiment was captured, far less poetically, by an active loyalist: "It's like the mother who hammers her kids all the time. She beats them, all that, but at the end of the day, the kids still love her."[62] Britain's public rejection of the self-described "most British of Britain's subjects" was affirmed in a June 2019 poll of 892 Conservative Party members in the UK— officially the Conservative *and Unionist* Party—finding that 59% would prefer to see Northern Ireland leave the UK if it was a necessary sacrifice to make sure Brexit happened.[63] The following September, an unnamed senior Conservative Party MP reporting overhearing Boris Johnson's then special advisor, Dominic Cummings, say: "I don't care if Northern Ireland falls into the fucking sea."[64]

While sectarian violence committed by loyalist paramilitaries has dropped to a large degree over the past decade or so even as their criminal enterprises have escalated, Brexit is a bracing wake-up call for them; a very threat to the heart of their constitutional identity. Old slogans of "We were born British, we will remain British, and we will die British!" are still being shouted, but with voices grown hoarse from futility. Still reeling from the identity assault of the 2012 flag protests, loyalists feel double-crossed yet again in what they perceive as the Withdrawal Agreement's (or what they derisively term "Boris's Betrayal Act") appeasement of republicanism. "The Johnson deal has reawakened Protestants' primeval fears of betrayal and loss; that the union—and with it, their country—is being taken from them through a combination of British weakness and Republican menace."[65] Brexit, rather than making Northern Ireland more distinct from the Republic of Ireland and preserving its place within the United Kingdom, is ending up making it more distinct from Britain and pushing it farther away into the Atlantic Ocean, and that is an identity biscuit very tough for loyalists to swallow. "It's a terrible irony," said Thomas Hennessey, a historian at Canterbury Christ Church University, "unionists and loyalists have always thought the main enemy was Irish nationalism, but it turns out it was really English nationalism, instead."[66]

Loyalists are particularly outraged by the belief that it is the prospect of dissident republican violence over a hard land border that drove Westminster to place the proposed border in the Irish Sea. This belief was reinforced when former Cabinet minister Sir David Lidington revealed that Theresa May's decision to rule out a no-deal Brexit was predicated, in large part, on fear of instigating dissident republican violence over a hard land border.[67] Jamie Bryson, a noted loyalist activist, spoke of the anger: "One of the main reasons we were told there can be no border on the island of Ireland is because dissident republicans may attack it, but yet there's been no consideration given to the loyalist community on how people may react to a border down the Irish Sea."[68] Elsewhere, Bryson reiterated: "Nobody wants to see violence, and nobody wants to go back to conflict. But people are being pushed into a corner, and they argue that if republicans threatened violence against a hard land border and they made concessions, then maybe if we threaten with violence they'll get rid of the Irish Sea border."[69]

If the threat of violence is what wins the day, then loyalist paramilitaries are certainly ready to answer the call by taking matters into their own hands. As one interviewee told me: "When loyalism becomes the 'minority,' demographically or politically, they will take on the old IRA role of 'freedom fighters' and turn this country upside down with their capacity for violence." And the distance, at least publicly, that political unionism has kept from loyalism over the years means that unionism will have little influence in mitigating loyalists' capacity for violence.

In October 2019, hardline loyalists said that they would engage in a "war of attrition" designed to "frustrate the operation of all cross community and cross border initiatives."[70] The following month, a mural on Belvoir Street in East Belfast, depicting two masked gunmen from the UVF, proclaimed: "The prevention of the erosion of our identity is now our priority." At a packed loyalist protest meeting in Portadown that same month, Bryson further fanned the flames: "The loyalist and working class unionist community—we have been criminalised, dehumanised, mocked, and sneered at, people have made fun of us, they've poked at us, they have done this consistently and then they wonder why they have created this monster."[71] Allison Morris forewarned of the potential for outbreaks of limited violence by loyalist paramilitaries: "Loyalist paramilitary organisations that continued to recruit long after the ceasefires have numbers that dwarf groups such as the New IRA. Thousands of members are still on the books with the capability to destabilise this place should they so wish. We are not talking about Troubles related violence. Loyalists operated during those years with the arm's length assistance of the state and the state is not going to help them now. But even acting unilaterally they could still bring disruption to cross border rail and roads links and to the port at Larne, conveniently located in a loyalist stronghold. They could destabilise an economy already damaged by Brexit and shatter 20 years of cross community peace building by further dividing our already fractured society."[72]

The Troubles began with Catholic frustration over a government that would not leave; if widespread violence returns, it is likely to be because of Protestant frustration over a government that would not stay. A loyalist paramilitary member told me: "If it ends up that the British state isn't there to protect us, then we'll protect ourselves." Another Belfast loyalist warned: "Ulster is ours, not theirs. [The republicans] have been trying to take my country away from me since 1968. It's a cert that troubles will start again. If the British government won't defend us, the UVF will."[73]

Vote for a United Ireland

The Good Friday Agreement recognizes the right of the people of the island of Ireland to decide the constitutional future of Northern Ireland. As human rights law expert Colin Harvey of Queen's University Belfast (QUB) summarizes: "Northern Ireland's continuing membership of the UK requires democratic interrogation."[74] This principle of consent allows for the right of self-determination by providing a political path to an exit from the UK and some form of reunification with the Republic of Ireland (and, by extension, with the EU). In order for a united Ireland to become a reality, votes (commonly referred to as "border polls") must be taken in Northern Ireland as well as the Republic.

In Northern Ireland, no political party has the power to call for a border poll on its own. Such a referendum can only be called by the Secretary of State for Northern Ireland and only in the case that she or he believes it appears likely to secure a majority. In the exact words of the Northern Ireland Act 1998, the Secretary of State may call a border poll "if at any time it appears likely to him [sic] that a majority of those voting would express a wish that Northern Ireland should cease to be part of the United Kingdom and form part of a united Ireland."[75] It is not clear just how much evidence, and of what type, it would take to compel the Secretary of State to call a border poll. Former Taoiseach Bertie Ahern (Irish equivalent for Prime Minister), one of the key architects of the Good Friday Agreement, suggests two conditions that must be met before a border poll is called: first, that Northern Ireland's institutions have been working sustainably for a prolonged period of time and, second, there is time for a significant period of expert planning about how a united Ireland would work.[76] Other indicators may include "a consistent majority in opinion polls, a Catholic majority in a census, a nationalist majority in the Northern Ireland Assembly, or a vote by a majority in the Assembly."[77] If the vote for reunification does not pass, the Secretary of State is prohibited from calling another border poll for seven years. In the Republic of Ireland, the mechanisms that would trigger a border poll are even less clear, though it is widely understood that the poll would have to be taken at around the same time as the voting in Northern Ireland. In both cases, the Good Friday Agreement's majority standard for democratic constitutional change is 50% plus one—not a supermajority (such as two-thirds or three-fifths), but a simple majority of just one vote.

The first, and to date only, border poll took place in Northern Ireland on March 8, 1973. Nationalist parties dismissed it as a futile performative exercise with predetermined results since there was a substantial reduction in polling stations, the results were not going to be analyzed at the constituency level, the questions being asked in the poll were so simplified as to be misleading, and it ought, they argued, to be the whole of the island of Ireland involved in making the decision for reunification. Political parties in the south were equally dismissive of the poll. There also was concern that the poll could lead to increased sectarian divisions and an escalation in violence. Indeed, a report about the poll stated it would have been almost impossible to "conceive of more unfavourable conditions" in which to hold the vote.[78] With all of this in mind, the nationalist parties in Northern Ireland called for a boycott of the border poll. As a result, the overall turnout of Northern Ireland voters was only 59%, and it was estimated less than 1% of the Catholic population voted.[79] Not surprisingly, of those who did turn out, an overwhelming 99% of voters favored remaining in the UK. Eddie McAteer, a nationalist political leader who supported the boycott, sarcastically suggested that the result "will surely settle the Irish border problem for another 10 minutes or so."[80]

While no border poll has been called since then (even though the British government had planned to do it every 10 years), the 1973 referendum did set an important though often overlooked precedent that would resurface in the 1985 Anglo-Irish Agreement as well as in the 1998 Good Friday Agreement. Namely, it "suggested that sovereignty rested with the people of Northern Ireland and not Parliament at Westminster."[81] The problems posed by Brexit, in the minds of many nationalists, have now provided an opportunity to argue that the time for the people of Northern Ireland to decide the country's constitutional future is here. As one interviewee told me, "Brexit has shined the light on the absurdity of partition." Indeed, Northern Ireland's "inbetweenness" on the outer margins of the British state and the very edge of the Irish state has never been more urgently relevant.[82]

The implementation of Brexit has clearly moved the needle on the possibility of a united Ireland or, at the very least, a border poll. As sociologist Katy Hayward of QUB asserted, "Brexit has made something that people will disagree about profoundly (i.e., Irish unity) increasing likely and increasingly consequential."[83] In 2016, only 21% of Protestants and 32% of Catholics believed Brexit made a united Ireland more likely. By 2018, as the reality of Brexit unfolded, those numbers had risen to 34% of Protestants and 46% of Catholics.[84] A September 2019 poll found 51% of Northern Irish respondents reporting that Brexit makes Irish unification in the foreseeable future "much more likely," with 58% believing Brexit "strengthens the case for Irish unification."[85] An October 2019 poll found that 65% of Northern Irish voters believed Brexit made Irish unity more likely within 10 years.[86] Most recently, a February 2020 poll found that 68.7% of respondents in Northern Ireland believe Brexit made a border poll more likely; that figure jumped to 74.6% of respondents in the Republic. That same poll found 82% of Northern Irish respondents and 83.4% of Republic respondents agreed that Brexit had intensified the debate about their country's constitutional future.[87] In general, an increasingly large majority of the public on both sides of the border believe Brexit has made a united Ireland, or at least the possibility of a border poll, more likely.

Statements of probability, however, should not be confused with favorability. Post-Brexit has seen a proliferation, and politicization, of opinion polling regarding popular support for reunification. Results serpentine across the interpretive landscape, at least partially influenced by methodological issues. Specifically, online polling generally shows much greater support for Irish unity while face-to-face polling tends to show significantly less. Columnist Paul Gillespie addressed the possible reasons behind this discrepancy: "Arguments continue on whether online panel surveys privilege more politically and socially engaged citizens to give pro-unity views, or whether face-to-face interviews underestimate such views—even if the latter do discern a slower change in similar directions."[88] More than an academic issue, the perceived validity of opinion polling matters because it is factor on which the Secretary of State's decision to call for a border poll could hinge.

Overall, opinion polling reveals that popular support for reunification remains a far cry from evidencing a consistent majority. As political scientist Jon Tonge outlines in a December 2019 piece: "Out of 12 opinion surveys conducted in Northern Ireland on the border issue since the 2016 EU referendum, only three have shown more in favor of a united Ireland than against. Of the nine studies showing more against unity than those backing the idea, the majorities of opposition have ranged from 3 percent to a whopping 41 percent."[89] Overall, however, recent polling trends do show a gradual, if underwhelming, shift toward unity. The relevance of this shift is underscored by the fact that the increasing numbers opting for a united Ireland are choosing the "unknown" rather than the more comfortably safe "known." In other words, when respondents are opting for a hypothetical, with very few of the specifics articulated, the presence of even a gradual shift toward unity speaks volumes on Northern Ireland's current constitutional status.

Polling trends also remind us that social identities in Northern Ireland are more nuanced than often portrayed, particularly when entwined with economic considerations. For instance, the notion that all Catholics would vote in favor of a united Ireland—and its corollary demographic belief that, once Catholics outnumber Protestants in Northern Ireland (likely to be confirmed for the first time in the 2021 census), reunification is inevitable—are misleading simplifications. In fact, most opinion polling data seem to show a pattern of far less than complete support for Irish unity from Catholics. As Irish historian Diarmaid Ferriter summarizes the trend of one long-term survey series: "Before Brexit there had been numerous Northern Ireland Life and Times (NILT) surveys indicating falling expectations of a united Ireland and an increase in the number of Catholics who favoured staying in the UK."[90] Even the most recent post-Brexit NILT survey (2019) found fewer than half (47%) of Catholic respondents believing the best long-term policy for Northern Ireland to be reunification with the rest of Ireland and 35% actually believing the better route lay in remaining part of the United Kingdom (either under direct rule or with devolved government).[91] Similarly, in terms of timing, fewer than half (43%) of Catholic respondents see a united Ireland as "very likely" or "quite likely" in the next 20 years.[92] One nationalist interviewee, describing the tension between the romanticized notion of reunification and its economic reality, recalled Northern Ireland Nobel peace laureate John Hume's well-known quip: "You can't eat a flag." For Hume, a founding member of the SDLP, a heady brew of nationalism had to be tempered with a reasonable dose of pragmatism.

On the Protestant side of the matter, nationalism seems, on the surface, to be more intemperate, with 87% of respondents expressing a desire to remain part of the UK and only 3% favoring reunification with the rest of Ireland.[93] Despite those stated desires, 24% of Protestant respondents admit seeing a united Ireland as "very likely" or "quite likely" in the next 20 years.[94] There are reasons to suggest, however, that it may be still somewhat misleading to assume that all Protestants would actually vote in favor of remaining in the UK and against a united Ireland when given the opportunity to do so. There are, in the descriptive words of one interviewee, a lot of "garden centre" unionists who will vote very pragmatically (albeit silently) when a border poll is called. Rather than voting from a place of loyal emotionality, they will, instead, ask if a united Ireland is better for them in a practical sense than re-maining part of the UK. In that regard, particularly after Brexit, assuming a traditional single-identity response from the Protestant and unionist com-munity may be as off-base as assuming the same from the Catholic and na-tionalist community.

In all the uncertainty, one certainty stands out: there are no guarantees that a united Ireland would be approved if a border poll was called today. A February 2020 poll conducted by the Belfast polling company LucidTalk indicated that 22.7% of Northern Irish respondents would not even support a border poll. Of those who favored a border poll, the biggest percentage (35.3%) opted for a poll within the next 5 years with increasingly smaller percentages favoring a poll within the next 10 years (16.8%) or 20 years (7.9%). An antsy 6.4% wanted a border poll taken in 2020. Questioned on how they would vote in a border poll, 46.8% would vote to remain part of the UK, 45.4% would vote for a united Ireland, and 7.8% were unsure how they would vote. Alliance voters, whose voice will be crucial in an actual vote, voted for a united Ireland over the union by more than two to one (47% vs. 22%), though, constitutionally, the Alliance Party is content to maintain the status quo for now. Commenting on the results of the poll, Harvey stated: "It increasingly looks like support for the current constitutional arrangements is on a knife-edge. That is simply remarkable. It shakes the legitimacy of the foundations of the existing constitutional order."[95]

Politically, the polar positions of the existing constitutional order could not be clearer, however. From the nationalist side, Sinn Fein has said it wants a referendum on Irish reunification within five years. As Deputy First Minister Michelle O'Neill declared in January 2020: "Irish unity has taken on a new dynamic as a result of Brexit."[96] If a hard land border had returned, then Sinn Fein would have pushed for an immediate border poll, couched in the promise that "Irish unity is the route back to the EU."[97] While a return to the EU might offer an economic benefit for both nationalists and unionists, it still remains too far of a reach to win over most unionists whose identity attachment to the UK runs so deeply. The other major nationalist-leaning party, the centrist SDLP, is more moderate in seeing reunification as a medium-term policy, allowing time to ensure unionists are part of the con-versation and preparation.

From the unionist side, political intransigence about a united Ireland re-mains firm, even though a secularized Ireland should, in theory, be a less threatening place for at least some Northern Ireland Protestants. The few

unionists who choose to pull their head out of the sand and take a more realistic tack about a united Ireland are roundly called out. In July 2018, for
instance, former First Minister and DUP party leader Peter Robinson, while
saying he did not believe Northern Ireland wanted to leave the UK, did suggest that unionists in the north should strategically prepare for that eventuality. "I don't expect my own house to burn down," he said, "but I still insure
it because it could happen." The knee-jerk response from unionism was swift
and vitriolic. DUP East Antrim MP Sammy Wilson said the comments were
"demoralizing" and akin to "inviting arsonists in to burn your house." He
continued: "It's not going to happen, so why should I prepare for it. I don't
prepare for a journey to the Moon because I'm never going to get on Richard
Branson's space rocket and fly to the Moon. So why would I prepare for a
united Ireland when it's not going to happen." Former Ulster Unionist
Party leader Lord Empey accused Robinson of becoming a "Sinn Féin echo
chamber."[98]

More recently, First Minister and DUP leader Arlene Foster, who turned
50 in 2020, says she does not expect to see a united Ireland, or even a border
poll, in her lifetime. "As you know the test for a border poll is that people
would vote for it in a majority," she said. "And there's no evidence of that. Yes,
people can have different opinion polls, but there's no tangible evidence if
you look right across Northern Ireland."[99] Drawing a line in the sand even
more clearly, party leader Steve Aiken said "nobody from the Ulster Unionist
Party is going to be involved in any conversation about a united Ireland—
not now, not ever."[100] It seems clear, however, that practicing unionism as
it has always been done will not save the union. Unionism is on the wrong
side of the future and must have the adaptive resiliency, including concrete
policy options, to accommodate that reality. As columnist Newton Emerson
argues, "unionism is having to accept change as a problem it brought upon
itself [through Brexit]."[101] The ability, or inability, of unionism to take on the
challenge of rethinking itself will go a long way toward understanding what
the north of Ireland will look like for future generations.

* * *

A vote for a united Ireland also would have to be approved by the Republic
of Ireland. And, despite the sentimentalized notion of a united Ireland that
plays well in principle and at campaign rallies, the reality manifests itself
quite differently in the political practices of the Republic. In the words of
Michelle O'Neill: "The only people not talking about Irish unity is the Irish

government."[102] As recently as December 2019, then Taoiseach Leo Varadkar (Fine Gael) said that he did not believe a border poll was a good idea and that the people of Northern Ireland should be encouraged, instead, to rededicate themselves to the Good Friday Agreement and powersharing.[103] Varadkar also has called for Sinn Fein to stop referring to the Republic as "the 'South of Ireland', 'Free State' or the 'Southern State.'"[104] A former republican political prisoner I interviewed in Belfast described the Irish government as having a "partitionist mindset." Several other interviewees expressed frustration that the ongoing political aloofness of the Republic only reaffirmed a prevailing belief that their neighbors to the south never saw the armed struggle in the north as "legitimate."

Indeed, as columnist Chris Donnelly opined in May 2020: "They've [the Irish government] been socially distancing from the north for a long time before Covid-19 became a thing."[105] People in Northern Ireland are very sensitive to this reality and take deep offense at the slightest hint of it. In September 2017, for instance, the popular Late Late Show on Raidió Teilifís Éireann (the national public broadcaster of Ireland) showed a map of the island of Ireland with Northern Ireland cut out. In place of the land border was a coastline. As author Anne Cadwallader sardonically tweeted: "RTE just drowned Seamus Heaney, Mary McAleese, John Hume, Van Morrison, George Best, Liam Neeson, Rory McIlroy."[106] Similarly, in May 2020, Varadkar, in referring to Belfast Fine Gael members, described them as "overseas" members just days after the party's Regina Doherty implied the inhabitants of the 26 counties alone constitute "the Irish people." Nationalists in Northern Ireland took exception, pointing out that Fine Gael translates as "Family/Tribe of the Irish" and, when formed in 1933, the party initially used the subtitle "United Ireland."[107] While Varadkar later issued an apology, many nationalists in the north, in a century-old historical episode of déjà vu, again felt left behind by their neighbors to the south.

This divide is particularly noticeable in Fine Gael's and Fianna Fail's (two centrist parties, born from Ireland's civil war, who have taken turns ruling Ireland since the foundation of the state) increasingly strained political relationship with the left-leaning Sinn Fein. Historically cool to any political discussions about a united Ireland, and certainly with no detailed plan for such, the Republic has been able to keep Sinn Fein and its relatively meager electoral impact at an arm's distance politically. However, Sinn Fein, long the largest nationalist party in Northern Ireland, has recently emerged as a serious political player in the Republic. In the February 2020 general election,

Sinn Fein's stunning electoral gains broke the long-standing Fine Gael–Fianna Fail duopoly, resulting in a near three-way tie. Sinn Fein, using social media to target young voters with an anti-establishment populist agenda centered on tackling a broken healthcare system and rising housing costs, attracted the largest number of first preference votes, though Fianna Fail narrowly won the largest number of seats in the Dail Eireann, the dominant branch of the legislature in Ireland. With no one party even coming close to the 80 seats necessary for a working majority, however, all three parties were left to try to form a minority government based on coalitions.

Both Fine Gael and Fianna Fail, despite a long history of mutual mistrust, stood firm in their united position that they would not form a government with Sinn Fein. This triangulated "my enemy's enemy is my friend" position was based on policy disagreements as well as moral objections over Sinn Fein's historical, and likely, continuing links with the IRA and its leadership. Fine Gael and Fianna Fail both suspected that, as the Army Council was the behind-the-scenes military decision-making head of the IRA, there is a parallel hidden structure of decision-making for Sinn Fein. Varadkar has characterized Sinn Fein as "not a normal party" since their decision-making is "not necessarily made by elected politicians." Similarly, Fianna Fail leader Michael Martin: "I could never be sure with Sinn Féin in terms of who you are dealing with. Is it unelected officials in Belfast who rule the roost, who control the levers of power within that party?"[108] In addition to the fact that leaders are selected and not elected, many also have noted that internal dissenters typically end up expelled or alienated from Sinn Fein's decision-making processes.[109]

In a May 2020 interview, Sinn Fein leader Mary Lou McDonald, a favorite of Gerry Adams, declared the IRA campaign was "justified" and openly admitted the involvement of ex-IRA members in the party's decision-making processes but painted it as "evidence of the huge success of the peace process" even as she steadfastly denied they are making decisions for elected representatives.[110] For many, however, this is less a sign of the success of the peace process and more a sign of political control not yet surrendered by the IRA. Indeed, many of the people I interviewed on both sides of the political spectrum confirmed the existence of a shadowy command-and-control structure to Sinn Fein decision-making—an unaccountable politburo—in which the "hard men" of the IRA Army Council who "served their political apprenticeship in the Maze Prison" still maintain predominant influence.[111] One republican I interviewed readily admitted: "Sinn Fein's political strategy comes straight from the Felon's Club" [a republican bar and restaurant in West Belfast]. For DUP party member Nelson McCausland, these links remain particularly problematic. "So long," he writes, "as Sinn Fein clings on tenaciously to such thinking and so long as it sacralises the Provisional IRA, it will remain a barrier to building a better Northern Ireland."[112]

In pursuit of a coalition government in the Republic, Sinn Fein was left out in the cold as it was impossible to build a working coalition with so many small parties and independents. Their role now is as the main opposition party, built on the strength that they are the only Irish party with major political influence both north and south of the border (there is now a Sinn Fein member of parliament in all 32 counties of both Northern Ireland and the Republic). Combining their seats, Fine Gael and Fianna Fail, only eight seats short of a majority, entered coalition talks with the Green Party, holder of 12 seats, looking to form a working government for the next five years. On June 15, 2020, each of the three party leaders formally signed off on a draft program for the coalition government, entitled "Our Shared Future."[113] The document spoke of a "shared island" rather than a "united Ireland" and specific references to Northern Ireland were markedly limited (mentioned only 17 times in 126 pages).

On June 26, 2020, the three parties announced their members had voted by large majorities to endorse the coalition deal, and, the following day, Fianna Fail leader Michael Martin was elected Taoiseach. After his election, Martin had the opportunity to nominate 11 personal choices to the 60-seat Seanad Eireann—Ireland's upper house of government. While expectations were widespread that one of those choices would be a Northern Ireland voice, likely a unionist, Martin did not nominate anyone from north of the border. Critics railed that Martin's decision undercut the coalition's commitment to improving cross-border integration and, in effect, left any talk of a shared island as just charade. Morever, since being elected Taoiseach, Martin has repeatedly affirmed that he would not press the British government to call a border poll for at least the next five years. Rather, as he announced in Dublin Castle on October 22, 2020, his "Shared Island" initiative prioritizes working "with all communities and traditions on the island to build consensus around a shared future," rather than getting bogged down in contentious constitutional or territorial questions over a united Ireland.[114]

In addition, the lack of political and moral respect for Sinn Fein among the Republic's political elite does not bode well for a move to a united Ireland. Sinn Fein's core political aim is Irish unity, but they cannot accomplish that without the support of the Republic to prepare and plan for Irish unity. And sometimes Sinn Fein's tunnel vision on a united Ireland works against nurturing that support. This was illustrated most recently by Sinn Fein's insistence on using COVID-19 as an opportunity to call for an all-island approach to healthcare, none too obliquely couched in renewed calls for a united Ireland. Mary Lou McDonald made the political point directly: "When Brexit happened, people said this is an accelerant in terms of the unity debate, because it was so obvious with the danger to the border. I think this [the pandemic] dwarfs Brexit in terms of reflecting the danger of partition, the fact that it's not sustainable, and the necessity for us to work as one island."[115] Columnist Ruth Dudley Edwards finds such a claim especially crass, galling, and even counterproductive for Sinn Fein's standing in the south: "As things stand, all the party leaders seem to have achieved by their constant carping, brazenness and rudeness and banging on about a united Ireland, at a time when politicians are trying to stop people dying and avoid crashing the economy, is to convince most southern politicians that it would be madness to go into coalition with them."[116] Similarly, columnist Tom Kelly, former vice chair of the SDLP, took McDonald to task: "Sinn Fein needs to learn that not every opportunity to score points about building an united Ireland has to be hammered home."[117]

The political hesitancies and passive support emanating from the political elites of the Republic also are matched, to some degree, on the streets of Ireland. As political scientist Brendan O'Leary points out, there are a good number of people in the Republic who "may be described as satisfied nationalists, loyal to, and content with, the twenty-six-county state."[118] In addition, the diversity of the Republic will come into play: "Protestant, liberal, socialist, postnational, and anticlerical intellectuals are in greater abundance in Ireland than at any previous time. Their views matter and will matter on reunification."[119] While a May 2019 exit poll of Irish voters found 65% indicating they would vote in favor of a united Ireland if a referendum was held the next day, a February 2020 exit poll during the general election found only 57% of Irish voters agreeing that there should be referendums on Irish unity on both sides of the border within the next five years.[120] The lack of consensus on the need for a border poll reflects the approach-avoidance tension, affirmed by nearly everyone I interviewed in the Republic, between the idyllic vision of a united Ireland and the impact of its day-to-day reality. People know what they "ought" to vote for (as one interviewee ardently told me: "It's ours and it's always been ours, it's time to reclaim it!"), but what they will vote for, particularly weighing their own best social and economic interest, may be quite different. As columnist Fintan O'Toole argues: "To put it bluntly (as no one ever does) southerners have no interest in inheriting a political wreck, or becoming direct participants in a gory sequel, Troubles III: the Orange Strikes Back. They will not vote for a form of unity that merely creates an angry and alienated Protestant minority within a bitterly contested new state."[121]

For some, there are serious questions about how well the Republic would welcome an influx of unionists with deeply ingrained British identities. This conundrum became painfully clear in early 2020, following a national uproar over a planned commemorative event at Dublin Castle. For the first time in the history of the Republic, pre-partition police forces—the Royal Irish Constabulary (RIC) and Dublin Metropolitan Police (DMP)—were to be commemorated as part of the Decade of Centenaries program. After invitations went out, however, there were an avalanche of withdrawals protesting the event as "revisionism gone too far" and expressing "serious concerns" over the forces' pre-partition role against those fighting for independence from British rule in Ireland.[122] Of particular concern was the RIC's armed auxiliary forces, renowned for their brutality and lack of discipline, including the commission of retaliatory atrocities (authorized and unauthorized) against civilians in the aftermath of IRA attacks. Eventually, the Irish government cancelled the event and began planning an alternative commemoration for a later time, while Sinn Fein continues to call for its outright cancellation. The controversy stirred by the event prompted a frustrated Varadkar to say it was a setback for unity and conciliation, making a united Ireland further away than it was before. Recognizing there are "one million people on the island who identify as British and as being from a unionist background," Varadkar declared that a united Ireland must be one that recognizes and finds a way to appreciate that shared history.[123]

For many in the Republic, however, the greatest concern about a united Ireland remains an economic one. As one person I interviewed in Galway, in the west of Ireland, said: "It's clear Northern Ireland will be right back in our lap sometime relatively soon. They cannot survive as an independent state and the United Kingdom is falling apart. East Germany gave West Germany a severe case of economic indigestion and I'm worried that the Republic picking up the costs of Northern Ireland will be even worse." Her worry is certainly not unfounded; in the 30 years after the fall of the Berlin Wall, some €2 trillion was spent rebuilding the economy of the east.[124] While Northern

Ireland's economy is far better off than that of East Germany's at the time of reunification, Britain's subvention to Northern Ireland is in the region of €11 billion annually, accounting for between 20% and 25% of Northern Ireland's GDP. Ferriter points out the harsh economic question of "how the Republic would manage to absorb the cost of unification and replacing the UK subvention in the short term . . . with predictions that it could reduce the Republic's living standards and national income by up to 15 per cent."[125] A 2019 report by Trinity College Dublin suggested that, without some sort of continuing subvention from the UK (perhaps supported by EU funding), a united Ireland would cost as much as €30 billion a year and cause the complete collapse of Northern Ireland's economy.[126] While economic models vary on what, exactly, the costs of reunification would be and what, exactly, the regional impacts would be for the south and north, there is no disagreement on the fact that there would be substantial costs and significant regional impacts.

Urging patience, financial journalist Paul Gosling has said it will take a 10-year plan to make a united Ireland economically viable. "In my eyes," he writes, "Northern Ireland is a dysfunctional society, kept segregated, with a duplicated and wasteful structure of public service delivery, a failing health service, weak economy, low productivity, absence of regional policy and in places under the continued grip of paramilitaries. . . . This set of deep-seated institutional problems will take years to resolve. That is why a 10 year programme makes sense. As these failings are corrected, we will reduce the 'subvention'—the subsidy Northern Ireland receives from the British Government."[127]

* * *

The constitutional future of Northern Ireland could go any number of different ways. Sir Keir Starmer, the leader of the UK Labour Party, for instance, has called for a new federal structure for the UK, devolving greater powers to the nations and regions of England, Scotland, Wales, and Northern Ireland after Brexit. In his plan, all four constituent parts of the UK would hold equal sovereignty under a written constitution.[128] At the other end of the spectrum, it could be that Northern Ireland's constitutional future is tied to the dissolution rather than the restructuring of the UK. The central threat to the cohesion of the UK could be the emergence of Scottish nationalism. Following the December 2019 landslide victory of the Scottish National Party, Scotland is challenging Westminster to approve a second independence referendum.

With 55% of Scottish voters rejecting independence in the initial 2014 refer-endum, there is an expectation that, in light of Scotland's overwhelming op-position to Brexit (62% voted remain), a second independence referendum might well pass. If that eventuated, given the deep historical and cultural ties between Scotland and Northern Ireland's Protestants, it would be yet another heavy identity blow to unionism.

Were the UK to have such a "monumental self-immolation," and recog-nizing that Scotland has no stated desire to unify with Northern Ireland, there is the chance that Northern Ireland might emerge, for the first time in its complicated history, as a sovereign, independent state "owing allegiance to neither the Republic of Ireland nor to Great Britain."[129] This would be "the breakup of the UK's two Unions: the Union of Great Britain, and the union of Great Britain with Northern Ireland."[130] While—given Northern Ireland's fragile political, economic, and social situation—most consider this a very remote possibility, columnist Sean Byers argues: "If Scotland were to leave Union anytime soon, the north of Ireland would be sure to follow. Realistically, this is where the immediate hopes of constitutional change lie for Irish republicans of varying shades."[131]

Much more likely, however, Northern Ireland's constitutional future, if it changes, will be tied to a vote for a united Ireland; a potential end to what an interviewee described as the country's "temporary little arrange-ment." As columnist Chris Donnelly contended after the February 2020 Irish elections: "Increasingly, political parties will find themselves thinking 32 as a consequence of the Dáil's new arithmetic. That will be the enduring legacy of this election."[132] Indeed, the circumstances for a border poll are inching ever closer. Consideration will have to be given to what the referendum questions would be and who would be eligible to vote. Some would even argue that a referendum with two binary choices—a united Ireland or no—is a very limited conceptualization of constitutional change and artificially restricts visions of what "united" and "Ireland" might become.

To be sure, the deliberative process for any potential constitutional transi-tion is crucial and may be particularly so on the southern side of the border. As Fianna Fail Senator Mark Daly forewarned: "The government must learn the lesson of the disastrous Brexit referendum in Britain, any referendum requires long-term detailed planning in advance. A referendum on a united Ireland should only be held at the very end of a long process."[133] Many, in-cluding Sinn Fein, advocate for that process to include an all-island Citizen's Assembly to deliberate on constitutional changes and plan for Irish unity.

Ahern, conversely, believes that a panel of academics would be the most appropriate forum for such deliberation.[134] Regardless, as Harvey says: "This island is heading towards these referendums. Whether that is within five or 10 years is a matter for political debate. There is no excuse for avoiding the work involved in managing the potential for constitutional change that will arise."[135] Eventually, whether the result of a coming poll or the next one, constitutional change for Northern Ireland, in some form or other, is a near-certainty within the next decade.

If both Northern Ireland and the Republic of Ireland ever voted in favor of reunification, the devil would then rear its ugly head in the details. The Good Friday Agreement states that it "will be a binding obligation on both Governments to introduce and support in their respective Parliaments legislation to give effect to that wish."[136] This means the exact terms of reunification would then have to be worked out in the respective governments, likely followed by another referendum for approval in the north and yet another referendum for approval and a constitutional amendment in the Republic. There also is the formality, at least assumed, that London must agree to the reunification. (It is hard to imagine a scenario in which they would not, as most believe the British see Northern Ireland as of no use to them anymore. Still, some skepticism rears its head from time to time. As one Dublin interviewee pointedly reminded me: "British have always broken treaties; the Good Friday Agreement will just be the next one they break." Another republican interviewee in Belfast said: "The Brits didn't respect the majority view of Northern Ireland regarding Brexit, so why do we expect they would respect a majority vote for leaving the UK?") Assuming all the consents are given, however, there still would not be an immediate transfer of full sovereignty. As Seamus McGuinness of the Republic's Economic and Social Research Institute has pointed out, Hong Kong's sovereignty transfer from the UK to China took 13 years, and a similar transitional timetable for Northern Ireland might be unsurprising.[137]

If it does come, what might a united Ireland look like? A united, independent, and sovereign Ireland has not existed for hundreds of years, so there is no ready template. Surely, governance would have to be reconsidered at a fundamental level. While many naturally assume the six counties of Northern Ireland would be absorbed into the Republic, resulting in a unitary state, that certainly is not the only viable scenario. "Other worlds are possible," columnist Sophie Long argues. "These include non-territorial autonomy, joint authority, city states, direct democracy, participatory democracy or a federal system. No one system will guarantee a political utopia, but offering a broader range of options, alongside a deliberative process will increase the likelihood of better outcomes."[138] There are, for instance, arguments to be made favoring the idea that the Northern Ireland Assembly would still continue as a devolved regional parliament—but within Ireland rather than the UK. A February 2020 poll found that, in the case of a united Ireland, 37.6% of respondents in Northern Ireland would want a federal arrangement leaving a power base in both Dublin and Belfast, while that figure increases to 40.7% of those polled in the Republic. Only 17.8% of Northern Ireland respondents would be in favor of a centralized government, while 33.2% of those in the Republic would favor such a system.[139] In August 2017, a joint committee of the Irish parliament even suggested "that the intergovernmental British-Irish Council could continue, allowing for an outgoing British role in the matters of Northern Ireland to reassure the unionist community."[140]

In addition to the thorny questions of governance are the even thornier questions of identity and the myriad symbols related to it. "When I opened my curtains in the morning [after Northern Ireland joined the Republic]," asks Mike Nesbitt, a former leader of the Ulster Unionist Party, "is the postbox still red or is it green?"[141] Does reunification bring a new flag? A new anthem? A new football and rugby team? How do the courts, army, health services, and public services reflect the new state? Are public buildings renamed, and, if so, for whom? Are memorials built, and, if so, what or who do they commemorate? What do the police uniforms look like? How are symbols of the "state" distinguished from symbols of "nationality?" What are the official languages (assuming plurality) of a united Ireland? What holidays are designated as national? In short, "identity is about little things as well as big ones, and there would be an almost limitless number of them to fiddle with and take umbrage over."[142]

Whatever form it takes and symbols it adopts, there is widespread agreement that a united Ireland, to be peaceful and prosperous, must be an inclusive Ireland. As Michelle O'Neill said: "It [a united Ireland] has to be one where those who have an Irish identity and those who have a British identity feel part and parcel, feel that they have their place, and it's valued and cherished."[143] Similarly, for Ahern, a united Ireland is one "where we can live together, work together, share together and understand our differences and diversities."[144] The extent to which that inclusivity can be pulled off is the extent to which stability, rather than instability, will be the hallmark of the island's future.

Unfortunately, the hope and optimism with which many nationalists face the future is not matched within unionism. For unionists, their future is one of uncertainty and threat; unsure of how unionism is accommodated if the entity known as "Northern Ireland" no longer exits. As historian Liam Kennedy of QUB argues: "Not unlike the weather most days in Ireland, the future seems far from settled. The distant skyline might be green, it might be orangeish-green, or greenish-orange, or some new colour compound prepared by Dublin and London. It will certainly not be orange."[145] When unionists listen to a Sinn Fein councilor say that hearing the term "Northern Ireland" is like the sound of nails on a chalkboard or they see Mary Lou McDonald parading with a banner reading "England Get Out of Ireland," they do not feel a sense of inclusivity.[146] Even though a February 2020 poll revealed that only 2.1% of respondents in the Republic believed the unionist identity would be given no respect in a united Ireland, unionists in the north do not believe they have a place in a united Ireland.[147] And, to this point, nationalists have been remiss, deliberately or not, in articulating what that place might be. And into that void creeps fear and suspicion and a sense of being disrespected. As Alex Kane argues: "My identity disappears in a united Ireland. I have yet to hear a convincing argument about how that identity can be protected and promoted outside the United Kingdom."[148] More om-inously, as one former loyalist political prisoner confided to me: "When the boot is on the other foot, they will do to us what we did to them."

Conclusion

These three accelerants are cross-cutting and intersecting, each feeding off the other and multiplying the accelerating impacts. Acute economic de-terioration, particularly felt in working-class communities, will make paramilitarism a viable economic option for the disenfranchised. In turn, paramilitarism and its corresponding violence and criminality will blight communities and lead to further economic deterioration. A potential border poll will only accentuate fears of economic instability and, most notably, will enhance outbreaks of paramilitary identity-based violence from both sides. Sovereignty based on national identity would be at stake; nothing less than the constitutional future of the country. And when that happens, as Duncan Morrow warns, "there is an unavoidable risk that the enormity of the cause will justify escalating violence."[149]

In the context of these accelerants further undermining the structural integrity and stability of Northern Irish society, there are a soberingly wide range of triggering factors that can make the return of violent conflict in contemporary Northern Ireland likely or imminent. Among these would be the restoration of direct rule from Westminster (increasingly unlikely but not an impossibility); a dissident republican hunger strike that might reawaken the echoes of 1981 and force Sinn Fein to make a public show of support and solidarity; the implementation of a standalone Irish language bill without a corresponding equivalent for Ulster Scots; a Sinn Fein representative as First Minister (meaning Sinn Fein has the largest party in the assembly); political exclusion of one or more parties from state administration, either through appointed posts or elected office; commemorative events surrounding Northern Ireland's centenary in 2021 (celebrated by unionists but churlishly referred to as the "anniversary of the creation of the rotten orange state" by Sinn Fein MP Chris Hazzard); or the identity crisis resulting from a 2021 census that reveals, for the first time, Catholics outnumbering Protestants in Northern Ireland.[150] The most significant potential triggers, however, are the direct outgrowth of the accelerants we have discussed, particularly those related to the constitutional future of the north of Ireland.

There is significant concern, for instance, that the current conditions for Irish unity stipulated by the Good Friday Agreement, 50% in favor plus one, could be an unwitting trigger for the onset of violence. As one unionist politician told me: "Politics now is all about a 50% + 1 mentality . . . keeping it if you're the DUP or getting it if you're Sinn Fein." Moreover, as Seamus Mallon, former Deputy Leader of the SDLP, argued less than a year before his passing in 2020, constitutional change on the basis of a simple majority will not create a peaceful and prosperous united Ireland. "My concern," he writes, "is that a very narrow vote for unity would lead to more division, instability and probably violence." An avowed nationalist, Mallon proposed a "parallel consent" amendment to the Good Friday Agreement in which the consent of both traditions—nationalist and unionist—would be necessary for a constitutional move to a united Ireland. He pleaded: "My nationalist community, now they are moving into the ascendant, must show the generosity to unionists that was sadly absent from the way in which they were treated by the unionists during 50 years of one-party rule."[151]

Mallon's proposal drew the expected uproar from many in the nationalist community who were irate at the suggestion that a united Ireland be put on hold until the majority of unionists are in favor of it. His concern, however, regarding the crudeness of a simple majority for such a monumental decision is justified. While Gerry Adams's reply to Mallon asserted that a narrowly won unity referendum would not lead to "any support for a return to the conflict of the past," such a perception seems disingenuously naïve to the reality that loyalists will not countenance unification under any circumstances, but, least of all, if the vote for unification is so marginal.[152] Especially if there has been insufficient consensus building in the runup to the referendum, unionist and loyalist response could lead to, at the best, low-level unrest and, at the worst, widespread violence. When the heart of their British identity is under threat, loyalists will mobilize, and, as one former political prisoner told me, "the lesson loyalists learned from republicans was the power of guns and bombs to effect political and social change." As loyalist activist Jamie Bryson warned in January 2020: "I would imagine there would probably be civil war first before unionists and loyalists would ever walk into a united Ireland."[153]

On the dissident republican side, hard-liners believe Irish self-determination is independent of a border poll (though they will certainly respond in kind to loyalist violence against such a poll). Paddy Gallagher, spokesman for Saoradh, a far-left republican party said: "As a republican, I am not comfortable asking my British occupier, 'Can I have my country back?' Why should the Irish people be forced to vote in a British border poll to determine whether our country should be free from British rule?"[154] Rather than a political path to a united Ireland, dissidents still stand firm in the tradition of physical force republicanism—armed violence, rather than the ballot box—to win back what is seen as rightfully theirs. Even if they do not enjoy widespread support from the nationalist community, dissident republican activity still will destabilize nationalist areas in the north as well as inflame unionist and loyalist fears and resentments.

In fact, as of this writing, there has been a significant uptick in paramilitary posturing, threats, and violence on both sides. In May 2020, the SEA UDA was widely believed to be responsible for threats issued against journalists working for the *Sunday Life* and *Sunday World* newspapers due to coverage of the paramilitary group's alleged criminal activities. It also was believed the SEA UDA issued subsequent threats against Assembly members from the SDLP, the UUP, the DUP, and Alliance for supporting the journalists.[155] A wave of terror unleashed by the UVF in Belfast over a 72-hour period in June 2020 included shots fired at a house, a car burned, a man beaten in a punishment attack, and four people ordered out of country.[156] In-fighting between loyalist paramilitaries continues to threaten the at-risk communities in which they are based, even as the groups escalate their recruitment of young members. A UDA mural in the Glenfada area of Carrickfergus, complete with a masked gunman, reads: "Better to die on your feet than live on your knees in an Irish Republic. Join the U.D.A." Also, in May 2020, the dissident republican group Oglaigh na hEirann was responsible for the murder of Kieran Wylie, a former member of the organization, in west Belfast. Suspected of being an informant, Wylie was gunned down in his home, shot several times at close range, in front of two of his children. The following week, in rural Fermanagh, armed and masked members of the Continuity IRA were photographed "patrolling" roads and firing shots in a cemetery. The organization, building on the ill-gained publicity gleaned from its failed "Brexit day" bomb, has been recruiting and regrouping in that area, poised to "operate at any time day or night."[157] All the while, the New IRA continues to loom as the most dangerous and well-resourced of the dissident republican paramilitary groups.

In February 2018, *The Irish News* columnist Leona O'Neill addressed Northern Ireland as it was: "This place is complex, more divided than ever and on a dangerous trajectory. Our peace has always been paper-thin fragile. We need not hand these problems to the next generation so that they struggle too. We need to sort this mess out. . . . We've come so far from the dark days that no one wants to remember, but it seems that we are on the edge of some kind of abyss again. We're never far from that edge."[158] In 2020, as Northern Ireland nears its centenary, the "mess" has only worsened and the "edge" only drawn nearer. Avoiding the abyss will require deep wells of attention to the accelerating and triggering events described in this chapter and even deeper wells of commitment to proactively take preventive structural and policy action to address those events. Only then will we know what sort of world might appear on the other side.

Notes

1. "Report of the Special Rapporteur on the Right to Education," A/74/243 (July 29, 2019), 5.
2. African Development Bank Group, "Drivers and Dynamics of Fragility in Africa," *Africa Economic Brief* (2013), 3.
3. Duncan Morrow, "The Rocky Road from Enmity," in Cillian McGrattan and Elizabeth Meehan (eds.), *Everyday Life After the Irish Conflict: The Impact of Devolution and Cross-Border Cooperation* (Manchester: Manchester University Press, 2012), 30, 34.

4. African Development Bank Group, "Drivers and Dynamics of Fragility in Africa," 4.
5. GDP measures the monetary value of all goods and services made within a country over a specific period.
6. Fund for Peace, "CAST: Conflict Assessment Framework" (2014), 10. The document was accessed at https://fundforpeace.org/2014/03/10/cast-conflict-assessment-framework-manual-2014-reprint/ on June 20, 2020.
7. Allister Heath, "Russia's Economic Crisis Could Easily End in Yet Another Sovereign Default," accessed on February 15, 2015, at http://www.telegraph.co.uk/finance/economics/11297915/Russias-economic-crisis-could-easily-end-in-yet-another-sovereign-default.html
8. See, for instance, Namsuk Kim and Pedro Conceicao, "The Economic Crisis, Violent Conflict, and Human Development," *International Journal of Peace Studies* 15 (2010), 29–43.
9. Dan Smith, *The Penguin State of the World Atlas*, 9th ed. (Brighton, UK: Myriad Editions, 2012), 66.
10. NISRA, "NI: In Profile, Key Statistics on Northern Ireland" (February 11, 2020), accessed on May 3, 2020, at https://www.nisra.gov.uk/sites/nisra.gov.uk/files/publications/NI%20IN%20PROFILE%20-%20February%202020_0.pdf
11. Francess McDonnell, "Homegrown Talent Stands High in Otherwise Difficult Year," *The Irish Times* (December 27, 2011), accessed on May 3, 2020, at https://www.irishtimes.com/business/homegrown-talent-stands-high-in-otherwise-difficult-year-1.15716
12. Caoimhe Archibald, "We Have the Opportunity to Build a Fairer Society for Our Future Generations," *Belfast Telegraph* (May 26, 2020), accessed on May 26, 2020, at https://www.belfasttelegraph.co.uk/opinion/comment/we-have-the-opportunity-to-build-a-fairer-society-for-our-future-generations-39233688.html
13. Quoted in Ann Marie Gray, Jennifer Hamilton, Grainne Kelly, Brendan Lynn, Martin Melaugh, and Gillian Robinson, "Northern Ireland Peace Monitoring Report, Number Five" (October 2018), 18, accessed on December 18, 2020 at https://www.community-relations.org.uk/publications/northern-ireland-peace-monitoring-report
14. Ibid., 18–29.
15. Data taken from "One Third of North's Adults Doesn't Have a Job," *The Irish News* (February 10, 2018), accessed on December 18, 2018, at http://www.irishnews.com/news/2018/02/20/news/one-third-of-north-s-adults-doesn-t-have-a-job-1259038
16. See Anne Devlin, Keara McKay, and Raymond Russell, "Multiple Deprivation in Northern Ireland," Research and Information Service Research Paper, Northern Ireland Assembly (June 1, 2018).
17. NISRA, "NI: In Profile."
18. Clodagh Rice, "Northern Ireland Economy 'Enters or Is Entering' Recession," *BBC News* (September 9, 2019), accessed on May 3, 2020, at https://www.bbc.com/news/uk-northern-ireland-49609767
19. Clodagh Rice, "Northern Ireland's Economy Could Be Slipping into Recession, Says Survey," *BBC News* (October 16, 2019), accessed on May 3, 2020, at https://www.bbc.com/news/uk-northern-ireland-50069050

20. Gary McDonald, "Tumbleweed Continues to Blow Through North's Shopping Centres and High Streets," *The Irish News* (November 11, 2019), accessed on May 3, 2020, at http://www.irishnews.com/business/2019/11/11/news/tumbleweed-continues-to-blow-through-north-s-shopping-centres-and-high-streets-1760815

21. Ryan McAleer, "'Immediate Action Needed to Reinvigorate North's Stagnant Economy' Warns Chamber President," *The Irish News* (January 2, 2020), accessed on May 3, 2020, at http://www.irishnews.com/business/2020/01/02/news/-immediate-action-needed-to-reinvigorate-north-s-stagnant-economy-warns-chamber-president-1802149

22. Filippo Biondi and Ines Goncalves Raposo, "The Impact of Brexit on Northern Ireland: A First Look," *Global Business Outlook* (no date), accessed on May 3, 2020, at https://www.globalbusinessoutlook.com/the-impact-of-brexit-on-northern-ireland-a-first-look/

23. Ryan McAleer, "No-Deal Brexit Will Put 40,000 Northern Ireland Jobs at Risk, Says Report," *Belfast Telegraph* (July 11, 2019), accessed on May 3, 2020, at https://www.belfasttelegraph.co.uk/business/northern-ireland/no-deal-brexit-will-put-40000-northern-ireland-jobs-at-risk-says-report-38301277.html

24. Lucinda Creighton, "The Harder the Brexit, the Harder the Impact on Northern Ireland," *Intereconomics* (2019), 62–63.

25. "New Decade, New Approach" (January 2020), 8. Accessed on May 5, 2020, at https://assets.publishing.service.gov.uk/government/uploads/system/uploads/attachment_data/file/856998/2020-01-08_a_new_decade__a_new_approach.pdf

26. John Breslin, "Coronavirus: Northern Ireland Economy Facing £5.4bn Hit and a Jobless Rate of 12%, Says Report," *Belfast Telegraph* (June 1, 2020), accessed on June 3, 2020, at https://www.belfasttelegraph.co.uk/business/northern-ireland/coronavirus-northern-ireland-economy-facing-54bn-hit-and-a-jobless-rate-of-12-says-report-39248521.html

27. Emma Deighan, "NI Coronovirus Economic Hit Will Be Staggering, Says Bank," *Belfast Telegraph* (April 28, 2020), accessed on May 3, 2020, at https://www.belfasttelegraph.co.uk/business/northern-ireland/ni-coronavirus-economic-hit-will-be-staggering-says-bank-39161943.html

28. Margaret Canning, "Economic Meltdown in Northern Ireland Was Steepest in UK, Says Economist," *Belfast Telegraph* (May 11, 2020), accessed on May 15, 2020, at https://www.belfasttelegraph.co.uk/business/northern-ireland/economic-meltdown-in-northern-ireland-was-steepest-in-uk-says-economist-39195162.html

29. Adam Jones, *Genocide: A Comprehensive Introduction*, 2nd ed. (New York: Routledge, 2010), 569.

30. Ervin Staub, *Overcoming Evil: Genocide, Violent Conflict, and Terrorism* (New York: Oxford University Press, 2011), 116.

31. Allison Morris, "Lyra McKee Murder Shows We Must Intervene in Derry and Turn Young Away from Violence," *The Irish News* (April 25, 2019), accessed on May 3, 2020, at http://www.irishnews.com/opinion/columnists/2019/04/25/news/allison-morris-we-must-take-this-opportunity-to-intervene-in-derry-and-turn-young-people-away-from-violence-1605361

32. Alex J. Bellamy, "Mass Atrocities and Armed Conflict: Links, Distinctions, and Implications for the Responsibility to Prevent" (The Stanley Foundation, February 2011), 13, accessed on May 5, 2020, at https://stanleycenter.org/publications/pab/BellamyPAB22011.pdf

33. The complete text of the third annual Independent Reporting Commission (IRC) report can be accessed at https://www.ircommission.org/sites/irc/files/media-files/IRC%20Third%20Report.pdf, accessed on December 18, 2020. Quoted material is taken from pp. 17–18 of that report.

34. A complete listing of the 14 proscribed groups can be found at http://www.legislation.gov.uk/ukpga/2000/11/schedule/2, accessed on May 5, 2020.

35. "Independent Reporting Commission, Third Report" (November 17, 2020), 18.

36. Data can be reviewed at https://www.psni.police.uk/inside-psni/Statistics/security-situation-statistics/, accessed on May 5, 2020.

37. Alex Kane, "A Quarter-of-a-Century After the Good Friday Agreement, the Deadly Hand of Paramilitarism Still Has a Grip on Too Many Lives," *Belfast Telegraph* (May 21, 2020), accessed on May 22, 2020, at https://www.belfasttelegraph.co.uk/opinion/comment/a-quarter-of-a-century-after-the-good-friday-agreement-the-deadly-hand-of-paramilitarism-still-has-a-grip-on-too-many-lives-39221849.html

38. The complete text of the second annual Independent Reporting Commission (IRC) report can be accessed at https://www.ircommission.org/publications/irc-second-report, accessed on February 16, 2020. Quote is taken from p. 9.

39. Allison Morris, "To Tackle Sectarianism We Must First Stop Paying Paramilitaries to Behave," *The Irish News* (May 16, 2019), accessed on June 3, 2020, at http://www.irishnews.com/opinion/columnists/2019/05/16/news/allison-morris-integrated-education-should-be-the-norm-1620674

40. Quoted material in this paragraph taken from an assessment commissioned by the Secretary of State for Northern Ireland, titled "Paramilitary Groups in Northern Ireland" (October 19, 2015), 4, accessed on May 5, 2020, at https://static.rasset.ie/documents/news/paramilitary-groups-in-northern-ireland-20-oct-2015.pdf

41. "Dissident" groups are distinguished from "dissenters" in that the former overtly support violence while the later oppose violence while still maintaining critiques of Sinn Fein and the peace process. See Paddy Hoey, "Dissident and Dissenting Republicanism: From the Good Friday/Belfast Agreement to Brexit," *Capital & Class* 43 (2019), 73–87.

42. Secretary of State for Northern Ireland, "Paramilitary Groups in Northern Ireland" (October 19, 2015), 1, accessed on December 20, 2020 at https://assets.publishing.service.gov.uk/government/uploads/system/uploads/attachment_data/file/469548/Paramilitary_Groups_in_Northern_Ireland_-_20_Oct_2015.pdf

43. Mark Edwards, "Gun that May Have Been Used to Kill Lyra McKee Found Close to Children's Den in Derry," *Belfast Telegraph* (June 8, 2020), accessed on June 8, 2020, at https://www.belfasttelegraph.co.uk/news/northern-ireland/gun-that-may-have-been-used-to-kill-lyra-mckee-found-close-to-childrens-den-in-derry-39266800.html

44. BBC News, "Dissident Group Oglaigh na hEirann Calls Ceasefire" (January 23, 2018), accessed on May 5, 2020, at https://www.bbc.com/news/uk-northern-ireland-42786530

45. See John Cassidy, "Seven Jailed Over MI5 Bugging Operation Targeting Continuity IRA," *Belfast Telegraph* (November 13, 2020), accessed on December 18, 2020 at https://www.belfasttelegraph.co.uk/news/courts/seven-jailed-over-mi5-bugging-operation-targeting-continuity-ira-39743872.html

46. Gerry Moriarty, "Who Are the New IRA and What Have They Done?," *The Irish Times* (April 23, 2019), accessed on May 5, 2020, at https://www.irishtimes.com/news/ireland/irish-news/who-are-the-new-ira-and-what-have-they-done-1.3869569

47. Palko Karasz, "Explosive Packages in U.K. Are Claimed as I.R.A. Attack, Policy Say," *The New York Times* (March 12, 2019), accessed on May 5, 2020, at https://www.nytimes.com/2019/03/12/world/europe/uk-explosive-packages-ira.html

48. Connla Young, "New IRA Admits Murder of Journalist Lyra McKee and Offers 'Sincere Apologies,'" *The Irish News* (April 23, 2019), accessed on May 5, 2020, at https://www.irishnews.com/news/northernirelandnews/2019/04/23/news/dissident-republican-new-ira-group-admit-murder-of-journalist-lyra-mckee-and-offer-sincere-apologies--1603611/

49. Ciaran Barnes, "Spooks Spend Two Nights Hunting for New IRA Bomb in North Belfast," *Belfast Telegraph* (October 25, 2020), accessed on December 18, 2020 at https://www.belfasttelegraph.co.uk/sunday-life/news/spooks-spend-two-nights-hunting-for-new-ira-bomb-in-north-belfast-39663393.html. Operation Arbacia was a joint operation between the PSNI, An Garda Siochana, and MI5.

50. Allan Preston, "Concern as New IRA Gets Weapons from Hezbollah," *Belfast Telegraph* (September 14, 2020), accessed on December 18, 2020 at https://www.belfasttelegraph.co.uk/news/northern-ireland/concern-as-new-ira-gets-weapons-from-hezbollah-39527531.html

51. Secretary of State for Northern Ireland, "Paramilitary Groups in Northern Ireland," 2.

52. Stephen Dempster, "Loyalist Paramilitary Groups in NI 'Have 12,500 Members,'" *BBC News* (December 2, 2020), accessed on December 18, 2020 at https://www.bbc.com/news/uk-northern-ireland-55151249

53. Allison Morris, "Loyalist Paramilitary Groups Raking In £250,000 a Month in Member 'Dues,'" *The Irish News* (December 3, 2020), accessed on December 18, 2020 at https://www.irishnews.com/news/northernirelandnews/2020/12/03/news/loyalist-paramilitary-groups-raking-in-250-000-a-month-in-members-dues--2149229/

54. Quoted material in this paragraph taken from Vincent Kearney, "Loyalist Paramilitaries: 'Once You Join It's Impossible to Get Out,'" *BBC News* (February 1, 2019), accessed on May 5, 2020, at https://www.bbc.com/news/uk-northern-ireland-politics-47072147

55. "Independent Reporting Commission, Second Report," 6.

56. Dan Haverty, "Paramilitaries Are Surging Again in Northern Ireland: And It's Not Because of Brexit," *Foreign Policy* (May 24, 2019), accessed on May 5, 2020, at https://foreignpolicy.com/2019/05/24/paramilitaries-are-surging-again-in-northern-ireland/

57. Connla Young, "'IRA' Easter Statement Described as 'Delusional,'" *The Irish News* (April 14, 2020), accessed on May 6, 2020, at http://www.irishnews.com/news/northernirelandnews/2020/04/14/news/-ira-easter-statement-described-as-delusional--1900826

58. Mark Daly, Pat Dolan, and Mark Brennan, "Northern Ireland Returning to Violence as a Result of a Hard Border Due to Brexit or a Rushed Border Poll: Risks for Youth" (February 18, 2019), 5. Accessed on May 8, 2020, at https://senatormarkdaly.files.wordpress.com/2019/02/unesco-chairs-report-brexit-return-to-violence.pdf

59. Channel 4 News, "New IRA Says Border Infrastructure Would Be 'Legitimate Target for Attack'" (October 16, 2019), accessed on April 24, 2020, at https://www.channel4.com/news/new-ira-says-border-infrastructure-would-be-legitimate-target-for-attack

60. Rory Carroll, "Belfast Bonfire 'Victory' Masks Tide Turning Against Loyalist Twelfth," *The Guardian* (July 12, 2019), accessed on May 7, 2020, at https://www.theguardian.com/uk-news/2019/jul/12/loyalists-celebrate-victory-after-belfast-council-tried-to-ban-bonfire

61. An image of the mural can be found at https://extramuralactivity.com/2012/09/25/ulster-girl/, accessed on May 7, 2020. A similar mural, titled "Ulster to Britain," also can be found on Thorndyke Street in East Belfast.

62. Tom McTague, "Northern Ireland Offers a Warning that Few are Hearing," *The Atlantic* (December 9, 2019), accessed on April 24, 2020, at https://www.theatlantic.com/international/archive/2019/12/northern-ireland-offers-warning-few-are-hearing/603196/

63. Susan Thompson, "Poll: Most Tories Would Sacrifice Union with Northern Ireland for Brexit," *The Irish News* (June 18, 2019), accessed on April 23, 2020, at http://www.irishnews.com/news/brexit/2019/06/18/news/poll-most-tories-would-sacrifice-union-with-northern-ireland-for-brexit-1644668

64. Allison Morris, "DUP Should Be Nervous About Boris Johnson's Brexit Backstop Intentions," *The Irish News* (September 12, 2019), accessed on May 7, 2020, at http://www.irishnews.com/opinion/columnists/2019/09/12/news/allison-morris-vital-services-struggle-as-westminster-descends-into-farce-1709613/

65. McTague, "Northern Ireland Offers a Warning that Few are Hearing."

66. Jonathan Gorvett, "Northern Ireland Is in a Culture War. Brexit Is Making It Worse," *Foreign Policy* (January 31, 2020), accessed on December 18, 2020 at https://foreignpolicy.com/2020/01/31/northern-ireland-culture-war-brexit/

67. Harriet Line, "Fear of Violence in Northern Ireland Led to Theresa May Deciding Against a No Deal," *The Irish News* (November 11, 2019), accessed on May 6, 2020, at http://www.irishnews.com/news/brexit/2019/11/11/news/fear-of-violence-in-northern-ireland-led-to-theresa-may-deciding-against-allowing-the-uk-to-crash-out-of-the-eu-without-a-de-1761669

68. James Angelos, "Will Brexit Bring the Troubles Back to Northern Ireland?," *The New York Times Magazine* (December 30, 2019), accessed on May 6, 2020, at https://www.nytimes.com/2019/12/30/magazine/brexit-northern-ireland.html

69. Ceylan Yeginsu, "In Northern Ireland, Brexit Deal Is Seen as 'Betrayal,'" *The New York Times* (October 24, 2019), accessed on May 7, 2020, at https://www.nytimes.com/2019/10/24/world/europe/northern-ireland-brexit.html

70. Allison Morris, "Loyalists Plan 'War of Attrition,'" *The Irish News* (October 23, 2019), accessed on May 7, 2020, at https://www.irishnews.com/news/northernirelandnews/2019/10/23/news/loyalists-plan-war-of-attrition--1745909/

71. Ben Lowry, "Loyalist Protest Meeting in Portadown Against Boris Johnson's 'Betrayal Act' Was Packed and Angry," *Belfast News Letter* (November 25, 2019), accessed on May 7, 2020, at https://www.newsletter.co.uk/news/opinion/columnists/ben-lowry-loyalist-protest-meeting-portadown-against-boris-johnsons-betrayal-act-was-packed-and-angry-2021523

72. Allison Morris, "Hyped Up Talk of Unionist Betrayal Could Have Dangerous Consequences," *The Irish News* (November 28, 2019), accessed on May 7, 2020, at http://www.irishnews.com/opinion/columnists/2019/11/28/news/allison-morris-hyped-up-talk-of-unionist-betrayal-could-have-dangerous-consequences-1776681

73. Lorraine Mallinder, "What the UK's New Power Deal Means in the DUP's Belfast Heartland," *The World* (June 27, 2017), accessed on May 14, 2020, at https://www.pri.org/stories/2017-06-27/what-uks-new-power-deal-means-dups-belfast-heartland

74. Colin Harvey, "Finding a Way Back to the EU," in John Mair, Steven McCabe, Neil Fowler, and Leslie Budd (eds.), *Brexit and Northern Ireland: Bordering on Confusion?* (London: Bite-Sized Books, 2019), 92.

75. Accessed on May 13, 2020, at http://www.legislation.gov.uk/ukpga/1998/47/schedule/1

76. Sinead Ingoldsby, "While Brexit Is a Threat to the Good Friday Agreement 'It Can be Managed,'" *The Detail* (February 28, 2020), accessed on May 18, 2020, at https://www.thedetail.tv/articles/while-brexit-is-a-threat-to-the-good-friday-agreement-it-can-be-managed

77. Institute for Government, "Irish Reunification" (June 18, 2019), accessed on May 13, 2020, at https://www.instituteforgovernment.org.uk/explainers/irish-reunification

78. See Rory Winters, "If Brandon Lewis Calls a Border Poll, It Won't Be Northern Ireland's First," *The Detail* (February 25, 2020), accessed on May 18, 2020, at https://www.thedetail.tv/articles/if-brandon-lewis-calls-a-border-poll-it-won-t-be-ni-s-first

79. BBC, "1973: Northern Ireland Votes for Union," accessed on May 13, 2020, at http://news.bbc.co.uk/onthisday/hi/dates/stories/march/9/newsid_2516000/2516477.stm

80. Quoted in Diarmaid Ferriter, *The Border: The Legacy of a Century of Anglo-Irish Politics* (London: Profile Books, 2019), 85.

81. Quote cited by The Constitution Unit, "'Taking the Border Out of Politics'—The Northern Ireland Referendum of March 1973" (November 21, 2019), accessed on May 13, 2020, at https://constitution-unit.com/2019/11/21/taking-the-border-out-of-politics-the-northern-ireland-referendum-of-march-1973/

82. Colin Coulter and Peter Shirlow, "From the 'Long War' to the 'Long Peace:' An Introduction to the Special Edition," *Capital & Class* 43 (2019), 19.

83. Katy Hayward, "Northern Ireland," in Anand Menon (ed.), *Brexit: What Next?* (February 2020), 39, accessed on December 18, 2020 at https://ukandeu.ac.uk/wp-content/uploads/2020/02/Brexit-what-next-report.pdf

84. 2016 and 2018 data were accessed on May 15, 2020, and can be found at https://www.ark.ac.uk/nilt/2016/Political_Attitudes/UNIRLIKL.html and https://www.ark.ac.uk/nilt/2018/Political_Attitudes/UNIRLIKL.html, respectively.

85. Lord Ashcroft, "My Northern Ireland Survey Finds the Union on a Knife-Edge" (September 11, 2019), accessed on May 14, 2020, at https://lordashcroftpolls.com/2019/09/my-northern-ireland-survey-finds-the-union-on-a-knife-edge/

86. *Belfast Telegraph*, "Poll: 65% of Voters in Northern Ireland Believe Brexit Makes Irish Unity More Likely Within Ten Years" (October 27, 2019), accessed on May 14, 2020, at https://www.belfasttelegraph.co.uk/news/northern-ireland/poll-65-of-voters-in-northern-ireland-believe-brexit-makes-irish-unity-more-likely-within-ten-years-38635481.html

87. Sinead Ingoldsby, "Results of a Future Border Poll on a Knife Edge," *The Detail* (February 24, 2020), accessed on May 15, 2020, at https://thedetail.tv/articles/a-majority-favour-a-border-poll-on-the-island-of-ireland-in-the-next-10-years

88. Paul Gillespie, "Brexit Impact on Northern Ireland Not as Big as We Think," *The Irish Times* (February 29, 2020), accessed on May 15, 2020, at https://www.irishtimes.com/opinion/brexit-impact-on-northern-ireland-not-as-big-as-we-think-1.4188055

89. Jon Tonge, "After Brexit, What's Left for Northern Ireland's Unionists?," *Foreign Policy* (December 21, 2019), accessed on May 19, 2020, at https://foreignpolicy.com/2019/12/21/northern-ireland-unionism-irish-unity

90. Ferriter, *The Border*, 133.

91. See https://www.ark.ac.uk/nilt/2019/Political_Attitudes/NIRELND2.html, accessed on June 20, 2020.

92. See https://www.ark.ac.uk/nilt/2019/Political_Attitudes/UNTDIREL.html, accessed on June 20, 2020.

93. See https://www.ark.ac.uk/nilt/2019/Political_Attitudes/NIRELND2.html, accessed on June 20, 2020.

94. See https://www.ark.ac.uk/nilt/2019/Political_Attitudes/UNTDIREL.html, accessed on June 20, 2020.

95. All material in this paragraph taken from Ingoldsby, "Results of a Future Border Poll on a Knife Edge."

96. Michelle O'Neill, "Irish Unity Has Taken on a New Dynamic as Result of Brexit," *Belfast Telegraph* (January 31, 2020), accessed on May 13, 2020, at https://www.belfasttelegraph.co.uk/opinion/comment/irish-unity-has-taken-on-a-new-dynamic-as-result-of-brexit-38912191.html

97. BBC News, "Brexit: Sinn Fein Repeats Call for Border Poll If No Deal" (July 30, 2019), accessed on May 13, 2020, at https://www.bbc.com/news/uk-northern-ireland-49165607

98. Quoted material in this paragraph taken from *The Irish News* (July 30, 2018), accessed on May 13, 2020, at http://www.irishnews.com/news/2018/07/30/news/sammy-wilson-hit-out-former-dup-leader-peter-robinson-warns-north-should-prepare-for-possibility-of-a-united-ireland-1393984

99. Gareth Gordon, "Arlene Foster: I Won't See a Border Poll in My Lifetime," *BBC News* (February 27, 2020), accessed on May 13, 2020, at https://www.bbc.com/news/uk-northern-ireland-51661578

100. Newton Emerson, "Unionists Surprisingly Interested in a 'United Island,'" *The Irish Times* (April 23, 2020), accessed on May 11, 2020, at https://www.irishtimes.com/opinion/newton-emerson-unionists-surprisingly-interested-in-a-united-island-1.4235186

101. Ibid.
102. O'Neill, "Irish Unity Has Taken on a New Dynamic as Result of Brexit."
103. Michael McHugh, "Majority in North Do Not Support United Ireland, says Leo Varadkar," *The Irish News* (December 27, 2019), accessed on May 13, 2020, at http://www.irishnews.com/news/northernirelandnews/2019/12/27/news/majority-in-north-do-not-support-united-ireland-says-leo-varadkar-1800429
104. Paul Ainsworth, "Taoiseach: I'm Sincerely Sorry for Referring to North as 'Overseas,'" *The Irish News* (May 11, 2020), accessed on May 11, 2020, at https://www.irishnews.com/news/northernirelandnews/2020/05/11/news/taoiseach-i-m-sincerely-sorry-for-referring-to-north-as-overseas--1933513
105. Chris Donnelly, "Dublin Has Been Socially Distancing from the North Long Before Coronavirus," *The Irish News* (May 11, 2020), accessed on May 11, 2020, at http://www.irishnews.com/opinion/columnists/2020/05/11/news/chris-donnelly-dublin-has-been-socially-distancing-from-the-north-long-before-coronavirus-1931829
106. Cited in Christopher Woodhouse, "Anger as RTE Cuts Northern Ireland Out of Map," *Belfast Telegraph* (September 3, 2017), accessed on May 11, 2020, at https://www.belfasttelegraph.co.uk/news/northern-ireland/anger-as-rte-cuts-northern-ireland-out-of-map-36095292.html
107. Bimpe Archer, "Leo Varadkar Accused of 'Insulting Nationalists,'" *The Irish News* (May 9, 2020), accessed on May 11, 2020, at http://www.irishnews.com/news/northernirelandnews/2020/05/09/news/taoiseach-describes-northern-nationalist-as-overseas--1932152/
108. Quoted material taken from Simon Carswell, "Why are Fine Gael and Fianna Fail Refusing to Go into Coalition with Sinn Fein?," *The Irish Times* (January 26, 2020), accessed on May 11, 2020, at https://www.irishtimes.com/news/politics/why-are-fine-gael-and-fianna-f%C3%A1il-refusing-to-go-into-coalition-with-sinn-f%C3%A9in-1.4151911
109. Tom Kelly, "Why Michael Martin's Elevation as Taoiseach Marks Nothing Less than the End of the Irish Civil War," *Belfast Telegraph* (June 16, 2020), accessed on June 16, 2020, at https://www.belfasttelegraph.co.uk/tablet/comment/why-micheal-martins-elevation-as-taoiseach-marks-nothing-less-than-the-end-of-the-irish-civil-war-39288439.html
110. Hugh O'Connell, "The Big Interview: Sinn Fein, the IRA and Me—Mary Lou McDonald," *Belfast Telegraph* (May 24, 2020), accessed on May 26, 2020, at https://www.belfasttelegraph.co.uk/news/northern-ireland/the-big-interview-sinn-fein-the-ira-and-me-mary-lou-mcdonald-39229711.html
111. Quoted material taken from Liam Kennedy, "The Future Might be Green, It Might be Orangeish-Green, or Greenish-Orange . . . What It Will Not Be Is Orange," *Belfast Telegraph* (May 11, 2020), accessed on May 20, 2020, at https://www.belfasttelegraph.co.uk/opinion/comment/the-future-might-be-green-it-might-be-orangeish-green-or-greenish-orange-what-it-will-not-be-is-orange-39194744.html
112. Nelson McCausland, "It's Attitudes Like Mary Lou's That Are the Real Obstacle to a New Northern Ireland," *Belfast Telegraph* (May 28, 2020), accessed on May 28, 2020,

at https://www.belfasttelegraph.co.uk/opinion/columnists/nelson-mccausland/its-attitudes-like-mary-lous-that-are-the-real-obstacle-to-a-new-northern-ireland-39238907.html

113. The document was accessed at https://static.rasset.ie/documents/news/2020/06/programmeforgovernment-june2020-final.pdf on June 20, 2020.

114. Michael Martin, "We Need to See More Reflection in South for any Shared Future," *Belfast Telegraph* (October 22, 2020), accessed on December 21, 2020 at https://www.belfasttelegraph.co.uk/opinion/comment/we-need-to-see-more-reflection-in-south-for-any-shared-future-39653028.html

115. Sam McBride, "Coronavirus: Sinn Fein's Claim Pandemic Boosts Chance of Irish Unity 'Crass,'" *Belfast News Letter* (April 27, 2020), accessed on May 11, 2020, at https://www.newsletter.co.uk/news/politics/coronavirus-sinn-feins-claim-pandemic-boosts-chance-irish-unity-crass-2550401

116. Ruth Dudley Edwards, "He's Keeping a Lowish Profile, but Gerry Adams Still Remains Very Significant Within Sinn Fein," *Belfast Telegraph* (April 27, 2020), accessed on May 11, 2020, at https://www.belfasttelegraph.co.uk/opinion/columnists/ruth-dudley-edwards/hes-keeping-a-lowish-profile-but-gerry-adams-still-remains-very-significant-within-sinn-fein-39158239.html

117. Tom Kelly, "In These Long Days of Lockdown, Counting the Hours to Irish Reunification Is Hardly a Priority . . . It's All About Health, Health and Health," *Belfast Telegraph* (April 28, 2020), accessed on May 11, 2020, at https://www.belfasttelegraph.co.uk/opinion/comment/in-these-long-days-of-lockdown-counting-the-hours-to-irish-reunification-is-hardly-a-priority-its-all-about-health-health-and-health-39162033.html

118. Brendan O'Leary, *A Treatise on Northern Ireland, Volume 3* (London: Oxford University Press, 2019), 347.

119. Ibid., 349.

120. Fionnuala O'Connor, "Amid the Election Drama, There Are Signs of Change on a United Ireland," *The Irish News* (May 28, 2019), accessed on May 13, 2020, at https://www.irishnews.com/opinion/columnists/2019/05/28/news/fionnuala-o-connor-amid-the-election-drama-there-are-signs-of-change-on-a-united-ireland-1629087 and Simon Carswell, Brian Hutton, and Freya McClements, "More than Half of Voters Want Border Polls North and South," *The Irish Times* (February 9, 2020), accessed on May 14, 2020, at https://www.irishtimes.com/news/politics/more-than-half-of-voters-want-border-polls-north-and-south-1.4167428

121. Fintan O'Toole, "United Ireland Will Not Be Based on '50 Percent Plus One,'" *The Irish Times* (August 15, 2017), accessed on May 21, 2020, at https://www.irishtimes.com/opinion/fintan-o-toole-united-ireland-will-not-be-based-on-50-per-cent-plus-one-1.3186234

122. Ronan McGreevy, "How Did Plans to Remember the RIC and DMP Become So Controversial?," *The Irish Times* (January 7, 2020), accessed on May 18, 2020, at https://www.irishtimes.com/news/ireland/irish-news/how-did-plans-to-remember-the-ric-and-dmp-become-so-controversial-1.4133248

123. *BBC News*, "Leo Varadkar: United Ireland 'Further Away' After RIC Controversy" (January 8, 2020), accessed on May 18, 2020, at https://www.bbc.com/news/world-europe-51035886

124. *The Economist*, "Briefing: A United Ireland" (February 15, 2020), 18.

125. Ferriter, *The Border*, 135.

126. Bimpe Archer, "United Ireland Would Cost Up To €30 Billion a Year and 'Collapse North's Economy,'" *The Irish News* (September 17, 2019), accessed on May 14, 2020, at https://www.irishnews.com/news/northernirelandnews/2019/09/17/news/united-ireland-would-cost-up-to-30-billion-a-year-and-collapse-north-s-economy--1714127/

127. Paul Gosling, "A 10 Year Programme for a New Ireland 'Makes Sense,'" *The Detail* (February 26, 2020), accessed on May 18, 2020, at https://www.thedetail.tv/articles/new-ireland

128. Rowena Mason, "Keir Starmer: Only a Federal UK 'Can Repair Shattered Trust in Politics,'" *The Guardian* (January 26, 2020), accessed on May 14, 2020, at https://www.theguardian.com/politics/2020/jan/26/rebecca-long-bailey-calls-for-greater-powers-for-scotland-and-wales

129. "Monumental self-immolation" comes from Angelos, "Will Brexit Bring the Troubles Back to Northern Ireland?" (December 30, 2019); the latter quote is taken from John Baillie's *Solution for Northern Ireland: A King's Perspective* (London: Book Guild, 1994), 13.

130. O'Leary, *A Treatise on Northern Ireland, Volume 3*, 353.

131. Sean Byers, "New Approach, Old Problems," *Tribune* (January 17, 2020), accessed on May 15, 2020, at https://tribunemag.co.uk/2020/01/new-approach-old-problems.

132. Chris Donnelly, "Mary Lou McDonald Has Delivered a Significant Advance for Modern Irish Republicanism," *The Irish News* (February 17, 2020), accessed on May 13, 2020, at http://www.irishnews.com/opinion/columnists/2020/02/17/news/chris-donnelly-mary-lou-mcdonald-has-delivered-a-significant-advance-for-modern-irish-republicanism-1843122

133. John Monaghan, "Anyone Believing Irish Unity Will Happen by 2021 'Should Go To a Trip in Space for a Decade,' says Former Taoiseach Bertie Ahern," *The Irish News* (December 23, 2019), accessed on May 18, 2020, at https://www.irishnews.com/news/republicofirelandnews/2019/12/23/news/anyone-believing-irish-unity-will-happen-by-2021-should-go-for-a-trip-in-space-for-a-decade-says-former-taoiseach-bertie--1797547

134. Ingoldsby, "While Brexit Is a Threat to the Good Friday Agreement 'It Can be Managed.'"

135. Ingoldsby, "Results of a Future Border Poll on a Knife Edge."

136. The full text of the Good Friday Agreement can be found at https://assets.publishing.service.gov.uk/government/uploads/system/uploads/attachment_data/file/136652/agreement.pdf, accessed on May 19, 2020.

137. Seamus McGuinness, "Four Known Unknowns of the Cost of Irish Unity," *The Irish Times* (September 26, 2019), accessed on May 18, 2020, at https://www.irishtimes.com/opinion/four-known-unknowns-of-the-cost-of-irish-unity-1.4030297

138. Sophie Long, "I'd Suggest That We Don't Limit Ourselves to a Snapshot Referendum with Two Choices Available," *The Detail* (February 24, 2020), accessed on May 18, 2020, at https://www.thedetail.tv/articles/i-d-suggest-that-we-don-t-limit-ourselves-to-a-snapshot-referendum-with-two-choices-available

139. Ingoldsby, "Results of a Future Border Poll on a Knife Edge."

140. Institute for Government, "Irish Reunification" (June 18, 2019).

141. *The Economist*, "Briefing: A United Ireland," 17.

142. Ibid.

143. Angelos, "Will Brexit Bring the Troubles Back to Northern Ireland?"

144. Monaghan, "Anyone Believing Irish Unity Will Happen by 2021."

145. Kennedy, "The Future Might be Green."

146. Lisa Smyth, "Unionists 'Disrespected' by Sinn Fein Northern Ireland Tweet, Says Councillor," *Belfast Telegraph* (May 15, 2019), accessed on May 19, 2020, at https://www.belfasttelegraph.co.uk/news/unionists-disrespected-by-sinn-fein-northern-ireland-tweet-says-councillor-38112035.html

147. Sinead Ingoldsby, "Legacy Issues Not a Priority for People North or South of the Border," *The Detail* (February 25, 2020), accessed on May 28, 2020, at https://www.thedetail.tv/articles/legacy-issues-not-a-priority-for-people-north-or-south-of-the-border

148. Alex Kane, "Sinn Fein Good at Arguing for United Ireland—It's Unionists That Worry Me," *Belfast Telegraph* (January 31, 2017), accessed on June 9, 2020, at https://www.belfasttelegraph.co.uk/opinion/news-analysis/sinn-fein-good-at-arguing-for-united-ireland-its-unionists-that-worry-me-35410623.html

149. Duncan Morrow, "The Rocky Road from Enmity," in McGrattan and Meehan (eds.), *Everyday Life After the Irish Conflict*, 21.

150. For more on the role of political exclusion leading to failed peace agreements, see Charles T. Call, *Why Peace Fails: The Causes and Prevention of Civil War Recurrence* (Washington, DC: Georgetown University Press, 2012); Hazzard's quote comes from Suzanne Breen, "How It Took Coronavirus Pandemic for DUP and Sinn Fein to Realise They Can Work Together," *Belfast Telegraph* (June 10, 2020), accessed on June 10, 2020, at https://www.belfasttelegraph.co.uk/opinion/comment/how-it-took-coronavirus-pandemic-for-dup-and-sinn-fein-to-realise-they-can-work-together-39273814.html

151. Quotes taken from Seamus Mallon, "Why a Simple Majority in Favour of United Ireland Will Not Deliver the Future We Deserve," *Belfast Telegraph* (May 18, 2019), accessed on May 19, 2020, at https://www.belfasttelegraph.co.uk/opinion/news-analysis/seamus-mallon-why-a-simple-majority-in-favour-of-united-ireland-will-not-deliver-future-we-deserve-38122624.html

152. Gareth Cross, "'It's Equality Stupid—Gerry Adams Rejects Mallon's Proposal to Amend GFA Vote on Irish Unity," *Belfast Telegraph* (May 23, 2019), accessed on May 19, 2020, at https://www.belfasttelegraph.co.uk/news/northern-ireland/its-equality-stupid-gerry-adams-rejects-mallons-proposal-to-amend-gfa-vote-on-irish-unity-38141294.html

153. Dan Haverty, "With Parliament Voting for Brexit, Is Irish Unification Inevitable?," *Foreign Policy* (January 9, 2020), accessed on May 19, 2020, at https://foreignpolicy.com/2020/01/09/irish-unification-brexit/

154. Ibid.
155. *Belfast Telegraph*, "Loyalists Issue Threats Against Sunday Life and Sunday World Journalists" (May 8, 2020), accessed on May 9, 2020, at https://www.belfasttelegraph.co.uk/news/northern-ireland/loyalists-issue-threats-against-sunday-life-and-sunday-world-journalists-39191888.html
156. Ciaran Barnes, "UVF Gang in 72-Hour Terror Rampage," *Belfast Telegraph* (June 21, 2020), accessed on June 21, 2020, at https://www.belfasttelegraph.co.uk/sunday-life/news/uvf-gang-in-72-hour-terror-rampage-39301471.html
157. Allison Morris, "Continuity IRA 'Patrol' Roads in Rural Fermanagh," *The Irish News* (May 21, 2020), accessed on May 21, 2020, at https://www.irishnews.com/news/northernirelandnews/2020/05/21/news/continuity-ira-patrol-roads-in-rural-fermanagh-1946743
158. Leona O'Neill, "If You've Declared 'It's Derry, Not Londonderry' or Vice Versa Then You're Part of the Problem," *The Irish News* (February 20, 2018), accessed on May 20, 2020, at http://www.irishnews.com/lifestyle/2018/02/20/news/leona-o-neill-what-kind-of-future-are-we-creating-for-our-kids--1258668

Conclusion: "I Hope It Wasn't All a Waste"

Northern Ireland at Its Centenary

On March 21, 2017, more than two months after he resigned his position as deputy First Minister of Northern Ireland, Martin McGuinness, surrounded by his family, died at the age of 66 in Derry's Altnagelvin hospital, reportedly from amyloidosis (a rare genetic disorder that leads to an abnormal buildup of protein deposits in the tissues and vital organs). His death would be marked with words of commemoration and appreciation from around the world. Former US President Barack Obama issued a statement praising McGuiness as a "man who had the wisdom and courage to pursue reconciliation for his people."[1] Closer to home, even among unionists, the former IRA commander who had turned peacemaker was, in the words of one politician I interviewed, remembered as "a man we could do business with." Within hours of his death, the family of the late Ian Paisley, firebrand founder of the Democratic Unionist Party (DUP), sent warm messages of condolence. His son, Ian Paisley Jr., later would remark that McGuinness had been on a "remarkable journey that not only saved lives but made the lives of countless people better."[2] Paisley's widow, Eileen, later visited the McGuinness home to show solidarity with the family. Queen Elizabeth sent a private letter of condolence to McGuinness's widow, Bernie.

The day of McGuinness's funeral, March 23, was the closest Derry has ever come to a state occasion. As the procession made its way from the McGuinness home on Westland Avenue to St. Columba's church, with tens of thousands lining the streets, among his relay of pallbearers carrying the tricolor-draped coffin were family members as well as Sinn Fein colleagues Gerry Adams, Mary Lou McDonald, and Michelle O'Neill. At the funeral service, Father Michael Canny noted: "There are people in this church today whose presence would have been unthinkable only a generation ago."[3] Most notable among those was Arlene Foster, leader of the DUP and First

A Troubled Sleep. James Waller, Oxford University Press (2021). © Oxford University Press.
DOI: 10.1093/oso/9780190095574.003.0008

Minister of Northern Ireland. As she arrived to take her place at the service, one person clapped, and then another, and then nearly all in attendance were applauding with cheers and a standing ovation. One person present at the service told me that Foster seemed surprised and relieved at the unexpected warmth of the response. An editorial by *The Guardian* proclaimed her choice to attend the service, about which she had hesitated publicly, as "magnanimous, dignified and right."[4] Former US President Bill Clinton spoke at the funeral and commended Foster for having the courage to attend as well as hailing McGuinness as someone who "expanded the definition of 'us' and shrank the definition of 'them.'" Clinton challenged the mourners: "If you want to continue his legacy, go and finish the work he has started."[5]

To be certain, Martin McGuinness's legacy was a complex one, demonized and deified in equal measure. A life lived in two halves as someone who took then saved lives. His gravestone attests to such, including "Oglach" (the term used by the IRA to describe its volunteers) as well as "MP MLA Minister" (his elected political positions) in its dedication. In marking his death, some remembered the first half of that life. In the Fountain estate of Derry, a tiny unionist and loyalist enclave, for example, one man recalled: "I lost many friends, all decent people—working class people—who joined the UDR [Ulster Defence Regiment] or police reserve. McGuinness signed their death warrants. You'll find a lot of sore hearts around here and we're not ready to forgive and forget."[6] The second half of that life, though, was remembered by many as a life lived as a man of peace. As former UK Prime Minister Tony Blair recalled: "I will remember him . . . with immense gratitude for the part he played in the peace process, and with genuine affection for the man I came to know and admire for his contribution to peace."[7]

Two months before his passing, during the annual commemoration of Bloody Sunday in Derry on January 29, I had the chance, introduced by a mutual friend, to meet McGuinness. He was clearly in ill health, recognizing, as did those around him, that this would be the last commemorative event for which he would be alive. Despite it all, he took a few minutes to chat, ask about the work I was doing, and express his appreciation for my interest in the future of a country he had torn apart and then helped rebuild. As we parted, he warmly grabbed my hand and said, simply and poignantly, with a faraway look lost in a world of distant memories: "I hope it wasn't all a waste."

* * *

Hope. The loaded word that ended the introduction to this book now begins its conclusion. As we have seen, hope is hard-won in contemporary Northern Ireland but resides nevertheless. Rays of hope are particularly noted by those who take only a passing glance. For instance, in July 2019, for the first time since 1951, the British Open golfing championship returned to Northern Ireland. The common media narrative focused on how Northern Ireland has "changed" since the Troubles have been left "behind" amid a "flourishing" peace process. Commentators repeatedly remarked on "how far Northern Ireland has really moved on the last 20 years" and marked the Open as "a major unifying milestone in Northern Ireland's lengthy transition from war to peace."[8] Rory McIlroy, Northern Ireland's favorite golfing son, in speaking of the Troubles, said "We're so far past that and that's a wonderful thing."[9] He went on to say that, today in Northern Ireland, "no one cares who they are, where they're from, what background they're from . . . you can have a great life and it doesn't matter what side of the street you're from."[10]

Along with Rory McIlroy, this is a rosy picture of the Northern Ireland for which we hope. We want our post-conflict societies to be healed, reconciled, made whole again. Unfortunately, however, this is more a projection of our hopes than a reflection of reality; the propaganda of peace rather than its eventuation. As I have argued throughout this book, Northern Ireland as it is remains Northern Ireland just as it was. All the divisive attitudes that were there before 1998 are still there; perhaps even more pronounced. Nations, like people, may change somewhat, but not in their essential characteristics. And Northern Ireland's essential characteristic, since its birth in 1921, has been deep divisions.

Recognizing the reality of contemporary Northern Ireland as it is should not minimize the myriad ways in which Northern Ireland does compel us to hope, however. As we have seen throughout history, the road to a sustainable peace is a long and winding one, rife with potholes and perils. Peace is a prolonged process and not a one-off event. Ending armed conflict is hard because you are making peace with enemies, not friends. Trust is not easily come by and history not easily overcome. The absence of violence does not automatically equate to the presence of stability, mutual understanding, and a shared future.

As a result, history is filled with the detritus of failed peace agreements. Since 1945, there have been more than 800 peace agreements signed in fragile and conflict-affected settings around the globe. In the first 12 years or so after the end of the Cold War, as many peace agreements were signed as in the previous 200 years.[11] Despite their proliferation, however, it is estimated that 54% of peace agreements break down within five years of signature.[12] Even for those agreements that do hold, seldom do they lead to the depth of true reconciliation necessary to inoculate a post-conflict society against the return of violence.

Most recently, for example, Colombia's 2016 peace deal to end a 52-year-old conflict between the country's most powerful rebel group, the left-wing Revolutionary Armed Forces of Colombia (FARC), and the government has begun to erode on all sides. A lack of political support for the peace process, as well as a failure to reintegrate FARC fighters, has led to increasing destabilization and a return to violence. Similarly, the world's newest country, South Sudan, has been caught in the grip of violence since shortly after its birth in 2011. Multiple ceasefires and peace agreements have been signed and violated since the start of conflict in 2013. While the rival parties finally agreed to a coalition government in February 2020, the desolation left by the conflict leaves many believing peace will be difficult to sustain for the long term. In fact, as of this writing, militant groups who were left out of the coalition government continue to engage in widespread massacres that kill hundreds and displace thousands, further destabilizing an already fragile peace.

So, in a comparative sense, Northern Ireland deserves credit that the Good Friday Agreement, despite, in some regards, rewarding separateness over integration, has, by and large, held for more than 20 years. In the words of political scientist Bill Rolston, the "creative ambiguity" of the Agreement has "held the peace together in a wobbly fashion."[13] There are lessons to be learned from the resilient reality that Northern Ireland has not descended back into the violence which defined it for 30 years. Since that time, the country has made absolute progress and there remains strong positive energy and a steady, if occasionally wavering, beam of resilience and hope that lights many sectors of its society.

Yet it seems that light has become too dim for the path forward. There is a dangerous trajectory in contemporary Northern Ireland that has regional, global, and, most importantly, human implications for how we understand the transitions a society goes through in moving from conflict to a stable, enduring, and sustainable peace. The wobbly-ness of that peace has become shaken by accelerants that reveal the underlying vulnerabilities related to memory, governance, and social fragmentation. To be clear, I have not argued that contemporary Northern Ireland is a failed or failing statelet that can no longer perform basic functions due to widespread violence. It is, though, a fragile and flailing one, closer to breakdown than a breakthrough.

While it may be beyond the beginning, it is certainly not yet in sight of the end. The strained filaments of the peace process may yet be holding, but its ongoing and future implementation is tottering and unstable. Doubts over its viability as a distinct geographic, economic, and political entity have never been greater. Author Colum McCann's words from 2014 still ring true today: "It's a small sky over Northern Ireland, but there's a lot of smoke."[14]

* * *

In August 2019, columnist Alex Kane reflected on his country's journey from the beginning of the Troubles until then: "It would be wrong to conclude that Northern Ireland hasn't changed over the past 50 years; and changed for the better. All those changes are to be welcomed, not least the fact that murder is not a regular occurrence. We don't gather around the radio and television at 11 PM to hear about the latest atrocity; and nor do we need to sit in an armchair in the front room or kitchen until we hear the sound of loved ones returning safely. That said, it would be wrong to conclude that those days will never return. There is still a belief in the civic/political/business/community mainstream, along with key elements of both the British and Irish governments, that a return to the bad days and bloody ways remains unlikely. I don't share that belief. In exactly the same way that few people predicted what followed the seismic changes in 1968/69, few people seem willing to admit that the road ahead could be dreadful."[15]

Indeed, at the outset of what would come to be known as the Troubles, no one predicted the violence would last for 30 more years and claim the lives of 3,532 people. As one academic I interviewed said: "No one saw the Troubles coming, so it's fair to ask if maybe no one sees it coming now. Maybe we have the same blinders on." This time, however, must be different; we have to see beyond whatever blinders we have on. As columnist Allison Morris argues: "We now have that wonderful gift of hindsight, we can see familiar patterns emerging and so there is no excuse not to deal with them, this time in a way that will have meaningful impact going forward. . . . If we ignore what is happening . . . having seen what might result if it is allowed to flourish then we've no one to blame but ourselves."[16]

Peace is harder won than war and maintaining the peace is harder than gaining the peace. Gaining the peace in Northern Ireland was damned hard and the maintenance of that paper-thin peace seems the definition of a Sisyphean task. Now gapingly open are old wounds of national identity, never fully healed. There is legitimate worry the violence is only buried under shallow layers of memory, not gone. As I have argued throughout the book, "those bad days and bloody ways" are perilously close to returning. Peace is far more than a breath away. The risk of a return to violent conflict is progressively accumulating in a rising tide, and resilience is rapidly receding. Critics will contend I have emphasized risk at the neglect of resilience. To be sure, I may have missed the mark, to some degree, on both sides of that equation. To be equally sure, however, there is a strong evidence-based argument to be made, as I have tried to do, for the reality that, rather than moving toward a shared future, contemporary Northern Ireland is at increased risk of being dragged back into a violent past.

Seen through the lens of this empirically and experientially informed, nonpartisan analysis of risk and resilience in contemporary Northern Ireland, it seems like a very long time ago that there was any horizon of "hope." In its place is exhaustion—a weary rumination on the past rather than the present, a stale identity-based system of power-sharing in governance, and a fatigued social fragmentation that simply makes it easier to live among "us" rather than reach out to "them." As one interviewee told me: "Living in a 'post-conflict' society just leaves you knackered."

As we saw in our discussions of memory in Chapter 3, all violence has a history. And in contemporary Northern Ireland, that history was born in the persecution of the "other" and normalized in ways that became part of the everyday lived experience. A conflicted past became a contested present and a thief of the future. Popular historical memory commodified violence and made it tolerable for public consumption. "Remember" became a loaded word, politicized and weaponized and territorialized and militarized for glorification of "us" and vilification of "them." Memory does not have to be so relentlessly tyrannical. As a 2014 concept note for a UN Security Council briefing pointed out: "What the United Nations has not understood well enough is how it can help forge a deeper reconciliation among ex-combatants and their peoples based on an agreed or shared narrative, a shared memory, of a troubled past. This is especially relevant to sectarian, or ethnic, conflicts, as well as wars driven by extreme nationalism or ideologies."[17] Reconciliation implies, however, that the two parties were in a state of conciliation at some previous point; that there was an earlier version of history in which combatants were colleagues, enemies were friends. In the north of Ireland's history, notes of conciliation are drowned out by the cacophony of the irreconcilable. Divisions are needled throughout the fabric of that history, and people ruminate in memory, chewing the cud of history and losing the present—and the future—to the past.

Related to issues of governance discussed in Chapter 4, former US Senator George Mitchell, drawing on his experience negotiating the Good Friday Agreement, has said ending violent conflict requires two critical components: committed political leadership and grassroots efforts that build bridges between peoples. Both approaches are necessary but neither is sufficient.[18] In the midst of the COVID-19 pandemic, while there remain some squabbles and ongoing Executive dysfunction, there are hopeful signs of a renewed commitment by political leadership to a shared future in Northern Ireland. The halls of Stormont are characterized more by a quiet truce than by the clamor of open hostility. The crisis may yet build a more stable platform for power-sharing and a unity of purpose, one forged rather than forced. As Allison Morris writes: "They [Arlene Foster and Michelle O'Neill] seem to have found a common ground and more importantly a relationship that didn't exist before the crisis."[19] While their joint appearances may make for good optics, however, governing by compromise remains a step too far for the voting blocs that both parties have built by playing to the extreme, particularly in regard to the core question of constitutional status: Does the north of Ireland best belong as part of the United Kingdom or a united Ireland? As Alex Kane argues, that "constitutional gulf... remains as wide and as divisive as ever" and will remain long after the pandemic wanes.[20]

In the runup to the Good Friday Agreement, civil society, both as an outside force holding the political parties to account and as formal participants in the peace negotiations, had a significant influence on how the peace process unfolded. Today, however, the trade unions, churches, cultural organizations, nongovernmental organizations, arts, and peace groups have increasingly evacuated the public sphere over the past decade and no longer mediate between the individual and the state. By and large, civil society has become disengaged with politicians and the political process. The most recent Peace Monitoring Report, for instance, noted the ongoing absence of the Civic Forum.[21] Suspended in 2002, the advisory forum was a consultative body (mandated in the Good Friday Agreement) to represent a wide range of civic voices, and, in its absence, civil society faces a lack of access to legislative and policy power. Moreover, the reduction of funding streams continues to challenge the role of civil society in contemporary Northern Ireland. While the "New Decade, New Approach" deal mentions the need for "structured civic engagement" in the sustainability of Northern Ireland's political institutions, many fear it will be among the lowest of priorities in the newly restored government.[22] As one interviewee summarily told me: "Civil society in Northern Ireland has died. The only advances they've left behind are thousands of people skilled at filling out funding applications." If there is to be a brake on future violence, it will have to come from the more grassroots, informal community level where ordinary people, rather than civil society organizations, band together to ensure there will not be a return to the violence of the past.

As addressed in Chapter 5, social cohesion is born from, or perhaps even gives birth to, a collective that is bound together in a community of shared obligation, purpose, and opportunity. A belief that we have much more in common than that which divides. In the words of Alex Kane, social cohesion "requires collective acknowledgment of past wrongs, collective determination to work together in a common cause and collective commitment to working together to rebuild a country that is emerging from conflict. It requires certainty that violence no longer remains an option for elements on both sides. It requires political and electoral stability. It requires demonstrable evidence of a change in how the former opponents think and do business together. It requires a drift to the centre rather than a polarising around the fixed positions of the past. It requires a swell of goodwill from a post-conflict generation who want to avoid the mistakes of their political/electoral predecessors."[23] Unfortunately, little, if any, of that is present in contemporary Northern Ireland. As of this writing, the pandemic has, as it has done for the rest of the world, hit "pause" on all aspects of social life in contemporary Northern Ireland. Twelfth of July parades have been cancelled and bonfire celebrations limited to small back garden gatherings. In the everyday quiet, however, divisionism and sectarianism have retreated to social media to huddle in their tribal groups and continue to fan the flames of identity division. As a result, the pandemic's rallying call, "We're All in This Together!," rings as hollow to many ears as it did in pre-pandemic social life.

In the face of these substantial risk factors and the accelerants and potential triggers discussed in Chapter 6, it may be that the impact of the Troubles also, in an optimistically counterintuitive way, has a positive influence on resilience. Risk engineers Nassim Nicholas Taleb and Gregory Treverton contend that past shocks to a society may prove to be a stabilizing influence. Their unique notion of "no stability without volatility" is grounded in research suggesting that "[c]ountries that have survived past bouts of chaos tend to be vaccinated against future ones. Thus, the best indicator of a country's future stability is not past stability but moderate volatility in the relatively recent past. . . . States that have experienced a worst-case scenario in the recent past (say, around the previous two decades) and recovered from it are likely to be more stable than those that haven't."[24] Countries that survive a conflict may find a strength that could not be discovered elsewhere; an antifragility culled from the chaos of disorder. In the case of Northern Ireland, there may be, as Taleb and Treverton suggest, a "virtue of volatility" in which the post-traumatic shock of the Troubles could actually work to inoculate against resorting to such violence again. "Countries that sustain chaos without falling apart," they write, "reveal something about their strength that could not be discovered otherwise."[25] For that prior conflict to be transformative rather than perpetually divisive, however, requires deep wells of commitment to justice, truth, and memory.

* * *

While there is certainly a lot to learn *about* Northern Ireland as a post-conflict society, there is even more for us to learn *from* Northern Ireland. To treat Northern Ireland as peculiarly unique in the world's historical and contemporary contexts is to neglect the universality of segments of its experience. Highlighting its singularity is also to veer uncomfortably close to an unwarranted sense of judgmentalism. Northern Ireland's story, while important in its own right, also has deep meaning that matters for the rest of the world.

Northern Ireland reminds us how easy it is for the world to fall into the panic–neglect cycle that we often see, for instance, in response to public health crises. The panic phase of the cycle draws our attention, but, in the neglect phase, we turn our attention elsewhere once the violence is seemingly over, or at least transposed into political and verbal embodiments of violence. And, unfortunately, there are far too many places currently in the panicked grip of crisis to which the world can turn its attention. Just in the past few years, civilians have found themselves under attack in Chechnya, the Democratic Republic of Congo, Kenya, Ethiopia, Cote d'Ivoire, Kyrgyzstan, Bahrain, Somalia, Afghanistan, Nigeria, Zimbabwe, China, the Philippines, Colombia, Macedonia, Pakistan, Libya, North Korea, Ukraine, Tajikistan, and a wide swath of territory controlled by the Islamic State of Iraq and the Levant (also known as ISIS). Of particular concern are escalating situations of large-scale violence in South Sudan, Sudan, Burma, Syria, the Central African Republic, Burundi, Iraq, and Yemen. The sad truth is that there are fragile, failing, and failed states in every direction the world wants to look.

It is not that the world is staring at the wrong things; indeed, our immediate attention should be on those places in immediate crisis. When we let ourselves only focus on the crises in front of us, however, we avoid recognizing that effective conflict prevention is not just about how we respond during a crisis in real time, but it also is about how we build crisis-resistant societies beforehand and how we rebuild post-crisis societies in ways that stabilize, heal, rehabilitate, and inoculate against the recurrence of a future crisis. In this cyclical framework, the work of conflict prevention is constant, even in the most seemingly stable of societies. So, it is not simply a matter of having strong fire brigades to put out the fires, but also of instituting healthy fire codes and safety practices prior to the fire. And, when those codes and practices fail and the fire is finally extinguished, there is the important practice of rebuilding the community in ways that prevent the recurrence of future fires.[26]

Understanding conflict prevention as a necessary practice at each stage of the conflict cycle reminds us that, if we neglect the dozens of post-conflict spots around the globe that lay forgotten because the "crisis" is over, we do so at our collective peril. Some of these post-conflict societies have transitioned, often with international assistance, to a measure of stability. Many others, however, lay dormant, tensions unresolved, only awaiting a trigger to sink again into violence. The cessation of conflict is not the solution to all the drivers of that conflict. Moreover, prolonged conflict exacerbates the potency of many of those drivers, leaving them even more entrenched in the post-conflict society. To complicate matters, the violence often leaves gaping holes in the infrastructure necessary to rebuild a post-conflict society. Recognizing these challenges helps us understand both the glacial pace of post-conflict recovery as well as why this tenuously volatile period leaves a society at substantially higher risk of a recurrence of violence.

Northern Ireland's past and present are a mirror of the world's past and present, as well as a bracing harbinger of our shared futures. Its story is timely and timeless. While history does not precisely repeat itself, it certainly has a rhythmic quality from which we can discern transnational and transhistorical patterns applicable to other contexts. From Northern Ireland we can learn what happens when identity politics prevail over democracy, when a paralysis in governance leads to a political vacuum that leaves spaces open for extremist voices to dominate, when de facto social segregation becomes accepted as "safer than the alternative," when acclimatization to violence becomes a generational legacy, and when questions of who we are become secondary to who we are not. We can learn the limits of what "peace" can be in a society where the underlying structural divisions and drivers that led to conflict have not been constructively addressed.

Unfortunately, as *Belfast Telegraph* columnist Eilis O'Hanlon argued in June 2020, "it's hard to escape the conclusion that, instead of learning from the tragic experience of Ulster, the whole world is turning into Northern Ireland writ large, with everyone retreating into hermetically sealed factions based on the sectarian identity and a one-sided grasp of the facts, while batting away all uncomfortable moral and political dilemmas with whataboutery."[27] Indeed, across the globe, amidst fears of scarcity and insecurity, identity has been weaponized into toxic tribalism across a spectrum of societies. Extreme partisan polarization has become the norm rather than the exception in far too many countries. Democracy is suffocating under a burgeoning movement of right-wing, anti-establishment populism. The notion that countries should privilege democracy over all else is no longer unquestioned, and support for autocratic alternatives continues to rise. In the words of Michael Abramowitz, president of Freedom House: "Democracy is in crisis. The values it embodies—particularly the right to choose leaders in free and fair elections, freedom of the press, and the rule of law—are under assault and in retreat globally."[28] Their 2020 "Freedom in the World" report documented the 14th consecutive year of a global decline in democratic governance and respect for human rights.[29] All of these trends depict a world full of flashpoints with increased risk for the onset of violent conflict.

As an American, born and raised in the South, I am all too painfully familiar with the lived experience of a deeply divided society, contested memory, and social fragmentation. Living in 2020 America is also to share the lived reality of flawed and divisive governance born from a legacy of identity-based politics. Our arrogance led us to think we lived in a dream and most of the rest of the world in a nightmare; only now do we seem to be facing the unglazed realism that we do, in fact, live in a collective nightmare. The myth of "American exceptionalism," always refuted by its history, has now been revealed in the riots on its streets and the dysfunction in its greatest corridors of power. As Reverend Al Sharpton decried at the June 2020 homegoing celebration for George Floyd, a black man murdered by a Minneapolis police officer, contemporary America has "wickedness in high places."[30] If ever we were a democratic role model for the rest of the world, we no longer are.

In many ways, Americans and the Northern Irish are authoring similar books on harming the other as well as inflicting self-harm; though, to be honest, America's culture of violence and deep divisions has long-outpaced that of Northern Ireland. Still, however, the resonance is there. As *The Irish*

News columnist Allison Morris writes: "Watching as injustice, discrimination and violent state actions rip through American cities and town, is shocking and yet disturbingly familiar."[31] Similarly, for columnist Jim Gibney, watching US protestors "facing state forces defending a system based on white power, privilege and racial and economic inequality" brought to mind the 1971 protestors against internment in Northern Ireland who "faced state forces defending a prejudiced system based on sectarianism, privilege and power."[32] In June 2020, that historical resonance became visual as the "Capitol Hill Autonomous Zone" in Seattle, a neighborhood taken over in protests over police brutality and racial injustice, posted a sign at its border reading "You Are Now Entering Free Cap Hill."[33] The sign's shape and coloring perfectly mirrored the internationally known wall reading "You Are Now Entering Free Derry," first posted in January 1969 on the gable-end of a derelict house in Derry's Lecky Road as a symbol of resistance and hope (Figure C.1).

* * *

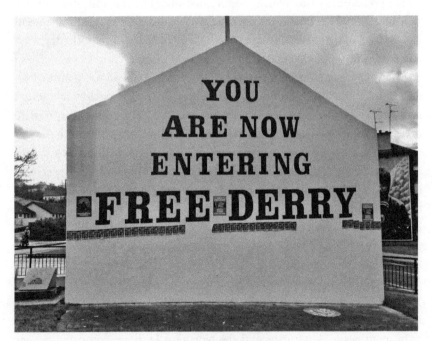

Figure C.1 Free Derry Corner, a historical landmark in the Bogside neighborhood of Derry.
Photo by author, January 28, 2017.

While the late Seamus Heaney, Northern Ireland's Nobel Prize-winning poet, cautions us that "history says, don't hope," he also reminds us that "the longed-for tidal wave of justice can rise up, and hope and history can rhyme."[34] The risk factors we have reviewed related to memory, governance, and social fragmentation—along with the accelerants and potential triggering events—indicate an increased likelihood of a return to violent conflict in Northern Ireland. They do not, however, predetermine that eventuality. Violence is a human problem and, as such, offers hope for a human solution. There is no inevitability in human affairs. Every country has the capacity for possibility; every story the room for a better ending. For contemporary Northern Ireland to find its way to that better ending will require an adaptive resiliency, an ability to bend and come back. And, following the tsunami-like impacts of Brexit and the COVID-19 pandemic, that adaptive resiliency will be necessary now more than ever. As *Belfast News Letter* columnist Sam McBride urges, "there is now a rare moment of opportunity for visionary politicians to use their power to reshape how we live and work. This is a moment which for many politicians never arrives even in a long political career: The chance to dramatically reshape society and fix some of what they knew to be broken."[35]

The hard work of preventing a return to violent conflict is not what makes headlines, but it is what prevents the worst of headlines from being made. Addressing the destructive legacies of contested memory, flawed governance, and divisive social fragmentation requires long-term strategies of building underlying structures of durability that increase the capacity and resilience of societies to inoculate themselves against the risk of violent conflict. Part II of the book, drawing from lessons gleaned from comparative research in post-conflict societies, described some of the possibilities for mitigating or countering such risk. A society cannot heal until it understands where the wounds are. Finding these wounds and effectively addressing them are long-sighted measures, often underappreciated or even unrecognized because they have led to a nonevent—the nonrecurrence of violence. We must come to see, however, that sustainable peace *is* the event. Indeed, the world's most important work is the work of peace; the work of turning strangers into friends. If the hard work to build a sustainable peace in Northern Ireland is not done, then McGuinness's fear, that it was "all a waste," will become realized and force many to question what lessons were learned from all the seasons of all the wasted years of violence, destruction, and death.

The Good Friday Agreement did not, by itself, move Northern Ireland from "conflict" to "post-conflict," no matter how many strokes of a pen or pages of attention were applied to it. It did not guarantee peace, stability, a shared future, reconciliation, and healing. It merely opened a space that made those hopes possible. Given the substantial commitment made by national, regional, and international actors in securing the peace agreement of 1998, we all have a vested interest in ensuring that peace in Northern Ireland not only be maintained but be transformed from simply relief over the absence of violence to the active and intentional creation of social and political systems that are inclusive, constructive, integrated, and, truly, peaceful.[36]

Today, however, that space seems to be rapidly contracting. Many continue to look back with disappointment and forward with fear. The perpetual roundabout that has been the history of the north of Ireland is now a pivotal crossroads. In a 2018 lecture at Queen's University Belfast, Peter Robinson, former First Minister and DUP leader, expressed his rising concern about the acceleration of sectarian division in the country. "We are at risk," he said, "of awaking the slumbering hostilities that we had all hoped would never again be aroused."[37] Indeed, more than two decades after the Good Friday Agreement, contemporary Northern Ireland finds itself in a shallow, troubled sleep, and its future, moving more quickly each day, is trending in a darker and more dangerous direction. As Northern Ireland approaches its centenary, how it awakes from that troubled sleep will determine whether it is on the edge of a new beginning or a painfully familiar old precipice.

Notes

1. Henry McDonald, "Bill Clinton Urges Leaders at Martin McGuinness Funeral to Finish His Work," *The Guardian* (March 23, 2017), accessed on May 25, 2017, at https://www.theguardian.com/politics/2017/mar/23/martin-mcguinness-funeral-former-foes-come-together-in-tribute-to-ex-ira-leader
2. Henry McDonald, *Martin McGuinness: A Life Remembered* (Belfast: Blackstaff Press, 2017), 141.
3. McDonald, "Bill Clinton Urges Leaders at Martin McGuinness Funeral to Finish His Work."
4. *The Guardian*, "The Guardian View on Martin McGuinness's Funeral: Enlarging the Definition of 'Us'" (March 24, 2017), accessed on May 25, 2020, at https://www.theguardian.com/commentisfree/2017/mar/24/the-guardian-view-on-martin-mcguinnesss-funeral-enlarging-the-definition-of-us.

5. McDonald, "Bill Clinton Urges Leaders at Martin McGuinness Funeral to Finish His Work."

6. Ian Cobain, "Martin McGuinness: 'We Knew He Was For Us and Would Never Let Us Down,'" *The Guardian* (March 23, 2017), accessed on May 25, 2020, at https://www.theguardian.com/politics/2017/mar/23/martin-mcguinness-we-knew-he-was-for-us-and-would-never-let-us-down

7. McDonald, *Martin McGuinness: A Life Remembered*, 141.

8. First quote taken from Chuck Culpepper, "British Open Is in Northern Ireland, and a Region Defined by 'The Troubles' Can't Quite Believe It," *The Washington Post* (July 17, 2019), accessed on July 20, 2019, at https://www.washingtonpost.com/sports/golf/british-open-is-in-northern-ireland-and-a-town-defined-by-the-troubles-cant-quite-believe-it/2019/07/17/8a4c428a-a8be-11e9-86dd-d7f0e60391e9_story.html; second quote taken from Ivan Little, "Lowry Unites Island in Joy as Co Offlay Golfer Wins the Open at Portrush," *Belfast Telegraph* (July 22, 2019), accessed on May 27, 2020, at https://www.belfasttelegraph.co.uk/sport/golf/the-open/lowry-unites-island-in-joy-as-co-offaly-golfer-wins-the-open-at-portrush-38332621.html

9. Brian Pinelli, "For Northern Ireland, This British Open Is More than a Golf Tournament," *The New York Times* (July 18, 2019), accessed on July 20, 2019, at https://www.nytimes.com/2019/07/18/sports/golf/british-open-portrush-rory-mcilroy.html

10. Culpepper, "British Open Is in Northern Ireland."

11. Dan Smith, *The Penguin State of the World Atlas*, 9th ed. (New York: Penguin Books, 2012), 70.

12. Dan Smith, *The Penguin Atlas of War and Peace* (New York: Penguin Books, 2003), 106.

13. Quoted in Vicky Cosstick, *Belfast: Toward a City Without Walls* (Belfast: Colourpoint Books, 2015), 173.

14. Colum McCann, "Ireland's Troubled Peace," *The New York Times* (May 15, 2014), accessed on May 27, 2020, at https://www.nytimes.com/2014/05/16/opinion/irelands-troubled-peace.html

15. Quoted material in these two paragraphs comes from Alex Kane, "Politicians Need to Get a Grip on Our Current Dire Situation, or the Consequences Could Be Horrendous," *The Irish News* (August 16, 2019), accessed on May 27, 2020, at http://www.irishnews.com/paywall/tsb/irishnews/irishnews/irishnews//opinion/columnists/2019/08/16/news/alex-kane-politicians-need-to-get-a-grip-on-our-current-dire-situation-or-the-consequences-could-be-horrendous-1685100/content.html

16. Allison Morris, "Lyra McKee Murder Shows We Must Intervene in Derry and Turn Young Away from Violence," *The Irish News* (April 25, 2019), accessed on May 31, 2020, at http://www.irishnews.com/opinion/columnists/2019/04/25/news/allison-morris-we-must-take-this-opportunity-to-intervene-in-derry-and-turn-young-people-away-from-violence-1605361

17. UN Document S/2014/30 (January 17, 2014), 2, accessed on December 21, 2020 at https://www.securitycouncilreport.org/un-documents/document/s201430.php

18. Fred Strasser, "Grassroots Work in the Israeli-Palestinian Conflict," United States Institute of Peace (March 23, 2017), accessed on May 28, 2020, at https://www.usip.org/publications/2017/03/grassroots-work-israeli-palestinian-conflict

19. Allison Morris, "Foster and O'Neill: A Stronger Leadership Forged from Crisis?," *The Irish News* (May 26, 2020), accessed on May 28, 2020, at http://www.irishnews.com/news/analysis/2020/05/26/news/foster-and-o-neill-a-stronger-leadership-forged-from-crisis--1951983

20. Alex Kane, "Don't Be Fooled by Joint Statements About Working Together . . . Covid-19 Changes Precisely Nothing Between Unionism and Republicanism," *Belfast Telegraph* (May 7, 2020), accessed on May 28, 2020, at https://www.belfasttelegraph.co.uk/opinion/comment/dont-be-fooled-by-joint-statements-about-working-together-covid-19-changes-precisely-nothing-between-unionism-and-republicanism-39188904.html

21. Ann Marie Gray, Jennifer Hamilton, Grainne Kelly, Brendan Lynn, Martin Melaugh, and Gillian Robinson, "Northern Ireland Peace Monitoring Report, Number Five" (October 2018), 206, accessed on December 21, 2020 at https://www.community-relations.org.uk/publications/northern-ireland-peace-monitoring-report

22. "New Decade, New Approach" (January 2020), 23, accessed on May 1, 2020, at https://assets.publishing.service.gov.uk/government/uploads/system/uploads/attachment_data/file/856998/2020-01-08_a_new_decade__a_new_approach.pdf

23. Alex Kane, "The Past Is Where We Go when There Is No Agreement on the Present or Future," *The Irish News* (December 1, 2017), accessed on May 28, 2020, at http://www.irishnews.com/opinion/columnists/2017/12/01/news/alex-kane-the-past-is-where-we-go-when-there-is-no-agreement-on-the-present-or-future-1199829/

24. Nassim Nicholas Taleb and Gregory F. Treverton, "The Calm Before the Storm," *Foreign Affairs* (January/February 2015), accessed on July 17, 2019, at http://www.foreignaffairs.com/articles/142494/nassim-nicholas-taleb-and-gregory-f-treverton/the-calm-before-the-storm

25. Ibid.

26. I have described these three forms of conflict prevention in more detail in James Waller, *Confronting Evil: Engaging Our Responsibility to Prevent Genocide* (New York: Oxford University Press, 2016).

27. Eilis O'Hanlon, "Minneapolis, Dominic Cummings, Emily Maitlis . . . Why Is the Whole World Suddenly Turning into Northern Ireland Writ Large?," *Belfast Telegraph* (June 1, 2020), accessed on June 2, 2020, at https://www.belfasttelegraph.co.uk/opinion/columnists/eilis-o-hanlon/minneapolis-dominic-cummings-emily-maitlis-why-is-the-whole-world-suddenly-turning-into-northern-ireland-writ-large-39248335.html

28. *Freedom in the World 2018*, accessed on May 27, 2018, at https://freedomhouse.org/report/freedom-world/freedom-world-2018

29. See https://freedomhouse.org/report/freedom-world/2020/leaderless-struggle-democracy, accessed on June 9, 2020.

30. The service was broadcast live from Houston, Texas, on National Public Radio on June 9, 2020.

31. Allison Morris, "Donald Trump's Version of the American Dream Is a Modern Day Nightmare," *The Irish News* (June 4, 2020), accessed on June 5, 2020, at http://www.irishnews.com/opinion/columnists/2020/06/04/news/allison-morris-trump-s-version-of-the-american-dream-is-a-modern-day-nightmare-1960966

32. Jim Gibney, "When I See the Protests in the US, I Remember the Rage in Short Strand on Internment Morning," *The Irish News* (June 15, 2020), accessed on June 15, 2020, at https://www.irishnews.com/opinion/columnists/2020/06/15/news/jim-gibney-when-i-see-the-protests-in-the-us-i-remember-the-rage-in-short-strand-on-internment-morning-1972621

33. Associated Press, "What's Next for Seattle Protestors' 'Autonomous Zone?'" *Los Angeles Times* (June 12, 2020), accessed on June 13, 2020, at https://www.latimes.com/world-nation/story/2020-06-12/q-a-whats-next-for-seattle-protesters-autonomous-zone

34. Seamus Heaney, *Opened Ground: Selected Poems, 1966–1996* (New York: Farrar, Straus and Giroux, 1998), 305–306.

35. Sam McBride, "Most Politicians Never Get This Rare Chance to Radically Reshape Society," *Belfast News Letter* (June 6, 2020), accessed on June 9, 2020, at https://www.newsletter.co.uk/news/politics/sam-mcbride-most-politicians-never-get-rare-chance-radically-reshape-society-2875836

36. This is the negative versus positive peace conceptualization as articulated most famously by Norwegian Johan Galtung, the founding figure of peace studies. See his "An Editorial," *Journal of Peace Research*, 1 (1964).

37. David Young, "Peter Robinson Suggests Fixed Generational Polls on Irish Unification," *The Irish News* (June 8, 2018), accessed on May 28, 2020, at https://www.irishnews.com/news/northernirelandnews/2018/06/08/news/peter-robinson-suggests-fixed-generational-polls-on-irish-unification-1350916

Index

For the benefit of digital users, indexed terms that span two pages (e.g., 52–53) may, on occasion, appear on only one of those pages.

Figures are indicated by f following the page number.